SAME RIVER TWICE

Same River Twice

THE POLITICS OF DAM REMOVAL
AND RIVER RESTORATION

Peter Brewitt

Oregon State University Press   Corvallis

Library of Congress Cataloging-in-Publication Data

Names: Brewitt, Peter, author.
Title: Same river twice : the politics of dam removal and river restoration / Peter Brewitt.
Description: Corvallis, OR : Oregon State University Press, 2019. | Includes
  bibliographical references and index.
Identifiers: LCCN 2018055308 | ISBN 9780870719578 (original trade pbk. : alk. paper)
Subjects: LCSH: Dam retirement—Political aspects—United States. | Stream restoration—
  Political aspects—United States.
Classification: LCC TC556 .B74 2019 | DDC 333.91/62160973—dc23
LC record available at https://lccn.loc.gov/2018055308

∞ This paper meets the requirements of ANSI/NISO Z39.48-1992
(Permanence of Paper).

First published in 2019 by Oregon State University Press
Printed in the United States of America

Oregon State University Press
121 The Valley Library
Corvallis OR 97331-4501
541-737-3166 • fax 541-737-3170
www.osupress.oregonstate.edu

To Kimie

Contents

Acknowledgments

The first person I need to thank is Daniel Press, my graduate advisor at UC Santa Cruz. Daniel accepted me into grad school, saw me through six years of academic indenture, encouraged my ambitions and ideas, and gave me academic freedom combined with constant support. Daniel, please read this over a Palomar margarita.

Thank you to Karen Holl, who welcomed a social scientist into her lab, chaired my exams (sorry for not bringing lunch), guided me into natural science, and showed me how to think about restoration ecology, and about ecological restoration.

Zdravka Tzankova took me under her wing partway down the river of grad school, introduced me to many fascinating facets of environmental policy, and boosted me through to the point of writing this work. Thank you, Z.

Much gratitude to William Lowry, the man who literally wrote the book on dam removal politics and later agreed to serve on my qualifying committee. I hope this work pairs well with *Dam Politics*.

The Press Lab overall was a joyful group to be part of and did a ton to help along this work, reading early chapters, batting ideas around, and making scholarship fun. Sarah Carvill, my officemate and academic sister, deserves her own sentence here for seeing the entire thing through to completion, and for always diving, at a moment's notice, into minute debates over scholarship and life. Watch out for the ghost of the spotted owl, Carvy. The whole Holl lab, as well, was crucial to my academic and personal life. The UCSC Environmental Studies department was a wonderful community. Cohort Mimosa, especially Tara Cornelisse, Leighton Reid, and Jorge Torres, were the best of colleagues and the finest of friends.

This book is founded on interviews with activists, scientists, managers, politicians, and many other folks from the world of rivers and dams. I am so, so grateful to all of them, and continue to be amazed that (almost) everyone involved agreed to sit down with a young scholar and tell their stories. Most of them are listed as interviewees, but many other people helped me along and shaped my understanding of the northwest and its rivers as well; thank you to all.

I must specifically thank John Esler, David Heintzman, and the late Julie Keil from Portland General Electric, who were endlessly accommodating and offered not just their time and documents but also many of the photos that grace this book. The same goes for Bob Hunter from Water-Watch of Oregon, who spoke with me three different times, including once in the very early days when I knew hardly anything, and who provided me boxes of documents from the issues over Savage Rapids Dam. Dan Shepard and Julie Webster of Grants Pass Irrigation District welcomed me into their domain and provided an academic treasure trove of dusty old binders, as well as sprinkling my research days with colorful and insightful observations on the politics of the Rogue. Virginia Egan, whose dissertation on the Elwha preceded my own, was kind enough to send it to me—as you'll see, it was very valuable as I wrote the Elwha chapter of this book.

Along related lines, I must thank all the archivists who helped me out along the way. The staffs of the Port Angeles branch of the North Olympic Library System, the University of Washington's special collections, Lisa Anderson of the *Sandy Post*, and Jeff Duewel of the *Grants Pass Daily Courier* were all extremely helpful. I must give particular recognition to the Josephine County Historic Society and Joan Momsen, who helped me find and access data on the Rogue and provided some of the images that illustrate this book. Joan's own books on the history of the Rogue were very useful— it is people like her, and organizations like the JCHS, who keep our country's history.

Funding for my research came from the Dr. Earl H. Myers and Ethel M. Myers Oceanographic and Marine Biology Trust and the UCSC Environmental Studies Department. I was able to spend seasons in the field thanks to this support. Later on, I presented some of this work at conferences due to grants from my present employer, Wofford College.

During my seasons in the field, I was very grateful for the hospitality of my friends Thor and Sarah Tingey (in Portland), and Jennifer Kidder and Nathan Forrest (in Port Angeles). Thank you for sharing your homes and for listening to me talk about dam removal. You're welcome on my couch any time.

I need to recognize the hard work of my research assistants, Kelly Huang, Taylor Long, Rikki Pritzlaff, Martin Sandoval, and Randall Walz. I appreciate you all. Victoria Salas took up the tedious work of entering my sources into Mendeley and did a great job—her work may have been the difference between my completing my doctoral dissertation on time and . . . not.

Many thanks to friends and colleagues who subjected themselves to prior versions of my chapters, and in some cases the whole book. Rob Karl and Ajay Singh, in earlier days, and Pete Bohler, Anthony Clare, Jon Eisenman, Rob Karl (again), Matt Kemp, Kevin Sullivan, and my sister, Anne Clare, later on. Massive thanks to Chelsea Colwyn, who read and commented on the entire book. You made this work much better.

Emily Witsell formatted the citations and created the index for this book—readers, if you find the book easy to use, thank her. I urge all other scholars to hire her for these services.

My colleagues here at Wofford College have been supportive and enthusiastic about this project. Thanks to Terry Ferguson, Kaye Savage, and Amy Telligman, with particular thanks to John Lane for sage advice on the publishing and editing process.

The people of Oregon State University Press were all wonderful to work with, from Mary Braun deciding to take a chance on an unknown scholar and acquiring this book for publication, to Susan Campbell copyediting my work and making it much sharper than it was before, Micki Reaman shepherding the book (and the author) through editing and publication, and Marty Brown coordinating the cover design and sending the book out into the world. Thank you all so much.

This book has been inspired by many, many environmental voices that have influenced me over the years, from Jean Craighead George to Edward Abbey to Marc Reisner to the Trespassers. A bibliography of works that have mattered to this project would be longer than the book, so I'll just say that I'm happy to have found fire and vision to take up this life and work.

My family—my father, Rob Brewitt, and my mother, Jeannie Muir—instilled me with a love of learning and adventure that will always be with me. My sister, Anne Clare, along with sisterly love and support, has read chapters from this book despite having nothing to do with environmental studies or dam removal, and donated a stretch of her living room floor in Seattle during my first fieldwork there.

I cannot thank my daughters, Penny and Lupin, for their help—they have never quite understood why Daddy needs to skulk inside on a day that would be perfectly good for running around—but I do thank them for their inspiration and for bringing joy to every day of my life. I love you two.

Finally and most importantly, thank you to my wife, the love of my life, Kim Brewitt. Kim has been a part of this project the entire time. Her doctoral work on the Klamath turned my head toward dam removal. She watched me read *Dam Politics* on our honeymoon. She and I snorkeled through remote steelhead streams in the wilds of Jefferson and moved up and down the west coast together. We sat across from each other over numberless cups of espresso as ideas became chapters became dissertations became publications. She has read all my work, taken up the parenting load while I've typed, and supported me in many other ways. We have so much fun together. I love you, Kimie.

SAME RIVER TWICE

1

The Storm

They waited on a storm. In Portland, engineers double-checked their calculations and environmentalists squirmed at their desks. In the little town of Sandy, Oregon, fishing guides stewed as they tied their flies. And in the shadow of 11,240-foot Mount Hood, scientists fidgeted with their equipment and cast anxious eyes at the murky waters of the Sandy River. They peered up at the clouds cloaking Hood's upper slopes, where the Sandy begins, and they wondered if those clouds would do the job.

When you take out a dam, you have to take out the silt behind it, and a century of erosion had left almost a million tons behind the Marmot Dam. They'd dismantled the dam months before, but the silt sat there still, held, for the time being, by a temporary earthen wall. The fear was that the silt would plug up the river permanently, leaving all the problems of a dam with none of a dam's benefits. For their restoration plan to work, the engineers and enviros and guides and scientists and all the other people who'd come together to restore the Sandy needed the river to swell with rain, thunder down through the gorge, and pop the silty cork.

Years before, when plans to remove Marmot Dam began to form, no one really knew what they were getting into. A few dams had been removed here and there, but in the late 1990s the idea was still a little bit revolutionary. The Bull Run Hydroelectric Project, of which Marmot Dam was the key part, was constructed before World War I—it started out making power for streetcars. Decades later, the streetcars disappeared, Portland became Portlandia, and Marmot Dam was still there. Its power-generating capacity, a big deal for 1912, seemed tiny eighty-five years later. Portland General Electric looked at its income from Bull Run, looked at how much it would cost to relicense the project, and decided to decommission it and take out the dam. Everyone soon found that the complications of removal were immense. The Sandy empties into the Columbia eighteen miles from downtown Portland, and every angler, kayaker, and river person in Oregon's biggest city felt they had some stake in the decision. What would removal mean for the fish, and for the fishing? What of the manmade lake, where local people learned to swim? How, exactly, should you take out a dam? It took years to wrestle out the answers, but by the fall of 2007, the only remaining problem was the house-sized load of silt. Engineers and enviros and fishermen looked to the mountain.

The mountain answered. On October 19, the skies opened up over Mount Hood, and as the river began to rise, gathering its strength, one of PGE's contractors cut a careful notch in the dirt retaining wall. You can watch what happened next on YouTube.[1] The Sandy rolled through, blasting the silt downstream. If you go there now, it's hard to see that there was ever a dam in the river at all.

Watershed

The dam removal phenomenon appeared more or less out of nowhere. There were only nineteen removals before 1980, a handful per year during the 1980s and 1990s[2]—and now, almost a thousand since 1999.[3] (See removals map on page 172.) The dam removal revolution continues to grow and strengthen with every breach. All removals transform a stretch of landscape; collectively, they are transforming the way a country manages its waterways and creating a new politics of dams, rivers, and ecological restoration.

This phenomenon raises vital political questions. How does dam removal become a serious possibility at all? What stakeholders and interest groups push for dam removal, and who opposes them, and why? What political instruments do they use? What political venues house dam removal debates, and what differences do these venues make? Dam removal has no precedent. In all of environmental history, we have never seen anything like this.

People and Rivers

Human beings are a riparian species—we rely on fresh water and make our communities near rivers. But the rivers are not always benevolent—T. S. Eliot's "strong brown god" sometimes rises and washes away the people who live on its banks, or dwindles to a trickle, leaving crops and livestock thirsty.[4] So we put dams in those rivers—to hold water for drinking and agriculture, to send floods away from our villages, to, eventually, use their force for ourselves; rivers were one of the first sources of energy people used beyond our own muscles or those of our animals. Ancient dams are still found all over the world. Lake Homs Dam, in Syria, is thought to have been built in the 1300s BCE, and continues to function in the twenty-first century.[5] The power to control rivers was the stuff of myth: as one of his twelve labors, the ancient Greek hero Hercules diverted the Alpheus River to clean the legendary dung of the Augean stables.

But altering a river means altering human uses and livelihoods— what of the people who lived downstream of Hercules' dam and found, one day, that their water did not flow, that their fish did not arrive? Dams have been a political issue for centuries. There were so many weirs in English streams that their removal was mandated in the Magna Carta— surely the first recorded case of dam removal politics.[6] But for most of the past thousand years, dam building has spread like, well, a flood. As European society industrialized, dam technologies improved enough that towns could be built around water-powered forges, and farmers could bring their grain to be ground up by water-powered mills. "Miller" is the seventh most common name in the United States.[7]

The trend carried across the Atlantic and into the New World, as European settlers dammed up America's rivers as fast as dams could be built. The native tribes who lived in the land that would become the United States had actively managed natural resources for thousands of years, including, in some places, manipulating their waterways. But an industrializing economy demanded control on a scale far beyond any that had been seen on the continent before. As Interior Secretary Bruce Babbitt once pointed out, "We have been building, on average, one large dam[8] a day, every single day, since the Declaration of Independence."[9] Mill Pond Dam, which still stands in Connecticut's Mill Brook, went up in 1677.[10] The dwindling riparian environment did not pass unmourned. Proto-environmentalist Henry David Thoreau, paddling the industrializing Concord and Merrimack Rivers of nineteenth-century New England, looked at the new dams rising from the waters, and asked, "Poor shad! Where is thy redress? Who hears the fishes when they cry?" Moving beyond lamentation, he wrote, "I for one am with thee, and who knows what may avail a crow-bar against that Billerica dam?"[11] But dam removal, like many of the ideas Thoreau wrote about, was not a popular sentiment in the 1830s. The damming went on apace, and the Billerica Falls Dam still stands in the Concord River.[12] The river's shad went extinct not long after Thoreau wrote his book.[13]

All through the nineteenth century, wildlife was extirpated all over America. Bison in Texas, elk in Pennsylvania, red wolves in North Carolina, passenger pigeons everywhere—you know the story. These disappearances came about as the sum of thousands of individual decisions to build a dam or clear a forest or dig a mine, but, along with farmers' and merchants' ordinary desire to live prosperous lives, environmental change was inspired by an ideology called manifest destiny—the idea that the North American continent (not to mention the tribes that, Europeans felt, had not even tried to develop it) was there to be mastered, and that it was the divinely ordained duty of Americans to conquer the land and turn wild nature to useful human ends. They believed in the "myth of plenty," the idea that there was no need to conserve resources because there would always be more beyond the frontier. Realizing Thomas Jefferson's old vision of America as a nation of small farmers, pioneers headed west, cleared the forests, ploughed the prairies, crossed the mountains, worked their fingers to the bone, braved the fury of the elements, suffered and prayed and strove and died, and made America. They really did.

But beyond the *Little House on the Prairie*-style homesteaders, and the American myths that sprang up like invasive grasses in the wake of the wagon trains, there were two crucial factors that are not much featured in children's books or western movies. One was that the pioneers would not have made much headway without the industrial products, capital, and markets provided by the cities. Barlow knives, which most Americans know from the novels of Mark Twain, originated in England;[14] Conestoga wagons came from Pennsylvania;[15] Colt revolvers were manufactured in Connecticut.[16] Once the forests were cut and the prairies farmed, the timber and grain and pigs and cattle went east to Chicago and New York.[17] Thomas Jefferson's great ideological rival, Alexander Hamilton, was never president, but history proved his vision—of an America founded on trade and linked to international industry and markets—correct. As anyone who has seen an advertisement for a pickup truck is aware, America likes to imagine itself as a nation of self-reliant farmers unsoiled by the city.[18] But it never was.

The other hidden factor in frontier history was that the pioneers relied on government support.[19] As they crossed the plains, they entered an arid landscape that did not suit their more or less European culture. For a while, in the 1870s and 1880s, some anomalously wet years prompted people to believe that "rain follows the plow," and that they could continue to farm and live more or less as they always had. But once this ecological naivety had dried up, along with their pastures, they faced a choice. One option was to abandon their farms, and of course, many did.[20] The other was to get help. For even the deserts of Nevada and Utah have some water—you can see it high above the farmed valleys, in the snowy slopes of the mountains. It is tauntingly incongruous on a 110-degree day in the red and brown canyon country. Legend has it that Utah's La Sal Mountains were named when Spanish explorers assumed that the white on their slopes was salt—they could not imagine that it was snow. But nonetheless, snow it was.

To channel the desert's water, to bring it down from the peaks and allow it to irrigate crops, was a landscape-scale project that few small farming communities could attempt. This kind of task required the resources of the state.[21] So, in 1902, to fill the West with small farmers, Congress passed the Newlands Reclamation Act, which established the Bureau of Reclamation and commanded it to turn the deserts to cropland. The Bureau of Reclamation transformed the region's arid countryside; to Oregon senator Mark Hatfield, "it was water impoundment that won the West."[22]

This was the crescendo of manifest destiny. The "re" in reclamation implies that the pure and original state of the landscape is irrigated farmland, that the land is being returned to its real form. But Jeffersonian ideology came with Hamiltonian consequences.[23] To fulfill its mission, the bureau, as well as other federal agencies with similar missions, built publicly funded water control infrastructure. Which is to say, dams.

Environmentalists

> . . . into the absolute epicenter of Hell on earth, where stands a
> dam. Conservationists who can hold themselves in reasonable
> check before new oil spills and fresh megalopolises mysteriously go
> insane at even the thought of a dam. The conservation movement
> is a mystical and religious force, and possibly the reaction to dams
> is so violent because rivers are the ultimate metaphors of existence,
> and dams destroy rivers. Humiliating nature, a dam is evil—placed
> and solid.
> —John McPhee, *Encounters with the Archdruid*, 1971

The manifest destiny ideology was strong but not monolithic. Over time, Americans began to appreciate their landscapes as beautiful and valuable on their own terms, and as symbols of national heritage. America had no castles or cathedrals, but it did have a continent of wild grandeur, from Niagara Falls to the redwoods of California.[24] And so, some of this nature began to be preserved. Yosemite[25] was preserved in 1863, Yellowstone in 1872, and a range of other landscapes, large and small, along the way. Of course, it was not just landscapes—the loss of American wildlife grieved many people across the country. The Lacey Act, the first major law to pro-tect migratory birds, was passed in 1900, and the first national wildlife refuge was created in 1903. Over time, all of this coalesced into what we now call the environmental movement.

That movement came of age in a dam fight. Yosemite National Park, two hundred miles east of San Francisco, embraces the upper watersheds of two rivers. One is the Merced, which runs through iconic Yosemite Valley. The other, the Tuolumne, has its own dramatic valley of granite walls and waterfalls, but this one is far less famous: its name is Hetch Hetchy. Four or five million people visit Yosemite National Park each year, but only about 1 percent of them go to Hetch Hetchy.[26] This is because it's under water.

The issue began because San Francisco sits on the tip of a peninsula, without any large bodies of fresh water of its own. This became a problem as the city's growing population, and ambitions for its future, began to put pressure on its water supply.[27] San Francisco's leaders, looking for more water, fixed on Hetch Hetchy Valley. In many ways, this was an ideal site: vertical, impermeable granite walls hundreds of feet high, a mountain wilderness upstream guaranteeing uncontaminated water, and no private landowner to have to buy out.[28] The Tuolumne, like most of California's big rivers, flows to San Francisco Bay, so the water would run to the city by gravity. But it was in a national park.

The political battle for Hetch Hetchy became the original national environmental issue, the template for all the spotted owls and Dakota Access Pipelines after. There was no doubt that such a dam would be useful, but what of the environmental loss? Should we allow a dam in a national park? The Sierra Club, founded in 1892 to enjoy and defend the mountains, roared with indignation and rallied people across America, people who would never go anywhere near Hetch Hetchy, to lobby Con-gress against the dam project. John Muir, seventy years old and already an environmental legend, lamented, "Dam Hetch-Hetchy! As well dam for water-tanks the people's cathedrals and churches, for no holier temple has ever been consecrated by the heart of man."[29] But they lost. The Raker Act, allowing the construction of a dam in Hetch Hetchy, passed in 1913. To John Muir, Hetch Hetchy was dead.[30] Dams would be an environmen-talist boogeyman for the rest of American history.

Muir passed away the next year; there are those who claim that he died of a broken heart.[31] The politicized Sierra Club went on to become perhaps the most influential environmental group in the United States. The ghost of Hetch Hetchy haunts environmentalists to this day. There is a quixotic organization devoted to tearing down the dam.[32] If you look around you'll find Restore Hetch Hetchy bumper stickers and mugs all over California.

But this sort of movement was deep in the future. Twenty years later, as America pushed through the Depression, dams became symbols of national salvation. Franklin Roosevelt's New Deal left many marks all over the country, but perhaps its most indelible image was and remains the gigantic Hoover Dam across the Colorado River. Hoover is a major tourist attraction to this day, so many Americans have at least seen pictures of it, but the numbers are worth listing. Hoover is 726 feet tall. Its reservoir, Lake Mead, covers 247 square miles—a fifth the size of Rhode Island. It produces four billion kilowatt-hours annually—enough power for 1.3 million people.[33] It is sometimes compared to the Great Pyramid at Giza.[34] While it may seem ridiculous to compare something that is eighty years old to something that is 4,500 years old, in the year 7018, Hoover will probably still stand, with a silted-up Lake Mead sitting behind it, in the Colorado River.[35] If that's what people still call the river then. And if there are still people.

The dam didn't just put tens of thousands of people to work; it didn't just produce a region's worth of power; it didn't just capture the water that would allow a desert railroad junction to turn into Las Vegas—it became the pride of America. Manifest destiny was alive, nature was still being conquered, and the desert country around the Grand Canyon—one of the last places to be explored by European Americans[36]—was being dammed, controlled, populated, and electrified.[37]

For their next trick, Roosevelt and his allies turned their attention north, to America's other great western river, the Columbia. The Columbia is the fourth-largest stream in the forty-eight contiguous states, discharging as much water as fifteen Colorado Rivers.[38] In its modern incarnation, it was formed when a massive lake in what's now western Montana burst past a collapsing ice dam, blew through the Cascades, and rolled on into the Pacific Ocean. This happened on several occasions over history, the most recent of which was about ten thousand years ago. There may have been people living there then who would have seen it.[39]

The explosion of water scoured eastern Washington, leaving behind a barren and strangely beautiful landscape called the Scablands. Like the deserts around the lower Colorado, the cold and arid steppe between the Cascades and the Rockies was only lightly settled even in the 1930s.[40] But the US Bureau of Reclamation built the Grand Coulee Dam, the "biggest thing on earth" there.[41] This, like Hoover, was a New Deal make-work and development project, and while it certainly played its part in creating the industrial Northwest, it was also made for propaganda. In 1941, the Bonneville Power Administration hired legendary folk singer Woody Guthrie to compose songs glorifying the effort, now-classic tunes like "Grand Coulee Dam" and "Roll On Columbia."[42]

Grand Coulee became the centerpiece of the Columbia Basin Project, a massive infrastructural program that turned the inland Northwest into productive farm country, cranked out more power than the region could easily use, and became part of the Northwest's identity.[43] The power found an outlet a few years later, making bombers to help the Allies fight World War II—and nuclear fuel, at the secret Hanford site, to help them finish it. For decades after and to this day, the Northwest got cheap river-generated electricity. All of this further enshrined dams as cornerstones of civilization and prosperity in western culture. Journalist William Dietrich calls the Northwest's relationship with dams a "romance."[44]

After the war, a buoyant America, flush with technological confidence, poured itself into building dams. From 1950 to 1979, 45,759 major dams went into America's rivers—1,525 a year.[45] The author Marc Reisner called these the go-go years, when zealous engineers were loath to let even a drop of useful water make its way to the ocean.[46] In the late 1940s, as the federal government planned a series of big dams along the Colorado River, the Bureau of Reclamation likely anticipated that the only problems would have to do with engineering, not politics.

They didn't reckon with the Sierra Club and its executive director, a Muir reincarnation named David Brower. "I hate all dams, large and small," he used to tell people.[47] One of the Colorado River Storage Project dams was slated for Echo Park, a stretch of the Colorado running through Dinosaur National Monument.[48] As its name implies, the monument was mainly distinguished by the remarkable abundance of dinosaur fossils there, but it also included a wild section of river and canyon. Not many people visited Echo Park, but those that had were dead-set against its being inundated by a federal water project.[49] Brower, and many allies, rallied a grassroots movement imploring the government to save Dinosaur National Monument and keep Echo Park wild. No one had ever fought against the construction of a big dam and won, but in 1956, that is what they did. Echo Park was removed from the storage project, and its rivers flow unimpeded through Dinosaur today. David Brower would be immortalized by the author John McPhee as "the Archdruid."[50] He would go on, in a stormy but extremely influential career, to accomplish many other feats of conservation—most notably, keeping dams out of the Grand Canyon—and to infuriate, alienate, and inspire people for decades.

But the dam that would plant dam removal in American minds would be one that David Brower, by his own account, allowed to happen.[51] Glen Canyon, on the border between Utah and Arizona, was not famous or popular: the legendary photographer Eliot Porter named his book about Glen Canyon *The Place No One Knew*.[52] It was not in a national park or monument. But by all accounts it was outstandingly beautiful, a gem of the American desert. The environmental movement did not quite realize this until it was too late, and despite some late protests, Glen Canyon stayed on the Colorado River Storage Project list. The 710-foot dam was completed in 1963. Its reservoir, Lake Powell, has become a popular spring break destination. Bureau of Reclamation commissioner Floyd Dominy famously said that "to have a deep blue lake, where no lake was before, seems to bring man a little closer to God."[53]

Environmentalists thought that it was bringing man a little closer to someone else. Brower regretted Glen Canyon's inundation for the rest of his life. He compared damming Glen Canyon to "urinating in the crypt of St. Peter's."[54] Environmentalists all over America were appalled, none more than the jagged, grouchy author Edward Abbey. Abbey, who liked to decry all the works of civilization since the establishment of agriculture,[55] worked, among other things, as a ranger at Arches National Monument (now a national park), outside Moab, Utah, before going on to great success as a novelist/polemicist. His two most famous books—a reflective, finely wrought series of essays called *Desert Solitaire* and a wild and screwy novel called *The Monkey Wrench Gang*—both express loathing for Glen Canyon Dam. The eponymous gang, a clutch of social misfits attempting to blow up the dam, are often considered the inspiration for environmental vandalism groups like Earth First!.[56] The book came out in 1975. By the time Abbey died, in 1989, the book had sold five hundred thousand copies.[57]

But at the time that *Monkey Wrench Gang* came out, while the environmental movement wielded great power in Washington, DC, its focus was on protecting wild land and limiting damage—not reversing development and restoring ecosystems, and certainly not on blowing up any dams. But the end of the go-go years was nearing. While Glen Canyon Dam and its Lake Powell crank out power and float houseboats to this day,[58] it would now, in the twenty-first century, be politically impossible to build another Glen Canyon Dam.

But as the environmental movement rose, into the 1970s and 1980s, it faced a backlash, especially in the rural West. American history is short. People who'd grown up in the go-go years, whose parents had received their water through the Reclamation Act, whose grandparents had moved with the gospel of manifest destiny, looked at public lands being managed as wilderness, at development being halted for the sake of endangered fish or turtles, and could barely believe it. Some of this manifested itself in what became known as the Sagebrush Rebellion, when some westerners argued that federal lands should be transferred to the states.[59] The related wise use movement, based partly in Seattle, argued for the primacy of private property rights and for the diminution of environmental regulation.[60] Many western counties passed various sorts of resolutions laying their claim to public lands and resources. They demanded not just access to federal lands, but privileged access, believing that resource extraction should get public support to ensure the primacy of a manifest destiny–style society in the rural West.[61] The political and ideological tug of war between environmentalists and the "wise users" shows no sign of stopping in the twenty-first century.

The Northwest

The Pacific Northwest is quite separate from the rest of the country, walled off by sparsely populated mountains and deserts to the east and the ocean to the west. The region's landscapes are unique, with its own chain of volcanoes, the Cascades, running from British Columbia to Northern California. If you see a ten-thousand-foot white pyramid on your horizon, you are in the Northwest. This geography makes the Northwest's rivers distinctively its own, as big streams like the Klamath and the Rogue and even the enormous Columbia run from the mountains to the sea entirely within the region.

As northwestern rivers run down to the ocean, salmon run back up. For many people, these animals define the region.[62] To celebrated Seattle author Timothy Egan, "the Pacific Northwest is simply this: wherever the salmon can get to."[63] There is a certain magic to salmon—the way they appear, running up out of the ocean,[64] year after year; the way they strive up against the flow, leaping over boulders and fallen trees and waterfalls; the way they find their natal stream, even after many years in the ocean, even hundreds of miles upriver; the way they spawn, despite being visibly torn and battered by the river—and the way that they die, after doing all this. Science has shown us that salmon don't necessarily fulfill all their mythology—some of them stray into new streams after they leave the ocean, some of them are not able to jump over obstacles in the river, many of them die before they manage to spawn—but they maintain a special place in the way America sees nature, and in the way the Northwest, at least west of the Cascades, sees itself.

When Europeans first reached the Pacific Northwest, they were amazed at the spectacle of its salmon runs.[65] Every stream, it seemed, no matter how small, was filled from bank to bank with shimmering fish. Annual returns of millions of salmon were common in big rivers like the Columbia and Sacramento.[66] Even smaller streams like the forty-five-mile Elwha hosted runs of more than one hundred thousand pink salmon.[67]

For many native tribes in the Pacific Northwest, salmon were a central fact of life, the foundation of their economies and culture.[68] For a subsistence society, it would be hard to imagine a better place to settle than a river where living protein surged up out of the ocean, season after season. Some rivers hosted enough different runs of salmon that people could expect to catch fish every day of the year. While some years were better than others—ocean conditions' effects on salmon remain poorly understood[69]—nonetheless, the salmon cultures were among the richest indigenous peoples in Native America.[70] The best fishing spots, like the famous Celilo Falls, near the present-day town of The Dalles, Oregon, attracted tribes from many miles away.[71]

It would be wrong to think of the pre-Columbian Northwest as a pristine wilderness. Native tribes fished intensively for thousands of years—modern scholars estimate that the number of salmon harvested by indigenous fishers, at least on big systems like the Columbia and Sacramento, was comparable to that taken at the height of the industrial era.[72] But this did not result in the collapse of salmon populations on any important scale. Part of this was simply that the fishery was dispersed along the whole length of the stream, up into Canada or the Sierra Nevada, rather than at the river mouth.[73] But just as importantly, the tribes generally fished with restraint, incorporating a variety of practices that sustained future populations.[74] For example, the First Salmon ceremony, practiced across the region, allowed fish to run upstream for a time before the catch could begin.[75] Some tribes also caught fish after they had spawned.[76] And as James Lichatowich points out, native salmon consumption did little to degrade salmon habitat; he considers the relationship between native people and salmon more like a case of coevolution than like the transactional or adversarial relationships between European cultures and wild species.[77]

All of this meant that, under native fishing regimes, large salmon and steelhead populations persisted in rivers across the region well into historic times, and in some cases, within living memory. It's common, in stories of early salmon runs, to read that you could walk across the river on the fishes' backs and never get wet.[78] More believably, some accounts indicate that a big run of salmon displaced enough water to overflow the riverbanks.[79] In some places, salmon were so abundant that early farmers used them as fertilizer.[80]

Salmon History

Europeans had seen big salmon runs before. Atlantic salmon (*Salmo salar*) once ran from northwestern Siberia's arctic coast down to Portugal.[81] When Julius Caesar arrived in Gaul (modern France), his legionnaires were amazed by the runs of Atlantic salmon in its rivers.[82] Salmon filled British streams—remember that they're in the Magna Carta. While their life histories were mysterious—the philosopher Boethius was amazed at how juvenile salmon went to sea and then, apparently, returned three weeks later as gigantic adults—it was well known that they needed access to their nesting sites.[83] King Robert the Bruce of Scotland decreed that salmon spawning streams should not be obstructed.[84] That was in the 1300s.

When Europeans crossed the Atlantic Ocean, they found salmon on the other side. Salmon lived from the Hudson River to northern Canada; they were swimming up New England's rivers when the pilgrims arrived in Massachusetts in 1630.[85] But by the early nineteenth century, most of New England's runs had collapsed.[86] The rise of mill dams in both Britain and New England not only barred salmon from spawning sites but also supported an industrial economy that dumped its waste into waterways. As the fish became scarcer, they became more valuable, putting economic pressure on dwindling populations.[87] When Thoreau paddled up the Merrimack, he noted that, while it had once been a rich salmon stream, they had become rare.[88] But the Northwest, and its Pacific salmon, remained preindustrial.

When European Americans reached the Pacific, they found themselves dealing with a whole new kettle of fish. There are five different species of Pacific salmon, from little four-pound pinks (*Oncorhynchus gorbuscha*) that spawn near the river mouth to enormous Chinook (*O. tshawytscha*) that weigh a hundred pounds and travel more than a thousand miles upstream.[89] Once adult salmon reenter the river, they do not eat, making their way to their spawning sites using only the calories they've consumed in the ocean.

Their journey is hazardous—everything from sea lions to ospreys to bears will eat a salmon. Once they've spawned, they cover their eggs and die, their carcasses washing onto the riverbanks—and nourishing their young. This upstream migration moves millions and millions of pounds of nutrients up from the ocean and sends them throughout the watershed. It's a profound influence on the region's ecology, nourishing species from eagles to insects and even riparian plants.[90]

Alongside the salmon come Pacific sea-run trout. These fish—cutthroat (*O. clarkii*), and especially steelhead (*O. mykiss*)—are anadromous, spawning in fresh water but spending their adult lives in the ocean, just like salmon. The important difference is that they can also spend all their lives in the river. Steelhead that live this way are better known as rainbow trout, and, having been stocked in rivers well beyond their native range, bring joy and frustration to anglers from New Hampshire to New Zealand.[91] The steelhead form of *O. mykiss* looks very different from the rainbow trout—it's twice the size, for one thing—but the species is the same. A steelhead population that finds itself walled off from the ocean by a dam will carry on as rainbow trout for generations, and may reestablish anadromy when the barrier is removed.[92] This biological plasticity makes *O. mykiss* politically and culturally flexible as well, passing between the jurisdiction of state fish and game agencies or the National Marine Fisheries Service depending on whether they go to the ocean. It also means that a beloved rainbow fishery may grow up in the stream above a dam, without the people who fish there being aware that their ten-pound trout might, under different conditions, run down to the distant ocean and return as thirty-pound sea monsters.[93]

Pacific salmon are resilient and adaptable—any animal that can live from the California chaparral to the arctic coast of Alaska would have to be. But after the arrival of Europeans, they were hit with a series of devastating ecological blows. The first came with the arrival of canning technology in the early nineteenth century. Anadromous fish are uniquely easy to catch in bulk: put a net across the river mouth, set up a cannery nearby, and you can remove all that protein from the river, can it, and disperse it all over the world. The fact that most of those salmon had not yet spawned was of little import to canners, at least in the short term. The canning industry quickly became regionally powerful, and although there were a variety of laws intended to maintain salmon runs, they were not very effective.[94] In some rivers, there was some push and pull between canners near the mouth and sport fishers upstream, but this tension eventually resolved itself as canneries demolished their rivers' salmon populations and put themselves out of business.[95]

The arrival of irrigated agriculture in river valleys diverted not just water but salmon themselves out of the stream, down canals, and onto farmers' fields. Urbanization and industrialization transformed the geography around key transitional sites in river landscapes—cities are often situated at confluences (like Portland) or at river mouths and bays (like San Francisco or Vancouver). By the late nineteenth century, northwestern salmon populations had plummeted. People realized this—as Taylor points out, the idea that Pacific fisheries are on the verge of collapse is a century old.[96] But while the species have never been in danger of worldwide extinction—there have always been plenty in Alaska, at least—runs in many rivers have in fact disappeared.

By the late twentieth century, Pacific salmon were absent from 44 percent of their historic habitat.[97] By 1991, 106 major Pacific salmon populations had been extirpated, and most of the rest were at risk of extinction.[98] That year, the Snake River sockeye (*O. nerka*) became the first evolutionarily significant unit (ESU, the government delineation for salmon populations) of salmon to be federally listed as endangered by the National Oceanic and Atmospheric Administration's (NOAA) National Marine Fisheries Service (NMFS). Northwestern fish advocates saw listing as their best option to save failing fisheries and, perhaps just as importantly, their watersheds. Wielding the Endangered Species Act as a weapon, they vigorously petitioned NMFS to list more and more runs.[99] A flurry of federal listings followed in the late 1990s; twenty-five Pacific salmonid runs were federally listed by 2000.[100] As of 2015, over 60 percent of runs were federally listed as endangered or threatened.[101]

One popular answer to this was to create more fish, in hatcheries. The idea behind hatcheries is simple enough—if you allow enough salmon eggs to hatch, and put enough young salmon in the river, then you will get more adult fish returning from the ocean. In the late nineteenth century, once the technical demands of hatching fish eggs in captivity were mastered, hatcheries became popular across the Northwest.[102] Hatcheries seemed like a great way to have your (fish)cake and eat it too—people looked at all the salmon eggs and juvenile salmon that, under natural conditions, died before maturing, and thought they could do better.[103] If a salmon's thousands of eggs were well tended, and smolts protected in hatcheries, surely the result would be enough adult fish for sport anglers and canners and ocean fishers to catch their share (though tribal fishers, in those more racist days, were not embraced).[104] A political, economic, and cultural eco-system grew up around hatcheries, as "fish culture" and "fish factories" were supposed to make raising fish as easy as producing corn on a farm, or cloth in a mill.[105] The fish were still being referred to as "product" in the late twentieth century.[106]

In reality, the results of hatchery production have been mixed. They have had some success in creating more fish, to be sure, and in some rivers most of the fish are hatchery stock.[107] But they have failed on many lev-els.[108] A large run of fish may be credited to the hatchery system when in fact success was due to favorable ocean conditions.[109] Salmon have to pass through a long chain of habitats between birth and death, and if a river is too warm, polluted, and fragmented by dams to produce a healthy popula-tion of wild fish, it will not be a good place for hatchery fish, either.[110] Moreover, the evolutionary conditions at hatcheries favor behaviors that will not serve fish well in the wild. For example, for hatchery fish, a shadow passing over the water may mean that food is about to be dumped in, and a fish that swims boldly toward that shadow will thrive.[111] In the wild, shadows over the water are seldom good for salmon. The density of fishes in a hatchery may also spread disease among smolts, which then spread it in the river.[112] Finally, many hatcheries have not used native fish runs. Salmon populations, both Atlantic and Pacific, are adapted to the ecologi-cal demands of their native streams, and putting fish into a river that may be faster or colder or siltier or have different seasonal fluctuations than they are equipped to handle is like trying to wedge in the wrong puzzle piece—you can do it, kind of, but it won't really work.

For all these reasons, hatcheries have been and continue to be very controversial in the Northwest. But, like canneries before them, hatcheries have political and economic supporters. A native tribe with a treaty right to catch salmon may not accept the idea of waiting for the uncertain and long-term prospect of a native fishery reviving—particularly when the decline of that run was not their doing. A fishing guide may need a catchable popula-tion of fish in order to make it through the year. A state wildlife management agency may face a constituency that expects to catch fish on the weekend, and may have its budget directly supported by that constituency's purchase of fishing licenses. Hatcheries have a recreational and educational role, as well—for many people, hatcheries are places you can take children to see salmon.[113] Practices that have caused problems for hatcheries in the past can be improved and are, to some extent, improving, as evolving science informs management techniques.[114] In some rivers, hatcheries will probably be a necessary bridge to a restored wild population. But will they be used that way? Can hatcheries get beyond the ideology of "fish culture" and human control of salmon? The controversy, and the lawsuits, roll on.

Hatcheries and dams have often gone hand in hand. If a dam excludes fish from spawning habitat—which, again, people knew to be a problem a thousand years ago—why not create artificial spawning habitat in a hatchery? Dams are useful nodes through which to sort and manage salmon; some dams even have their own hatchery built in. They are convenient collection points for hatchery stock—not only can you catch your adult fish at the base of the dam, you can expect that most of the fish you release there, having matured at the site, will return to it.

In the twentieth century, the Northwest's rivers, big and small, became increasingly managed for power, navigation, irrigation, and flood control—a series of "organic machines."[115] As this happened, its fish populations too became increasingly managed and controlled. But the decline of *Oncorhynchus* continued. The ocean catch ramped up in the twentieth century, as the fleets of all North Pacific nations, and some from beyond the region, used increasingly effective fishing technology to catch salmon on the open sea where regulation ranges from rare to impossible.[116] All of this means that the salmon crisis is often defined by four H's: harvest, hatcheries, hydropower, and habitat.

Dams Everywhere

The legacy of the New Deal and the go-go years is not just about big dams like Hoover and Glen Canyon. It is more subtle than that. There are fewer than two thousand hundred-foot dams in America.[117] While America had its eyes on big dams in big rivers, tens of thousands of smaller ones were rising in brooks and creeks and kills and runs all over the country. By the 1990s, the National Research Council estimated that 2.5 million dams—that averages out to fifty thousand dams per state—stood in America's waterways.[118] But this is only an educated guess. Most dams are not recorded anywhere. And while a little three-foot dam in some nameless tributary isn't a landscape-changer or economic engine like Hoover or Grand Coulee, it still holds up sediment, widens and slows the river, and bars the movement of a wide variety of animals.

Fast-forward to 2018, and they're all falling apart. An estimated 85 percent of American dams will be past their useful lives by 2020.[119] Many of these structures were built for purposes that no longer exist, but although regional economies have moved on, the dams still sit in their rivers, decaying, year after year. The US Army Corps of Engineers, which keeps an inventory of America's 87,359 major dams, rated over 27,000 of them as having "high" or "significant" hazard potential.[120] A productive dam that halts floods and makes electricity and diverts irrigation water is a valuable tool, but most American dams aren't like that.

On a subtler but just as politically important level, the go-go years made us a nation of lakes. But they aren't really lakes—referring to a dam's impoundment as a lake is a cultural distinction. In some countries, a lake is only a natural lake.[121] Many states have no natural lakes; there aren't many forces of nature that dig out basins and fill them with water. The lakes and levees beloved of characters in country songs were mostly engineered in the middle of the twentieth century. But even if a dam was originally built to produce power or hold drinking water or play some other economically productive role, its impoundment quickly becomes a recreational center for the community and a beloved quasi-natural feature. The most common primary purpose for a structure on the National Inventory of Dams is recreation.[122] We build our heritage quickly, in America.

Ecological Problems

All this aside, dams are a Pandora's box of ecological destruction. That dams change their landscape is obvious to anyone who looks: they flood the valley above them and turn floodplains and forests into an artificial lake.[123] Often, these lakes host an array of invasive species that thrive in still waters.[124] Dams sequester flows of silt, gravel, and woody debris—the raw material of river habitat.[125] Downstream, this leaves an "armored" riverbed, made only of large, immovable stones, and a deeper, narrower channel.[126] Sandbars and estuaries and beaches, even if they're many miles downstream, dwindle as their sand and silt washes away without being replenished.[127] Sometimes all of this is considered to be a trade-off for climate-friendly power—the alternative to a dam might be a coal-fired power plant, and all its carbon—but this is not necessarily the case. Plants rotting in the reservoir and releasing methane, among other processes, make some dams significant greenhouse gas producers.[128]

Just as silt is stuck above the dam, fish—unless they're spry enough to leap over it, or to climb a fish ladder—are stuck below it. This is especially bad for migratory species, like salmon, that must move upstream to spawn. There are many accounts of fish leaping—crash!—into dams and spillways in vain attempts to reach upstream spawning sites.[129] Some dams have fish ladders or other passage mechanisms built in, but overall these are not very effective, especially for species that cannot jump.[130] Dams disproportionately bar fish from certain types of habitat—upland forests with lots of melting snow and downstream floodplains, for instance.[131] As this happens, the salmon runs that rely on this kind of habitat suffer.

This is a problem not just for the fish, or even the river, but for the entire upstream ecosystem. Under natural conditions, flesh from salmon carcasses—most of them die after they spawn—spreads far beyond the water's edge, nourishing many other animals, and even plants, throughout the upstream parts of the basin.[132] Only 6–7 percent of all the millions of pounds of nutrients that salmon once brought up from the sea make it inland today.[133] Even small dams tire or delay fish as they strive to leap over them or school at the base of fish ladders.[134] Stuck at the dam site, the fish are in grave danger from predators, from mergansers to bears—a near-literal example of fish in a barrel.

For the fish that hatch upstream, migration down to the ocean, through or over the dam, is possible but dangerous. Agricultural diversions sometimes channel fish into canals and deposit them on farmers' fields.[135] Hydroelectric turbines can "chew up" fish[136] as they pass downstream, and nitrogen, dissolving under the pressure of spillways, can give fish gas bubble disease.[137] The water below a dam may also be artificially warm or cold depending on how water is released from the reservoir.[138] Along with the physical stress of high temperatures, cold-water fish must survive the diseases and parasites that thrive in warm water.[139]

Dam Removal

For all these reasons, political, ecological, and cultural, environmental advocates have opposed dams for a century. Dam removal, though, has been a twenty-first-century phenomenon. The beginning of the dam removal era came in 1999, when the Edwards Dam, which had stood in Maine's Kennebec River since the Van Buren administration, was decommissioned and removed.[140] This removal was done against the wishes of the dam's owners in order to restore native fish populations—exactly the sort of removal that environmentalists wanted to see. American Rivers, probably the foremost dam removal organization in the country, begins its dam removal list with 1999.[141] At the end of that year, the Heinz Center marshaled together a formidable set of scholars and thinkers to discuss and assess the new dam removal phenomenon.[142] After 1999, inspired and invigorated river advocates across America leapt into an assault on the nation's dams that continues into the present day.

Since 1999, the dam removal phenomenon has moved further in some places than others, clustering in several regions.[143] The Pacific Northwest is one of these. The Northwest has had a disproportionate number of dam removals: California,[144] Oregon, and Washington contain 4 percent of the nation's dams but have accounted for 11 percent of its removals.[145] In some ways this is surprising: along with the still-powerful cultural resonance of Grand Coulee and the dam-building go-go years, these states are the top three hydroelectric generators in the nation,[146] and their powerful agricultural sectors are heavily dependent on irrigation water caught and diverted by dams. People sing Woody Guthrie's dam-building songs around Cascade campfires to this day. At the same time, the environmental movement has been strong and dynamic on the West Coast, successfully promoting strict environmental laws and securing large tracts of protected land. The region also contains many tribal nations, which gained in power and political dynamism in the final third of the twentieth century. As these groups rose, they joined the battle over salmon, attacking the crisis through habitat conservation, eventually backed by federal listings. But much of the salmon habitat in the Northwest was altered by, or lost behind, dams. The goal of most of the dam removals in the Northwest has been to trade hydro for habitat, and get the salmon back.[147] The question was, and remains, how to do it?

Dam Removal Politics

When stakeholders begin to consider dam removal, they enter a policy wilderness. There are plenty of laws guiding dams' construction and operation, but few guiding their end. Once a dam is no longer economically productive, its owners can (and often do) walk away, as if leaving a broken-down car out on a public highway. Enough abandoned structures sit in the nation's waterways that river and fishery managers have coined the term "feral dams."[148] American environmental laws tend to invoke negative rather than positive authority—they stop bad actions rather than mandate good ones.[149] This basically defensive approach has served the American environment reasonably well, as major laws—the Clean Water Act, the Clean Air Act, the Endangered Species Act, and many more—fought pollution, habitat destruction, and so on, more or less as intended. But negative authority falls short when the goal is to reverse the past and restore a degraded ecosystem.

A notable exception to this situation—a settlement in the policy wilderness, if you will—is hydroelectric dams; these are licensed by the

Federal Energy Regulatory Commission (FERC) and undergo a relicensing process that offers dam removal advocates an opportunity to get politically involved. This is thanks to the far-sighted approach of lawmakers a century ago. When they passed the Federal Power Act in 1920, they wanted to encourage the development of water and power, but they did not choose to give private dam operators dominance over public waterways (or regional energy markets) into the indefinite and uncertain future. They established a system wherein licenses would come up for review and renewal—or, potentially, purchase by the government—after thirty to fifty years.[150] So when dam removal became an active idea, many decades later, it had an opening. For this reason, several larger and better-publicized dam removals, like the Edwards case in Maine, have been of hydroelectric dams. Even so, FERC's authority only extends so far—it can decline to renew a license, and the government can buy the dam, but it cannot mandate that anyone take the all-important step of paying to remove the decommissioned dam.[151] Beyond the vagaries of the FERC licensing process, the vast majority of dams have no clear policy pathway toward removal. Only a few thousand American dams produce hydroelectricity; again, the most common function for dams is recreation.[152] There is no Federal Recreation Regulatory Commission.

In the absence of policy, there will be politics, and river politics are, by their nature, tough and complicated. Rivers are classic common-pool resources: hard to privatize and widely used by the public at large.[153] Elinor Ostrom, the Nobel-winning scholar of resource use, points out that rivers and fisheries are especially challenging to manage, being inherently dynamic and difficult to contain. But of course, waterways provide many important societal functions, and it is necessary to govern them somehow.

Most American states, which own all surface waters within their borders, govern those waters under one of two regimes: riparian rights and prior appropriation.[154] When English settlers arrived in the rainy eastern half of the United States, they apportioned its waters the same way they had in England: through the common-law doctrine of riparian rights, wherein people with land on waterways could use the water however they saw fit as long as they did not unreasonably impair downstream users. But once they reached the arid West, the dead-grass landscape drove American pioneers to invent prior appropriation. This is first come, first served, basically, no matter how users affect people downstream—so long as the use is deemed beneficial by the state. For many decades, ecological conservation was not deemed beneficial, but in the later twentieth century, the definition of beneficial use expanded to include ecological purposes that kept water in the stream.[155]

These systems provide the foundation for dam politics and policy. Legally, dams' uses are beneficial, a routine part of water law and management. But while those uses are easy to see and evaluate—they are why dams are built, after all—dams' problems are harder to account for. Traditional dam functions cause problems for the environment and for society, and neither water rights regime has provided an effective way to account for all these problems or to make whole the people, and the species, who bear them. Under both systems, dam operators get the exclusive right to use a public resource for their own private ends, running the state's water through turbines or dumping it on their fields or stocking it with bass, regardless of what other river users might want.[156] Most of the dams on the National Inventory of Dams are privately owned,[157] and the overwhelming majority of unlisted, smaller dams surely are as well—public resources are not required in order to raise a three-foot push-up dam. This sort of situation will always create political tension.

Nature, Culture, and Restoration

The difference between dam removal and all the river politics that came before it is that dam removal reverses—not adjusts, not limits, but reverses—the political, economic, and ecological status quo. Its goal is to return the river to a more natural hydrological state, with unimpeded flows of water, species, and material. Of course, when people built the dam, they did so specifically in order to end the river's natural flow regime and replace it with their own, one that sent water wherever they wanted it, whenever they wanted it. To give up this control is nothing less than a fundamental reconsideration of the relationship between human beings and nature in America.[158]

At the beginning of American history,[159] nature was something to be feared; then, with the country's increasing mastery of the New World, something to be exploited; then, with the growth of environmentalism, something to be protected—protected from the depredations of other people.[160] From each of these perspectives, human beings are essentially separate from and antagonistic toward nature.[161] From the perspective of ecological restoration, though, people are vital parts—perhaps the most powerful parts—of nature, and should play a beneficial role in it.[162] Anyone who advocates for restoration crashes into traditional perspectives on nature, and the politics and policies those perspectives created. All these other views on nature remain present and powerful throughout American society.[163]

In restoration politics, the past becomes as much of a problem as the future. The act of ecological restoration implies that the traditional exploitative uses of nature were somehow wrong, or bad.[164] This can prompt angry resistance from those who believe in or benefit from that traditional use. Gretel Van Wieren describes a situation where a five-acre plot of native tallgrass prairie was planted, presumably for educational purposes, beside a school in Illinois. This plot makes up 0.000005 percent of the historic extent of tallgrass prairie, but its existence was seen by local farmers "as a moral indictment of their way of life and work, and more generally, of the American achievement of agricultural progress." Dam and reservoir users across America feel much the same way about their rivers.

How to Proceed?

So, given the combination of culturally powerful dams and a lack of reliable policy weapons, the question presents itself: Politically, how and why does dam removal happen? The simplest answer might be that the dams are getting old, but dams have been wearing out long before the dam removal era; in 1950, the young environmental movement could have targeted nearly three thousand major dams that were at least fifty years old.[165] The next answer might be that dams cause environmental harm, but again, this is something that has been known for many decades—angry fishermen dynamited a dam in Southern Oregon as early as 1918.[166] So, while age and ecology are surely contributing factors, they are not sufficient to explain the dam removal phenomenon of the past twenty years.[167] In this century, dam removal advocates have found new and effective ways to push for dam removal.

Once political negotiations get under way, though, the issues change. Many dams are marginally productive, imposing great ecological costs (as well as safety risks) in return for scanty economic benefits. So the converse question arises: How could dam removal *not* happen? But, despite these problems, some removal efforts have seen furious resistance and endured multi-decade delays. Dam defenders have had to be politically creative and energetic, just as removal advocates have.

These questions have not been satisfactorily answered; they have rarely even been raised. As the dam removal phenomenon continues to grow, it is important to understand the politics that shape it. In dam removal, the distribution of political power and the scope of conflict are fluid, and political players are forced to grapple with new and difficult emotional, ecological, economic, and engineering issues. The ways they do this—their values and motivations, their alliances, and their strategic and tactical decisions—make the difference between a dammed and a free-flowing river, with all that that brings.

The Waters Ahead

In chapter 2, I discuss the political lenses I use to examine dam removal: political frames, advocacy coalitions, and venue shopping. I also discuss the methods I used to study these cases.

In chapters 3, 4, and 5, I lay out the stories of the Elwha, Savage Rapids, and Marmot Dam removals. I place each dam removal in the context of its region, its history, and its natural environment, and identify important variables that defined the progress of each case. I also briefly discuss the removals' effectiveness as restoration actions.

In chapter 6, I analyze political variables, draw distinctions between cases, and offer hypotheses to be tested by future scholars. Each dam, each river, and each suite of stakeholders is unique, but a variety of political and policy issues were important across cases. These issues are likely to be important in many future situations, in dam removals and in other ecological restoration projects. I suggest approaches for understanding the politics of ecological restoration and recommend possible avenues for future study.

2

What We Think About When We Think About Dam Removal

Everyone thought Rick Rutz was crazy. In the mid-1980s, as he worked his way around Seattle, promoting a plan to remove the Elwha dams, even his fellow environmentalists told him that this was too much, that this would never work, that this would smirch the name of environmentalism and stop real, realistic, important work from happening.[1] Jeff Curtis, president of WaterWatch of Oregon, had a similar experience. As he lobbied for the removal of the Savage Rapids Dam, he found that his opponent, Representative Bob Repine (R-Grants Pass) couldn't believe this was happening.[2] When Portland General Electric decided to decommission the Marmot and Little Sandy Dams, they found that the stakeholders involved in the dam removal "had virtually no experience in how to make it happen."[3] As the removal of each dam rose to the political agenda, the first reaction was not anger or happiness, support or opposition—it was confusion.

Restoration Politics

Dam removal is new, but river politics are as old as the Nile, and uniquely complicated—nearly everyone who lives in a watershed can plausibly feel that they have a stake in the outcome of the issue. Overlapping claims to ownership, with the public's water flowing through a private dam, and that dam changing the river for other private landowners above and below it, enliven the issue as well.

The central problem with dam removal, again, is that it makes history go backward. Environmental advocates, from John Muir on, spent the twentieth century playing defense—working to protect landscapes and species before they disappeared, or to limit pollution and mitigate its effects. But in ecological restoration, environmentalists play offense, their goal nothing less than bringing nature back from the grave. In the past, a dammed valley would be mourned as dead and gone. Not anymore. Now it's just sleeping.

Restoration depends on understandings of an often-nebulous past and an always-uncertain future. Ecological restoration is notoriously plagued by clashing visions of what ecological restoration actually is.[4] Restoration advocates have to define the ecosystems of the past, to show how things that once were lost can live again, and to prove that those things are worth restoring. In many cases, this past ecosystem will be poorly recorded and difficult to define—who can say just how many salmon swam up the Rogue River before the arrival of Europeans? Once they successfully define the past, restoration advocates must then define the future—what is being restored, and how will it work in the twenty-first century? Some idealistic advocates may dream of the exact ecosystem from pre-Columbian times; others may want only to achieve an aesthetic and superficial restoration; others may care about one particular species, and want it as fast as possible. All can agree that what they want is restoration, but depending on how the undammed river takes shape, what may seem like a brilliant success to one group of stakeholders may seem like a dismal failure, or even betrayal, to others. To add to the vexation, dam removal, unlike other kinds of restoration, requires destruction—the dam must be demolished. Even more dramatically, it drains the impoundment—the "lake"—behind the dam. Just as dams transform landscapes, so does their removal.

Ecological restoration practitioners are trying to shake free of impossible expectations and ideological nostalgia, emphasizing the return of natural processes and managing for self-sustenance and resilience, to the extent that these things are possible in a twenty-first-century landscape, rather than a re-creation of a pre-Columbian wilderness.[5] As the fields of restoration science and environmental history mature, more stakeholders are coming to understand that Native America, while it certainly had more salmon in its rivers, pigeons in its skies, and bison on its plains than we see now, was very much a continent of managed landscapes, not a wilderness in any traditional sense.[6] Moreover, even if wilderness advocates' wildest dreams and their opponents' wildest nightmares were realized—if whole watersheds or mountain ranges were declared off-limits to all people—factors like the extirpation of some native species, colonization by exotic species from other regions, and changes in climate make the perfect reappearance of ancient ecosystems impossible. As most restoration stakeholders know, you cannot step in the same river twice. But for all that primeval wilderness never did and never will exist, it is a powerful American myth, one that lives in the hearts (more than the minds) of many environmentalists.[7] It is codified in law. The nation's highest-quality rivers are still designated "wild and scenic," and since 1964 its most natural land-scapes have been protected under the Wilderness Act. The wilderness ideal cannot be disentangled from restoration politics.

New Rivers

Politics grows out of history. Since colonial times, Americans[8] have tended to look at rivers primarily as sources of economic function; their hydrology and ecology only mattered insofar as they helped people make or lose money.[9] The "myth of plenty" mentality applied to rivers and fish just as much as it did to forests or bison herds. Rivers were transformed with minimal regard for the conditions that shaped the continent's streams, or their natural qualities. In many places, all that was left of a river's natural state were names—the Northeast, until recently, was full of Beaver Brooks that didn't contain any beavers.[10] Even when rivers were managed for recreation, their ecosystems might be entirely remodeled—in 1962, a poison called rotenone was poured into the Green River of Wyoming and Utah in order to eliminate "trash fish" and make way for more fishable, fry-able rainbow trout.[11] Eventually, played-out rivers all over America became little more than garbage dumps, filled with broken machines and industrial effluent.

But in recent decades, America's relationship with its rivers is becoming more holistic. Dan McCool calls this new regime, with its own dynamic politics, the River Republic.[12] This change has arisen alongside the growth of American environmentalism as a whole. As stakeholders built up the "Green State," the massive and durable political management apparatus through which Americans tend their environment, it has given river activists of all sorts many opportunities to get involved with their rivers, at all political levels.[13] In particular, the River Republic has risen with the growing national embrace of sustainability, a concept that is increasingly understood to incorporate social and environmental durability as well as economic strength. Indeed, the social and environmental qualities of rivers are precisely what new stakeholders are promoting in the River Republic. The change did not occur overnight, of course—its sources can be found as far back as the 1968 establishment of the Wild and Scenic Rivers Act, or even the fight over Hetch Hetchy. But the new era really embraces the 1990s and the twenty-first century. Developments from the formation of watershed councils to the popularity of whitewater rafting have opened and expanded river politics, and stakeholders as old as native tribes and as new as stand-up paddleboarders are bringing their values to the nation's waterways.

This new era in American river politics has attracted a good deal of attention from political scientists.[14] It will surely continue to do so. But the only scholar to treat dam removal in both depth and breadth was William Lowry, when he wrote *Dam Politics*. Lowry, grappling with dam removal just as the phenomenon was gathering head, pointed to dams' physical complexity and political receptivity as the key issues in restoration. He investigated eight dams, covering all regions of the United States, and showed, unsurprisingly, that rickety and unproductive dams, and higher degrees of stakeholder cooperation, were more likely to lead to dam removal. Brad Clark later refined Lowry's variables a bit, focusing on landscape-based factors.[15] But that's really been all.

Dam Politics was published fourteen years and more than 750 dam removals ago.[16] Since then, Lowry's work has been more cited than built upon. Research on dam removal politics and policy since then has been piecemeal and case-specific—only very recently has there been a serious effort to collect dam removal information.[17] The politics of dam removal are mostly uncharted waters.

To understand politics, you must know who you're talking about, what they want, and what they do. So I scrutinize these cases through three analytical lenses. The first and most basic lens is the stakeholders: Who takes part in dam removal politics? How do they form advocacy coalitions, and how do these coalitions evolve? The second lens is political framing: When stakeholders look at the dam, the river, and one another, what do they see, and what do they want? The final lens is venue shopping: As each issue evolved, where did stakeholders take it, and how did their choices of venue matter? These factors are, of course, tightly interrelated, each of them changing in concert with or in response to the others. Together, they show how my cases of dam removal happened in all their complexities and details, and allow me to lay out the political pathways whereby dam removal went from being a strange and unsettling idea to a concrete reality.

Advocacy Coalitions

Who cares about dam removal?

A natural question with which to begin. But before I even began this work, it was clear to me that the answer to "Who cares about dam removal?" was "Everyone." Dam removal has risen to public attention on a flood of controversy.[18] It is the sort of issue where every person you talk to offers to show you their own PowerPoint about just how right they are.[19] Even as dams alter landscapes on a watershed scale, dams' operations, and their removal, touch all the human interests in that watershed. Even passive or recreational users see their familiar river transformed once the dam comes out. How do they involve themselves in the politics of dam removal?

To analyze stakeholder dynamics, I chose the Advocacy Coalition Framework (ACF), created by Paul Sabatier and Hank Jenkins-Smith.[20] The ACF is one of the most popular frameworks with which to explain policy change, particularly on natural resource issues.[21] I don't use the entire ACF wholesale—it's built more for large trends than for individual cases, and to track policy change over a decade's time. But the useful tools the ACF offers let me cast light on my cases.

Essentially, the ACF sees politics as the result of conflicting stakeholders expressing and promoting their beliefs, and approaches political issues as those beliefs collide. The framework was formed in response to an era when political issues began to include more and more stakeholder groups, as opposed to those issues' being resolved by a small set of professionals.[22] It sees the people working for the same political goal (an advocacy coalition) as sharing policy beliefs on a deep enough level that they are willing to put time and resources into political action. The whole set of people and organizations involved in a policy issue, known as the policy subsystem, engage in policy learning as the issue unfolds, and become more adept at dealing with the issue and each other. The policy subsystem is the unit of analysis for scholars applying the ACF.[23]

This approach applies well to dam removal. As the issue is a new one, dam removal presents an array of interest groups doing new things and combining in new ways—forming a new policy subsystem, in fact. They inevitably engage in policy learning as they work through the situation. Dam removal calls on the beliefs of all stakeholders, and exposes just how much, and in what ways, they value the dam and the river. If dam removal were a straightforward technocratic matter, decided by engineers and economists, it would be a different political world.

The obvious advocacy coalition to focus on is the one that wants the dam removed—the advocates who raise the issue to the public agenda and push it through to its resolution. This focus suits a variety of policy change models, the ones that emphasize policy entrepreneurs.[24] However, it's important to pay equal attention to dam removal opponents. The fight to save a dam is just as new and strange as the fight to destroy one. The challenges facing people who love dams as they figure out how to express their values politically and decide how to connect with allies are as equally novel and politically relevant as those facing people who want them out.

Framing

A river's tale depends on who's doing the telling. One person may talk of a wild and dangerous stream that alternated between terrifying floods and miserly trickles before being tamed and steadied by a dam. Another might bemoan the decline of a vibrant, dynamic watershed that spread life all through the floodplain until it was degraded and shackled by a dam. Our two narrators, both intelligent, well-informed, well-meaning people who care deeply about the river, will tell the story with different heroes, different villains, different victories, different defeats—different worlds. They're talking about the same river, and the same historical events.

The difference is framing.[25] The frame through which stakeholders see an issue creates the moral and causal foundation for their political involvement—the beliefs they strive to realize and promote. To understand the stakeholders that form and drive dam removal's advocacy coalitions, we must understand their frames.

Natural resources conflicts hinge on framing, of course—one man's wise use is another man's wanton destruction. By the end of the twentieth century, nearly every significant goal and understanding of natural resource use was strongly supported in both policy and politics. Like layers of sediment in the earth, layers of policy have been laid down over history, and the interest groups, laws, and institutions that surround those policies have endured through the ages.[26] These policy layers begin as deep as the Constitution and even Roman law, but each generation has added its own alterations and additions to its parents' natural resource use regime. Often, this happens without eliminating the old regime.

For a dramatic example of this, consider the General Mining Act, passed in the Wild West days of 1872. This was, of course, a time when the environmental movement was in its earliest infancy, and the dominant use for public lands was to extract their natural resources. The act allowed prospectors to essentially buy federal land for $2.50/acre if they dug up minerals there. They did not have to pay the government any royalties. In the interim, public attitudes toward public lands have changed radically, and a great many laws and rules have been created to limit and regulate, and indeed to forbid, industrial development on public land. But as I write this, in 2017, the General Mining Act still offers miners federal land for $2.50/acre. They still don't have to pay any royalties.[27]

All of this infuriates environmentalists, when they think of it.[28] The General Mining Act would be unlikely to pass today. But this approach, turning public land into minerals and money is, of course, framed as the highest and best use of those resources by modern-day miners and their political allies. So it endures. Cases like these, where conflicting goals are supported by policy and by politics, are, in the phrase of Deborah Stone, a policy paradox.[29]

There are few starker examples of this paradox than the competing demands the modern Pacific Northwest puts on its waterways. Rivers are expected to store water and provide electricity for millions of people, irrigate vast expanses of agriculture, and nurture healthy populations of native salmon and trout, every year. These functions run directly counter to each other.

And this is the basic framing clash in dam removal: What is the river for? Both sides can argue that they are in favor of a river's traditional, true, best purpose. Each side presents a powerful symbol of national heritage. On the one hand, dams represent the working landscape, with nature guided to humanity's purposes.[30] On the other hand, the wild stream, alive with fish, can embody America's unique natural beauty.[31] A person's frame for the river carries with it the crucial issue of who gets to use the river—should it be the domain of business or the government, local people or all Americans?—and therefore, who can legitimately take part in important decisions. If you see the river as a key supporter of regional economic security, then an environmentalist who works in Washington, DC, and seeks to place an Oregonian river off-limits to hydropower development may be too far estranged from reality to merit a seat at the negotiating table.

As noted by Schon and Rein, and supported by the formulations of the ACF, these sorts of frames are terribly difficult to resolve because a clash of deeply held beliefs doesn't allow for much common ground—the two sides are effectively talking about two different rivers.[32] While, in practice, most stakeholders are reasonable enough to at least admit the validity of other people's perspectives, political conflict is not like competing bids for a contract. In politics, if you lose, it means that your beliefs, your values, even your identity, lose as well.

Stakeholders' understanding of a river's uses goes on to set the stage for the next framing issue: the definition of the problem. A problem rarely springs onto the world out of nowhere. Somebody must be unhappy with the status quo, and voice this criticism.[33] But such a person is only a lonely Cassandra until they reach a corps of allies, who agree that this is indeed a problem that must be solved.[34] Moreover, these allies must be strong enough to take political action[35] and to define their problem to the voting, paying public as one that can, and should, be solved.[36]

This is how issues morph, in two generations, from being accepted as a routine annoyance of everyday life to being seen as a shameful national embarrassment. Air pollution, which has been present as long as people have burned fuel for warmth but was controlled on a meaningful level only in the 1970s, is an example. This kind of successful reframing creates what Baumgartner and Jones, in their popular framework for analyzing policy change, call punctuated equilibrium[37]—wherein political life is seen as stable over a fairly long time, and then is disrupted by the arrival of some catalytic event.

A neat trick, to take something ordinary and sell it as an important problem. How do advocates pull it off? One key approach is to associate the problem with a strong and sympathetic policy image.[38] A good example is the oil-coated animals of Prince William Sound after the Exxon Valdez oil spill. People understand policy and problems in simplified, symbolic terms.[39] They have to—no person has all the necessary expertise to fully grasp all aspects of an environmental issue. They see the animals, they feel bad, they think oil spills are problems.

Having successfully framed an issue as a problem and brought it to the national agenda, the task of the stakeholder is to promote their solution. If they manage to take hold of the debate quickly enough, they can extend their frame to make their solution into an obvious choice.[40] However, having disrupted the political equilibrium, the policy entrepreneur is likely to be fiercely attacked by the defenders of the status quo. Thus a new political conflict is born.

Solving the problem often means blaming someone. If a problem is no one's fault, then no one can be held accountable for solving it. For instance, depending on the frame, natural disasters can easily be framed as acts of God, necessary evils, beneficial ecological phenomena, or the result of callous human negligence. Events like the Three Mile Island nuclear power station accident[41] and the Gulf BP oil leak[42] are even labeled acts of God. This is politically clever—these issues were patently not acts of God unless the Almighty builds faulty nuclear reactors and drills poorly secured oil wells. But if they're acts of God, then it follows that private stakeholders should not be forced to pay for them. If a problem is defined as human, then someone has done something wrong, or poorly, or negligently. In reality, not many environmental decisions are made with truly nefarious motives, but accusations of negligence or ignorance are common. The moral overtones of blame are likely to anger the target and spark an indignant response.

Some people might look at a dam removal decision and feel that it should be easy. All that is required, our optimist might say, is to ask ecologists, engineers, and economists what will happen if the dam is removed or re-operated, and then decide what to do. Will the removal be bad for the local economy? Will the fish return? Can the dam come out safely? Hardly anyone—the environmental advocates pushing for dam removal, the businesspeople who own the dam, the politicians who make natural resource laws—actually understand what will happen. So why not leave it up to the experts?

Of course, this isn't how it goes. While technical experts' involvement is indispensable in natural resource issues—indeed, it is often legally mandated—in the hands of clever stakeholders, science becomes one more political weapon with its own unique power. Advocates strive to frame their solutions as being scientifically correct, but are unlikely to change their beliefs to conform to science. It was a dam removal issue on the Klamath River that gave rise to the phrase "combat biology."[43] Funtowicz and Ravetz call this "postnormal science," where many people take part and stake some claim to authority.[44] Laypeople cannot really have much to add to a technical scientific debate,[45] but in America, they do so anyway, creating and interpreting science for their own purposes.

The way people frame the problem, the solution, the resource, and the experts is not only about expressing beliefs, of course, but also about gaining the support of powerful people. Frames change, and so does their effectiveness, depending on their setting and audience. This phenomenon is common enough—it is well known to any teenager who has tried to convince both his friends and his mother to agree to the same plan for a Saturday evening—but it is central to landscape politics and policy change. Policy entrepreneurs must take their case through multiple venues—just as a teenager requires the approval of both his mother and his friends in order to bring his plan to fruition. The multiple uses and identities of the river, the dam, and dam removal evolve and develop with the venues that house it.

Venue Shopping

In America, conflicts never need to end. The United States is blessed and cursed with an open political landscape.[46] Americans can comment on a timber sale in a national forest, join (or form) an advocacy group to lobby for stricter industrial waste storage standards, and write letters to the editor or even buy an ad in the newspaper to complain about windmills on a nearby ridgeline. They can promote their views on climate change through an array of social media, they can boycott companies that use palm oil, they can accost other people on the sidewalk and urge them to sign petitions in defense of tigers. They can sue the opponents all the way, potentially, to the Supreme Court of the United States. And, of course, Americans can vote for or donate to representatives at local, state, and national levels, and if they aren't satisfied, they can run for office themselves. A motivated stakeholder can go a long time before their resources or energy are exhausted.[47]

All of this puts a premium on venue shopping, which is to say, finding the most advantageous place in which to promote a cause.[48] Ideally, you'd find a venue where powerful decision-makers are unmoved by an opponent's political frame but sympathetic to your own.[49] Nature is many things to many people, and since the tides of history have laid down layers of policy that empower many different environmental perspectives, such venues are likely to be available. An excellent example of this is provided by Pralle: Canadian environmentalists promoted the preservation of Clayoquot Sound in far-off cities and overseas, where the public cared more about trees and wildlife than about income for British Columbian loggers.

Shifts in venues expand and reshape the composition of political coalitions as well; the most powerful thing that a new ally may bring to a coalition is access to an advantageous political venue. The most obvious political venues are legislatures (where a fortunate advocate can get their chosen solution enshrined in law, and publicly funded) and courts (where a judge can order one's opponents to surrender). At the same time, subtler and less direct venues may be just as powerful. Stakeholders can help carry their cause toward victory by doing something as simple as designing a clever bumper sticker.

The diverse issues associated with fish and water open a tremendous number of potential venues to dam removal stakeholders, and the unformed nature of dam removal politics means that removals' potential political pathways are wide open. It may be that a dam removal decision stays locally contained, with easy cooperation between private stakeholders and the relevant public agencies, in a venue like a watershed council. But larger dams, and the many stakeholders and issues that connect to them, are likely to attract controversy and require a political odyssey, with various gods and monsters lying in wait for the coalitions as they reach each venue.

Venue selection is the first and most important challenge in dam removal. With very few policies defining the end of a dam's life, anyone promoting dam removal must be imaginative, discovering or creating venues where they can successfully promote their views. Advocates may have wished a dam gone for many decades but have no established place to make their desire into a live issue. Without finding a political leverage point[50] at which to start the process, dam removal would be impossible. Perhaps the biggest lasting effect of the early removals I discuss in this work is that they showed the world where to go to take out dams.

Nearly as instructive as the venues actors select are those that they avoid. Naturally, actors will strive to stay out of venues where they will be defeated. But venues also dictate the terms of victory or defeat. A lawsuit, for instance, may provide a thunderous victory for an environmental advocate worried about an endangered species, but will that lawsuit yield the sort of textured long-term management plan that would offer the best chance for that species to thrive? How will it affect future relationships with other stakeholders present in that ecosystem? Coalitions' approach to venues can display advocates' core values, members' perspectives on acceptable solutions, and those members' roles in relation to other stakeholders and authorities.

Case Studies and Methods

I set out to understand dam removal politics by researching three major removals: Savage Rapids Dam, removed from southern Oregon's Rogue River in 2009; the Elwha/Glines Canyon complex, removed from Washington's Elwha River in 2011–2013; and Marmot, removed from Oregon's Sandy River in 2007. These were the three biggest functioning dams to be removed in the Northwest.[51] Under Lowry's formulation, these larger—that is, more physically complex—dams should be more difficult to remove, and for that reason, more politically revealing. As I traced the political process of each removal, I identified important political variables and generated hypotheses about the dam removal phenomenon.

I interviewed everyone I could find who had been involved with these dam removal decisions—to do case studies like these, you have to talk to people.[52] I began my work by contacting the key informants listed on American Rivers' dam removal database. I conducted semi-structured interviews, taking notes and recording the conversation digitally whenever possible. Interviews focused on informants' roles in the issue. Usually these roles were confined to particular episodes of the larger story. Very few people were involved in the entire twenty-year-plus span of the Elwha or Savage Rapids cases. In several cases, informants' age and the many years between the events described and the day of the interview (as well as subtler issues like confirmation bias, self-absorption, and a desire to be seen as having been right) meant that their accounts may not have been completely reliable.[53] At the end of each interview, I identified subsequent informants through snowball sampling.[54] Most of these conversations were in person; some were by phone. I gave informants the option of having the recorder turned off at any point in the interview, and a few did ask for this. In total, I interviewed about eighty people.

I confirmed and supplemented informants' accounts with archival research. I focused on newspapers, the only sources for week-to-week details of ongoing dam removal debates. I read each removal-related article to appear in each community's local newspaper: the *Grants Pass* (Oregon) *Daily Courier*, the *Sandy* (Oregon) *Post*, and the *Peninsula Daily News* (Port Angeles, Washington). I also read agency documents on each case, as well as press releases, personal letters, pamphlets, bumper stickers, and any other relevant sources that were available. I took care that each narrative chain was linked together by causal connectors to ensure that my accounts and conclusions are sound and reliable.[55] From these sources, I assembled a coherent narrative of each dam removal.

3
Big Fish, Big Dams, Big Problems

Congressman Norm Dicks tells the story of walking into a town hall meeting in Port Angeles, Washington, in the mid-1990s. Dicks had only recently become Port Angeles's representative, so he and the 120 or so people in attendance didn't really know each other yet. Before he could even reach the microphone, Norm tells me, "A guy jumps up and says, 'Let's tell the congressman how we feel about taking the dams out on the Elwha. All opposed?' A hundred and fifteen people stood up."[1]

The dams that all these people stood for were 210-foot Glines Canyon and 105-foot Elwha. When the citizens of Port Angeles looked at them, and the river churning through their turbines, they saw what dam builder Thomas Aldwell had seen: "peace and power and civilization."[2] For them, the lakes that rose behind the dams were places where human ingenuity had improved nature, and raised it to a higher level of purity and beauty. They wanted to be sure that their new congressman understood this.

But when other people looked at the Elwha, they saw something very different. To environmentalists, the Elwha was one of the wildest rivers in the Lower 48—the dams were the only significant development in the entire watershed. To anglers, the Elwha was a legend—a river that housed (before the dams) ten different runs of anadromous salmon, including a monstrous race of hundred-pound Chinook. And to the Lower Elwha Klallam Tribe, looking at the Elwha as it ran past their reservation at the estuary, the river was the foundation of their traditional economy, a central presence in their culture, and the legendary site from which the first people emerged.

When the Elwha dams eventually came out, many years after that meeting, the deconstruction came amid great fanfare and public excitement. Luminaries from Clallam County and well beyond came together to witness the removal. The tribe sang songs of celebration. Interior Secretary Ken Salazar warmly assured the crowd of the Obama administration's devotion to healthy rural landscapes and economies. A movie star made a speech. And Norm Dicks, now eighteen years older and in his last term in

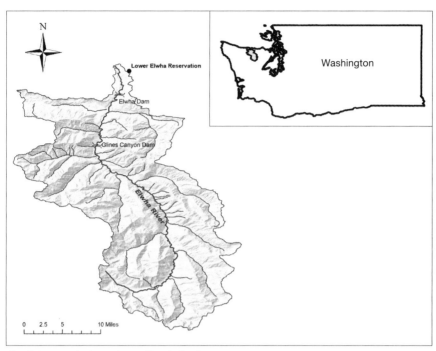

The Elwha watershed. Map by Bradley Blackwell.

Congress, helped kick off the demolition of the lower dam. Somewhat lost amid the cheers was the fact that the removal occurred only after decades of contentious debate, political maneuvering, tension, fighting, and fear.

Background

The Elwha runs north, spilling down from the glaciers of the Olympic Mountains to the Strait of Juan de Fuca. Its watershed covers 321 square miles, the largest drainage basin of the many rivers radiating out from the peninsula's mountainous center; it is forty-five miles long. Above the last few miles of the river, where Highway 1 crosses on its way around the Olympic Peninsula, the Elwha watershed lies almost entirely within the protective embrace of Olympic National Park, lending it an ecological purity shared by few streams of any size in the Lower 48.

The Lower Elwha Klallam Tribe and the other Klallam (sometimes written as s'Klallam)[3] tribes have lived on the North Olympic Peninsula for many thousands of years—the legal term is "time immemorial." There is some tendency, in modern times, to romanticize pre-Columbian life and make it out to be a paradise. Of course this is not realistic. However, it's fair to say that the Elwhas, and their fellow Puget Sound tribes, lived amid natural abundance that supported a rich existence. Indeed, they are reckoned to have been among the wealthiest societies in Native America.[4] The ecology of the Olympic Peninsula and the Salish Sea meant that there was game in the forests and seafood in the Elwha estuary and beyond. And, always, there were salmon.

The Elwha churned with fish. It's important, before diving in to this subject, to remember that preindustrial fish populations are difficult to gauge.[5] There were, of course, no scientists, in the modern sense of the word, monitoring *Oncorhynchus* populations in the old Northwest. What we have to go on are entries in pioneer journals and accounts from tribal elders, which, while valuable, are inexact and sometimes layered with nostalgic mythmaking. It's also worth bearing in mind that, historically, many streams up and down the West Coast hosted salmon runs that would have seemed enormous to pioneers from the fished-out streams of the East, let alone to twenty-first-century urban Americans.

However, by any standard, the Elwha really was an extremely rich salmon stream. Ten different runs of anadromous salmonids lived in the Elwha, including all five Pacific salmon species. The river was fishable throughout the year.[6] The ecological effects rippled up into the mountains as the relatively nutrient-poor Elwha watershed[7] was replenished annually by millions of pounds of spawned-out salmon, nourishing animals and plants throughout and beyond the riparian zone.[8]

The most famous of these fish were the Chinook salmon, known as kings. The Elwha is a rugged river, crashing down canyon after canyon from the Olympic peaks. Over the millennia, the caloric demands of swimming up it to spawn had built the kings into giants that weighed more than a hundred pounds.[9] King salmon in other rivers usually weigh about forty pounds. In the twenty-first century, Elwha elder Adeline Smith remembered seeing, as a young girl, fish nearly as long as herself.[10] When these huge Chinook were gaffed, tribal fishers would have to link arms to pull them up out of the river, tug-of-war style.[11] The river also hosted an enormous population of pink salmon. The run has been conservatively estimated at one hundred thousand adults in a year.[12] When the pinks came in, the river would be so alive with fish that horses would shy away from crossing it.[13] There were also coho, sockeye, and chum salmon, as well as char, winter and summer steelhead, and cutthroat trout—a river of scales and fins and protein, running uphill through the water. To the Klallams, the salmon were not just an economic essential, but a sacred gift, given to them by their maker.[14] Thus it was for many thousands of years.

Industrializing the Elwha

After the arrival of European and American colonists and the subsequent devastation of their traditional way of life, the Klallams, along with other tribes, were compelled to sign away their ancestral lands in the 1855 Treaty of Point No Point. In return they received reservation lands and cash. The treaty also held that "the right of taking fish at usual and accustomed grounds and stations is further secured to said Indians."[15] In the decades that followed the treaty, some Elwhas managed to retain something of a traditional subsistence fishing lifestyle; others homesteaded, much as Caucasian pioneers did.[16] They continued to live in the area between the Elwha River and the beaches of Port Angeles.

Around the turn of the twentieth century, Canadian businessman Thomas Aldwell moved to Port Angeles, staked a mining claim in the lower Elwha Valley, and set about acquiring land with the intention of building a hydroelectric dam there.[17] All of this was very much in the tradition of manifest destiny, to the point where Aldwell called his self-congratulatory autobiography *Conquering the Last Frontier*.[18] The settlers of Port Angeles, in the same tradition, wholeheartedly welcomed the project and looked forward to living in an electrified town.[19] Aldwell started construction in 1910 at a site five miles above the river mouth. Two years later, the 105-foot dam was nearly complete, but the work was shoddy—the dam was not built down to bedrock. The river pushed, the foot of the structure collapsed, and the new reservoir (which would be known as Lake Aldwell) blew down the valley, carrying with it every fish unlucky enough to be in the lower river. To the Elwhas, October 31, 1912,[20] became known as "the day the fish were in the trees."[21] Angry but undaunted, Aldwell rebuilt the dam, packing the hole with debris from the surrounding canyon.[22] The jury-rigged dam held. It would stand until 2011.

Political trouble began while the Elwha Dam was being built. Even in those pre-environmentalist days, Washington law required that dams include passage structures to let salmon and trout access upstream spawning habitat. Aldwell did not make much effort to comply. After a lengthy exchange with Washington fish commissioner Leslie Darwin, a man known to be serious enough to dynamite illegal dams, Aldwell figured a way to circumvent the law.[23] He declared that his dam was actually a collection tool for a future hatchery, and as such, did not need a fish ladder.[24] The promised hatchery was built in 1915, but it failed after only seven years.[25] No one ever moved to rectify this situation. In 1916, Aldwell sold the dam.

The Elwha Dam under construction. National Park Service.

In 1927, the Northwest Power and Light Company built 210-foot Glines Canyon Dam eight miles upstream, at river mile 13.5. With no more salmon in the upper river, there was no need to build fish ladders there. Under the terms of the 1920 Federal Power Act, Glines Canyon was granted a fifty-year operating license by the Federal Power Commission (later known as FERC). The Elwha Dam, having been built before 1920, was never licensed.

The Crown Zellerbach (CZ) paper company owned both dams by 1937; it would run them for most of their existence. At first, the dams' nineteen megawatts provided power to all of Port Angeles, but the town's consumption quickly outstripped the dams' production.[26] Ultimately, the dams' sole role would be to make power for the CZ paper mill in Port Angeles; they supplied a little more than a third of the mill's electricity.[27] The CZ mill employed some 320 people, making it the second biggest private employer in Clallam County.[28] The forest industry was the foundation of the North Olympic Peninsula's economy for most of the twentieth century.[29]

The truncated river retained strong salmon populations for a few decades. Longtime Port Angeleno Dick Goin, whose family homesteaded the river valley in the 1930s, fished an Elwha full of salmon. As a child he regularly caught Chinook weighing seventy and seventy-five pounds, and his friend Ernie Brannon gaffed a 102-pound Elwha Chinook. Brannon managed the state hatchery on the nearby Dungeness River, and for years

Glines Canyon before the dam, and with it in place. National Park Service.

he kept the giant fish preserved there to show to visitors.[30] But this rich fishery wouldn't last.

Swimming up the first five miles of the river, returning salmon would jump into the concrete and "throw themselves at it time and time and time again" in a futile effort to surmount the dam.[31] And as the Elwha dams stopped the fish from coming up, they also stopped sediment and debris from going down. Consider, again, what this means from a fish's point of view. Instead of a riverbed full of boulders and tree trunks to diversify the flow and quality of the water and to allow them to hide from predators— habitat heterogeneity is the technical term—the riverbed became a barren place for fish to live.[32] A particular problem was the lack of appropriately-sized gravel in which to make their nests.[33] Most of the good gravel in the lower five river miles eventually washed out to sea. The dams held back the gravel that would have replenished it. The only material that flowed into the lower river after 1913 came from bluffs and from some small tributaries that enter the river below the dam sites.

All of this degraded not only the lower river, but also features miles away from the Elwha. The town of Port Angeles is sheltered from the sea by a three-mile spit of land called Ediz Hook. The hook is formed partly of Elwha silt, carried east from the river mouth on the current. With dams holding back the silt, Ediz Hook began to wash away.[34] By the end of the twentieth century, the US Army Corps of Engineers was having to spend $100,000 per year to stabilize the Hook; the dams' effect accounted for about 28 percent of maintenance expenditures.[35]

In the early years of the dam, the Elwha's flows were dictated by Crown Zellerbach's power needs. At times, when CZ decided to hold more water and build up head above the dams, the lower river would be dry, and the fish left gasping on the banks.[36] It was illegal for members of the Elwha Tribe, who were not at that time citizens of the United States, to harvest stranded fish— they had to choose between watching the fish rot or surreptitiously making off with them.[37] This was profoundly unfair, but they had little recourse in those days. At other times, when CZ wanted to crank out more power, unannounced floods would thunder through the dam's spillway, imperiling people (often tribal fishers) working downstream.[38] This situation, of trying to fish an artificially dangerous and unnaturally managed river, formed part of the tribe's complaints well into the 1980s.[39]

At the same time, for many people in the North Olympic Peninsula, fishing was not so much an economic or leisure activity as a way of life. Thomas Aldwell himself acknowledged that fishing was one of the greatest attractions of the Olympic Peninsula.[40] In the early days, many people fished for subsistence—Dick Goin spoke of heading to the river with homemade tackle, as a young boy in the 1930s, to catch fish for his family's table.[41] By the 1960s, this was no longer necessary for most people, but sport and commercial fishing were entrenched as part of the region's economy and culture; one of the big social events of each year was the Olympic Peninsula Salmon Derby.[42] Infuriated by the destruction of the Elwha fishery, anglers sometimes collected dead juvenile salmon in buckets and mailed them to Washington Department of Fisheries (WDF) director Milo Bell. One fisherman's message to Director Bell: "I am sending a sample of some dead fish that were picked up yesterday. . . . There were lots of dead fish, Mr. Bell. You will receive these fish from time to time."[43] Some young people would try to personally run salmon above the dams in damp gunnysacks, but this, of course, was not effective.[44]

Those buckets of dead fish didn't bring about political change. Or ecological change—salmon runs continued to decline. The last big run of pinks, forty thousand returning adults, came in 1963. The pinks dropped off sharply after that.[45] The Elwha's sockeye became "essentially extinct."[46] No one knows when the last hundred-pound Chinook swam up the Elwha; they have not been seen in many decades. But in the 1960s, the political situation began to move.

Political Stirrings

In 1968, the Lower Elwha Klallam Tribe gained legal recognition from the United States government.[47] The tribe quickly sought federal grants to improve housing on their reservation, but found that the rickety condition of the lower dam—the one that blew out in 1912—made this impossible.[48] The dam leaked several hundred cubic feet of water per second: what amounted to a large creek, constantly filtering through the structure.[49] In the past, flooding had damaged the reservation and forced the emergency evacuations of low-lying homes.[50] The Elwhas worried about earthquakes as well. Western Washington is seismically active, and the prospect of a shake that might collapse the dam was terrifying.[51] They began to look into what they could do to nullify this problem. At the same time, the tribe remembered well the times when their traditional economy revolved around the Elwha ecosystem, and the tribe's top natural resource priority had long been the restoration of the river's salmon runs.[52] As the tribe later pointed out, the dams' hydropower was considered cheap by some people, but this was because the dam owners had externalized the dams' ecological costs, putting them on the Elwhas, and on other river users.[53] The social costs that grow out of these ecological problems are difficult to measure, but for indigenous communities they can be enormous.[54] To some Elwha tribal members, fish were at the same time a gift from the creator, a resource to protect, and a member of the family.[55] The loss of such a thing is difficult for people from other parts of society to comprehend.

In 1965, the US Supreme Court's Taum Sauk Decision (*Federal Power Commission v. Union Electric Company* 381 US 90) established that uses of the navigable streams of the United States for energy transmission required a license. This decision, Crown Zellerbach deduced, included the unlicensed Elwha Dam. The company began to apply for a license in 1968.[56] Their application required some editing, though, and the Federal Power Commission issued a notice of the application only in 1976.[57] As time went by, CZ began to think that FERC might not have jurisdiction after all— perhaps the Elwha might not count as navigable under the Federal Power Act?—and so the company filed for a declaratory order from FERC, stating that it did not have jurisdiction and so, of course, could not require the Elwha Dam to be licensed. The company was wrong—in 1979, FERC (as it was now called) stated that it did, in fact, have jurisdiction over the lower dam.[58] It did not issue a license, though.

Glines Canyon Dam's jurisdictional situation was complicated as well. The FPC had issued a fifty-year license in 1926, but the 1938 creation of Olympic National Park left the dam and its reservoir inside park boundaries. The government could not license hydro projects in national parks— but could it relicense existing dams? Crown Zellerbach hoped so. In 1973, the company applied for a new license for Glines Canyon. FERC issued a notice of application in 1978.[59]

When a project's license is considered for renewal, FERC is supposed to treat that project as if it were new—outdated features are not to be

grandfathered in. And in the 1970s, environmental laws were more exact-
ing than they'd been in the days of Leslie Darwin and Thomas Aldwell. CZ
consulted with the United States Fish and Wildlife Service (USFWS) and
with the National Marine Fisheries Service, as well as with the WDF, to
understand the state of the Elwha's fisheries and how to manage the dam.
It quickly became apparent that sorting out fish passage and maintenance
upgrades would be a challenge. In 1975, CZ reached a deal with the State
of Washington wherein it would mitigate its dams' impacts by helping
build a Chinook hatchery. CZ agreed to pay 23.6 percent of the hatchery's
construction costs (not to exceed $145,140) and annual operating costs (not
to exceed $33,500).[60] The agreement also established that CZ would operate
the Elwha Dam project in a run-of-river fashion: it would no longer alter
the river's flow to maximize power generation, but rather use the water
as it came down from the mountains. The Chinook hatchery would not
include any other fish species, and the agreement barred WDF from any
future involvement in Elwha fish restoration issues, but decision-makers at
WDF found the deal to be acceptable nonetheless. CZ would later point to
this agreement as evidence of its sensitivity to fishery and resource issues,
and to agency concerns.[61]

While all of this was going on, there came a decision that would permanently change the rivers of Washington State. As native tribes regained
some measure of political power in the latter decades of the twentieth
century, they sought to regain their traditional fisheries—tribal fishers
had found themselves continually in conflict with the state's fishing laws
through the 1960s. In 1970, a group of tribes sued the state, pointing out
that, when they had given up their land, under their treaties they had
retained "the right of taking fish at usual and accustomed grounds and
stations . . . in common with all citizens of the Territory."[62] These "usual
and accustomed grounds" clearly meant waters beyond the tribes' reservations. Restrictions on their fishing those waters would have to be lifted.
But what should "in common with all citizens" be taken to mean? In 1974,
Judge George Boldt of the US District Court for Western Washington ruled
in *United States v. Washington* that it meant the tribes were entitled to half
the fish in Washington.

Half! Before the Boldt Decision (as it became known), the tribes had
taken an estimated 2 percent of the state's annual catch. The implications of
a twenty-five-fold increase in the tribal catch boggled the minds of Washington's fishers. Boldt was upheld by the Ninth Circuit, and affirmed by the
Supreme Court in 1979.

In 1980, the Boldt Decision was given a second phase, known as the Orrick Decision. In response to Boldt, the State of Washington optimistically claimed that Boldt only meant that native fishers had the right to try to catch fish in these accustomed waters, whether there were fish in there or not, and that fish produced by state hatcheries were not subject to the ruling. Judge William Orrick (Boldt having retired) ruled that *United States v. Washington* did indeed include hatchery fish, and that, furthermore, it established the legal need for conservation of fish habitat. The terms of the treaties were intended to allow the tribes to continue to catch fish in order to sustain their traditional livelihoods—this, surely, had been the understanding of the long-dead tribal leaders who signed those treaties.[63]

The State of Washington was represented in the case by its attorney general, Slade Gorton. Gorton's role in the Boldt Decision helped build his political reputation as an enemy of the tribes,[64] a reputation that would resurface much later on the Elwha.[65] In the near term, these rulings intensified competition for scarce fishery resources and ratcheted up tensions that had long plagued the relationship between tribal and non-tribal fishers on Washington rivers, including the Elwha.[66]

The Lower Elwha Klallam Tribe was not party to *United States v. Washington*, but as the signatories of the Treaty of Point No Point, they were entitled to 50 percent of the river's fish through Boldt, and to a healthy ecosystem to produce those fish through Orrick. But in the 1970s, as they later pointed out, these rights were guaranteed, but not protected.[67] If there are no fish in a river, you cannot have 50 percent of nothing.[68] To secure their treaty rights, it would be necessary to restore the Elwha; a restored Elwha River, with its hundreds of thousands of salmon, had the potential to be economically and culturally transformative for the tribe.[69] But despite the encouraging legal rulings, this future remained very distant, and most Elwhas did not think dam removal was a realistic goal.[70] In 1974, the four tribal signatories of the Treaty of Point No Point (the three Klallam tribes and the Skokomish) formed the Point No Point Treaty Council (PNPTC) to manage the tribes' fisheries. In 1978 the Elwhas built a steelhead and coho hatchery to help provide the fish to which they were entitled under the treaty.[71]

In 1976, the tribe intervened in the Elwha Dam licensing decision.[72] The secretary of the interior, as the tribe's trustee (the Department of the Interior includes the Bureau of Indian Affairs), intervened as well. Uncertainty about jurisdiction over the upper dam was frozen in place as FERC issued CZ a series of annual operating licenses. In 1979, FERC decided that the two dams would be considered as one hydroelectric project, given the interconnection in their operations.[73] CZ agreed that this would be appropriate.[74]

The federal resource agencies grew uneasy—what would this all mean? In 1980, Assistant Interior Secretary Larry Meierotto wrote to FERC to say that, from the perspective of the Department of the Interior (incorporating the National Park Service, the BIA, and USFWS), the Elwha projects had caused massive problems for the resource base in the area, problems that had never been appropriately mitigated.[75] But this did not make much difference in policy or management—agencies are not in the business of pushing political change. FERC kept issuing annual operating licenses, and there was political stasis on the Elwha until the mid-1980s.

Battle Is Joined

The 1980s were a time of environmental ferment in the Northwest, with the Public Utility Regulatory Policies Act of 1978 (PURPA) and the Washington Wilderness Act of 1984 offering many opportunities for activists to engage in land protection and FERC licensing decisions.[76] PURPA, which encouraged the development of small-scale hydropower, released a flood of little dam projects nationwide. Washington, a state blessed with steep mountains and powerful rivers, was full of promising dam sites.[77] Activists like David Ortman of Friends of the Earth and Polly Dyer of Olympic Park Associates, while working on other land issues and involving themselves in other licensing decisions, thought about the two Elwha dams and began to muse upon whether there might be any way, politically, to get at them.[78]

In 1982, journalist Bruce Brown published *Mountain in the Clouds*, a vivid, adventurous account of the decline of the Olympic Peninsula's salmon. This was nothing less than the *Silent Spring* of the Elwha River. In the book, Brown tells the stories of many Olympic rivers, but the chapter on the Elwha, laying out the underhanded dealings that enabled Aldwell to build his dam, and the loss of the river's remarkable fisheries, stood out, to Washington conservationists, as a real-life environmental crime story. Many of them would credit it, many years later, with awakening them to the plight of the Elwha and its salmon and inspiring them to work on the issue.[79]

The person near-universally acknowledged as starting the environmentalist campaign to remove the Elwha dams was Rick Rutz.[80] Rutz was not a professional activist—he worked for Seattle City Light, the city's public utility—but on his own time, he worked with Friends of the Earth, the Mountaineers, the Seattle Audubon Society, and a variety of other environmental groups.[81] Rutz had been involved with a number of licensing decisions in the aftermath of PURPA and had gotten to know the possibilities and limitations of the FERC process. Looking over a Washington State map one day, he reflected that the Elwha Dam was unlicensed and that Glines Canyon Dam's license had not been renewed. So, he thought, the final licensing decisions must still be pending. Rutz felt that the environmental movement should take a hand in the matter and push to remove the dams.[82] Despite the fact that he was not a lawyer, he began to prepare a motion to intervene in the licensing process.

Rutz's intervention would be very late, of course, but the unresolved FERC process and the shaky status quo—all those temporary one-year licenses—offered him an excuse. In the mid-1980s he pitched Elwha intervention to various environmental groups in the Seattle area. Looking back on those days in 2011, he remembered that both the environmental community and the National Park Service thought he was crazy. This wasn't *The Monkey Wrench Gang*, this was real life. Environmental groups worried about looking ridiculous and reducing their ability to be taken seriously in other settings.[83]

After some effort, Rutz persuaded the Seattle Audubon Society, Friends of the Earth, the Cascade chapter of the Sierra Club, and Olympic Park Associates (OPA) to join his intervention. Each of these organizations had its own persuasive argument for legal standing in the Elwha relicensing process. Seattle Audubon had been running trips to the peninsula since the 1920s, Friends of the Earth had been intensely involved with hydropower issues, and Olympic National Park was the cause of OPA's very existence. The Sierra Club's credentials as perhaps the foremost environmental group in the United States spoke for themselves.[84] Each group contributed to building an active environmentalist role in the Elwha decision. Friends of the Earth had staff time available whereas the other organizations did not, so its operatives, Michael Rossotto, Jim Baker, and then Shawn Cantrell, took the lead in the environmental effort.[85] Friends of the Earth also possessed a Victor computer, a rare resource in 1986. This was one of the reasons Rutz had solicited its help.[86] OPA provided the regional connections to hire Len Barson, a former staffer for Congressman Al Swift (D-WA2), as the environmentalists' counsel.[87] Swift's district included Clallam County. The Sierra Club's Legal Defense Fund also provided some pro bono aid.[88] The conservationists held meetings to discuss the Elwha in the offices of Barson's law firm, Keller Rohrback.[89]

These groups, eventually to be known as the conservation interveners (CIs), filed to intervene in May 1986. Their timing was fortuitous—that autumn, the Electric Consumers Protection Act established that environmental and recreational values would be considered of equal importance to more traditional dam uses in licensing decisions. This reduced the dam owners' advantage and opened things up for environmental advocates.[90] The four original CIs became the core of an environmental coalition that drove the early stages of the dam removal fight. They would be joined in 1990 by Trout Unlimited, and, in time, by a cascade of environmental groups.

The Point No Point Treaty Council was preparing its own intervention in the mid-1980s, and there was some cooperation between the environmentalists and the tribes. Russell Busch, a lawyer from Evergreen Legal Services and the man who would represent the Elwha Tribe throughout the process, had been in touch with Rick Rutz. By some accounts, Busch and tribal biologist Steve Ralph helped Rutz prepare the CIs' intervention.[91] The tribe and the council intervened later in 1986.[92] The tribes welcomed Rutz and his allies to the fight.[93] CZ objected to these late interventions,[94] but as the conservation interveners pointed out, there had been no forward movement in the years since the license applications: they hadn't missed any developments that would make their intervention inappropriate.[95] The tribes' and environmentalists' interventions were accepted by FERC in November 1986.[96] Thus began the real battle over the Elwha.

Rising controversy over the Elwha hydroelectric licenses put land and resource agencies in an awkward position. The ecological and management status quo on the Elwha had not changed much for years, but the evolving, intensifying situation with the dam challenged agencies to reassess their approaches.[97] Part of this reassessment came as a result of changes in personnel—as the park's leadership changed, the Park Service's vision of restoration expanded. To some extent this was simply a matter of generational change, as nationwide shifts in environmental attitudes, from conservation to preservation to restoration, were reflected in applicants to the Forest Service, Park Service, and Army Corps of Engineers. Younger line staff and their traditionally trained superiors approached their jobs from profoundly different environmental perspectives.[98] By the 1980s, agency personnel who had begun their careers in the age of environmentalism and ecology were stepping into leadership roles, asserting themselves, and taking their agencies in new directions.[99] Resource agencies' missions tend to be broad and even contradictory, especially as new policies—the Multiple-Use Sustained-Yield Act or the Electric Consumers Protection

Act, for instance—are formed. This leaves a fair amount of room for interpretation, and depending on the tone and direction of the agency and department, the ambiguity can be paralyzing or liberating. In the case of the Elwha, the Interior Department was not opposed to restoration, but there was little sense that an agency staffer would feel free to speak out on an environmental issue.[100] But the agencies did begin to take a more active interest in the dams.

The various governmental units involved with the Elwha formed a working group for the restoration and relicensing effort as early as 1985.[101] The group covered biological and management issues. Represented were the National Park Service, the Point No Point Treaty Council, the Lower Elwha Klallam Tribe, the US Fish and Wildlife Service, NOAA's National Marine Fisheries Service, and the Washington Department of Game (later consolidated into the Washington Department of Fish and Wildlife). The agency group, which became known as the Joint Fish and Wildlife Agencies (JFWA), would work together throughout the process. In the mid-1980s, the lead agency was the National Marine Fisheries Service, under the leadership of lawyer Lori Bodi.[102] The JFWA made sure that their statements on the dams matched one another's, to present a united front to FERC.[103] They looked into the impacts of relicensing and removal, demanding information from FERC on all options to assess the case.[104] Members of the group met regularly with the CIs,[105] as the agency role was to distribute and exchange information with all interested parties. The CIs were able to take more active approaches to restoration than the agencies. As the agencies' stance moved toward restoration, each part of the coalition, in its own way, "pushed the snowball" of the Elwha dams.[106]

Issues

The unprecedented complexities of the Elwha Dam issue meant that the late 1980s and early 1990s were mostly taken up with wrangles over information and expertise, undertaken within the FERC process. FERC issued a scoping document on Elwha licensing in 1989 and a draft environmental impact statement (EIS) in 1991. Interim relief, intended to maintain the viability of the Elwha's fish and wildlife in the meantime, was requested by the agencies and discussed between 1987 and 1989. In the course of these documents' formation, the stakeholders debated an array of issues that would permanently shape the Elwha decision. The rest of the process, for the next two decades, would be devoted to resolving or working around these issues.

Jurisdiction

The primary question was whether the licensing could proceed at all—whether FERC had jurisdiction over Glines Canyon Dam. The law barring FERC from licensing dams in national parks was quite clear, but FERC, CZ, and electricity interests (including the Department of Energy, and some politically active local citizens) believed that renewing existing licenses for such dams was permissible.[107] The conservation interveners disagreed.

In 1986, Senator Dan Evans (R-WA), a former governor and longtime environmental advocate, suggested working around the jurisdiction issue by having the federal government buy the dams. This possibility had been specifically laid out in the Federal Power Act back in 1920, but in 1986 there was little support for the idea.[108] Evans, a keen outdoorsman, had long harbored a desire to see the dams removed from the river.[109] A few weeks after Evans's proposal was featured in the *Peninsula Daily News*, Clallam County locals Buck Adamire and P. V. Holden wrote to the editor decrying park expansion and, for Holden, equating the continued operation of the dams with national survival.[110]

Jurisdictional questions aside, in the North Olympic Peninsula runs a deep vein of skepticism toward the federal government and the National Park Service. The antigovernment views espoused by Adamire, Holden, and others like them would continue to color the issue for years. Federal acquisition of private property, whether of a dam or a homestead, was not politically popular in the Olympic Peninsula. The peninsula is about as far as you can get from the District of Columbia and still be in the continental United States. Many people liked it that way.

In 1988, the CIs filed a petition with FERC for a declaratory order that it (FERC) did not have authority to renew the Glines Canyon license. In 1989, Representative John Dingell (D-MI12), a powerful congressman who chaired the House Energy and Commerce Committee, asked the non-partisan Government Accountability Office (GAO) to look into the matter of whether the Glines Canyon Dam was in fact under FERC's jurisdiction. Later that year, FERC responded with an inconclusive statement that it might have jurisdiction given the ambiguity of the law and mixed agency jurisdiction over the lands containing the projects.[111] In early 1990, the GAO replied to Dingell, saying that, in its judgment, the dam was not in FERC's jurisdiction.[112] The CIs immediately issued a press release trumpeting the GAO's finding.[113] This finding wasn't binding, as the companies' representatives were quick to point out.[114] However, as the thoroughly researched and well-supported position of a neutral party, the GAO's report carried significant weight.

During these years, the mill changed owners several times. Crown Zellerbach joined the James River Corporation, which went through a variety of names and corporate identities in a few years. In 1988, the mill was sold to Daishowa, a Japanese company. Daishowa America, the company's arm in the United States, would not take possession of the hydro projects, though, until such time as the licensing situation had cleared up. In the meantime, James River Corporation and its successors continued to own the dams themselves.[115] Daishowa worked hard to establish itself as a good citizen of Port Angeles, reaching out to the community through such gestures as building athletic fields.[116] In some ways Daishowa's role as mill owner increased the pressure to resolve the issue—a Japanese company was considered by some to be less likely to stay patient with the vagaries of American politics over the long term.[117] Daishowa's representative in negotiation was Terry Bracy, a widely respected lobbyist and a man with a great deal of experience in and commitment to environmental issues.[118] Daishowa stayed engaged but quite neutral throughout the process.[119]

Restoration

> No one involved with the dams—Swift, business concerns, the National Park Service, the Federal Energy Regulatory Commission and environmentalists—disagrees with the goal of re-establishing fish runs.
> —Christman, "Elwha Plan," *Peninsula Daily News*, 1989

No important stakeholder, at any time, opposed the restoration of the Elwha fisheries. How such a restoration should be accomplished, though, and what sort of restoration would be feasible, was a source of passionate debate.

After the 1986 interventions, CZ responded by suggesting that the fishery be managed and restored with the dams in place.[120] This scheme evolved over the years as the relicensing question went through rounds of debate, study, and documentation. Restoration with the dams in place would be convoluted: reestablishment of upstream fish passage through some combination of trapping fish below the upper dam to haul them above it and fish ladders; Eicher screens (which keep downstream migrants away from hydroelectric turbines); and some dam reoperation, with water spilled in such a way as to benefit fish.[121] Of course, all of this would have been expensive for the company, rendering the dams less valuable.

The environmentalists and the tribes found this kind of scheme unacceptable—one tribal biologist would call such ideas "Band-Aids."[122] For the tribe, full restoration was defined by the return of a year-round Elwha fishery, with at least one species catchable in the river every day of the year; tribal fisheries manager Rachel Kowalski pointed out that this was why the tribe had settled at the river mouth, thousands of years ago, in the first place.[123] The tribe would not even accept 95 percent passage, the standard set by the agencies, for downstream migrants;[124] they pointed out the ecological value, to the salmon population, of early and late migrants' genes. These would be limited by CZ's plan.[125]

Fish passage was not the only problem. The agencies, and the tribe, pointed out many ecological and management issues stemming from the dams. Brian Winter, at that time a PhD candidate in fisheries at the University of Washington, reported the presence of many false redds, nests without viable salmon eggs, in the lower Elwha. These he blamed on unsuitable riverbed material. Rachel Kowalski pointed out the danger and property damage caused to tribal fishers by seasonal up-ramping of water releases from the dam. They recommended a range of initiatives—outplanting, habitat rehabilitation, land set-asides, and more—but emphasized that these expedients were temporary and inadequate.[126] Winter would eventually succeed Lori Bodi as the lead member of JFWA, and then rise to be the Elwha restoration project manager. He would oversee the removal effort for well over a decade.

The dam owners' restoration plans focused on restoration of Chinook and coho salmon, and steelhead trout: economically valuable species with strong chances of restoration and populations supplemented by hatchery production. The company did not consider pink and chum salmon (*O. keta*), which were still technically present in the Elwha, to be realistic restoration candidates.[127] NOAA had previously feared that the Elwha pinks were extinct—a disastrous population crash after 1981 dropped the formerly enormous run to a token few individuals; from 1989 to 1995, four pinks were seen in the Elwha.[128] To the tribe, the agencies, and the CIs, though, Elwha restoration meant full restoration.[129] The company was advised that its plan needed to include restoration of all Elwha runs regardless of its own opinion on whether the fish would come back.[130] FERC's 1991 draft environmental impact statement did not identify a preferred alternative, leaving the company to claim that the document supported dam retention, and the interveners to claim the opposite.[131] The CIs argued that the document proved that dam removal would be a "win-win" option wherein the community, the company, and the river would all benefit.[132]

The JFWA's comments, a year later, supported dam removal, and noted that the only interests served by retention would be those of the company. Moreover, they said, since James River would be transferring the dams to Daishowa in the event of a renewed license, it would presumably not be committed to or responsible for the future failure of any restoration plan that kept the dams in place.[133] This criticism raised echoes of Thomas Aldwell's short-lived hatchery from seventy years before. The environmentalists also criticized James River for failing to account for the future capital investments that would likely be required, especially on the decrepit lower dam, if the dams stayed in place.[134] Some years later, company representative Orville Campbell pointed out that the system of temporary one-year licenses and ongoing uncertainty made it hard for the companies to justify such capital investments.[135]

Some local people worried that the upstream population of resident rainbow trout would be harmed by any dam removal and the possible return of anadromous fish. To the JFWA, though, the priority was the reintroduction of the native anadromous runs; changes for these resident trout were not an issue.[136] James River criticized the engineering and ecological demands of dam removal as unfeasible, and maintained its belief that pinks, chums, and sockeyes were unlikely to be restored regardless.

As scientists analyzed the situation, restoration with the dams in place began to look like a catch-22. Periodically, the salmon of the Elwha would suffer from parasites or diseases, devastating that year's runs and forcing alterations in river management.[137] Such a year was 1987, and the company was forced to respond to an outbreak of gill disease by adjusting the operation of the lower dam to release cooler water.[138] While this spoke to the company's willingness to work with resource managers and help the fish, it also spoke to the changes the dams had wrought on the river—water at the surface of a reservoir, sun-warmed and still, is hotter than the moving water of a natural river, and parasites and diseases thrive in hot, still water. Later documentation would reveal that water releases from the surface of the reservoirs had raised the downstream temperature by as much as eight degrees Fahrenheit.[139] If the dam was re-operated to release cooler water, then any juveniles planted above the dams as part of a future restoration effort could be killed in the turbines—there was no safe operating regime that would allow for fish to migrate above and below the dams.[140] This conundrum helped convince some scientists that managing the Elwha into the cooler waterway salmon require would not be possible with the dams still standing.[141] The company suggested that the dams could act as a management tool and give agencies more options to deal with diseases, but the agencies dismissed this claim as being without scientific merit.[142]

A common refrain in some corners of the Olympic Peninsula was that the tribes, not the dams, were to blame for the decline in salmon. Noting that the salmon runs had declined decades after the dams were built, some people believed that the Boldt Decision and a subsequent rise in native fishing were the problem.[143] The tribes sometimes caught fish by using gillnets, which stretch across the mouths of rivers, to snare returning salmon. These nets are typically used and managed in such a way as to perpetuate the runs and let some fish spawn upstream,[144] but to casual observers it can appear that the nets catch all of a returning cohort of adults. Complaints about nets continued throughout the debate.[145] Foreign fishing vessels, lurking offshore, also provided a popular scapegoat.[146] Gillnets and ocean fishing had been controversial long before the 1980s, but the Elwha relicensing issue gave these controversies fresh life. Gillnets will remain a contentious issue in the Northwest for the foreseeable future.

Economics

During this time, northwestern environmentalists also found themselves fighting the furious "spotted owl wars." The northern spotted owl (*Strix occidentalis caurina*) was a topic from Northern California to the Canadian border, but nowhere were the political battles over the owl more fervently and ferociously waged than in the Olympic Peninsula. Swathes of the old-growth forests where the northern spotted owl lives still stood in Olympic National Forest. In 1990, the owl was listed as threatened, ending logging in these zones. This stoked predictable fury across Clallam County. It was a devastating time for the region's timber economy, putting hundreds out of work, creating a regional mindset of owls versus people and, in some quarters, casting environmentalists as inhumane zealots driven to return the land to wilderness.[147] The very epicenter of the owl wars was the small town of Forks,[148] in the rain forest fifty miles west of the Elwha River.[149] Journalist William Dietrich found people there wearing sweatshirts that read "Support Your Local Spotted Owl: From A Rope." Parades of logging trucks rolled down the streets of Port Angeles, on the way to blockade Interstate 5 and alert Seattleites to the battle in the woods.[150] The seemingly unrelated conflict poisoned and extended the dam removal debate, with salmon filling the political place of owls. Environmental advocates who'd been trying to remove the Elwha dams found themselves facing hardened opposition that reflexively hated them. Many Elwha stakeholders noted the owl while discussing Elwha Dam politics in 2011 and 2012.[151]

With the anger came fear: Would the controversy over the dams result in the mill closing? The company worried that if the dams' portion of their electricity became more expensive, it would raise operating costs enough to perhaps drive them out of business. They projected that replacing the Elwha's megawatts with power from Port Angeles City Light would increase their total operating costs by 5.4 percent.[152] In 1987, Crown Zellerbach asked the Clallam County Economic Development Council to review the effects of closing the mill. The council projected over one thousand jobs lost, constituting 7 percent of the county's work force and 11 percent of county wages.[153] A horrifying prospect.

Just as no relevant stakeholder opposed salmon restoration, no relevant stakeholder wanted the mill to close. The key to the continuous operation of the mill would be to replace the dams' power at a reasonable price. Dan Evans' idea arose again—what if the federal government took possession of the dams?[154] This idea, taken more seriously now, stemmed from an unnamed Fish and Wildlife Service official's suggestion to treat the dam removal like a standard water project, with a negotiated, funded solution.[155] The companies, the agencies, and members of Congress began to work up this plan,[156] and congressional staffers ran "shuttle diplomacy" efforts to get the CIs (who wanted the company to pay) to acquiesce to the plan and drop their effort to have the dams legally declared to be outside FERC's jurisdiction.[157] The people of the Olympic Peninsula were open to federal acquisition as well.[158] In later years, as dam removals became more commonplace, there was some criticism of the government's paying the company for its old dams, but as Congressman Al Swift said, no one in 1992 would have considered anything else appropriate—the purchase was not then seen as a windfall for the company, but as a political necessity.[159] Swift had been adamant that the federal government, not the people of Washington State, should bear the financial burden when the Elwha Act was passed.[160] The price of the dams was eventually set at $29.5 million.

Perceptions

The stakeholder groups involved in the dam removal looked at the dams, the lakes, and the river, and saw fundamentally different things. To the companies, the dams were power providers—for them the relicensing decision and all that came with it were a matter of business.[161] At the same time, the companies were aware of the mill's importance to the Port Angeles community, and of the dams' place in local heritage. James River's comments on the National Environmental Policy Act (NEPA) documents emphasized that the facilities in question were already operating, and raised the specter of dam removal causing floods, and of a regional power shortage in the future. The company emphasized that it did not believe that NEPA required FERC to include past impacts in its deliberations.[162] The company argued that FERC's draft environmental impact statement gave too little consideration to the cultural and historic values of the Elwha and Glines Canyon Dams, which were on the National Register of Historic Places; some in the Port Angeles community felt this way as well.[163] The companies asserted that "there is no legal basis for elevating the restoration of natural conditions in the Olympic National Park, which is based on NPS policy, above the statutorily protected historic values of these two projects, and the FERC decision making process must be readjusted to give equal and balanced consideration to historic preservation objectives."[164]

When the companies trumpeted the historic character of the dams, the CIs facetiously agreed that, yes indeed, "they are historic examples of indifference to environmental values and concerns."[165] When they looked at the dams, the environmentalists saw destruction. The CIs' "battle cry," many times repeated, was Free the Elwha, or Elwha Be Free![166] To environmentalists, the dams were like prison walls, or chains, confining the river and curtailing its "legendary" salmon.[167] The Sierra Club's publication *Cascade Crest* depicted the lower dam as a guillotine, with a collection of dead fish below.[168] An OPA mailing, offering "a once in a lifetime opportunity to help remove two fish-killer dams," featured a cartoon of water spilling out the middle of a broken dam and three smiling fish leaping merrily toward the hole.[169]

Once the dam/prison was razed, the salmon could come back. The return of the legendary runs was a key to the CIs' perceptions and promotions. Michael Rossotto, a Friends of the Earth staffer who helped coordinate the CIs in the mid-1980s, made sure that the environmentalists emphasized the remarkable qualities of the Elwha's salmon in their public communications.[170] Salmon restoration was particularly exciting for anglers, and Trout Unlimited joined the CIs in 1990. Anglers emphasized the unique nature of the Elwha, with its glacial headwaters, pristine watershed, and history of gigantic trophy Chinook—the sort of river that most American anglers were forced to seek in Canada or Alaska.[171] The prospect of thousands of fly fishers vacationing in Port Angeles rather than British Columbia added an economic angle to the promised environmental benefits of dam removal. The connection between fishing and environmental goals was strong through the 1980s and 1990s. When environmentalists look back on the process, particular credit goes to Trout Unlimited's local executive director, Bill Robinson, who forged an effective coalition of fishing-based groups, which tend to be more politically conservative and economically motivated, and traditional environmental groups.[172]

The legally dubious history of the dams' construction was a constant theme in environmentalists' story, and a spur to their political zeal.[173] The companies pointed out that such long-ago events were not supposed to matter under NEPA, but the illegal dam construction remained part of the dam removers' indignant rhetoric throughout the issue.[174]

Environmentalists often have to wrestle with the legacy of destructive practices that were normal and honorable in the past—eliminating predators, for example—and to argue that the world has changed, and that, while it's hard to blame people for what they did back then, now we know better. But here was a clean, direct story of ecological villainy. Damming the Elwha had been criminal from day one. The illegality of the Elwha Dam offered a rare sense of historical purity and consistency to the dam removal mission. The agencies were aware of the dam's murky history as well,[175] but vengeance was not a part of their mandates.

The tribe, of course, was viscerally committed to dam removal. The Elwhas, like many tribes, struggled with poverty and substance abuse, and at one point the tribe's unemployment rate was 63.5 percent.[176] The tribe linked this social disarray to the dams and the destruction of the riparian and estuarine ecosystems that had been the foundation of their economy for millennia.[177] Moreover, beyond the declining salmon runs and the shrinking estuary, the Elwha Dam had been built over the Elwhas' traditional creation site, the spot where, they believe, the god-like Changer created them.[178] The Elwhas found the companies' emphasis on the dams' historic role to be inappropriate and Eurocentric, especially in light of the Elwhas' far deeper and longer connection to the river.[179] Russell Busch wanted FERC to "have a clear understanding of how these dams have dominated, in a thoroughly negative way, the daily life and attempts at advancement of the Elwha Tribe," citing flooding, beach erosion, and drinking water impacts as well as the loss of fish and seafood species. He connected the breakdown of the Elwha fishing economy to "alcohol/chemical abuse, depression, eating disorders, nutritional deficiencies." Busch then detailed the Elwhas' dire poverty:

There is so little value available in the Indian community that the normal social mechanisms middle-class communities take for granted do not function. There is no "reserve" to meet the crises which poverty generates in a downward spiral. There is little money for social services. There is little money for planning, let alone the economic development that might follow. When a member of an extended family has an emergency, there may be no one with the money to help. Children learn defeat and powerlessness. Success and growth require resources. Those have been taken away.

All of this, said Busch, was not accounted for in FERC's documents.[180] The Lower Elwha Tribal Council commissioned a study on the socioeconomic aspects of the draft EIS, which supported Busch's points.[181]

When the *Peninsula Daily News* listed the dams' stakeholders in July 1989, it did not mention the role of the local community.[182] Perhaps because of the idea's strangeness, there was relatively little public attention paid to dam removal in Port Angeles until the early 1990s. When the idea of dam removal first arose, people in Port Angeles were incredulous.[183] Even such pro-salmon voices as Roy Nelson, president of the Olympic Outdoor Sportsmen's Club, supported conducting a dam removal feasibility study, "but [didn't] expect that to ever happen," saying, "Our club is working for a way to get the salmon over the dams to the water on the other side."[184] The club had taken part in other restoration projects in the area and had even helped remove a much smaller dam from nearby Ennis Creek,[185] but undamming the Elwha was too much for them to believe. Bruce "Mountain in the Clouds" Brown himself raised the option of removing the lower dam only and trying to pass fish around the upper one.[186] James River called dam removal "an extreme and unrealistic proposal"[187] by "extreme environmental groups."[188] Even the resource agencies, at the beginning, suggested only fish passage installments at both dams.[189] But after some thought, the JFWA specifically emphasized to FERC that dam removal should, in fact, be evaluated as a full restoration alternative for the Elwha.[190] NOAA later laid out the arguments—Glines Canyon's location in the park, inadequate passage, the dams' relatively paltry power production, and so on—but the first challenge, before those arguments could take effect, was to get everyone to take dam removal seriously.[191]

In the peninsula, the only significant agitation surrounding the dams came from the radical environmental group Earth First!, which was known in the Olympic Peninsula through their activism (some would say terror-ism) on forest issues.[192] The Earth First! activists, "swept up in the idea of seeing the Elwha free again, since the salmon runs are legendary there," put on a pantomime of the demolition of Elwha Dam.[193] The group later painted a crack on the face of the Glines Canyon Dam, with the message "Elwha Be Free!" beside it.[194] These sorts of political theatrics has been performed on controversial dams throughout the West—remember that Earth First! was born out of controversy over Glen Canyon.[195] In Port Angeles, though, playing at sabotage in this way seemed like the action of "sick mind[s]."[196]

Around 1990, as it became apparent that the dam removal idea was serious, anti-removal forces began to mobilize. The mere suggestion of dam removal made some people furious. To one local letter-writer, "all that Port Angeles has accomplished since their building is due to their [the dams'] tire-less efforts."[197] Concerns over the dams' status as private property concerned some people as well.[198] Letters to the editor lauded the dams' hydropower as clean energy.[199] The lakes formed above the structures were praised for of-fering "opportunities to experience nature in the raw."[200] Some pointed out that other rivers in the Olympic Peninsula had no dams and yet also hosted struggling fish populations.[201] There was also a widespread belief that the dams' power served as an emergency backup and stabilization supply for the city of Port Angeles, particularly the hospital.[202] This was not actually the case—the dams didn't make enough electricity to power emergency services, and were not connected with the Port Angeles grid in such a way as to send their power to, for example, a hospital, in case of an emergency.[203] To all these people, the dams provided many benefits at minimal cost.

This discontent did not (yet) coalesce into organized resistance, and dam removal advocates seized the political initiative. In 1989, at meetings to discuss the relicensing and restoration process, environmental groups rallied their supporters in Port Angeles and Seattle. At both meeting sites, the mood was overwhelmingly in favor of restoration and dam removal—Orville Campbell, who worked for James River, remembers that in Seattle, company representatives were the only ones who stood for the dam.[204] In Port Angeles, ten people spoke in favor of removing the dams while only two favored keeping them.[205] Attendees applauded the tribe and the environmentalists for their support of dam removal and fish restoration.[206] People at the meeting sported "Free the Elwha" buttons,[207] as they would for years afterward.[208]

Local supporters of dam removal organized themselves into an ad-vocacy group named "Friends of the Elwha." Sounds like Friends of the

Earth, does it not? This was not a coincidence. Friends of the Earth helped create Friends of the Elwha in order to add a local connection to the CIs, and to ensure some credible local pro-removal voices at public meetings.[209] As Port Angeles's incredulity turned to anger, Friends of the Elwha urged its members to be calm and polite, and to remember that "our opponents are the crazy ones, not us!"[210] They argued that "there is a good deal of sentiment within the community that the dams should come out."[211] Led by local environmentalist Jim Curnew, Friends of the Elwha strove to act as a counterbalance to the rising anti-removal voices in Port Angeles.

The Issue Expands

As debates and negotiations went on in Western Washington, the conflict began to worry Al Swift and Senator Brock Adams (D-WA). In early 1989, Adams visited Port Angeles and expressed his support for restoration, but specifically emphasized his hope to achieve restoration while keeping the dams in place.[212] At the same time, Swift proposed a study of the dams and the fish, noting the economic benefits of restored fish runs but underlining the importance of the mill—he would never support a restoration plan that could throw the mill's 320 employees out on the street, or degrade Port Angeles's water.[213] Swift was well aware of the precedents that the Elwha might set on jurisdiction, restoration, and dam removal, and was eager to work out the interagency dispute to avoid the need for legislation and, especially, litigation.[214] In 1989, he met with environmentalists Jim Baker and Michael Rossotto of Friends of the Earth, and with Rick Rutz, to inform them that he didn't feel dam removal was warranted, and that he was considering the introduction in Congress of a bill forbidding dam removal on the Elwha.[215]

This frightened the environmentalists. They had felt confident that they would be able to win a relicensing battle with FERC, but Al Swift and his federal bill were quite another matter. Baker thought, however, that in these meetings Swift was giving the environmentalists a chance, pushing them to find some resolution.[216] Baker considered the situation and suggested a creative solution (later dubbed the "creative solution")[217] that could preserve the mill and remove the dams. What if, he asked, James River could replace the dams' power by taking measures to conserve energy? The mill was relatively old and there was hope that it could re-operate and find significant efficiencies. Baker suggested that the company allow the Bonneville Power Administration (BPA) to audit its operations and identify any available savings.[218] The environmentalists, Baker said, believed that fifteen to twenty megawatts of cost-effective conservation were possible at the mill and that such an audit qualified for BPA funding.[219] But James River said no. The fact that the company resisted even a free audit seemed, to the CIs, to suggest that the company was not being entirely frank in its dealings.[220] They told Swift as much. Swift and Adams seized on the "creative solution" and began to push for it as a win-win option.[221]

In 1990, the Park Service, which had previously gone along with the plan of a new license for the upper dam and the installation of fish passage on both structures, reconsidered its position.[222] Maureen Finnerty, the new park superintendent, was more active on restoration issues than her predecessors had been.[223] In 1990, Olympic National Park released a statement unambiguously supporting full restoration through dam removal.[224] A Park Service representative pointed out that if restoration was attempted with the dams in place, even if everything worked perfectly, it would only restore two salmon runs out of the Elwha's historic ten. In her public statements, Finnerty did make sure to emphasize that the viability of the mill and its power supply were necessary for any plan, as far as the park was concerned.[225] By October 1990, the Park Service was running slide shows telling audiences that restoration would depend on dam removal.[226] A similar statement from the US Fish and Wildlife Service soon followed.[227] NMFS, for its part, had favored dam removal before either Interior Department agency.[228]

This move was serious—the Department of the Interior includes resource extraction agencies as well as resource conservation agencies, so it was bureaucratically important for bodies like the Fish and Wildlife Service to make sure that their science was sound before moving forward, and to focus on restoring fish rather than on any more emotional desire to remove dams.[229] As the agencies declared for dam removal, this indicated that the science warranted dam removal as well. The company and Congressman Swift expressed their disappointment at the agencies' taking sides, but continued to work on the issue regardless.[230] For Swift, the Park Service shift signaled that removal was likely to happen.[231] In 1991, with the Park Service, Fish and Wildlife Service, and Bureau of Indian Affairs all in favor of removal, the Department of the Interior wrote to FERC firmly establishing its opposition to relicensing.[232]

In 1990, the Elwha dams began to gain some national attention. The giant salmon, the national park, the Elwha tribe, and the novelty of dam removal attracted the attention of *New York Times* columnist Timothy Egan, a Washington State native.[233] Egan's writing, in turn, came to the notice of powerful senator Bill Bradley (D-NJ).[234] Bradley had been in-terested in tribal issues since his days as a professional basketball player, when he ran basketball clinics on reservations.[235] He was familiar with the Olympic Peninsula from taking family vacations there. The novelty of the situation excited Bradley—no one had ever taken down a major dam.[236] He was struck by the Elwha restoration's potential to, as he later put it, "bend the arc of history to bring justice to Indian people whose lives were so frequently and unhappily interwoven with the rivers that the United States chose to develop for water supply and power."[237] As the chair of the Senate Subcommittee on Water and Power and a powerful figure in the Democratic Party, Bradley was well positioned to move the issue. It also happened that he and Daishowa lobbyist Terry Bracy were childhood friends.[238] Bradley's aides began to contact Elwha stakeholders. Congress-man George Miller (D-CA), who chaired the House Interior Committee, also began to look in on the Elwha restoration.[239] This gave the Elwha a player in both chambers of Congress.

Back in Port Angeles, people began to worry. On April 28, 1990, the town hosted the Olympic Peninsula Families Solidarity Rally, intended "to save our Olympic Peninsula and jobs from the Politicians, Preservationists and other liars." Attendees were encouraged to bring effigies for burning, and a sense of humor.[240] These people's desire for local primacy, though, could only go so far—the Elwha was, mostly, a Park Service watershed, and the dams' fate was in the hands of the NPS and with FERC. Nonetheless, the removal issue popped up occasionally in the Washington State legislature. In 1987–1988, the state senate looked into a bill studying the feasibility of dam removal.[241] This effort died after a barrage of lobbying from James River, which claimed that removal would cost too much.[242]

In 1991, the Port Angeles city council got earnestly involved in the Elwha decision. The major concern for the city, aside from potential un-employment, was municipal and industrial water supply.[243] Port Angeles' water came from Ranney wells.[244] The two artificial lakes behind the Elwha dams served as large settling pools, catching sediment and making down-stream flows of water artificially clear. Dam removal would release decades of silt from behind the dams and potentially overwhelm the Ranney wells. The city council demanded the water supply be guaranteed at all times. There was no objection to this from anyone—indeed, the Elwha tribe's law-yer, Russ Busch, noted that the Elwhas got their water from the river too.[245] During this process, the city, which had long identified its own interests with those of the mill, came to realize that, in fact, the mills were under no particular obligation to the city—that they would be unlikely to take any kind of loss to secure Port Angeles' water quality. Port Angeles would need to look out for itself.[246] The city hired a lobbyist to keep an eye on their interests as the issue was hashed out in Washington, DC.[247]

The company, reluctant to lose its electricity, continued to urge FERC to license its dams. In May 1991, the CIs and the tribe, confident that they would win the licensing battle, petitioned the Ninth Circuit Court of Appeals to review FERC's rulings on jurisdiction over Glines Canyon Dam.[248] The CIs were aware that this aggressive move would give some of their allies "heartburn"—some in the coalition had hoped to continue to negotiate, as the companies had seemed somewhat amenable.[249] But the petition went ahead, and the following month, the Department of Justice, representing the Departments of Interior and Commerce (which is to say, NOAA), filed its own petition with the Ninth Circuit.[250]

A court decision could transform the situation; consider James River's predicament if it suddenly found itself in possession of a legally inoperable dam in a national park.[251] Such a ruling would be exactly the sort of political blunt instrument that Al Swift and Brock Adams had feared.[252] In his nightmares, Swift saw a sweeping legal decision forcing the end of hydropower, the shutdown of the mill, and an expensive explosion of environmental strife: a true "lose-lose" scenario. Daishowa and James River also feared resolution by "meat ax" rather than by scalpel.[253] The tribe uneasily envisioned a long and expensive run of litigation, and feared that James River might abandon the dams, with untold consequences for the mill and community, litigation into the future, and no restoration.[254]

The Elwha Act

The surest way to avoid this political and environmental disaster was to pass a law. Adams and Swift, in regular contact with all parties, began to craft legislation that could remove the dams and preserve the mill. As a member of the House Energy and Commerce Committee, Swift (like Bradley) was well placed to do this. The two men also sought funding commitments from the president and from the Office of Management and Budget.[255] Each of the legislators was deeply and personally committed to finding a successful resolution. Bradley was passionate about Native American and water issues. Swift was zealous in defending his constituents and their landscape. Adams, who had long been an environmental advocate, saw the Elwha as his chance for a legacy achievement. Adams had been embroiled in an unsavory sex scandal that year,[256] and knew that he would be leaving public service in 1994. He is widely assumed to have wanted to go with his name attached to something positive.[257]

Public campaigning ramped up all around. The CIs rallied support from their constituents.[258] Lead environmentalist Shawn Cantrell, looking to get a strong bill introduced in Washington, DC, urged a united front with the tribe and the agencies.[259] Elwha tribal members traveled to Washington, DC, to speak at hearings. One elder said "I've been waiting all my life to tell this story."[260] The *Seattle Times* editorial page threw its weight behind removal.[261] At the request of OPA leader Polly Dyer, Senator Dan Evans, now working with Seattle radio station KIRO, made an editorial broadcast advocating dam removal.[262] The city of Port Angeles sent a delegation to Washington, DC, met with their representatives, and demanded that the city's water be protected.[263] The city had to threaten to withdraw its support from the project entirely, but in the end it got its water.[264] James River, seeing political support for dam removal rising, considering the costs it would incur if it were required to put in fish passage and perform other upgrades, and believing that it could secure its power supply, decided to support Swift's legislation, which guaranteed compensation for the dam and power for the mill.[265]

Even local long-time removal opponents threw up their hands and moved on to suggesting options for the disposition of project land after dam removal.[266] Local political activist Buck Adamire, who would go on to fight the removal for many more years, wanted the land returned to the public. Public status, to him, included Olympic National Forest, but not Olympic National Park. In 1992, a few regional economic interests spoke up in support of dam retention—the Northwest Public Power Planning Association passed a resolution to preserve hydroelectric projects, and ITT Rayonier, a forest products company and the largest private employer in Clallam County, intervened in the case in early 1992.[267] But this sort of involvement, late in the game, did not sway decision-makers. All long-standing interests were now joined in one coalition for dam removal.[268]

The last front of political resistance now was in the United States Congress itself. Practically every member of Congress has dams in their district, and the potential precedent of a bill requiring dam removal made some members, especially westerners, deeply uncomfortable.[269] Along with a cultural and generational allegiance to dams and water control in general, representatives could easily imagine their opponents in the next election pointing at their Elwha vote and warning their constituents that their own local dams would be next.

The solution came in the text: the Elwha bill would require restoration of the river, which everyone could support, but it would not mention dam removal. All key decision-makers were well aware that restoration could not happen with the dams in place, but this kind of political massaging eased in the necessary votes. The mill, for its part, would be guaranteed cheap power.[270]

Some skepticism remained, though. John Dingell, in particular, resisted Swift's demands, protesting that the bill wasn't ready.[271] Dingell had long been Swift's political ally and even patron, and he was well apprised on the dams from continued consultations with the GAO.[272] He had even sent a sharp letter to FERC chairman Martin Allday, criticizing the commission's unresponsiveness to the agencies' points and demanding that FERC work with them,[273] but he remained skeptical of the dam removal plan and,[274] according to Tom Jensen, hoped to use the Elwha as political leverage to move along other, unrelated issues.[275] Swift insisted that the bill would pass, and after what is often referred to in our nation's capital as "a frank exchange of views," the two men came to an agreement.[276] In a dramatic session at the very end of the 102nd Congress, the Elwha River Ecosystem and Fisheries Restoration Act, PL 102-495, finally came to the floor of the House of Representatives. Co-sponsored by Bradley and the entire Washington delegation (other than Speaker Tom Foley), what would become known as the Elwha Act passed the House and the Senate. It was signed into law by President George H. W. Bush on October 24, 1992.

The overjoyed dam removal coalition vaulted into celebration. Olympic Park Associates billed the act as "the product of more than five years' work by a varied group of organizations: government agencies (NMFS, NPS, WDFW, USFWS), Native Americans (the Elwhas), peninsula residents (Friends of the Elwha), and conservation and wildlife organizations."[277] The CIs and the tribe issued a press release two days later. In it, Shawn Cantrell said, "Congress and the president are clearly stating that environmentally destructive action of the past can be rectified, that past mistakes can be corrected." Tribal representative Robert Elofson affirmed the action as part of the federal government's trust responsibility under the Treaty of Point No Point, and went on to say, "This bill recognizes the devastation to our cultural, social and economic well-being, along with the negative impacts on the salmon runs and ecosystem, caused by the Elwha dams." Tribal chair Carla Elofson called it "a long-sought first-step toward restoring the heart of the Elwha S'Klallam people—the wild salmon." She was sure to acknowledge the efforts of Adams and Swift as well as Bill Bradley and Representative Norm Dicks.[278] The tribe later hosted a celebratory dinner, presenting Swift with a hand-painted canoe paddle.[279] In Seattle, the Mountaineers hosted "The Elwha Party," inviting "all conservationists, environmentalists, boaters, hikers, campers, fish-lovers, dam-haters, park-users, tree-huggers, and anyone else who supports FREEING THE ELWHA."[280] Rutz also received a certificate of appreciation from his fellow environmentalists.[281] David Ortman offered a poem:

> So raise a toast, it's time to boast;
> Of eyes and fish, both steely;
> Hoist your glass, don't let it pass:
> May the wine and river flow freely![282]

The parties to the FERC jurisdiction suits sought and received a stay. The case was later ruled moot after the Elwha Act took matters out of the court's hands.[283] The next step, as required by the act, was for the secretary of the interior to produce a report, due in 1994, detailing what, exactly, Elwha restoration would entail. The CIs and the tribe began to pursue appropriations to perform the necessary battery of studies for the report. Under the new Clinton administration and its environmentally enthusiastic Interior Secretary Bruce Babbitt, political conditions appeared promising.[284] In January 1994, the secretary personally assured lead environmentalist Shawn Cantrell of a strong desire for removal to happen on "his watch" and added that he wished to be the one to set off the demolition.[285] Cantrell believes that, in retrospect, Babbitt's zeal for dam removal may have been counterproductive, provoking and hardening removal opponents.[286] The environmentalists began to discuss expanding intervener meetings to include the companies,[287] and the agencies worked with the CIs in drafting the Elwha Report.[288] The CIs looked to put together a joint statement with the tribe, the companies, the city of Port Angeles, and the State of Washington, in hopes that "Congress would be impressed by a single joint letter from the unique 'coalition' we would represent."[289]

Around this time, the environmental community began to feel a little marginalized. They complained that the story coming through in the draft Elwha Report portrayed the debate as taking place between FERC and the resource agencies, disregarding the CIs' contributions.[290] They continued to advocate for dam removal, but their role was no longer clear in this new and less adversarial situation.

REALpolitik

In January 1994, Babbitt's Interior Department sent the completed *Elwha Report* to Congress. The report confirmed that, sure enough, the only alternative for full restoration was dam removal. The highlight of the nearly two-hundred-page document was a table that clearly and accessibly displayed restoration prospects for all ten of the Elwha's anadromous fish runs. The table indicated that, with both dams removed, prospects for recovery were good or excellent for nine out of ten runs. They were much worse with either or both dams standing.[291] Versions of this table would continue to appear in subsequent EISs and papers.[292] The *Elwha Report* underlined that the settlement had been negotiated, not litigated, and called the solution a "win-win." Buoyed, Senator Patty Murray (D-WA) looked to introduce an amendment to the Elwha Act to ease along funding for the dam removal.[293] But this was the last good news the dam removal coalition would receive for some time. The political world was turning.

In the same month that Babbitt released *The Elwha Report*, the *Peninsula Daily News* reported that support "runs deep to keep two Elwha dams" in the North Olympic Peninsula, with some citizens calling the removal plan a "land grab."[294] This discontent was stoked and expressed by a group calling themselves Rescue Elwha Area Lakes (REAL). REAL was composed mostly of "local folks," "old-timers who have hated the government from way back when," for whom the dams and lakes were familiar and comfortable parts of the landscape.[295] Anti-removal letter-writers and commenters had been simmering in the North Olympic Peninsula for years—REAL actually formed in 1992—but did not have the political force or opportunity to assert themselves until 1994.

Led by Marv Chastain, himself a former Seattleite who had retired to Port Angeles, REAL deployed a wide variety of arguments in favor of dam retention. Turning the environmentalists' support of charismatic wildlife against them, REAL spoke in defense of trumpeter swans (*Cygnus buccinator*), which used Lake Aldwell during migration.[296] This attracted concern from the national Trumpeter Swan Society as well.[297] The swans, large and proverbially graceful birds, helped identify REAL as an environmentally sensitive group. The potential disappearance of swan and others species' lake habitat was used to cast doubt on the conservation interveners' true intentions—if the CIs were against the birds, could they be legitimate?[298] REAL thought not. The conservation groups were labeled "so-called" environmentalists, a phrase that had been in use since at least 1990.[299]

REAL also waded into the scientific debate, claiming that the dams did not harm salmon runs and arguing that removal would, in fact, hurt the fish by inundating downstream reaches with silt.[300] REAL also suggested that silt releases would result in higher water levels and flooding of downstream property, including the Lower Elwha Reservation.[301] To arguments about the lack of spawning gravel in the lower river, removal opponents suggested that it would be cheaper and easier to dump "a few truckloads of gravel" into the stream.[302] This belief, that you could have the salmon and the dams at the same time, was an old one in Clallam County, and some REAL members had held to it for years.[303] They pointed out successful examples of fish passage in other dams and rivers,[304] and engaged an independent fish biologist, Robert Crittenden of nearby Sequim, Washington, to produce a new restoration plan. Crittenden's plan promised affordable salmon restoration while retaining the dams. Chastain said that he expected to "get a big charge the first time I see salmon in the river swimming above the dams."[305]

REAL drew political strength from the antigovernment feelings that had festered in the North Olympic Peninsula since, at least, the early days of Olympic National Park.[306] The owl wars had left the newest, rawest wound, but the environmental politics of the peninsula were also enlivened and embittered by controversies over private inholdings,[307] the management of introduced mountain goats, and the potential reintroduction of wolves.[308] People also worried about the role of the United Nations (Olympic National Park is a UNESCO World Heritage Site) and its rise to power in the United States.[309] Park opponents collected all their issues with the park and flung them into the same rhetorical cauldron, complaining that the park "digs deeper into our pockets while kicking us in the teeth."[310] This anger combined with layman's assumptions about the destructive potential of dam removal and public affection for the reservoirs to create widespread fury. REAL passed around a pro-dam petition and got hundreds of signatures.[311] By the mid-1990s the town of Port Angeles was awash in signs demanding to keep the dams.[312]

REAL recorded videos presenting their views on the lakes, the dams, and the park, and distributed them as widely as possible. They found sympathetic audiences among conservatives and in the hydropower industry—even Tacoma City Light helped hand out REAL's tapes.[313] Lauri Phillips, a Republican running against Dicks in 1994, promised to distribute tapes to members of Congress and their staffs in Washington, DC.[314] REAL's movie warned that dam removal would leave muddy, dusty messes after the reservoirs drained, and predicted the end of swans, ospreys, and other species that people in Clallam County were accustomed to seeing around Lakes Aldwell and Mills. The decline of the salmon runs was blamed on overfishing and on burgeoning populations of marine mammals. REAL pointed out that the salmon had held on in the river for decades after the dams, and that there were undammed rivers in the Olympic Peninsula with low fish populations. They pointed the finger of blame at what they called the "Virgin Earth Cult," saying that environmental extremists were the real villains of the Elwha.[315] Chastain (as of 2014) continues to maintain that the dam removal was, and is, part of a larger plot, the Wildlands Project, which aims to evict rural people and return the western United States to wilderness.[316]

The Park Service, for its part, carried on implementing the Elwha Act. Once sufficient funds had accrued, the NPS prepared two environmental impact statements, one (the programmatic EIS) on Elwha ecosystem restoration, and the other (the implementation EIS) on how restoration implementation would work. In October 1994, the Park Service released the draft programmatic EIS, which again asserted that removal was the only way to fully restore the fishery and that the chances for recovery for most runs were hugely better with both dams removed.[317] But the prospect of actual removal seemed a long way off. James River worried that with the dams in limbo, neither saved nor removed, they would have to shut down the mill, and told Norm Dicks so.[318] In the midst of this ferment, the *Peninsula Daily News* released an editorial broadly supporting dam removal but raising doubts about funding.[319] This was prescient.

Slade Gorton

In 1994, Newt Gingrich and his Republican colleagues swept into power in Washington, DC. The Gingrich revolution empowered and emboldened the antienvironmental movement nationwide, at all levels of government—this was the prime of the wise use movement as well. On this wave rode the greatest challenge to the Elwha Dam removal: Senator Slade Gorton (R-WA). Gorton had co-sponsored the Elwha Act, along with the rest of the Washington delegation, but had not been enthusiastic about it. In part, his support had been a favor for former colleague Brock Adams.[320] Gorton simply expressed his support for removal as the least-bad option at the time.[321]

Gorton's power base in conservative Eastern Washington was facing its own dam removal question. The Snake River, a major tributary of the gigantic Columbia River, is partly controlled by four large and controversial hydroelectric dams. Environmental groups have targeted these dams for many years. Gorton's constituents worried that dam removal on the Elwha would set a precedent for the Snake. He was also, as a fiscal conservative, concerned about the costs of removal. Gorton sat on the Senate Interior Appropriations Subcommittee, placing him in prime position to put his thumb over the metaphorical money hose. After the Gingrich revolution, Gorton swiftly withdrew his support from the Elwha Act. When Congressman Norm Dicks, in the aftermath of the Republican landslide, asked Gorton about this shift, Gorton's response was, "Welcome to the party."[322] In 1994, Dicks lost Clallam County (but comfortably won reelection), and deprioritized the Elwha effort.[323] He suggested that fish ladders might have to be the best option.[324] Although the project retained support from Democrats and from Secretary Babbitt, in 1995 Gorton's resistance was enough to halt a dam removal, especially an expensive and controversial one like the Elwha.

From his chair on the subcommittee, Gorton released Elwha money in a trickle. For instance, in fiscal year 1997, the president's budget included $110 million for Elwha Dam removal.[325] The Senate committee released $4.7 million.[326] The next year, the president requested $24.9 million—Gorton released $3 million.[327] In a 1995 press release, Gorton laid out his Elwha priorities: first, that the mill stay in Port Angeles; second, that the Port Angeles community approve of the decision, especially dam removal; third, to accomplish "a degree of fish restoration." He specifically stated he did not believe that dam removal would achieve these goals, "given current fiscal constraints."[328] This was a neat formulation for Gorton to use, since he personally embodied those fiscal constraints. The mill's survival was not really at issue. As congressional aide Tom Jensen notes,[329] the Elwha Act was very much a business-friendly measure, with significant concrete benefits for the company, the mill, and the Port Angeles economy. But the Gingrich revolution and the wise use movement were, of course, about more than business.

The political ruckus raised by REAL gave Gorton political cover. He said that he wanted the decision to be made by the people of Clallam County.[330] Gorton's opposition helped REAL by giving them more time to work—if the government had purchased the dams by 1995, REAL's situation would have been very different. But there was no unity of action between Gorton and REAL. REAL did bring its case to Gorton, and was assured of his intention to keep the dams standing, but did not make any constructive plans with the senator.[331] REAL's hope of success lay in convincing enough people to agree with them that the river would be better off with the dams in place, and that the Interior Department should embrace relicensing the dams and restoration with the dams in place. REAL did a good job of convincing people, or at least rallying people who agreed with them, but didn't manage to move from this into an effective long-term political strategy to relicense the dams. In the meantime, they continued to say "not only no, but Hell No."[332] It is certain that REAL and its sympathizers stood to support the dams when Norm Dicks strolled into his public meeting that day in Port Angeles in 1995.

The Citizens' Advisory Group

Alarmed conservation advocates and the tribe continued to seek restoration funding from the government and support from the public.[333] However, for all that they urged people to write letters and tried to spread the message that more fish meant more jobs, even creating a Fish = Jobs logo,[334] they did not gain much leverage in Slade Gorton's office. In June 1995, the Park Service released its final restoration EIS, confirming that nine out of ten salmon runs would have good or excellent prospects for restoration with both dams removed. Gorton was not moved, and neither were the anti-removal citizens of Clallam County. The scenic lakes and the memories local people had made there proved difficult to challenge. The CIs tried to make sure to call them reservoirs, in hopes of establishing a distinction between artificial and natural lakes.[335] This rhetoric didn't make a difference. The CIs considered other angles from which they might litigate the issue along, but they didn't see a way that any such choice might lead to the dams coming out. Even if they won, and forced dam removal through legal action, the companies may not have had the money to pay for it, and it wasn't clear that anyone else would, either—eventually they were going to need federal funding.[336]

Through it all, the North Olympic Peninsula community had really not been in position to speak for itself. The peninsula's elected representatives had not thrown their weight to one side or the other. The Port Angeles City Council, throughout the process, kept its issues carefully circumscribed—in favor of jobs and water supply, and advocating no specific action on the dams.[337] The town's Chamber of Commerce released a 1996 position statement emphasizing that it wanted a stable supply of water and power and compensation for the company's losses, so it still supported federal purchase of the dams, but not necessarily dam removal.[338] Friends of the Elwha spoke on behalf of their local members, but in a Port Angeles full of anti-removal signs, they could not claim to represent the broader community.

The only strong and coherent voice that had been speaking more or less on behalf of the whole northern Olympic community was REAL. Of course, REAL had no authority to speak for anyone beyond its members, but it filled a political vacuum in a way that Friends of the Elwha did not. In September 1994, the *Peninsula Daily News*, looking to present a balanced account of the Elwha controversy, ran a large feature built around two interviews: Park superintendent Maureen Finnerty, and REAL's Marv Chastain.[339] By mid-1995 Chastain, confident of success, said of the dam removal, "That body is dead there, let's drag it off the floor," and urged everyone to implement REAL's restoration scheme.[340]

Stakeholders across the Elwha's political spectrum agreed that delay helped no one and that a decision over the Elwha's future should be made soon, for the sake of the community and the fish alike.[341] In 1995, as removal advocates cast about for options, Bill Robinson of Trout Unlimited; Willy O'Neil of the fish advocacy group Long Live the Kings; Joe Mentor, a Republican operative and Olympic Park Association board member; and Bart Phillips, the executive director of Clallam County Economic Development Council, began to concoct a plan. The men wanted to consult the community directly, in order to offer a coherent and well-informed local statement on the Elwha that might "provide some cover"[342] for legislators to appropriate money to buy the dams and fund removal.[343]

O'Neil, Robinson, Mentor, and Phillips' idea was to assemble an advisory committee of well-respected community leaders to consider the issues, hear from each significant stakeholder group and from technical experts, and then weigh in on the Elwha and the jobs at the mill.[344] This seemed like the sort of thing that might be effective in dealing with Slade Gorton—Gorton and others in the Washington delegation had been requesting local guidance on the Elwha issue.[345] The tribe was very skeptical of the plan, and so were some of the conservation groups, but in 1995 they didn't have many other options.[346] Marv Chastain was skeptical too,[347] but REAL didn't have a clear path through the impasse, either. After a series of meetings, the four planners began to approach the first few potential committee members, local residents widely respected for their character and integrity. Trout Unlimited pieced together some funding to support the group's efforts,[348] and the twelve-member Elwha Citizens' Advisory Group (CAG)[349] was formed. Most of its members were broadly impartial on the subject of dam removal, with a handful of exceptions: Orville Campbell, a long-time representative of both James River and Crown Zellerbach, who presumably wished to see the dams purchased on behalf of his company;

Glenn Wiggins, the head of Slade Gorton's Clallam County Advisory Committee; and Harry Lydiard (a former county commissioner) and Jim Walton (a former chair of the Washington Fish and Wildlife Commission), both conservationists. But each of these men was considered open-minded and fair. Moreover, the members of the group were mostly businesspeople who could be expected to potentially change their minds, if not their feelings, when presented with evidence.[350] The group as a whole was very difficult for political critics to attack.[351]

Like most other stakeholders, the CAG members felt that the status quo of uncertainty and antagonism benefited no one. They were motivated to help move Port Angeles, Clallam County, and the Elwha River toward some sort of resolution, but they were not quite sure what status or power they really had. In late 1995, the committee contacted the Washington congressional delegation and the secretaries of Commerce and the Interior, to ascertain that these decision-makers would be open to the advice of such a local group as themselves. The answer was positive. Buoyed by this approval, the CAG held a series of meetings to agree on an approach. They put together a list of seven goals and objectives:

1. To maintain family-age jobs.
2. To provide efficient and reliable electric power for current and potential future Elwha Dam users.
3. To find fiscally responsible and achievable solutions for fish restoration.
4. To secure adequate good quality water for Elwha Basin water users.
5. To identify specific measures to address local concerns about implementation or modification of the Elwha Restoration Act.
6. To make the solution cost-effective for the nation's taxpayers.
7. To remove the threat of litigation for current dam owners and economic uncertainty for the community resulting from the unresolvedness of the issue.[352]

The CAG then invited all stakeholders to share their perspectives on the Elwha. They received presentations from the company, the tribe, the environmentalists, the paper companies, REAL, the Bonneville Power Administration, and the National Park Service, and hosted a well-attended town meeting as well.[353] From all this, the CAG established that the companies preferred to sell the dams and rid themselves of the situation rather than relicensing them. In April the committee published its findings, saying that the case for restoration by dam removal was ecologically "compelling," raising concerns over the cost, and suggesting a phased plan for dam removal:

Phase 1: The federal government should buy the dams, begin restoration actions, and perform studies to inform the future.

Phase 2: Continue to work on fish outplanting and water quality improvements.

Phase 3: Remove Elwha Dam and study the middle Elwha and its tributaries.

Phase 4: Evaluate the Elwha Dam removal, continue water quality protection and restoration actions. Continue to monitor and assess through the life cycle of initial outplanted fish.

Phase 5: After a full assessment, remove Glines Canyon Dam.[354]

This cautious approach offered some satisfaction for nearly everyone (except REAL), and the CAG was generally accepted as solidly representing the community.[355]

The conservation interveners worried about the CAG's position being taken as more authoritative than that of long-standing Elwha stakeholders like the company, the tribe, or themselves.[356] They pointed out that, while the CAG viewed the Elwha as a local concern, in fact it was a regional and national one.[357] In public, though, the CIs promoted this takeaway from the CAG report: that the community wanted to remove the dams.[358] The report gave the companies new hope that the issue might be resolved, and the dams finally purchased.[359] It offered the tribe, fishers, and scientists the prospect of a roadmap to restoration and a free-flowing Elwha River. The tribe came out in support of the finding, with the caveat that they would prefer only one dam removal project to disturb the river rather than a phased approach.[360] The agencies, also, wanted the dams to be taken out concurrently—it would demand less documentation, less money, less time, and less perturbation of the river[361]—but the CAG reasoned that a more extended plan would be less expensive per year, and therefore perhaps easier to fund.[362]

The CAG's report was the turn of the tide.[363] For all that Marv Chastain derided it as "a left-handed way of getting citizen approval,"[364] the CAG's report fatally weakened REAL. REAL's status had been inflated by its claim to be the voice of local people. This gave it more influence, more political weight, than ordinary advocacy groups that only claimed to represent themselves. Associating itself with the regional economy and regional beliefs, REAL built itself into a counterweight to the removal coalition despite limited resources and political connections. The group claimed to have done its scientific homework, and had made a confident case that its approach to restoration would be the best one.[365] But its authority in all of these claims was hollowed out when the CAG took up the same questions and arrived at different answers. Bart Phillips noted that the CAG had, in fact, absorbed a presentation from REAL during its process (another example of REAL receiving the same political status as other longer-standing stakeholders), and had included REAL's ideas in its deliberations.[366] REAL could not reasonably argue that they had been ignored or marginalized.

At the same time as the CAG released its recommendations, the Park Service released its draft implementation EIS.[367] This document indicated that dam removal would be a surprisingly easy engineering job, clearing the silt using natural erosion rather than carrying it out in trucks or through some other laborious method. Brian Winter was delighted.[368] The EIS also forecast economic benefits to the community—the removal itself would bring an influx of cash during deconstruction, followed by increases in sportfishing and tourism that would drive an increase of an estimated 446 permanent jobs and $4.6 million in payroll.[369] The net economic gain in recreation and tourism dollars had already been estimated at $133 million.[370] In response to public comments criticizing the removal project's $113 million price tag, the Park Service noted that adding passage to the dams would indeed cost less—$38 million—but would produce 12 percent of the fish.[371] Marv Chastain called the implementation EIS "an environmental obscenity," and a "disaster that would wipe out the best five miles of Chinook spawning habitat in the state."[372] In fact, the EIS noted, rivers tended to recover from traumatic silt events in two to seven years.[373] The document prompted Representative Rick White (R-WA), a moderate Republican from Western Washington,[374] to publicly urge Elwha removal as a "perfect laboratory" for northwestern salmon restoration.[375] He believed in Elwha Dam removal as a beneficial move and, as a politician, planted his environmental flag there.

Thwarted, REAL took its efforts to Olympia in 1997 and worked with its representatives, Republican Jim Buck and Democrat Jim Hargrove, to pass a bill mandating that REAL's restoration plan be implemented as an interim management option. The plan envisioned a system of planting fish eggs upstream, and using screens with a trap-and-haul or fish ladder system to allow for safe migration, much like the companies' suggestions during the FERC process ten years before.[376] But the state had no power to do any such thing. NMFS, which would have to approve any such changes, had rejected most aspects of REAL's plan long before. Besides, the other essential Elwha stakeholders had not been consulted on the matter.[377] As the editors of the *Peninsula Daily News* noted, this amounted to REAL (and Buck and Hargrove) making an effort to show that it cared about restoring fish. REAL represented to legislators that it had the backing of Clallam County commissioners,[378] but the commissioners quickly moved to distance themselves from REAL. The bill died in committee.[379]

Actual power continued to rest with federal appropriators. The CAG decision offered Slade Gorton a way to maintain his commitment to rural communities while agreeing to dam removal, and his initial reaction was to voice support for funding federal acquisition of the dams, and restoration work.[380] But that year he released only another $4 million for purchase, about the same amount he'd released in the past. At this rate, removal supporters noted, it would take the federal government eight years just to buy the dams.[381] Along with limiting appropriations, Gorton tried to get rid of the issue by including, in the 1997 appropriations bill, a clause authorizing the State of Washington to purchase the dams for one dollar each, after which the state would be responsible for removal and restoration. This idea presented many obvious complications. Shawn Cantrell, while he was sure that the state would not buy the dams, worried that all this might indicate to other skeptical members of Congress that the Elwha dams had now become a state matter, and that there was no need for the federal government to pay attention to it.[382] Either way, the State of Washington did not want the dams, at any price.[383]

Funding

Slade Gorton no longer had any real justification for opposing the dam removal coalition. Gorton had admitted that he was impressed by the CAG's compromise,[384] and he could not but concede that all stakeholders (except for still-defiant REAL) were united in favor of the federal purchase of the dams and their removal. But he continued to try to have it both ways. President Clinton's 1998 budget included $154 million for Elwha removal.[385] In February, Gorton agreed to go along with dam removal and announced, at a town hall meeting in Port Angeles, that there would be acquisition funding.[386] He said that he hoped this would satisfy the "environmental extremists" in the Clinton administration.[387] But then, in April, he introduced S1904, a bill amending the 1992 Elwha Act in such a way as to allow federal purchase of the dams under the condition that "a Federal or State agency shall not require, approve, authorize, fund, or undertake any action that would" alter any Snake or Columbia dams.

This political poison pill predictably drew criticism from conservation groups, who saw it as a naked attempt to hold the Elwha restoration "hostage" to events around other dams on another watershed.[388] The James River Corporation, which wanted to wash its hands of the Elwha dams, demanded clarification on what this meant for them.[389] Gorton's S1904 also mandated twelve years of evaluation between the removal of the Elwha and Glines Canyon dams, mirroring the CAG's recommendation. Norm Dicks called the bill "outrageous" and "obviously political," noting that the removal of one of the Snake or Columbia dams would require congressional approval regardless of this bill.[390] Senator Murray and Representative Elizabeth Furse (D-OR) also vocally opposed Gorton's bill.[391] Gorton claimed that he, having agreed to Elwha removal, now needed his opponents to work with him.[392] The bill died in committee but stood as a reminder of Slade Gorton's loyalties, priorities, and power.

It was the last card Gorton played. Acknowledging that he would need to work with the pro-removal Clinton administration,[393] he fully dropped his opposition to Elwha removal in June 1999.[394] Gorton placated his constituents in Eastern Washington by explaining that there wasn't enough time left in the last years of Clinton's presidency for anyone to take out the Snake dams. If Al Gore was elected in 2000, he said, that might change matters, but in the meantime he would no longer block Elwha removal funding.[395] Some felt that Gorton did this in order to give himself an environmental sheen for his 2000 Senate race.[396] On October 16, 1999, Norm Dicks, Slade Gorton, and Bruce Babbitt agreed that the dams would be purchased by February 29, 2000.[397] Removal stakeholders began to shift their outlook on dam removal from whether it would happen at all, to when to do it, and how.[398]

In February, Secretary Babbitt, the companies, and the tribe signed a declaration marking the federal purchase of the dams and beginning to shift them into the responsibility of the Bureau of Reclamation, the branch of the government that would operate them until they were removed. With federal acquisition, Babbitt crowed, "we have irretrievably and inexorably crossed the divide which will result in the removal of these dams and the restoration of these salmon and steelhead runs." Babbitt also optimistically stated that the dams were likely to come out in two to four years—perhaps in 2003.[399] Daishowa America president David Tamaki said, "We stand next to a hydroelectric dam that now more closely resembles a bridge that in the future will connect our differing interests and concerns; economic, environmental, tribal, ecological and government."[400] Slade Gorton, who did not attend the ceremony in person, pledged to support President Clinton's $15 million budget request for the Elwha, but presciently doubted that the project would be finished in only a few years.[401] He warned Babbitt against casting his eyes on the Snake dams, though, writing to tell him, "You will not be making a similar trip across the Cascade Range with a hammer[402] in your hands."[403] But the purchase of the dams, while a necessary step, did not equate to the restoration of the river. As one Port Angeles letter-writer said, the best way to help the Elwha fish was going to be to vote for Gorton's opponent in the next election.[404]

The next month, the Fort James Corporation (the latest iteration of the paper company) handed operations over to the Bureau of Reclamation. BPA would sell the dams' power, and any money the dams made would go to the National Parks Foundation.[405] Brian Winter declared that, with both dams removed, the Elwha would be the first dams taken out to restore an ecosystem from the mountains to the sea—a triumph for ecological restoration.[406] Winter received credit from many of the other Elwha stakeholders for leading the restoration project through years of challenges and on to completion.[407] Having worked for the tribe, then for NMFS, and then for the National Park Service, Winter came to personify the agencies, and indeed, the restoration effort.

To the tribe, the dams' transfer to federal hands brought them closer to the natural ecosystem that their ancestors, and indeed still-living elders, had seen. While to many people the restoration project was about salmon, the tribe's understanding of the Elwha was more holistic. The return of natural flows down the watershed would also restore the estuary and the nearshore environment, supporting shellfish and other seafood. Tribal restoration director Michael Langland quoted an elders' saying, "When the tide is out, the table is set," but noted sadly that by now, in 2000, there were no more shellfish or crabs to be had at the much-reduced river mouth.[408] To tribal councilman Russell Hepfer, the return of the Elwha also meant the renewal of the tribe's culture, but he noted that, after all this time, he wouldn't believe anything until he saw it.[409] The tribe's traditional subsistence economy would be buoyed by the return of marine and aquatic life, but so would their twenty-first-century market economy, with opportunities opening for commercial fishing and guiding. From the tribe's perspective, there was little distinction between the economic, ecological, and cultural benefits of dam removal—Frances Charles later said, "We, as Tribal Council and staff, are following the path of our elders set for us to protect and preserve our natural habitat."[410]

Anti-removal agitation, futile though it now was, boiled on in early 2000, stoked by Gorton's capitulation and announcements that the Interior Department would buy the dams. Angry letters flooded into the offices of the *Peninsula Daily News*. The paper collected and featured these letters in the days after the purchase announcement.[411] The removal project, letter-writers said, would destroy "beautiful lakes" (another writer called them "pristine") and deny people the fun they'd had there. Another writer, bemoaning the politicization of the river, was sure that both fish and dams would thrive with the addition of "a little common sense" and a state fish and wildlife director elected by Washingtonians—not the federal government. Another yearned for the days when the peninsula was allowed to log its own forests and fend for itself without depending on the government, and compared people holding Save the Dam signs to the famous image of a Chinese student in front of tanks in Tiananmen Square. He also brought up the price of restoration, estimating that the price of dam removal would be $133 per fish, and $11 per fish in lost electricity.[412] Another writer estimated anywhere from $256 to $333 per fish.[413] Most colorfully, past REAL president Don Rudolph, calling on the phrases of conservative broadcasting icon Paul Harvey, purported to tell "the rest of the story," saying that the "wise wizards of Washington, DC," had come to town, deriding Bruce Babbitt as the secretary of the "inferior," and saying that Slade Gorton had been "brainwashed" into believing that dam removal would help fish. He claimed that the people of Port Angeles remained heartily opposed to dam removal.[414] "Stop Elwha Dam Removal" flyers continued to appear on windshields and bulletin boards around Port Angeles. These were apparently distributed by one B. J. Allen, who had not been interested in dam politics until he attended the February 2000 transfer ceremony.[415] Ray Beaumariage of Port Angeles claimed that he had submitted a resolution to save the dams to the state grange years before, and that it had passed strongly.[416] The grange didn't have any power in this situation, of course, but in the past, granges had been influential in rural America, and presumably carried moral weight for some traditionalists in Clallam County.[417] While some letter writers did favor dam removal,[418] their voices were not as vehement as those of removal opponents.

Don Rudolph might have been right that the people of Port Angeles still broadly opposed dam removal, but their political leverage was gone. The Clallam County commissioners, for their part, bided their time until

The Elwha Dam, 2005. Photograph by Larry Ward. Wikimedia Commons.

September 2000, when they sent a position letter to Slade Gorton and other decision makers endorsing the concurrent removal of the two dams.[419] Orville Campbell, of James River, the CAG, and Port Angeles, noted that it was nice for the county to take a position, but that they were about six years late.[420]

Some people continued to raise fears about sediment releases and floods.[421] And indeed, the hydrology of removing dams this big would surely be a challenge—no one had done such a thing before. Resource agencies received funding in 2000 to study flooding in the Elwha watershed.[422] Later on, levees were raised to protect downstream property from rising waters.[423] Such studies were not sufficient for some locals, though—to Ethan Harris of nearby Sequim, Washington, "a frog living along the bank knows as much about the effects of the dam razing as a bunch of elite environmentalists pushing an agenda."[424]

Gorton lost his 2000 reelection campaign to Maria Cantwell (D-WA), and the only thing left was to implement the removal. Elwha appropriations now went through Representative Norm Dicks, who fortuitously chaired the House Subcommittee on Interior and Environment Appropriations. Dicks, a passionate fisherman who hoped to catch a hundred-pound Chinook someday himself,[425] had long supported dam removal, but he now faced the concrete challenge of funding an enormously expensive project.

In the first decade of the 2000s, Dicks set about appropriating money, putting together about fifteen separate appropriations of roughly $20 million each. This approach was calculated to keep the project moving but to not use too much of the National Park Service's annual budget on one project in one park.[426] To strengthen and broaden political support, Dicks brought his subcommittee colleagues to the site, and got them, Republicans and Democrats, on board with the project.[427] In the end, Dicks received widespread credit as a political "hero," the only person who could and did ensure that removal funds actually arrived.[428]

How to Free the Elwha

> But what was a great idea back then, is a terrible idea in the year 2001.
> —Orville Campbell, "Hydro(power) Had No Friends,"
> *High Country News*, 2001 (quoted in Burke)

With Dicks ensuring the flow of money, managers set about planning the on-the-ground restoration. The actual dam removals would cost $26.9 million—less than a tenth of the eventual cost of the project.[429] The biggest expenses came from ancillary projects, most notably new water treatment plants, necessitated by the dam removal. Environmentalists were skeptical about these "gold-plated" facilities.[430] But heavy silt releases during the dam removal meant that water treatment would be difficult.[431] The tribe's steelhead hatchery and the state's Chinook hatchery were also very expensive. The bill for the entire Elwha restoration would eventually be an estimated $324 million.[432]

Studies went on throughout the decade in response to changing needs and circumstances—for example, bull trout (*Salvelinus confluentus*) and Puget Sound Chinook were listed under the Endangered Species Act in 1999[433]—but while the Elwha project as a whole received a lot of federal money, the scientific studies attached to the project were inconsistently funded.[434] Other monies went toward other restoration preparation. A nursery raised native plants to revegetate new riverbanks,[435] logjams were placed in the lower river to improve habitat below the dams,[436] and hatchery operations were altered to better replicate the fishes' natural environment by, for example, making them wary of shadows.[437] A diverse team of agency and tribal scientists monitored the river in anticipation of massive changes after removal.[438] Local students from grade school to college levels took part in citizen science projects to measure the river's features before, after, and during dam removal.[439]

The environmentalists continued to promote the dam removal to their constituents and to the public. Here, they hoped, was a success story that could fire up their community and perhaps boost interest in other elements of the northwestern environment—how restored Elwha Chinook might contribute to orcas in Puget Sound, perhaps.[440] American Rivers, the nation's leading advocate of natural rivers and by this time the lead environmental group on the Elwha, put together three-dimensional visualizations of the Elwha Valley along the way to restoration, hoping to promote the removal project and educate the public.[441] Olympic National Park too, looking to raise the Elwha's profile, commissioned artist Larry Effert to make a painting of a restored Elwha River Valley.[442] These efforts were intended to make restoration projects more concrete and reassure skeptics that the project would not leave an ugly mud flat behind it.[443] Some local people continued to express fear and sorrow, with the dam removal being cast as a "national disaster" and the dams as "two old friends," which "need to be shown the respect they deserve in their final year of life."[444]

The contract for the water treatment plant was awarded in 2007, and ground was broken the following year.[445] At the groundbreaking ceremony, Norm Dicks made sure to credit Brock Adams and Al Swift for their crucial roles in passing the Elwha Act fifteen years before.[446] Some observers lauded the water treatment contract as the true beginning of the dam removal—the first physical work to be done on the project.[447] The start date for the actual removal was pushed back to 2009 because of water quality and treatment issues and new fish listings,[448] and then again to 2012.[449] These delays concerned the tribe and other removal advocates, but there was not much that anyone could do to make the money flow faster.[450] In the end, the removal date settled in 2011, thanks to the federal stimulus of 2009. To the delight of all removal advocates, this provided a $54 million dollar bump that put the project over the top.[451]

As Port Angeles got used to the idea of dam removal, in some quarters it grew to be a source of pride. One science teacher called it "a golden opportunity to be part of something big," saying, "The Elwha project is known around the world, and it is in our backyard."[452] The Elwha's worldwide importance was often mentioned as boosting the river and its community.[453] A local environmental education organization featured the Elwha watershed in its programs, working with the tribe to integrate culture and science in their programs.[454] Later on, volunteer opportunities to remove nonnative plants from the Elwha valley were promoted with the words, "Be a part of history. Even the fish will thank you."[455] NPS spokesperson Barb Maynes

The Elwha Dam during removal, 2011. Taken from an Olympic National Park web camera. Wikimedia Commons.

promised massive ecological effects: "more fish, more birds, more insects, more bears, more of everything."[456] In 2010, plans began for the celebration of the actual dam removal. Olympic National Park promoted the theme "Last Dam Summer," and began to distribute buttons for people to wear to spread the message.[457] These echoed the pro-removal buttons environmentalists had worn to meetings twenty years before. The local marine life center offered interpretive models of the river and its flows, to be used for public education.[458] Two Republicans who hoped to take Norm Dicks' seat criticized the removal and the science behind it, but Dicks comfortably won reelection in 2010 nonetheless.[459] Removal advocates, so close to success, congratulated and thanked themselves for years of hard work.[460] The contract to remove the dams was awarded at the end of the summer of 2010.[461] The dams' crushed concrete would go to paving roads, saving taxpayers an estimated $1.5 million.[462] At the end of 2010, the Park Service announced its slogan for the Elwha restoration project: "Natural Wonders Never Cease."[463] In June 2011, the dams' generators shut down for the last time.[464]

Dam Removal

On September 17, 2011, the removal of the Elwha Dam was inaugurated as the culmination of a weekend of festivities, which ranged from emotional poetry readings at the Elwha Klallam Heritage Center to a lewdly

The Elwha Dam site after removal, 2013. Wikimedia Commons.

good-natured burlesque show at a Port Angeles bar.[465] The removal ceremony, "a major interagency effort,"[466] was attended by many dignitar-
ies from Elwha and Washington State politics. President Barack Obama,
who had joked about salmon governance in his 2011 state of the union
address,[467] sent Interior Secretary Ken Salazar to represent the administration. The weekend of celebration was overwhelmingly cheerful, and casual
observers in Port Angeles that weekend would have found little evidence
that there had been much controversy to the project at all, other than some
speakers' oblique references to long struggles and perseverance. Some saw
signs of a social transition—nearly everyone, in town as well as beyond it,
had come to accept and even embrace the dam removal.[468] For Lower Elwha
Klallam Tribe chairwoman Frances Charles, the restoration was an answer
to the tribe's many decades of prayer and tears.[469] Bill Bradley spoke, saying, "In this time, it is time for beautiful fish to restore the circle of energy
and nutrients, prompt the rich life of the sea to flow up into the mountains,
and the mountains, enriched again, to move stone by stone, grain by grain,
down to the sea. It is time for the river to return to life."[470]

The final approach for the actual dam removal was essentially concurrent removal, with the Elwha Dam to come out first, followed quickly by
the Glines Canyon Dam. The actual physical removal occurred in a series of
carefully directed demolitions, intended to lower the water level in Lakes

Aldwell and Mills. This approach allowed workers to release the silt on a schedule that left "fish windows," times when returning salmon and trout could return to spawn without too much disruption.[471] Elwha Dam was completely removed by March 2012, and Glines Canyon came out in the summer of 2014. The world watched on webcams as the dams came apart, the lakes turned to rivers, and the deltas and the estuaries and coastal environments evolved.[472] Where Lakes Mills and Aldwell once sat, there is now a rapidly resprouting riparian valley.[473]

Some controversy lingers. The water treatment facilities, gold-plated or not, have failed to handle the undammed Elwha; they have performed poorly and cost a lot. There is, as of 2018, a lawsuit in process between the City of Port Angeles, the tribe, and the Park Service, trying to settle who should take possession of the facility and pay the costs of water treatment.[474] There is a moratorium on fishing in the Elwha, now scheduled to last until June 2019.[475] The Elwha's state and tribal hatchery programs have been the subject of lawsuits; some groups want restoration using only wild fish. The plan promulgated by the agencies and the tribe is immensely more ecologically advanced than the bad old days in the early twentieth century. It does use a nonnative run, Chambers Creek steelhead, along with Elwha stock.[476] In 2017, the Ninth Circuit ruled in favor of the federal and tribal plan to continue using hatchery releases to supplement wild fish.[477] The salmon and steelhead, for their part, swiftly recolonized the middle and upper Elwha and its tributaries, spawning where their ancestors had more than a century ago.[478]

Conclusions

> Interior is deliberately destroying industrial civilization.
> —Melanie Caltrider, commenting in USDOI NPS 1995

While the politics of the Elwha were complicated, its ecology is relatively simple—with the dams as the only important human impact in the watershed, it really is the ideal restoration laboratory,[479] so conditions should be good for restoring fish to their historic habitat. The river's progress as it evolves post-dam will help answer many of the ecological questions that worried river stakeholders in the 1980s and 1990s. Situated on the north-facing slope of the Olympic Mountains, it should even be pretty robust in the face of climate change.[480] It will be as close as there is to the old dream of a salmon park, a stronghold river that protects salmon the way that wildlife refuges protect whooping cranes or bison.[481]

Scholar Virginia Egan[482] identifies three time periods that shaped the progress of the Elwha removal question: FERC relicensing, the Elwha Act, and the creation of an action plan for dam removal. I find it more useful to view the process as a series of hurdles removal advocates needed to leap— the passage of the Elwha Act, the defeat of REAL and its allies, and the acquisition of sufficient funding to purchase and remove the dam. Each of these processes depended on advocates' working with one another's political perspectives to grow and maintain the pro-removal coalition, and diminish the power of removal opponents. Over time, dam removal went from an extremist proposal to an expensive but sensible mainstream idea. In 1986, dam removal was crazy. In 2011, the year the Elwha Dam removal began, forty-nine other dams came out too, from Washington to Alabama.[483]

Despite twenty years of turmoil, the Elwha's dam removal coalition did not have to shift much. In 1986, the tribes (represented by the PNPTC and the Elwhas) and the four original CIs were essentially alone in the field of political battle against the company, with relevant agencies and politicians expressing varying amounts of sympathy but not taking an active hand in the issue. As the Elwha moved beyond the routine FERC relicensing process, politicians from Slade Gorton to Bruce Babbitt became increasingly important, and resource agencies declared that they favored removal. The removal coalition swelled dramatically as it brought on agencies, politicians, and paper companies, but while these groups brought their own issues to the coalition, they did not have to compromise their core values. After the Elwha Act, of course, the emergence of REAL and the CAG redirected and concentrated the debate. But these were really the only game-changing additions to the Elwha's advocacy coalition dynamics after 1992. The coalitions continued to add allies—removal advocates were joined by fishing interests like the Northwest Sportfishing Industries Association (NSIA) and the Pacific Fishery Management Council[484] and recreation groups like American Whitewater[485] and the Surfrider Foundation,[486] while removal opponents looked for support in granges, rural electric cooperatives, and realtors' organizations.[487] None of these additions changed the project in important ways. Newer groups added their voices and resources, but were not sufficiently influential to write new chapters in the political history of the dams.

In the end, all these stakeholders came together to form a mega-coalition that could raise money in Washington, DC. To do this without taking leave of their core values demanded some careful political work, and each group had to come to an understanding of the dam removal as serving

Glines Canyon Dam before removal, 2011. NPS web camera.

their true interests. To take one small and specific example: in 1987, the Association of Western Pulp and Paper Workers tried to intervene in the FERC process in favor of license renewal. It then supported the Elwha Act in 1992.[488] But in 1994, when Shawn Cantrell sounded out the Pulp and Paper Union for support, its representative told him that the union was taking a low-profile approach to the issue: management still wanted the dams out, but his membership was in favor of keeping them.[489] Had the union been vocally in favor of keeping the dams and allied itself with REAL, perhaps local government would have joined the effort and political support to buy the dams would never have coalesced. Such shifts in perspective and emphasis were necessary to keep the mega-coalition more or less intact—with funding contingent on pacifying Slade Gorton and then on fighting for a large piece of the Park Service budget, any serious dissenting voice could have fatally delayed the removal.

The dam removal coalition essentially operated in two wings—the JFWA, with their responsibility for science and management, and the CIs, with their political activism and creativity. In between, as Lori Bodi noted,[490] was the tribe (including the PNPTC), which contributed technical expertise as well as applying political pressure.[491] Broadly, the CIs carried more of the political load leading up to the Elwha Act and then again in the

The Glines Canyon Dam site after removal, 2016. NPS web camera.

"creative solution" that created the CAG, and the agencies were responsible for carrying on scientific work, setting the terms of restoration, and implementing the Elwha Act.[492]

Of course, the dam removal coalition was not a united political juggernaut—the political role of resource agencies is very different from that of advocacy groups, and even more different from that of a sovereign nation like the Lower Elwha Klallam Tribe. The various actors did work together over the course of the issue, beginning with the PNPTC helping Rick Rutz write the initial conservation intervention in the mid-1980s[493] and ending with Dick Goin receiving a carved cedar fish from the Elwhas in 2011. But as Katherine Ransel of American Rivers put it, "The idea of stakeholders holding hands is a load of crap."[494] Shawn Cantrell gets credit for holding the greens together,[495] but even within the CIs, there were differences of opinion: some environmentalists, confident in their strength, would have preferred to let the question of FERC's jurisdiction play out in the courts instead of having the government buy out the companies.[496] More proactive agency personnel like National Park superintendent Finnerty and her management assistant Cat Hawkins-Hoffman shared information with the CIs.[497] This connection put actors in roles where they could be effective— the CIs saw their role as pushing issues and making points that the agencies

were "unwilling or unable to make."[498] The tribe, using the fishery and the
rickety lower dam just above the reservation, leveraged its treaty rights to
pressure decision-makers, a political power source totally different from
that of agencies or private groups.[499] There was some sense that if ever
negotiations really fell apart, the tribe would be able to send the matter to
federal court immediately.[500] The agencies, of course, had to pursue goals
within the scope of their missions and mandatory responsibilities, and had
little opportunity to be creative or proactive in changing the political situation. At the same time, the CIs could not do the necessary science or set
public policy. The coalition members needed each other.

The Elwha process is a good example of the old saying that success
has many parents.[501] Throughout, small political changes could have resulted in the end of the dam removal effort, and many people and organizations justly take pride in saving the dam removal effort. Stakeholders' roles
ebbed and flowed. By 2011, the CIs had had a very limited role in the
politics of the Elwha for over a decade. They could devote themselves only
to public relations, as well as urging Dicks and other politicians to keep the
money flowing.[502] This being the case, it was not surprising that the CIs
felt a little bemused, a little forgotten, when in 2011 the Elwha restoration
was publicized as the work of the politicians, the agencies, and the tribe.[503]
There were few environmental activists honored at the dam removal event,
though Norm Dicks did make sure to credit the conservation groups in his
remarks at the time.[504]

The Elwha dams had to be a federal issue—once the CIs and the tribe
made relicensing into an open controversy, the matter could only be resolved
in federal court or in the United States Congress. Between the anadromous
fish, the tribe, and the national park, there was no other way, and ultimately, the make-or-break venues for dam removal were congressional appropriations committees. But dam removal would have passed through the
appropriations process far more easily if it hadn't gotten stuck, like a salmon
at the foot of a dam, in the angry streets of Port Angeles. The public clamor
in Clallam County, amplified by REAL, squeezed appropriations and halted
the removal project for years. While the tribe and the CIs probably would
have won a lawsuit, this would have made it hard, perhaps impossible,
to get federal money for dam removal. Conciliating the local community
required the creation of a new venue, the CAG, that catered specifically to
local feelings. This represented a failure of established venues—the hearings and written comment periods of the NEPA process, for instance—to
accommodate these feelings and to express them in a sufficiently coherent

and representative way. The CAG had no formal power, and was well conscious of this, but it did a job that could be done nowhere else. Only once the group had nodded, grimacing, at dam removal could the issue emerge from the Olympic Peninsula and take up residence in Washington, DC. The locals' veto power meant that the terms of dam removal were advantageous for Port Angeles. The most expensive piece of the Elwha project, and the first to be physically built, was the city's water filtration facilities.[505]

Once REAL's effort to rally the North Olympic Peninsula community failed, few other venues were available. Frustrated removal opponents repeatedly tried to settle the Elwha issue in the State of Washington; the antienvironmental right wing of American politics has long embraced states' rights and state jurisdiction. But when local advocates called for state control, they showed themselves as having a naïve and fanciful understanding of the rights, roles, and responsibilities of state versus federal bodies.[506] There was no important state jurisdiction in the Elwha case, and even if there had been, Washington was and remains a liberal state.[507] Governor Booth Gardner, a Democrat, was an enthusiastic supporter of Elwha Dam removal as the Elwha Act was being debated.[508] The WDF deal of the mid-1970s was the only way in which the State of Washington participated meaningfully in the Elwha decision, and that, of course, was in a very different political context.

The cultural values held by these local advocates were deeper than the issue of the dam removal. Antigovernment voices saw the dam removal as one more case of the plot by urban elites, big government, and even the "Virgin Earth Cult" to control their homes.[509] The Elwha dams joined mountain goat management, wolf reintroduction, new land acquisition, the spotted owl, inholdings, and every other issue that had caused tension between the community and the park since the 1930s. To some extent, this perspective (other than the cult part) is reasonable. A lot of the pro-removal coalition was centered in Seattle or Washington, DC, and, as the *Peninsula Daily News* noted, much of the Seattle media favored dam removal.[510] Geographically, Seattle and the peninsula are not far apart—many a Seattleite looks out their kitchen window at the glaciers of the Olympic Mountains across Puget Sound. But culturally, they are two different worlds. Even moderate North Olympic Peninsula locals are rankled when city-dwellers equate their peninsula with Olympic National Park.[511] The emotional roots of the Sagebrush Rebellion, usually associated with the Intermountain West, and the wise use movement[512] have long been present in the Olympic Peninsula. This current of discontent produced REAL, which was powerful enough to delay dam removal for years, despite having little quantifiable connection to the dams and very few resources—they raised a total of only a few thousand dollars.[513] REAL's successes are a tribute to the power of grassroots activism, its political savvy, and the resonance of its broader message.

The fact was that many people in the North Olympic Peninsula valued the dams and the power more than the natural river. As one sign above a Port Angeles highway read, "Remove the dams and eat your salmon in the dark."[514] Nearly everyone involved enjoyed fishing and outdoor recreation, too; some simply saw the dams and the lakes as a better setting for such activities. The idea that you'd want to remove a dam to restore nature when a perfectly beautiful natural lake was already there seemed nonsensical to REAL and its allies.

Cultural conflict between pro- and anti-removal actors was even deeper when it came to the tribe. Resentment between the tribe and some local people had existed long before the Elwha Act,[515] and the removal offered some people an opportunity to hurl accusations about destructive fishing practices and greedy natives, on the one hand, and about racism and sabotage, on the other.[516] Who counted as local became a tangled issue, as well—Port Angelenos may have complained about local people being ignored, but who could be more local than the tribe? There was a perception that the Port Angeles community looked at the tribe and said, "Oh, are you still here?"[517] It is difficult to gauge the role of racism in the issue, but there is no doubt that there are strong tensions between the tribes and the Caucasians of the Olympic Peninsula. The massive importance the tribe placed on the dam removal—the goal of bringing back their ancestral river and the prosperity it had once supported, the memories of elders who had seen the giant salmon and the fish filling the Elwha—was something that few other people, including the tribe's political allies, could fully grasp. The complex indigenous relationship to rivers and dams continues to grow in political importance worldwide.[518] The Elwha tribe's persistence, like the fish waiting at the base of the Elwha Dam,[519] its unique moral and political status, and its culturally distinct long-term sense of time were crucial to maintaining the dam removal effort through to the end.[520] Whether the effort was successful, and tribal members once again go down to catch hundred-pound kings, will be seen in years to come.

4

Savage Rapids, Savage Conflict

Savage Rapids was an obstinate dam. It was first condemned in 1994, when the Grants Pass Irrigation District (GPID), which owned the dam, agreed to remove it. But it was saved. Again, in 1997, GPID decided to remove its dam. And again, it was saved. Finally, in 2001, the irrigation district once more promised to remove Savage Rapids Dam. This time there was no reprieve, but it was only in 2009, after decades of acrimony and toil, that Savage Rapids actually fell.

The removal of Savage Rapids Dam destroyed no jobs, bankrupted no businesses, released no toxins. The dam's function, to divert the waters of the Rogue River into GPID's canals, continued as before—the district, using pumps, delivered the same amount of water to its patrons. But hundreds of people had fought furiously, for years, risking their bank accounts, their reputations, even their friendships, in the process. Their motivation, while not easily defined or quantified, was simple: people loved the dam.

The Rogue Valley

The Rogue River rises in Crater Lake National Park, flows west out of the Cascades for 215 miles, and empties into the Pacific Ocean just north of the California border. Most of its five-thousand-square-mile watershed is quite wild, with mountains in the upper reaches and temperate rain forest near the mouth. The Rogue was one of the eight original rivers to gain Wild and Scenic status in 1968. It hosts some of Oregon's largest populations of anadromous salmon and trout.[1] Most of the people in the Rogue Valley live in the middle reaches of the river, where Interstate 5 runs through the cities of Grants Pass, Medford, and Ashland. This little stretch of Southern Oregon, far from the state's power centers in Portland and Salem, enjoys its own distinct landscape and identity.

The Rogue Valley of a century ago was thirsty for water. An editorial in the *Grants Pass Daily Courier*, titled "Water Everywhere," compared the people of the valley to Coleridge's Ancient Mariner, distressed that

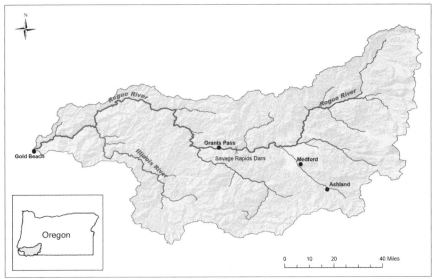

The Rogue River watershed. Map by Bradley Blackwell.

the Rogue's water ran along, useless, into the sea.[2] In 1916, the farmers of Grants Pass formed an irrigation district covering eighteen thousand acres of dusty Southern Oregon.[3] By 1921, the district had raised enough money to build a diversion dam at Savage Rapids. The dam was raised higher in each summer irrigation season in order to lift the level of the reservoir and allow water to run into irrigation canals. This process formed a lake that would become a popular recreation spot.

Grants Pass greeted the construction of the Savage Rapids Dam with great fanfare; in the *Daily Courier,* many articles boosted the irrigation project, and the paper covered the dam's construction avidly.[4] A crowd of three thousand turned out to watch the dedication ceremony,[5] and in 1922, the irrigation district printed Christmas cards displaying their new dam.[6] People in remote Southern Oregon, only a generation removed from the homestead days, doubtless sent these cards back East with a certain pride, to show that now they too lived in a modern community and that they (and their crops) would no longer live and die at the whim of the weather. In 1929, the State of Oregon awarded GPID a water right allowing it to divert 230 cubic feet per second (cfs) of the Rogue River, an allotment of 1/80 cfs per acre.

All of this spelled disaster for the Rogue's salmon and steelhead trout. The dam diverted juvenile fish into irrigation canals, from which they were pumped up and spilled out across the land—one farmer spoke of scooping hundreds of salmon fry out of his field, and local children would find little fish on the ground after irrigation.[7] Downstream migrants that escaped the canals churned through the dam's turbines and were turned into "fish salad."[8] Savage Rapids' fish ladder delayed adult fishes' migration upstream, keeping them waiting at the base of the dam.[9] For anglers (and other, more natural, predators) it was like fishing in an aquarium. The dam also heated the river downstream, releasing sun-warmed water from the still surface of Savage Rapids Lake. This increased physical stress on migrating salmon, which are cold-water fish.[10]

In 1934 a new fish ladder was built on the dam's south side, but a 1941 investigation from the Oregon Game Commission still found 14–38 percent mortality at the dam.[11] By 1949, the cost of fish passage was onerous enough that GPID asked the Bureau of Reclamation (BOR) to help repair its dam, incurring a debt that it would carry into the 2000s.[12] In the 1970s, BOR put together a report on renovations that would fix fish passage, but there were no acceptable bids to make these upgrades, so the issue was dropped.[13] Major repairs and fish passage problems continued through the twentieth century. In 1982, for example, 1,500 adult steelhead trout were trapped because of malfunctioning ladders, prompting a rescue operation by GPID and the Oregon Department of Fish and Wildlife (ODFW).[14] In the mid-1960s, ODFW biologists had rated Savage Rapids Dam the biggest fish passage problem on the entire Rogue River.[15] The label "fish killer" would stick to the dam for the rest of its existence and beyond,[16] though it was sometimes known as the "smolt pulverizer."[17]

There had always been conflicts between fish and dams in Southern Oregon. Historically, the Rogue had hosted immense runs of salmon and steelhead trout, enough to sustain a cannery near the river mouth and a sportfishing economy upstream.[18] In the 1930s, fishing on the Rogue was good enough to attract famous anglers like movie star Clark Gable and Western novelist Zane Grey, men who presumably could have chosen to fish anywhere they wanted.[19] Zane Grey had a cabin on the Rogue and set one of his novels there: *Rogue River Feud*. But the many users claiming the Rogue, upstream, downstream, and otherwise, put the river's fish, and its fishermen, under pressure. *Rogue River Feud*, in fact, is about conflicts between canneries and upstream fishers. As early as 1910, a group called the Rogue River Fish Protection Association formed to help defend the Rogue's fisheries.[20] In 1916, fishermen were suspected of blowing up a small structure called the Ament Dam in order to restore fish passage.[21] Whether they did it or not, it didn't make much difference for the fish: through the twentieth century the Rogue's fish populations plummeted, like many throughout the Pacific Northwest. Commercial fishing had ended by 1935.[22] A disgusted Zane Grey moved north to find better fishing on the Umpqua River.[23]

Explaining the decline of a salmon run is rarely simple. Changing land uses throughout the Rogue watershed, and fluctuating ocean conditions, undoubtedly played their parts in the fishery's decline, but so did dams. In the 1970s, the Cole Rivers Hatchery was built upstream of Grants Pass, and the Rogue's salmon runs were artificially augmented with hatchery stock. This put more fish in the river, but at some ecological cost.[24] Through the twentieth century, fishing groups worked with GPID to restore fish passage and habitat around Savage Rapids and Grants Pass—for example, the Rogue Flyfishers and the local chapter of Northwest Steelheaders pitched in to help rebuild the dam's fish ladders in the 1980s—but such efforts came nowhere near perfecting fish passage at the dam.[25]

All the while, Grants Pass, and the irrigation district, were changing. The Rogue Valley of 1921 had been an agricultural place, but over time GPID's community of patrons became more and more urban and suburban. The Middle Rogue is an island of aridity in Western Oregon.[26] The Grants Pass town slogan is "It's the Climate,"[27] and its dry, temperate conditions, more like California than Portland, began to lure retirees to Southern Oregon.[28] These same conditions had made irrigation, and the dam, necessary in the 1920s, but sixty years later, very few GPID patrons were actually farmers.[29]

This sort of social shift is an ongoing trend across the rural West.[30] GPID patrons subdivided and sold their land. By 2012, the Irrigation District's average parcel size was about one acre.[31] Many of these small-scale landowners did not actually receive irrigation water—GPID is not responsible for getting the water up to its patrons' lawns or fields, and a retiree may not care to buy and operate their own pumping system.[32] This unusual situation is sometimes compared to a school district, where landowners' taxes support the local school whether they have children there or not.[33] As early as 1980, GPID board chair Paul Brandon told Oregon Water Resources Department (OWRD) administrator Larry Jebousek that the board believed GPID was no longer "a viable irrigation district" and discussed converting it into some other body that was more appropriate for the new Grants Pass.[34] The dam was aging, and despite continual maintenance efforts, removal had been discussed as early as 1975.[35] And the dam was already political—the fishing groups that had helped GPID with upgrades criticized changes that might hurt the fish, including the potential installation of hydroelectricity in the mid-1980s.[36]

892 SAVAGE RAPIDS DAM, ROGUE RIVER FROM PACIFIC HIGHWAY, OREGON

PHOTO BY WESLEY ANDREWS

A postcard of Savage Rapids Dam printed some time in the 1940s. Josephine County Historical Society.

All of this left a policy paradox: the Rogue River and the Savage Rapids Dam were different things to different people.[37] To some, this was a mostly wild river that provided fish, with a dam that was somewhere between an imperfection and a problem. To others, the Rogue was a reservoir of irrigation water that also allowed them to swim and water-ski, and the dam was a tool to hold on to it. These two identities, and the management approaches they demanded, were, of course, in direct conflict. As salmon runs dwindled, farms became subdivisions, the dam aged, and the environmental movement rose on the horizon, contrary demands and ideologies collided.

Savage Rapids on the Policy Agenda

In the late 1970s, the OWRD began to perfect GPID's water right. This is a process requiring water right holders to prove that their water goes to the beneficial uses for which it was allocated. OWRD is supposed to perform this service for each water right soon after the right is issued, but such inspections were often not a high priority. The state's survey revealed that GPID only irrigated about 7,755 acres. Oregon still calculated irrigation water at 1/80 cfs/acre, so OWRD's 1982 final proof survey reduced GPID's water right to 96.94 cfs.[38]

GPID had feared this possibility for years. The district felt that it needed extra flow, beyond the water it actually used for irrigation, to account for seepage and to push water out to the far end of the canal system.[39] The district board applied for a larger water right, but, having little confidence that seepage and water transport demands would convince the state to allot them extra water, they sought other solutions as well. There was some discussion of going above the Water Resources Department and seeking a legislative solution to keep their larger water right, but this did not come to anything.[40] In the early 1980s, GPID worked out a creative deal with Oregon Fish and Wildlife wherein ODFW would apply for a water right of 83 cfs for habitat enhancement, to be delivered through GPID's canals. This 83 cfs, ODFW claimed, would maintain wildlife habitat in and around the canals, connecting streams and recharging groundwater. Along the way, the water would conveniently provide a boost for GPID's irrigation water.[41] With this deal in place, the board withdrew its application for further water appropriations.[42] ODFW went along with this solution, though it did raise removal as an option for the dam in 1985.[43]

The deal with ODFW raised one of the subtlest and most difficult issues of the entire process: that GPID's leaky canals meant a greener Rogue Valley. The people of Grants Pass lived in a verdant community watered by moisture seeping from the canals while enjoying California-style weather that should, in a state of nature, have made a green landscape unlikely—very much having their cake and eating it too. Most Grants Pass citizens were not GPID patrons. They received this scenic gift for no effort, and free of charge.

The result was that people saw Savage Rapids Dam as a creator and guarantor of beauty and civilization. The dam had turned the arid Rogue Valley into a green paradise; even, by some accounts, a Garden of Eden.[44] A frequently repeated story in the area is that local Indians had called the region something like the "brown desert"[45] or "The Land of Little Brown Sticks,"[46] but that this wasteland had been redeemed by irrigation and Savage Rapids Dam. There does not seem to be any hard evidence for such an appellation among the Rogue's native tribes,[47] but the popular perception that the dams and the irrigation district made and kept the Rogue Valley green offered a durable and compelling policy image. Later on, at the height of the controversy, some pro-dam advocates were sure that the very idea of a return to the natural desert landscape would shame dam removal advocates into admitting that they were wrong after all and that the dam should stay.[48] It was inconceivable to them that anyone would prefer a dry landscape to an irrigated one.

GPID's water right partnership with ODFW ran until 1985, when ODFW told the district that actually, it could only apply for beneficial use of about 20 cfs through the canals, and that this use would be only in particular streams.[49] After two more years of discussion, ODFW director Randy Fisher stated that it was "important for us to keep in mind that DFW attempted to assist GPID in finding a solution to a very difficult problem [in the 1980 agreement]. . . . DFW can legitimately appropriate only 20.5 cfs. I hope that we can put the 1980 agreement behind us."[50] This left GPID and its water right question back where it had begun in the late seventies. In 1987, GPID applied to the state for a supplemental water right of 90 cfs.[51]

In 1988, the Bureau of Reclamation began the Josephine County Water Management Improvement Study (JCWMIS), which targeted, among other things, improved fish passage at Savage Rapids.[52] Embracing the opportunity to resolve (or at least delay) its problems, GPID joined the project.[53] In 1990 the State of Oregon granted GPID a temporary supplemental right, allowing it to divert at its historic level on the condition that it continue the water management study, with the eventual goals of implementing conservation measures to lower its water consumption, and to fix fish passage. There is some precedent for the state conditioning water rights on making fish passage or other natural resource improvements in the public interest.[54] This move provoked some grumbling—there are those who doubt that such conditions should be part of water rights[55]—but the study and the temporary water right went ahead.[56] To fund its part in the study, GPID charged patrons an extra $25.[57]

Save the Rogue

In early 1989, WaterWatch of Oregon (a group devoted to maintaining and restoring natural flows in the state's rivers), Rogue Flyfishers, and the American Fisheries Society met with OWRD to discuss their thoughts on the water right issue.[58] These fishing and river groups wanted to remove the dam and allow the fish to migrate freely, and the political uncertainty over GPID's water right offered them the policy leverage with which to accomplish that. They made it clear that they were prepared to go to court, if necessary, to enforce the state's decision to reduce GPID's water right to 97 cfs.[59] GPID had been friendly with anglers in the past—remember, these were the people who helped fix up the dam in earlier years—but upgrading a fish ladder and cutting a water right are very different matters. After the conversation, the district board forebodingly noted that "we [are] not going to be able to live with their comments."[60]

The groups were trying to save fish through the doctrine of beneficial use, making, as Whitworth notes, creative use of an old law.[61] The supplemental water right would only seep into the canals, and not benefit GPID in any direct way, so an argument against the water right had a good chance of holding up in court. Despite the State of Oregon's ability to deny or alter water right applications on behalf of the public interest, environmentalists found private pressure to be a key part of ensuring that the state (and later, the federal government) actually enforced the law.[62] Indeed, for always-busy agencies like OWRD, enforcement is often "complaint-driven."[63] The key, from the environmentalist perspective, is to find a powerful enough complaint. GPID's water right was certainly powerful. If the district were forced to divert only the 100 or so cfs they actually put to beneficial use, too much water would seep into the canal bed to reach the extremities of the canal network, and the district would be unable to function.[64] This strategy was and remains an anomaly—there are few political mechanisms through which outside stakeholders can push for the removal of old diversion dams.

At this time, the Oregon Department of Fish and Wildlife was also becoming more proactive in attacking fish passage problems. Under the leadership of Chief of Fisheries Jim Martin, ODFW assembled a "hit list" of the most problematic dams in the state, including Savage Rapids.[65] The department estimated that the dam's removal would boost the Rogue's salmon and steelhead populations by 26,700 adult fish.[66] The ODFW hit list rankled people in the Rogue Valley—they did not want the fate of their dam and river to be decided by outsiders, especially government bureaucrats.[67] At one local rally, Martin was burned in effigy, an event that he remembered proudly in 2012.[68]

As the JCWMIS continued into the early 1990s, the situation was uneasy but relatively stable. Savage Rapids was still a primarily local issue, as the lead voices for removal were either explicitly based in the Rogue Valley (Rogue Flyfishers, for instance) or were Oregon-specific bodies with strong presences in the area: environmental groups like WaterWatch, or fishing groups like Curry Guides Association.[69] The environmental groups did receive some sympathetic advertisements from the outdoor gear company Patagonia, which is active in environmental issues.[70] Even Patagonia's support sparked resentment in Grants Pass, much as Jim Martin's hit list had; people didn't see how it was the place of a faraway sporting goods company to influence events on the Rogue.[71]

Bob Hunter, a lawyer, boater, and fisherman from nearby Medford, represented WaterWatch. Hunter had grown up in Michigan but had been living and fishing in Oregon since the 1970s. While many people worked to take out Savage Rapids Dam—Tom Simmons, also of WaterWatch, gets credit as an early leader[72]—Hunter was the widely acknowledged face of the effort, seen as representing all the private stakeholders that wanted to see the dam removed.[73] One of the few people who was present through the entire multi-decade political process, Hunter gained respect not just from his environmental allies but from his opponents as well. He remained fair, respectful, and clear-headed even in the most stressful of times.[74]

Save the Dam

GPID still wanted to keep the dam. So did the Grants Pass community. As early as 1991, dam supporters were holding candlelight vigils for Savage Rapids Dam.[75] Dam savers organized into grassroots nonprofit groups with names like the Save Savage Rapids Dam Committee and the Three Rivers Watershed Council and held a series of public rallies, and meetings in area granges.[76] This galvanized local opinion and took Savage Rapids Dam from a relatively private and contained issue to a matter of public debate.[77] Some of the protesters were small entrepreneurs whose recreation-based businesses benefited from summer traffic at Savage Rapids Lake; others were lakeside property owners worried about what would happen to their wells or property values when the lake disappeared.[78] Some lakeside landowners had built boat landings, which would be useless with no lake.[79] There were voices in GPID that wanted to sue OWRD, or file an injunction against their opponents, but they could find no legally defensible reason to do these things.[80] By the same token, there was no path through which the lakeside property owners who had enjoyed the benefits of groundwater recharge and recreation could put a legal claim on them—it wasn't their water, and while they'd used it freely, they did not have any right to or responsibility for it.

The most aggressive of the small pro-dam groups was the Association to Save Savage Rapids Dam and Lake (ASS). Led by fiery local Republican John DeZell, the association filed a SLAPP (strategic lawsuit against public participation) against a long list of opponents, from Secretary of the Interior Bruce Babbitt to local environmentalist Andy Kerr.[81] The ideological slant of the SLAPP is well expressed by legal analysts Phillip Bender and

Phillip Berry: "ASS's SLAPP 'may represent the high water mark of SLAPP litigation, being based, apparently, upon the theory that anyone who even speaks, however abstractly, about removing a dam . . . for whatever reason is subject to suit for alleged conspiracy.'"[82] Indeed, the stated intention of the suit—to stop environmentalists from speaking—was patently frivolous,[83] and it did not succeed.[84] SLAPPs can be lengthy and expensive, though,[85] and the dam removal coalition took this suit as an attempt to harass and silence them.[86] Indeed, this is why SLAPPs exist—to defeat cash-poor opponents in a legal war of attrition. ASS's resorting to a SLAPP reflects the weakness of the dam savers' legal and political position—they could hold rallies, or lobby the GPID board, or write op-eds in the *Daily Courier*, but there was no policy mechanism that they could confidently use to advance their case. If they'd had a better choice, they probably would have taken it.

All this represented a political role reversal. The traditional narrative of environmental politics is one of scrappy upstart environmentalists protecting landscapes—forests, deserts, seashores—from extractive interests who wish to destroy those landscapes for their own purposes. But ecological restoration flips this around, and in the case of Savage Rapids, it was environmental groups on the attack and their opponents playing defense. In Grants Pass, as the dam savers adjusted to their new role, they consciously took on many of the political trappings of environmental groups. The leader of one microscale pressure group, the Save Savage Rapids Dam Committee, promised to turn environmentalists' tactics on them and snare these "masters of deceit" and "parasites" in court—rhetoric reminiscent of environmental firebrands like Edward Abbey.[87] The Three Rivers Watershed Council's name makes it sound like some sort of natural stewardship group, not an organization dedicated to fighting dam removal. The dam savers protested, over and over, about how much money environmental interests had and how difficult it was to compete with their resources.[88] There were even suggestions, later on, that dam savers would chain themselves to the dam, defying the backhoes, much as some environmentalists sit in redwood trees to prevent them being felled.[89]

Deciding on Dam Removal

Meanwhile, the JCWMIS was split into a water conservation study, performed by David J. Newton Associates, and a study on fish passage, performed by BOR. BOR published a progress report on fish passage in 1992 and released a planning report/draft environmental impact statement to the public in 1994. The EIS identified dam removal, with the installation of pumps to maintain GPID's irrigation activity, as the preferred alternative—it was projected to cost $10 million, while refurbishing the dam to create adequate fish passage would cost an estimated $15 million.[90] The EIS projected a 22 percent increase in fish escapement above the dam site after removal.[91] Moreover, if GPID took out the dam, the improvement to natural resources and the associated benefits to the public interest would be enough for OWRD to allow GPID its supplemental water right.

GPID didn't have an extra $10 million, let alone $15 million, so the obvious move was to ask the federal government for it. Mike Jewett of the Oregon Water Resources Commission (OWRC) impressed upon GPID the necessity of having environmentalist support if they wanted to successfully seek federal funding.[92] Some environmentalists, Bob Hunter among them, indicated that they would be very open to helping GPID gather these funds to pay for dam removal—and, by the way, to ensure the survival of the district.[93] To other environmentalists, the survival of GPID was not important.[94] Andy Kerr of the Oregon Natural Resource Council suggested simply expanding the Grants Pass municipal water system and doing away with the irrigation district entirely.[95] This attitude was not calculated to build friendships with GPID. Moreover, as GPID's lawyer Chris Cauble noted,[96] the end of the district would leave less impetus to remove the dam—the removal would still be expensive and difficult, but no one would be legally responsible for it.[97]

Late in 1993, with the study winding down, the GPID board had to face some hard truths on the Savage Rapids question. To continue irrigating, they needed water. They were using more water than OWRD allowed. Even if the state did issue them an expanded water right, that right would probably be shot down after an environmental lawsuit. If they did somehow manage to keep the dam, they would have to make expensive upgrades, and without environmentalist support they would be hard-pressed to get the necessary external funding to make those upgrades.[98]

Raising the money internally was unlikely. A survey of GPID patrons, reported by board member Bill Hiljus in late 1993, indicated that only 28 percent of respondents were willing to pay to save the dam; 34 percent wanted to save it but specifically declined the option of paying to do so.[99] A variety of local advocates took up the cause of dam retention but were frustrated in their attempts to find the $15–17 million that was by then estimated as the cost of fixing fish passage.[100] The *Grants*

Pass Daily Courier's headline summed up the situation nicely: "Dam Fans Scratch Heads, Raise Fists."[101]

Seeing no way around the state's demands and needing to keep their water, the GPID Board regretfully voted to remove the dam in January 1994.[102] But the vote came with a list of conditions, which GPID laid out in a full-page ad in the *Daily Courier*. Most prominently,

> A permanent water right of 149 cfs, with sufficient in-stream flow to provide it.
>
> Outside funding for pumps, power, restoration, and a park above the dam.
>
> Agency and environmentalist guarantees of support and noninterference.
>
> Debt forgiveness from BOR work in the 1950s.
>
> The right to change its mind if funds for fish passage improvements on the dam were found in the community.

In the same ad, the district claimed that it was responsible for making the Rogue Valley a verdant and attractive place, and urged the public to support it.[103]

In October, the Oregon Water Resources Commission accepted GPID's plan and extended its permit to 1999 under the condition that the district implement a water conservation plan and fix fish passage by removing the dam.[104] Senate Appropriations Committee chair Mark Hatfield (R-OR) stood ready to gather funding for the project if stakeholders could reach a consensus on replacing the dam with pumps.[105] As noted above, the pumping alternative opened fish passage and was much cheaper for the district. Moreover, according to the environmental impact statement, dam removal also created greater fishing and whitewater recreation opportunities, potentially providing a significant economic boost for the local community.[106]

But the local community hated it.

Why?

The Grants Pass community's resistance toward dam removal had deep and tangled roots. In the late 1980s and early 1990s, dams were a minor environmental issue in the region, overshadowed by the political Ragnarok of the owl wars (see chapter 3). As in the Olympic Peninsula, the tension and distrust the owl wars caused and exacerbated among communities, environmentalists, and government agencies, the battle lines they drew, and the political mind-sets that were created and entrenched, remained violently alive when dam removal rose to the political agenda a few years later. One of the centers of the owl wars had been Roseburg, Oregon, an hour north of Grants Pass. In 2011 and 2012, many stakeholders from the Savage Rapids debate spoke of the spotted owl as a touchstone in their political careers and environmental consciousness.[107] As early as 1991, Oregon governor Barbara Roberts replied to GPID secretary Bruce Buckmaster's concerns about federal salmon listings under the Endangered Species Act by assuring him that "like you, we do not want this to become another 'Spotted Owl.'"[108] So in Grants Pass, bitterness and suspicions were already simmering, and when the issue politicized, salmon swiftly replaced owls as a symbol of government interference.

Further complicating matters was the mercurial history of Elk Creek, an upstream tributary. A dam on Elk Creek had begun to be built in 1982, as the "age of dams" was coming to an end.[109] Environmentalists fought it through the 1980s, and in 1987 they succeeded in getting an injunction that halted construction partway,[110] much to the chagrin of many Rogue Valley residents. Stakeholders on both sides of the issue lumped the survival of Savage Rapids and the completion of Elk Creek together throughout the process.[111] Elk Creek Dam was never completed; in 2008 it was notched to open fish passage and then abandoned.

To many people in Grants Pass, the issue was not just Savage Rapids Dam so much as Savage Rapids Lake. GPID irrigators' water supply was assured under BOR's pumping alternative, but the seasonal "lake" would be impossible to replace. This issue was raised within the GPID Board when the fate of the dam was debated in 1994. In a letter to their fellow board members, Catherine Davis and Bill Hiljus said,

> The dam has been a fixture in this community for many, many years and thousands of people have fond memories of family picnics on the summer lake, or learning to water-ski there, and of watching fish jump the ladders. Many people had also built boat docks on the lake, and enjoy the still water view during the irrigation season. These are the images that tug at our hearts.

They went on, in the rest of the letter, to urge their colleagues to look beyond nostalgia and embrace the facts laid out by the Bureau of Reclamation, and reminded them that GPID did not exist to provide recreation.[112] But to the candlelight protesters beyond GPID's offices, recreation was exactly what the irrigation district provided. Local politician Royal

DeLand suggested that local dam supporters organize into a recreation district and buy the structure themselves. It is very unlikely that they had the resources to do this. While the heart-tugging attachment to the lake was certainly genuine, to some extent the desire to reject dam removal was also symptomatic of a larger rejection of the government. As seen by DeLand, "These people are just sick and tired of the government telling them what color toilet paper to use and when to use it."[113]

Pressed by anglers, environmentalists, and the State of Oregon, the dam savers groped about for new weapons as the public rhetoric heated up. After the vote to remove, GPID board member Don Greenwood resigned, joined up with the anti-removal Three Rivers Watershed Council, and began to circulate a save-the-dam petition through the community. He later claimed to have ultimately collected some thirteen thousand signatures.[114] Greenwood also sought and received the support of *Sneak Preview* publisher Curtis Hayden, whose free newspapers reach some ninety thousand Rogue Valley residents each month.[115] From his editor's chair, Hayden condemned the dam removal plan and its proponents.[116] While Greenwood's efforts may have given heart to the dam savers of Grants Pass, the actual GPID Board kept only very loose connections to these outside pressure groups. Individual board members did want to keep the dam—they hoped that these groups somehow succeeded—and no one could doubt that Grants Pass and Josephine County wanted to keep Savage Rapids Dam. But officially, GPID had committed to removal, and the board knew that the district would lose its supplemental water right if it went back on this commitment.[117]

Don Greenwood's petition had little political effect, and the protesters continued to be stymied by the fact that they had no legal claim to the dam or the water. Some resorted to scaremongering. This, it was said, would be the first domino in an onslaught of restoration that would topple every dam in Oregon.[118] John DeZell suggested that the environmentalists were not interested so much in fish passage as in destroying private property rights and the capitalist system.[119]

GPID countered such claims in a full-page advertisement in the *Grants Pass Daily Courier*, reminding readers that the district's canals made the Rogue Valley green instead of "a dry gulch," and that to keep doing this GPID needed a large enough water right to keep those canals full. The price of that water right was fish passage, and the cheapest fish passage came through dam removal. The district emphasized that their acquiescence had come only with stringent conditions.[120] GPID's ad was accompanied by a guest opinion piece by board member Bill Hiljus, laying out these points in more detail. While Hiljus acknowledged the fun that the lake had provided, he pointed out that the protesters had not produced any resources or ideas that could change the situation in any meaningful way.[121]

GPID's public relations efforts didn't work; at a public hearing in early 1995, many commenters failed to understand that the Rogue Valley would stay just as green with pumps as with the dam—that the same water would flow down the same canals.[122] The decline of GPID's farming base did not alter the community's aesthetic preferences: as patron Esther Bristol said, "'They' say 'Irrigation is not needed since farms have ceased to exist.' Don't 'they' know it is the same thirsty land, whether farms or many households?"[123] The economic productivity of irrigated land didn't matter to people outside GPID—the look and feel of the landscape did. The Josephine County commissioners passed a resolution urging the salvation of the dam, listing recreation, verdant land, and water supply for fire suppression[124] among the benefits provided by the dam.[125]

To some extent the conflict was generational. Simply put, the Greatest Generation loved dams.[126] Many of the strongest voices in favor of Savage Rapids Dam were older people, known to GPID staff as "the W2 guys," or the "Iwo Jima crowd," who made their stands on principle without much reference to the specifics of Savage Rapids Dam.[127] To ninety-six-year-old former GPID board member L. H. Kirtley, "I don't care where it is, to take out any dam . . . there's no reason in the world."[128] Carl Stein, who would later serve on the GPID Board, avowed that he was "not in favor of the removal of the dam under any circumstance."[129] Such ideology, embraced by local leaders who had grown up in a far more rural Rogue Valley, was not susceptible to economic arguments, let alone to promises of future salmon runs. Some of them had been alive when the dam was built, and would have remembered the fanfare and excitement that had come with it. The dam and the lake meant more to them than 150 cubic feet per second of diverted water.

Later in 1994, dam retention advocates attempted to recall what they saw as an insufficiently steadfast GPID Board.[130] Previous GPID Board elections had usually been quiet affairs, with little voter interest or turnout—board members had essentially been appointed, or volunteered.[131] The recall effort failed, but the politicization of board selection was a sign of things to come. Bill Hiljus, who had voted for dam removal with clear eyes and a heavy heart, wrote another op-ed for the *Daily Courier* in November 1994, asking who the dam savers would blame when the valley turned brown (as it surely would if GPID lost its water right and stopped diverting water) and pointing out that the board had taken courageous, financially responsible steps, especially in view of the fact that district patrons were not willing to pay for fish passage upgrades. He noted that the board and the district faced many kinds of pressure—the water right, future upkeep, and (he was prescient in this) possibly, in the future, endangered fish. He urged support for the board and its decision.[132]

For all the difference it made, Hiljus' column might as well have been birdsong. Three days later, Don Greenwood wrote a counter-article, predicting that the pumping alternative would result in more expensive patron buyouts, and the collapse of the district, leaving Grants Pass with an arid landscape. He also cast doubt on the dam's impact on salmon. Greenwood claimed that he enjoyed popular and political support.[133] But as he himself said, "Unless we can gather some kind of power to combat the power that the bureau [OWRD] has, they're going to get their way."[134]

Turning to Salem

Just the sort of power Greenwood was hoping for arrived in November 1994. The nationwide conservative uprising spearheaded by Newt Gingrich rippled down to the Oregon legislature, where Brady Adams, Republican of Grants Pass, was elected president of the state senate. Feeling that local people were being pushed around by outsiders, Adams threw his support behind the dam.[135] A popular, influential local banker, Adams was an ideal figure to represent the dam savers in the state capitol. Adams had previously been approached about the dam by some environmental groups, but had formed a dislike for them and their cause immediately. He'd found them antagonistic and overconfident in manner, and saw them as separate from the Grants Pass community.[136] Adams was not the only person who felt that environmentalists were abrupt and peremptory in their approach to the community,[137] but the feelings of a powerful senator matter politically.

Joined by fellow Grants Pass Republican representative Bob Repine, Adams set out to craft legislation that would protect the people of the Rogue Valley.[138] He pushed through bills guaranteeing GPID a water right of 150 cfs (SB1005) and making dam removal subject to the approval of the legislature before being ordered by any state agency or local government (SB1006). Adams also engineered Senate Joint Rule 12, forbidding state agencies (like OWRC) from adopting any administrative rule without the legislature's consent, and he sent a directive to the agencies forbidding them from putting state money toward dam removal without legislative approval.[139] All of this was very much in line with the broader conservative movement, which has long been skeptical of unelected bureaucrats. The Savage Rapids Dam issue's sudden movement to a powerful state-level venue stoked hope in the hearts of dam savers in Grants Pass, but it put the dam's future in the hands of the Oregon government. Few Oregon legislators could be expected to be as sympathetic to GPID as Brady Adams was, and the bills still required their votes, and the governor's signature.

Despite Adams' machinations, GPID had to continue to pursue dam removal to keep its supplemental water right—the district was afraid to even study dam-saving ideas publicly, fearing that this would open it to claims that it was not in due diligence.[140] Board members who wished to speak out on the situation outside of meetings were advised to consult with GPID's lawyer to understand the parameters of what they were and were not allowed to say.[141] This tension was demonstrated in a pair of letters from board chairman Tom McMurray to US representative Wes Cooley (R-OR). The first letter, written February 16, 1995, noted GPID's decision the previous year to remove the dam, and said that when the district had assembled a working group to remove the dam, they hoped for his support in securing federal funding. No one is carbon-copied on the nine-line letter.[142] Five days later, McMurray wrote another letter to Congressman Cooley, this one two pages long, with copies going to Brady Adams, Bob Repine, and the GPID Board. Here McMurray admitted frankly that his previous letter was only sent to fulfill OWRD's demand for due diligence. He stated that the funding help they really wanted was to keep the dam, asserted that they had the support of the commissioners of Josephine and Jackson Counties, the city of Grants Pass, and the current GPID Board, and hoped that GPID would get help from Salem in saving their dam.[143] McMurray would later claim that the state "blackmailed" GPID into voting for dam removal.[144]

The Task Force

Back in Salem, Brady Adams's campaign to save the dam ran into Governor John Kitzhaber, a staunch environmentalist whom dam savers bitterly accused of displaying a "Take Out Savage Rapids Dam" bumper sticker on the wall of his office.[145] Dam removal proponents showed up in force to testify against Brady Adams's bills: the only dam savers who testified were Tom McMurray, and Adams himself.[146] Kitzhaber vetoed SB1005, the bill guaranteeing GPID its water, and made it clear that SB1006, putting dam removal decisions in the hands of the legislature, would not pass as written. This brought the situation to an impasse. Law and economics were clearly on the side of dam removal, but with local sentiment dead against it, funding the removal with public money would be politically impossible, as Kitzhaber's administration acknowledged.[147] Realistically, GPID could pay neither for removal nor for fish passage mitigation.

Kitzhaber decided that Savage Rapids needed more time and consideration, so he and Adams created a venue in which all these interests could apply themselves to the problem, rewriting SB1006 to create a special Savage Rapids Dam task force.[148] The governor and the senator appointed the task force in December 1995: some local agency staff, some environmental and fishing representatives (Bob Hunter among them), and a large proportion of Grants Pass citizens, some of whom had previously been vocal advocates of keeping the dam. Here was an effort to create the space to form one coalition out of the many Savage Rapids stakeholders, in hopes that they would overcome cultural differences through discussion and mutual education. The task force could circumvent many political challenges and finish the Savage Rapids conflict—if the task force could reach a durable agreement.

Assembling task forces and similar bodies has been a relatively common strategy in western land issues,[149] and it has seen some notable successes, most famously in Northern California's Quincy Library Group,[150] which works on forest issues.[151] At that time, Governor Kitzhaber and the many interest groups involved with Oregon's salmon were planning what would become the Oregon Plan for Salmon and Watersheds.[152] As a part of his broader approach to natural resource issues, Kitzhaber hoped that he might help restore Oregon's salmon runs, get out ahead of federal endangered listings, and avoid federal management of Oregon fisheries.[153] The task force was one step in this direction.

The task force went to work under the chairmanship of Dennis Becklin, a Grants Pass businessman, GPID patron, recreational fisherman, and associate of Brady Adams.[154] Becklin's son was a river guide, which Adams expected would lead him to lean toward dam removal.[155] As chair, Becklin emphasized the need to ensure that all task force members were educated on the issues, and they consulted with professionals in many relevant fields, from ecology to engineering.[156]

Despite this, the group did not come to unified conclusions. Some members were dubious of estimates on how much damage Savage Rapids did to fish—the estimates, they pointed out, were based on data from other

Savage Rapids Dam. Josephine County Historical Society.

rivers.[157] Other members were deeply concerned about the possible release of contaminated sediment behind the dam. While there was no indication that the sediment behind the dam was dangerous,[158] this fear would continue to dog the removal well after the dam came out.[159] The deliberations of the governor's task force counted as due diligence on the part of GPID, so the district continued to divert water as in the past.

In October 1996, the task force released its report, and it was messy. While the report admitted that the dam was indeed a problem for fish, it recommended dam retention with the addition of rebuilt fish ladders, pumps to propel irrigation water instead of turbines, and some other salmon safeguards.[160] When the document was finalized in December, Michael Evenson of ODFW and Al Cook of OWRD signed it only with the explicit understanding that their agencies would not be obliged to provide resources to support this plan.[161] Costs also worried Gordon Anderson, the mayor of Grants Pass, and he signed with the statement that he was concerned about the expenditures of taxpayer dollars without (in his view) sufficient demonstration of need.[162] Emerson Roller of Grants Pass and Lyle Woodcock of the Josephine County Farm Bureau refused to sign at all, believing that more study of fish mortality at the site was needed—BOR's estimates had left them unconvinced that the dam was a fish killer at all.[163] Bob Hunter, Bernie Moore of Rogue Flyfishers, and fisherman Dale Smith refused to sign for the opposite reason—they believed that the dam was a fish killer and had to be removed.[164] The task force's recommendations were in no way legally binding, and Kitzhaber did not accept them.[165]

The upshot was that the task force changed almost nothing, serving only to prolong the debate and inflame opinions on both sides. The police had to be called in to at least one GPID board meeting in the mid-1990s,[166] and another ended with the audience throwing folding chairs at one another.[167] GPID tried to reconcile varying visions of the dam's future by bringing in the Rogue Valley Council of Governments (RVCOG) to facilitate discussion, fact-finding, and (potentially, eventually) funding. RVCOG is an apolitical group made up of over twenty governmental or quasi-governmental organizations in the Rogue Valley. RVCOG met with GPID roughly once a month through 1997, but the volatile political climate made consensus impossible. Brady Adams tried to revive his dam-saving legislation, but to no avail.[168] The dam savers had little chance of winning with John Kitzhaber in Salem, but with Brady Adams in the Oregon legislature, the dam wouldn't come out as long as the status quo held.

The SONCC

In 1997, NMFS listed the Southern Oregon Northern California coho salmon (SONCC) (*O. kisutch*) as threatened under the Endangered Species Act. NMFS wrote to GPID, acquainting the district with this new situation and noting the district would need an incidental take permit to operate its dam.[169] The listing could have come as no surprise to task force members, who had been warned about this possibility by agency personnel well before it happened.[170] Indeed, there had been concerns about Rogue fish being listed since the early 1990s.[171] The SONCC listing supported environmentalists' contentions about the dire state of Rogue River fish, made NMFS into environmentalists' ally, and opened federal court as a promising future venue in which to push for dam removal. The presence of a listed species and the fact that the dam's operation now constituted a taking under the Endangered Species Act permanently shifted the parameters of the debate.

When McMurray testified before the Oregon senate in 1995 (as a private citizen, not the sitting GPID chair) and said that the board individually wanted to save the dam, he noted that the recent coho run had been the Rogue's largest since counts began.[172] This objection—that the government claimed that the coho was threatened but that people could see the population thriving—would come up repeatedly.[173] The fish that people saw in the river were partly hatchery stock—in fact, the Cole Rivers Hatchery produced so many excess coho that they were processed into cat food. Savage Rapids Dam savers questioned just how endangered such a fish could be.[174]

The issue reflects a significant political weakness of the evolutionarily significant unit (ESU) system by which NMFS lists endangered anadromous salmonids. Biologically and logistically, the ESU system is sensible—each ESU embraces a group of rivers that are near one another and, because salmon stray into nearby streams when they return to spawn, have relatively genetically uniform fish. The SONCC ESU extends from the Mattole River in Northern California to the Elk River just north of the Rogue. But this system means that some individual streams, particularly if they have active hatchery programs, may well host large cohorts of listed fish.[175] The system opens NMFS to severe criticism by people who see these fish. The fine GPID would pay for taking an endangered SONCC was expected to be $100,000 per fish.[176] Such a penalty, if enforced, would quickly ruin the irrigation district.

Endangered coho aside, the save-the-dam coalition was emboldened by the task force's report, which some people seemingly confused with a final, legally binding decision.[177] On July 22, 1997, the GPID Board reversed its 1994 decision and voted three to two to keep Savage Rapids Dam.[178] This did not move the Water Resources Department, though; Al Cook, representing the agency, noted that GPID still had to demonstrate progress toward dam removal in order to keep its water right, no matter how the current board felt about the matter.[179]

The vote was a bold move, but it had no workable plan behind it. Brady Adams had explained to GPID that, despite his support, the state would not supply much money to retain the dam as long as Kitzhaber was in office.[180] GPID secretary-manager Dan Shepard reflected at the time that Adams was beholden not to GPID, but to his district and the region as a whole, and that the senator's vision might emphasize recreation and a green Rogue Valley, not necessarily a prosperous irrigation district—that he might well accept a future with the lake, but without GPID.[181] In Washington, DC, Senator Gordon Smith (R-OR) indicated his willingness to support keeping the dam if it became a federal question, but noted that this would be more difficult under the Clinton administration.[182] GPID's lawyer, David Moon, pointed out that it would be hard to convince the state to let them have an extra 52 cfs regardless of funding, and that while some people believed that the state did not have authority to mandate dam removal, in his view it certainly did. Moon was subsequently criticized by the board for having a negative, unsupportive attitude.[183] Board members discussed hiring a biologist to gather data that could support their pro-dam arguments.[184] They looked to implement the task force's recommendations—pumps, ladder upgrades, and a standing dam.

To pay for anticipated legal and scientific bills, GPID raised its patrons' rates, though the rise would account for only about a fifth of their projected expenses.[185] This worried some larger patrons, such as the Grants Pass Golf Club—they needed the water for their business to survive, and they wanted it as cheaply as possible. Buying out of the district would be expensive as well.[186] As one patron said,

> If one board of directors voted to remove the dam because that
> was the cheapest way of providing the water, then another
> board should not come in and make us pay $7 million more
> than necessary to provide the same water, but with a lake. . . .
> If the people wanting to retain the dam feel it is that important
> to the community, then let them buy the dam from the GPID
> and pay to save it themselves. But I can tell from the tone of
> the opposition, they think they are on a mission from some god
> to control locally a state-owned waterway and are using GPID
> funds instead of their own to try and prove it.[187]

Two weeks later, after some agonizing, board member Bill Braun-berger changed his mind, presciently stating that he saw nothing but legal expenses for years into the future if they continued to defend the ageing dam.[188] He further noted that

> the dam was built for a 50 year period and it has served us for
> 75 years. The dam is beginning to give us a lot of problems,
> there is hidden costs to retaining the dam that we don't even see
> at the moment. I even went out and talked to the service men
> that have done work on the dam. They can tell you things about
> that dam that will turn your hair on end.[189]

On August 12, the board voted three to one to formally rescind its July decision to retain the dam, board member Sam Attolico having died between meetings.[190] Dam removal advocate Leon Guillotte later took

Attolico's seat. Steadfast dam supporter Marjorie Spickler (the lone vote to keep the dam) made a statement echoing German theologian Martin Niemoller. It is worth quoting in its entirety as a remarkable example of the ideology guiding part of the dam debate:

> You all know that there is more involved here tonight than just water and the fish and I am thankful that the people that are sitting around this table weren't part of our founding fathers or we would all be a British Colony. Before the vote, I would like to recall [indecipherable][191] memory of the 40s. He said when Hitler went after the Polls [sic], he didn't protest, because he wasn't Polish. When Hitler went after the Germans, he did not protest, because he was not German. When Hitler went after the Christians, he did not protest, because he was not a Christian. When they came after him there was no one to protect him. We have the very same situation developing with this type of a meeting this evening.[192]

Dam supporters, undaunted, began an effort to recall board chair Tom McMurray—the same one who had played a double game by writing letters seeking support for removal and for retention. Despite his personal support for the dam, McMurray had finally voted for removal, believing that there was no way to overcome the SONCC listing.[193] Dam supporters criticized him for caving in to the government and to WaterWatch.[194]

These shifts, based on the comings and goings and feelings of individual board members, reflect the complicated position of the GPID board in relation to the advocacy coalitions on both sides. Every other group, from ASS to WaterWatch to OWRD, approached the issue and joined coalitions based entirely on their values or organizational missions. The board, pushed and pulled by legal obligations, economic realities, public opinion, the desires of district patrons, and members' individual beliefs, maintained an uneasy position throughout the issue, tied in different ways to each coalition and pressed from all sides.

From the outside, an increasingly active Dennis Becklin cast doubt on the waffling board's credibility and competence.[195] He announced his candidacy for a position on the board in that year's elections. The *Grants Pass Daily Courier* characterized Becklin as "a vocal and avid supporter of dam retention."[196] Becklin offered a plan to take care of fish passage for $12 million—cheaper than the task force's plan.[197] The Bureau of Reclamation found Becklin's "bare bones" plan for dam retention unacceptable.[198] Becklin embraced the idea that GPID was more or less morally responsible to the community as a whole for providing recreation and quality of life. Legally, of course, GPID was beholden only to its patrons and its regulators, not to, say, private well owners, or the Jackson County commissioners. As Tom McMurray pointed out in a *Daily Courier* op-ed, the cities and counties of the Rogue Valley did "not pay one dime for this water. Only GPID patrons contribute."[199]

In September, Becklin and Spickler sued the GPID board, alleging conspiracy.[200] The suit went nowhere, but it established Becklin as a man of action. NMFS began to ask GPID for its fish passage plans and pointed out that the task force's upgrade plan could be considered a starting point but would not be sufficient to comply with the Endangered Species Act.[201] As the debate boiled on and letters to the editor of the *Daily Courier* grew increasingly passionate, Curry, Jackson, and Josephine Counties endorsed the effort to save the dam, crystallizing local support for Savage Rapids Dam.[202]

Enemies

In this increasingly controversial phase of the dam removal issue, Spickler's heated allusion to Hitler was not out of the ordinary. Without much of a technical or scientific defense available, dam savers warned of vague conspiracies with existential consequences, an old tradition in American politics.[203] One commenter opined, "We should save the dam just to help save America."[204] Dam opponents were repeatedly described as Nazis during the course of the Savage Rapids controversy; they were "throwbacks from the Hitler and Imperial Japanese regimes,"[205] and their tactics had "the markings of Karl Marx and of Joseph Goebbels of Nazi Germany."[206] These insults were rarely aimed at specific people or organizations but at broader, shadowy groups. Real organizations like WaterWatch were labeled as "pink,"[207] "wacos [*sic*],"[208] "wild-eyed environmentalists from San Francisco and Los Angeles,"[209] and "self-appointed environmental terrorist[s]."[210] It was suggested that they were part of "an agenda that worships Mother Earth instead of God."[211] Even their credentials as environmentalists were called into doubt. "So-called environmentalists," it was said, were trying to remove Savage Rapids Dam, for nefarious reasons all their own.[212] Task force member Lyle Woodcock said that he believed that environmentalists were in it for money and that they really hoped that fish would never be saved; he blamed declining salmon runs on foreign fishing and marine mammals.[213]

Rogue dam savers cast their opponents as outsiders interfering with local matters—urban greenies or intrusive government bureaucrats.[214] While such views are strong in many places, they are particularly potent in Southern Oregon, which has long perceived itself as separate from the rest of the state. Understandably so. In the days before the interstate highway system, the Rogue Valley was a long trip from the big cities of the Willamette Valley—250 miles, over several mountain passes.

Parts of Southern Oregon (along with the counties of northernmost California) semi-seriously identify as Jefferson, a mythical fifty-first state independent of faraway Salem. Jefferson's borders shift depending on who's discussing it, but, driving north from Sacramento, you know you're there once you pass the massive State of Jefferson sign on Interstate 5 near Yreka, California. The local public radio station covering this part of the country calls itself Jefferson Public Radio. The Jefferson state seal, commonly seen on flags and hats and logos all over the area, sports two X's, signifying that Jefferson has been "double-crossed" by the government. If Jefferson became real, it would be a conservative state culturally dominated by ranching and other resource extraction, but with an interesting political seasoning of hippie marijuana farmers and alternative spiritual communities, which dot the hills between Mount Shasta and Crater Lake. Your typical Jeffersonian, it's said, carries two things in their pockets at all times: a pistol and a crystal.[215] The common thread, of course, is the rejection of mainstream society.

There has been active separatist agitation in Jackson County (where Savage Rapids Lake sat) since at least 1854.[216] The most serious uprising came in the fall of 1941, when a club of Grants Pass boosters called the Oregon Cavemen proposed secession, and Jeffersonian activists with rifles blockaded the road north from California. The grievances were poor infrastructure maintenance and, in a prelude to the wise use movement, a failure to develop Jefferson's natural resources.[217] Pearl Harbor brought an end to the armed struggle, as everyone turned to bigger things.[218] Interstate 5 was built after the war; nowadays you can drive from Los Angeles to Portland in one long day. But rural Jefferson still feels neglected by urban politicians, and still wants to extract its natural resources. Jeffersonian rhetoric has risen again in the decade of the 2010s, as the same sorts of grievances that have upended politics all over America have resurfaced there.[219]

There's always been an element of whimsy to Jefferson—the 1941 Proclamation of Independence included the line "Patriotic Jeffersonians intend to secede each Thursday until further notice."[220] But while Jefferson may be a joke to some, the separatist idea has become a consistent and public part of the region's identity, and anyone living there is constantly reminded that they've been double-crossed by Salem and Sacramento. While the secessionist movement didn't become an important political voice in Savage Rapids, its ideology resounded through the rhetoric opposing dam removal on the Rogue River.

To some in Grants Pass, even other parts of the Rogue Valley were suspect. Bob Hunter of WaterWatch, a resident of nearby Medford, was still viewed as an outsider.[221] This may be partly due to the historic atomization of Rogue Valley society. There is remarkably little connection between the upper, lower, and middle Rogue, a subtle but important issue in forging consensus over land management.[222] Grants Pass is only ninety river miles above the town of Gold Beach at the mouth of the Rogue, but it takes three hours to drive there—longer than to far-off Eugene. Even within the Middle Rogue Valley, people from the liberal enclave of Ashland are seen as hippies and Grants Pass conservatives are labeled Cavemen.[223] Future GPID board member L. H. Kirtley, complaining about outside control of the dam, lumped Medford in with Salem and Montana as places from which GPID shouldn't have to take orders.[224]

All of this put resource agencies in a challenging political position. Agency representatives did not (and cannot) advocate publicly for anything beyond their findings and their official missions; when the task force released its recommendation of dam retention, all agency representatives signed it. But in this case, agencies' findings and missions tended to put them on the same side as the environmentalists. As the political pressures surrounding GPID's water right and the SONCC seemed, more and more, to push harder and harder in the direction of dam removal, dam savers vilified the agencies as well as the environmentalists.[225] Such a transition, a far cry from the days when ODFW went out of its way to help GPID keep its water right, is emblematic of the broader embrace of environmental goals by land and resource agencies in recent decades.[226] While NMFS and OWRD could not stand shoulder-to-shoulder with WaterWatch, the dam savers felt that they did. Even Representative Bob Smith (R-OR), in a sharp letter to NMFS, suggested that the agency had predetermined the fate of the dam.[227] In GPID meetings, people complained that "all fish agencies and environmental groups are working to see that Savage Rapids Dam is going to be removed."[228]

To some extent this belief, that the agencies, or at least agency personnel, wanted dam removal, was accurate. As noted above, Jim Martin of

ODFW spoke openly of his goal, supported by his agency's mission, to take out dams in order to preserve and restore Oregon's fisheries.[229] But this sort of direct advocacy was unusual. Martin had the professional and mandatory authority and political backing to publicly call for dam removal, and he brought controversy on himself when he did so.[230] Most agency personnel kept a lower profile and worked for their mandatory responsibilities, but occasionally their personal desires leaked out. Brady Adams remembers seeing a fax from a government employee, on Fish and Wildlife Service stationery, with drawings of fish with little hearts in them, appealing for people to support dam removal.[231] Another agency employee, rarely named but frequently cited, did refer to himself and his colleagues as "dam busters" in an email.[232] He was quickly chastised, but the political damage had been done.[233] An older generation of managers tended to see their job as the provision of natural resources for users—timber for loggers, ducks for hunters—rather than the protection, or restoration, of natural resources for the public. The shift from managing natural resources to conserving them, noted above, was driven partly by the rise of agency personnel—like the "dam buster"—raised and trained in an environmentally conscious world.[234] Several resource agency representatives, who have taken part in a variety of dam removal negotiations, now display concrete chunks from these dams as trophies on prominent shelves in their offices.

In October 1997, OWRD held a hearing on GPID's water right. Becklin, who was by this point something of a free-range political operative, had his credibility questioned by OWRC commissioner Mike Jewett. He responded by saying that dam removal would happen one of two ways—either after a thorough examination of the sediment, or over his dead body.[235] As noted above, there was no indication that the sediment was dangerous, but Becklin made an issue of it. After the hearing, OWRD amended the 1994 water right by setting out timelines by which to measure GPID's progress in due diligence.

The next month, GPID's patrons recalled pro-removal board chair Tom McMurray by a vote of 115 to 68.[236] Don Greenwood, the one who had circulated the Save the Dam petition, replaced McMurray on the board. In November's board elections, Becklin displaced Leon Guillotte, and staunch dam defender L. H. Kirtley defeated Nancy Tappan, both by significant margins.[237] Kirtley asserted that the dam did not kill fish and was sure that no judge "with any sense at all" would deny GPID its extra water.[238] Guillotte and Tappan had favored dam removal. Tappan, a vineyard owner, needed a secure water supply to sustain her business—how it arrived was not important.[239] Worried over the future of the district, she noted that many of the dam savers were not professional irrigators, and that they fought for the dam without weighing the consequences if GPID lost its water.[240] Guillotte, a colorful character, said that this loss proved that "the majority of the people that voted are dumber than a codpiece," urged them to look up the definition of "codpiece" in the dictionary, and said that the patrons were "lemmings following the pied piper [presumably Becklin, whom Guillotte disliked] over the dam."[241] The GPID board was now stocked with dam savers.

The Becklin Board

In the first GPID board meeting of 1998, Dennis Becklin grasped the district's "helm with an iron hand."[242] He presented a new district mission statement, one that incorporated the dam's non-irrigation amenities (such as recreation) that enhanced the quality of life in Grants Pass, and called the distribution of GPID's water "an inviolable community trust vested in GPID by its patrons and by the community at large."[243] Becklin asked each GPID employee for "total dedication to the cause." He committed to "a constructive dialogue" with NMFS and OWRC and had (said the *Daily Courier*) "the open aim of preserving current water rights while staving off demands for dam removal."[244] Becklin was named the sole spokesman for the district.[245] GPID fired its longtime lawyer and replaced him with Becklin's attorney, Chris Cauble.[246] The new board voted to inspect the dam and fish passage facilities daily, as part of an effort to operate the structure for optimal fish passage while providing irrigation water. Board meetings were moved from once a month to once a week.[247] Two weeks later, GPID terminated its relationship with RVCOG, which was guiding talks away from lawsuits (and therefore toward removal), and decided to handle the issue by itself.[248] Going forward, Becklin would sometimes refer to "this board," distinguishing it, and its way of doing business, from its predecessors.[249] The new board of Becklin, Kirtley, Spickler, and Greenwood (Braunberger resigned at the end of 1997 and was not replaced for a year) had by now engaged in a great deal of policy learning, particularly through Becklin's experience on the task force, and felt well equipped to move forward through the political landscape in which they found themselves.

But still, the board had to demonstrate due diligence in pursuing removal to keep the water right. WaterWatch, feeling that GPID had failed in this, asked OWRC to begin a contested case hearing on the water right, to be finalized in November.[250] GPID went ahead with studies of potential dam upgrades, hoping for funding through Brady Adams.[251] This was insufficient—in November, the OWRC denied GPID's water right, saying that it had not, in fact, done due diligence.[252] GPID sent the case on to the Oregon Court of Appeals.

With a federally listed salmon swimming up over the dam, the board also had to deal with NMFS and the Endangered Species Act. In late 1997, GPID hired Harza Engineering to help form their habitat conservation plan (HCP) and set about reengineering the dam's fish passage.[253] GPID also hired S. P. Cramer and Associates (now Cramer Fish Sciences) to ascertain the level of coho mortality at the dam. Cramer found very little,[254] but was criticized for its methodology and for having performed its studies after the fish were expected to have passed above the dam.[255]

The fact that this latest and most significant threat came via the federal government was not lost on the patriotic conservatives of Grants Pass. In an op-ed, Marjorie Spickler announced that "I, for one, still stand tall when I salute our flag. I still suppress tears when Old Glory is unfurled or when 'The Star-Spangled Banner' is played. I resent giving up our rights to Washington—and ultimately to the United Nations." She called Savage Rapids a test case for federal takeovers and warned that all major rivers and dams would follow.[256] This perspective was difficult for natural resource agencies or dam removal advocates to counter.

In 1998, a messy process unfolded wherein Becklin and the board attempted to shore up fish passage more or less on their own, and to present their plans to NMFS as they went along.[257] NMFS, unimpressed, pointed out the inadequacies of GPID's plans in an increasingly exasperated correspondence.[258] NMFS emphasized that any interim fish passage measures had to be accompanied by an effective commitment to no net take of coho, which, it eventually became clear, probably meant dam removal.[259] Becklin fired back some defiant letters, continued to raise the specter of destructive sediment releases after the dam came out, and forged ahead on all fronts.[260] He personally funded a study of the dam's sediment load, which resulted in no finding of toxicity.[261] Becklin insisted that the salmon were at the heart of GPID's concerns, trumpeted the district's "mission to protect every salmon and steelhead possible," and said that if "a small band of dam haters" would not support these efforts, then they were not real environmentalists.[262] He lauded his board for its "courageous battle."[263] During this time, Brady Adams found GPID some state money to acquire better fish screens that would help guide salmon safely across the dam.[264] To NMFS, these screens were "a waste of money."[265] While some of GPID's efforts to improve fish passage were indeed helpful, and acknowledged as such by NMFS, it undertook fish management without effective cooperation with the agency.[266] In April 1998 NMFS, deciding that legal action was the only way to protect the SONCC, filed for an injunction against GPID in federal court.[267] Will Stelle, NFMS's regional director, again called Savage Rapids the worst fish killer on the Rogue, and asserted that "while Oregonians work hard to save these imperiled runs, this dam completely undercuts those efforts. Everyone knows it, and knows that it's time to fix it."[268] The environmental law group Earthjustice, representing WaterWatch and some other environmental organizations, intervened in the case.[269] GPID responded by claiming that NMFS had never intended to work with them and had always intended to remove the dam, noting the above-mentioned "dam busters" email.[270]

When GPID raised the dam for the 1998 irrigation season, it knew that it might be violating the Endangered Species Act.[271] In May, irrigation was halted for ten days after Judge Michael Hogan of the Ninth Circuit, saying that both GPID and NMFS bore some fault, ordered the parties to work together.[272] NMFS bent enough to allow irrigation for the remainder of the 1998 season while GPID performed some interim fish mitigation, and the two sides continued to negotiate.[273] In September Earthjustice, unsatisfied, announced its intention to sue GPID for violating the Endangered Species Act.[274] Curry Guides and other fishing groups also joined the suit.[275]

GPID's fight against NMFS, OWRD, and the environmentalists grew increasingly expensive, and patrons, especially the ones whose businesses relied on irrigation, grew increasingly worried.[276] In 1998, GPID was paying four lawyers: a water specialist, two endangered species specialists, and Cauble.[277] From 1988 to 1999, patron fees skyrocketed from $35 to $115 per acre.[278] In August 1998, Becklin admitted that GPID was $225,000 over budget.[279] Earlier in the year, the board had reached out to the larger irrigators directly, but had not been able to give them much concrete assurance that they would get their water.[280] Some concerned patrons organized into a group called Citizens for Responsible Irrigation (CRI) to combat the Becklin board.[281] They argued that the purpose of GPID was to provide water and that the board should stop "throw[ing] away" their money in a high-risk, low-reward battle for the dam.[282] Patrons began to buy out of the district in increasing numbers.[283] GPID's board meeting minutes betray a growing personal animus between the board and some of its opponents both in and out of CRI, inflaming an increasingly tense situation.[284]

GPID sought other sources of funding. Lakeside property owners, having as much to lose as anyone, seemed a possible source, but GPID had no leverage to extract money from non-patrons, and these property owners' commitment to the dam dissolved when they were asked to open their wallets. In the late summer of 1998, the board made a supplemental assessment, asking patrons for an extra $20 per acre. This, on top of the risk of losing the water right, provoked a backlash against the board, and against Becklin personally.[285]

Dennis Becklin's personality and leadership style created strong opinions in almost everyone who met him, inspiring and infuriating people in equal measure.[286] Some people criticized his "swaggering, publicity seeking and publicly antagonistic behavior."[287] They resented paying for what they believed to be a personal emotional crusade.[288] Becklin's public statements were cautious and equivocal, but he was widely considered to be, at heart, a champion of keeping Savage Rapids Dam.[289] Some suspected that Becklin's interest in Savage Rapids came because he owned property below the dam and therefore enjoyed good fishing as up-migrating fish massed below the dam, and a quiet river because the dam prevented motor boats from roaring downstream.[290] Another board recall effort, aimed at Becklin and his allies, began in the summer of 1998.[291] GPID, always in a tenuous political position, split into factions, with a vocal group of patrons, including some of the largest irrigators left in the district, advocating for dam removal to secure their irrigation water.[292]

The New Old West

Grants Pass is in Oregon (and in Jefferson) but it is also part of a region known as "the New West." The New West phenomenon, sometimes typified as "ranches to ranchettes," happens when white-collar, amenity-driven outsiders move into rural regions in the American West.[293] This is to be seen most famously in places like Boulder, Colorado, and Jackson Hole, Wyoming, in addition to many other examples. Often, such scenery-loving migrants could be expected to favor environmental causes. But not in Grants Pass. Retirees, while new to Josephine County, brought along their generational conservatism and pro-dam ideology.[294] These were amenity-driven migrants, but among the amenities they enjoyed were quasi-natural flat-water recreation ("Our beautiful dam with a big lake"[295]) and the green landscape provided by leaky canals.[296] Some of these people served on the GPID Board—Don Greenwood was one—but were less invested in the irrigation district as such. State representative Dennis Richardson (R-Central Point) would later distinguish between the *dam* savers and the *district* savers.[297]

GPID's twentieth-century transformation into a collection of hobby farms and half-acre lawns lengthened and complicated the dam removal issue.[298] There is a widespread belief that if GPID's patrons had still mostly been farmers, they might have struck a deal quickly and secured their water, whether delivered by pump or by dam.[299] To board member and vineyard owner Nancy Tappan, the fact that few GPID patrons really needed the water in order to get by freed those who favored keeping the dam to fight alongside Dennis Becklin on ideology alone.[300] By the same token, though, a "real" irrigation district might have gathered the political clout to counter the environmentalist challenge in the 1980s and secured their extra 50 cfs with minimal fuss. As Jim Martin observed, agriculture is a powerful force in American water politics.[301] Active farmers would have had a far more legitimate economic argument for needing the water and would also likely have had a better working understanding of the water rights system: Dan Shepard acknowledges that GPID failed to effectively educate its patrons on this sort of technical issue.[302] Bearing out this line of thinking, the larger remaining irrigators—a golf club, a vineyard, a cemetery (a very New West set of businesses)—lobbied to retain the water as cheaply as possible.[303] To them, the dam was not the issue.[304] But they were in a minority.

At the same time, the nature-based economy that characterizes the New West had always been there, as Clark Gable, Zane Grey, and their local fishing guides knew. Bob Hunter and Bernie Moore were both classic New West migrants, having both moved to the Rogue Valley from Michigan and joined Rogue Flyfishers. The fishing economy mattered too, and the people who relied on it wanted restored salmon runs. In 1999, Rogue Valley native Dave Strahan and Maddy Sheehan of the NSIA wrote guest opinions for the *Daily Courier* noting that as sport-fishing professionals they made a living from the Rogue, and that to them and their industry dam removal was not just a matter of environmental nature worship but of sustaining their business and of bringing tourist money to Southern Oregon. They criticized "the illusion of lakeside living" that allowed a fish-killing dam to stay standing.[305]

The dam savers did not accept that the dam was a fish killer.[306] This was in spite of many studies, which they specifically rejected, and even in spite of eyewitness accounts of dead juvenile fish in irrigation ditches and turbines.[307] Scientific conclusions in the EIS were seen as illegitimate because they drew on other rivers, despite assurances from ODFW that other rivers provided legitimate models for the Rogue, and reminders that over many years of study at Savage Rapids itself, biologists had firmly established that the dam was deadly to fish.[308] The anti-removal Three Rivers Watershed Council spoke of getting their own assessments to prove their predetermined point[309]—a perspective reminiscent of creationist pseudoscience. To borrow a phrase from the Klamath, one watershed to the south, this was "combat biology."[310]

For the dam savers, fish passage was unimportant. They would be happy enough to have it (no one was opposed to a healthy fish population), but the dam and the lake were the issue. Mainstream scientific arguments did not resonate, partly because many people in Grants Pass had personally watched the migrating fish "taking their time" and swimming up the dam's fish ladders.[311] The ladders were even something of a tourist attraction. To some local people, the ladders visibly worked, and it was foreign fishermen in the ocean who were to blame for declining salmon runs.[312] Indeed, to some people in Grants Pass, the ladders not only worked, they were necessary to keep water levels sufficient for salmon.[313] Dam savers demanded visible evidence of dead fish, which to them meant bodies strewn around the dam.[314] Later, Dave Strahan filmed mergansers taking advantage of the migratory bottleneck at the dam site and eating juvenile fish in bunches, but this did not have much effect.[315] The subtler ecological impacts of migration delay on salmon survival and the destruction of smolts on their downstream migration (confusingly called "invisible fish" by Bob Hunter[316]) were not communicated effectively by the environmental groups or the agencies. The dam's identity as a fish killer with terrible passage was a core belief for the removal coalition, and they would not waver on the point—perhaps this was why they had a hard time explaining it. When the dam supporters got their own science in the form of the Cramer study on juvenile mortality, it served to confirm what they already believed. Bob Hunter compared this science to that wielded by big tobacco.[317]

By the late summer of 1998, facing angry patrons, the board started to back down, tiering the supplemental assessment in such a way that it brought in less revenue while failing to mollify the big irrigators or anyone else.[318] As *Daily Courier* editor Dennis Roler pointed out, the situation had forced GPID between a rock and a hard place—either lose the water and disappear, or agree to remove the dam and go broke trying to pay for removal. Unless, of course, GPID could put together a plan to gain external funding. For his own part, Roler hoped things would work out so that Grants Pass could somehow stay green.[319] In 1999 the Oregon legislature passed a bill guaranteeing GPID its extra 52 cfs, but it was a symbolic effort—there was no doubt that Kitzhaber would veto it.[320] Becklin decried the "attempt to coerce the district into a forced removal of Savage Rapids Dam without appropriate compensation. . . . The GPID Board of Directors will not be swayed by coercion of the governor, his bureaucratic agencies and from environmental extremists."[321]

Resolution

In 1998, Judge Hogan ordered the parties into mediation—a forceful move to push stakeholders into a venue where they had to form consensus, coalesce into one coalition, and create a negotiated resolution. Had the Endangered Species Act case played out in court, it would have resulted in either an unscientific and damaging precedent (had the court decided in favor of GPID) or the unpopular destruction of an irrigation district (had the court decided in favor of NMFS and the environmentalists). Here was something like another task force[322] but with a more experienced suite of stakeholders motivated by the looming threat of the district's collapse—probably with no mechanism to fund dam removal afterward—if negotiations didn't work. During mediation, the Bureau of Reclamation performed a new study of the Savage Rapids silt load, finding little total sediment and low levels of toxicity; dam removal would not release poison downstream.[323]

At the end of 1998, a few GPID patrons reported Becklin's somewhat ad hoc fish passage work to the Oregon State Board of Examiners for Engineering and Land Surveying, saying that Becklin made false claims to being an engineer.[324] Becklin, for his part, didn't believe that anything he was doing constituted a violation of Oregon's engineering laws.[325] This fairly petty micro-issue hardened battle lines within GPID—some patrons were for Becklin and the dam, some against him.

After months of closed-door negotiations (there was a gag order on participants, and the dam removal was no longer an allowable subject at GPID board meetings) and relative calm, Becklin seized the initiative in July 1999 and released his own plan for dam removal.[326] The plan was so broad and expensive—it included subsidized electricity for the pumps and $10 million to build a riverside recreation area including a water slide—that some did not believe it to be a legitimate offer.[327] Rather, Becklin's plan was seen more as a shield for dam savers, who could say that they had agreed to removal but been rejected by the environmentalists and the agencies. The district court's response was to instruct Becklin to comply with the gag order.[328]

At about this time, the pump system inside the dam broke down, much to patrons' dismay. Normal service was not restored for two weeks.[329] In September, the dam's fish screens were damaged by moss, again shutting down GPID's canals. The dam was starting to look like a financial liability. Patrons kept trying to buy out of the district, to the disappointment and disgust of the board.[330] GPID sued the buyouts, arguing that they were maliciously orchestrated by Leon Guillotte and the CRI, and that "this group . . . made something of a sport of attacking the GPID."[331]

In November 1999, Judy Gove, a CRI leader, was elected to the GPID Board on a dam removal platform.[332] She referred to her victory as "a crack in the dam."[333] Seeing the way things were going, Becklin revised his dam removal proposal, taking out the water slide,[334] and drummed up support from his political allies in Salem. Brady Adams called the plan "the minimum needed to protect the interests of the community and the district," and state representative Carl Wilson (R-Grants Pass) said, "to the federal government . . . if YOU want it removed, YOU pay for it."[335] Becklin also wrote an op-ed in the *Daily Courier* reiterating his previous points and claiming that his plan would be fair for everyone. At a rally in December 1999, Becklin spoke of "a very strong umbilical cord between the community and this dam."[336] Many people would not support even this removal plan—though some did hope that the plan might be too expensive for the government, forcing it to give up and let the district keep the dam.[337]

The board submitted the revised dam removal plan to its patrons in January 2000. The patrons, sick of the conflict and the legal fees, supported the plan, 1,821 to 1,088.[338] Becklin found that, according to GPID's bylaws, the board chair could only sit for two years.[339] Don Greenwood replaced him, and shortly thereafter, Becklin resigned from the board. Greenwood's stance had moderated over the years, and his task now, as he saw it, was to save the district.[340]

WaterWatch and its allies, now armed with evidence that 63 percent of GPID patrons favored dam removal, pressed on with their removal case.[341] They were very dubious of Becklin's plan itself, worrying that it was all a political game to keep the dam, but felt that the vote and Gove's election indicated a shift in the patrons' feelings.[342]

During this time, the OWRD water right case was still proceeding. GPID, knowing that it could not sufficiently strengthen its case for extra water, asked for an extension nine times without filing a brief. The absurdity of this was pointed out at the time by Bob Hunter.[343] The Oregon Court of Appeals threw out the case for want of prosecution in June 2000.[344]

GPID appealed to the Oregon Supreme Court. This stayed the water right decision for the 2000 irrigation season,[345] and gave GPID time to work with the agencies and WaterWatch while retaining its ability to irrigate.

In late May 2000, one of the dam's turbines broke, leaving a third of patrons without water.[346] The bill to appropriately replace the 1920s-vintage turbine would be over $200,000.[347] The patrons were furious.[348] At an energetic meeting, they decried the board's "love affair with an aging dam," and claimed that if the 1994 and 1997 votes to remove Savage Rapids had been honored, then none of this would have happened.[349] The turbine wasn't repaired until mid-July.[350]

With the board majority and district's patrons having agreed to it, federal legislators and state agencies began to take steps toward dam removal, releasing funds for pump design studies.[351] In Washington, DC, Senators Smith (R-OR) and Wyden (D-OR) introduced the Savage Rapids Dam Act of 2000.[352] In Grants Pass, the board worked amicably with WaterWatch. When the bill was introduced, GPID put out a joint press release with WaterWatch and Trout Unlimited to mark the occasion.[353]

The dam savers' political efforts from the past ten years required some undoing. The GPID board wrote to the Rogue Valley counties' commissioners asking them to reverse their previous pro-dam stances.[354] The Oregon Farm Bureau was concerned about the example of an irrigation district being pushed to remove its dam and skeptical about the dam's effect on fish; it complained to Smith and Wyden. The five state legislators representing Southern Oregon wrote to their counterparts in Washington, DC, disavowing the Farm Bureau's stance on behalf of their constituents.[355] They knew that the dam needed to come out to save the district and make peace.

Removing the Dam

In July 2001, the board voted to join a consent decree with the other stakeholders, formally and legally agreeing to dam removal. Kirtley and Spickler were still unhappy. In the last few meetings before the vote, Kirtley spoke of the nearby Klamath, where another battle over water allocations and dam removal was heating up. This, of course, wasn't GPID's problem, as Judy Gove (who had voted for removal) pointed out, but Kirtley, who valued all dams, saw dam removal as part of much larger regional problem.[356] Kirtley and Spickler voted symbolically against removal and then resigned, applauded by a large number of the people at the meeting.[357] The rest of the board voted in favor, noting that an agreement would end all litigation, ensure 150 cfs of water, and put GPID in the good graces of the National Marine

Fisheries Service.[358] To Dan Shepard, the situation was simple: "We're basically out of funds. We have to secure water and we have to run a business. We gave it the college try and lost. That's that. We're going forward. . . . The majority of the patrons of this district are tired of kicking the dog. They want the water."[359] Kirtley and Spickler's replacements on the board favored dam removal. The next month, the board voted to return to the old, pre-Becklin mission statement, removing the clauses that gave GPID responsibility for the well-being of the broader Grants Pass community.[360]

On August 27, 2001, everyone—GPID, NMFS, OWRD, Bureau of Reclamation, and WaterWatch—signed the consent decree. A ceremony marking the agreement was held in October in Governor Kitzhaber's office. While many individuals in the community still wished to keep the dam, the consent decree enforced consensus and allowed the signatories to frame themselves as one united coalition, which politicians and the public could view with favor. Kitzhaber was delighted, saying that

> the Rogue River is one of Oregon's most spectacular natural
> treasures. The waterway is legendary for its scenic beauty,
> fish and wildlife and amazing whitewater. Today I'm pleased
> to be here with conservationists, irrigators, and federal
> representatives to announce a landmark agreement to restore
> and protect this incredible river, while still allowing farmers to
> meet their water needs.[361]

After years of conflict, everyone was happy to have it over—Don Greenwood referred to the consent decree as a "peace treaty"[362]—and the signing ceremony was something of a "joyous occasion."[363] The consent decree allowed GPID to continue to operate the dam until 2006, giving everyone time to gather federal support for the removal.

The next step was to pass federal legislation, so the stakeholders went to Washington in force. One condition in the consent decree (insisted on by the fish interests) was that GPID had to hire lobbyists to better secure federal funding and keep the district financially vested in the dam removal effort. GPID had to pay these lobbyists a minimum of $50,000 a year.[364] GPID engaged Michelle Giguere and Dan James, both of Ball Janik, a Portland and Washington, DC, law firm. While the lobbyists went to work, national environmental organizations with a stronger presence in Washington than WaterWatch stepped forward to appeal for dam removal. They were led by American Rivers;[365] Trout Unlimited also contributed.[366] These groups had always been involved in the removal effort, but until this point they had not had any role to play that was not better filled by WaterWatch. The collaboration was smooth, particularly as Bob Hunter enjoyed close ties to these national organizations: his sister-in-law was the senior director of American Rivers' dam programs, and his former WaterWatch colleague Jeff Curtis worked for Trout Unlimited.[367] Economic dam removal advocates like the Northwest Sportfishing Industry Association and local fishing interests like Curry Anadromous Fishermen joined the lobbying effort as well.[368] The pro-removal groups' strengths and priorities complemented one another well, and helped the coalition gel as they moved forward.[369]

Looking to expand the coalition, GPID sought support from such irrigation industry bodies as the Oregon Water Resources Congress and the National Water Resources Association.[370] The American Farm Bureau itself would not express support, but stayed neutral.[371] Hundreds of GPID patrons also wrote to Congress individually.[372] The fear of Grants Pass returning to its historic arid conditions, once a driving image for dam savers, was now used to urge appropriations for dam removal.[373] Among the many stakeholders lobbying for funding, much individual credit went, as it had throughout the process, to affable GPID manager Dan Shepard.[374] Shepard had kept the district operating through many political shifts, and his testimony and august personal presence made a strong impression on lawmakers and agency personnel when he represented the district in Salem and in Washington, DC.[375]

Congress presented its own challenges. The mega-coalition was challenged not only to raise funding, but to assure skeptical members of Congress that Savage Rapids would not necessarily be a springboard to other bigger removals on rivers like Washington's Snake.[376] Members of Congress were uncertain and skeptical of supporting any removal, but key Oregon Republicans Gordon Smith and Greg Walden, having confirmed support for removal from the local community, were convinced that by now all stakeholders really wanted this.[377] With the Oregon delegation behind the dam removal there was little outright resistance in Congress.[378] Giguere found it useful to point out to conservatives that the consent decree was signed under the Bush administration, not under Clinton, an important political distinction in the early 2000s.[379] However, as Oregon no longer had an appropriator in the House or the Senate, funding was more difficult to come by.[380]

Senators Smith and Wyden introduced dam removal legislation in various forms several times, using frames that appealed to each side's values. In 2002, they took dam removal out of the bill's name, calling it the "Grants Pass Irrigation District Improvement and Rogue River Restoration Act" to keep the focus positive from all angles.[381] Senators Smith and Wyden and Representatives Walden and DeFazio, in a letter to the Bush administration, stated that "the Savage Rapids Dam Consent Decree stands as a unique example of how natural resource disputes can be resolved in a way that keeps the local agricultural community viable, while achieving important goals for the restoration of anadromous fish runs."[382] To conservatives, then, the act secured irrigation water for farmers, and to liberals, it restored the Rogue River ecosystem. As Wyden said, "The funding is a tribute to a community that came together to find a win-win solution for fish and farmers."[383] It is likely that Wyden and his colleagues, who had been aware of the Savage Rapids debate for nearly a decade by then, knew that there were very few farmers in the district. But casting the bill as a defense of farmers would make the deal more palatable to colleagues who represented agricultural irrigation districts. John Kitzhaber, as noted above, had engaged in similar rhetoric. The Savage Rapids legislation passed in 2003 as part of an Energy and Water Development Appropriations bill. BOR was now authorized to proceed with dam removal.

The final challenge was to gather money. The Oregon Watershed Enhancement Board (OWEB) had pledged $3 million for dam removal in 2002, demonstrating the State of Oregon's earnest support of the project. This counted heavily in Washington, DC.[384] To provide extra motivation, OWEB's money was not to be made available until the actual structure was being removed.[385] But in the early 2000s, Congress's focus on the new war on terror made appropriations harder to find.[386] Money came in small chunks for studies and pump installation in 2004 and 2005, though these were greeted with gratitude and taken as proof that the project really would happen in the end.[387] GPID received several extensions of its right to operate the dam—since the district was obviously, strenuously, doing its due diligence by seeking funding, there could be no reasonable objection from the state.[388] In 2006, real money finally came through: GPID received $13 million that summer. By the fall the contract to construct the pumping station was awarded;[389] $15 million came the next year.[390] The last $3 million came with the American Recovery and Reinvestment Act of 2009—the Obama stimulus—which also helped fund the Elwha project, as well as the removal of another Rogue River dam, Gold Ray.[391]

In 2005, Dennis Becklin released an editorial on one of several now-defunct news websites he ran.[392] He predicted ruin for Grants Pass as GPID water would disappear and the people's wells would dry up, accused

The deconstruction of Savage Rapids Dam, 2009. Flickr Creative Commons.

Kitzhaber of participating in a fraudulent listing of the SONCC, claimed that the GPID board had accepted "total and unconditional surrender to WaterWatch . . . total and unconditional capitulation to the US Government . . . and total and unconditional surrender to the state of Oregon." He predicted "a financial death spiral" for GPID, followed by a return to the "red desert" landscape, and told the people of Josephine County to remember that their apathy was to blame when they ran out of water. After providing his account of the years of enmity he had faced from dam removal proponents, he claimed not to care about these problems anymore.[393] Becklin later moved away from Grants Pass.

The summer of 2008, the last for Savage Rapids Lake, was filled with sentimentality. People waxed nostalgic about water-skiing and boating down on the lake, and continued to criticize the dam removal decision.[394] Some people noted perceptively that the pumps would be expensively powered by coal from Wyoming rather than by the flow of the Rogue River.[395] Of course, the pumps did bring their own problems: they sometimes malfunctioned, especially as the river's sediment began to move.[396] A local archivist, seeing history in the making, put together a book featuring old photos of the Rogue River dams.[397]

On October 9, 2009, Savage Rapids Dam was removed. The lobbyists had looked into getting the dam demolished by the Department of

The Savage Rapids Dam site after removal, 2010. Wikimedia Commons.

Defense as a training exercise,[398] but in the end, the removal was planned as a straightforward deconstruction project, with coffer dams rerouting the Rogue and the concrete being broken down and taken out. The edges of the dam were left standing at the water's edge. Two days later, a jubilant flotilla of some eighty dam removal advocates floated down through the open (and unstable) Savage Rapids Dam site in drift boats, rafts, and kayaks.[399] Some at this event felt that the community, after all those years of conflict, had come back together and come around on the dam removal.[400] Chinook salmon spawned almost immediately in the reach formerly occupied by Savage Rapids Lake.[401] As of 2014, there were abundant redds in the lake site, "almost to the point where can't count them all."[402] Anecdotally, Rogue fish seem to be doing well—returning earlier and healthier[403]—but salmon lives are complicated, and there have been many factors at play on the Rogue, including other dam removals.[404] It's hard to say how much is due to the removal of Savage Rapids Dam now that the Gold Ray Dam, which had a fish counting station, is down.

As Brady Adams later observed, the dam removal has not been the failure that its critics predicted, but it has not been perfect, either.[405] The sediment, while nontoxic, has been slow to move downstream, one of the pumps didn't work, and the electricity to run the pumping station has been expensive. However, the pumps are unlikely to fail the way the old

turbine did in 2000. The electric bills encourage the pursuit of efficient water use—GPID's bills go down when it pumps less water.[406] But for GPID,
these issues are relatively small compared to the existential post-removal
crisis many had feared.

The district continues to send its water down the irrigation canals,
boaters and salmon drift past the dam site unimpeded, and Grants Pass
remains as green as it can be. In 2011 Tom McMurray, once again chairman
of the GPID board, credited WaterWatch and the negotiated settlement
with saving the district.[407] At the same time, as Dan Shepard has observed,
WaterWatch's work with GPID gives it credibility in the Rogue Valley and
allows it to make progress on future projects without being seen as the villain that killed the district.[408] Several other dams have been removed in the
Rogue Basin. As a result of his personal style while pushing for the removal
of the dam, Bob Hunter now enjoys a fine reputation as a fair, consistent,
collegial, and principled environmentalist.[409] As Jim Martin of ODFW put
it, Hunter was "firm on policy and easy on people."[410] On Hunter's car, a
bumper sticker that long bore the message "Take Out Savage Rapids Dam!"
has been amended to read "Took Out Savage Rapids Dam!" But there was,
of course, some discontent after the fact,[411] and dam nostalgia remains. In
2012, two photographs of Savage Rapids Dam still hung on the wall of the
GPID office.[412]

Conclusions

The Savage Rapids Dam conflict was open and wide-ranging, offering actors
an array of political options but demanding creativity and shrewdness in
choosing between them. Stakeholders faced a complicated situation, even
by the standards of dam removals, from the beginning: discussions of the
issue could begin only when environmental groups identified a venue in
which they could contest GPID's water right. While there had always been
an undercurrent of discontent with Savage Rapids Dam, there had never
been a clear way to force the issue until the 1980s. From then on, state and
local agencies and lawmakers all played important roles before a massive
effort to collect federal funds and remove the dam.

Beyond the inherent tension arising when private dams meet public
waters, dams create separate benefits that are used and viewed like public
goods but are not, in fact, owned by the public. GPID's leaky canals did
(and still do) green much of Grants Pass, but this is not GPID's job. Dams are
rich in policy paradoxes—they are many things at once.[413] It is extremely
difficult to reconcile things like water-skiing and groundwater recharge

with economic and legal decisions about dam management. Savage Rapids' many functions let different Grants Pass community members form different relationships to, and perceptions of, the dam and the river.

The result was clashes of values and beliefs. One of WaterWatch's slogans is "Rivers need water,"[414] but people in Grants Pass asked, "How can they withhold water God gave us and let it run into the ocean?"[415] Such dissonance yielded fears of hidden agendas,[416] as people on both sides of the issue could not accept their opponents' statements at face value. Failure to understand how an environmentalist might be deeply, profoundly opposed to damming rivers, and care about salmon restoration more than about preserving Savage Rapids Lake, led their opponents to search for their "real" motivations. A conspiracy to return the Rogue Valley to wilderness and spread communism seemed a more plausible story than environmentalists working toward ecological restoration.

The political systems governing water rights and fish passage allowed all stakeholders a variety of venues in which to fight for their beliefs. Those who found themselves abandoned or unrepresented by existing organizations could continue to engage in the political process by joining or even founding an advocacy organization that did reflect those beliefs—organizations like ASS, begun by disgruntled members of the Grants Pass community. While such organizations had limited political options, they helped push the debate from Grants Pass to Salem. The GPID Board itself offered concerned patrons both an outlet for expressing their views and a convenient way to access power—and to wield it if they were elected. A post on the board was relatively accessible; even in the heightened tensions of late 1997, some board elections had fewer than two hundred votes cast in total.[417] Most people didn't care enough to vote, but the ones who did mattered a lot. The intensely local debates and relationships that changed the course of GPID also meant that well-connected stakeholders could effectively reach the public by such simple expedients as letters to the editor or the local promotion of their own plans—as occurred when Dennis Becklin suggested his dam removal/water park plan in 1999.

Mirroring the dam's dual public-private status, the shakily defined semigovernmental role of GPID added a layer of complexity to the issue. GPID essentially had the power to levy taxes on anyone who bought property in the district, but this system made less and less sense as patrons stopped farming. A school district may be broadly accepted as a public good toward which most people are willing to pay even if they do not have children, but in Grants Pass, people in urbanizing neighborhoods were not so willing to pay for water that neither they nor their neighbors needed. At the same time, GPID operated within the narrow limits set by state and federal laws and agencies, and had to run like any other regulated business. Irrigation districts are beholden to their patrons, much as a corporation is beholden to its shareholders. Patrons and shareholders might each buy out at any time, so it is necessary to keep them happy.

Throughout the process, scientific and technical information was used as political ammunition. This is not uncommon in environmental issues,[418] but in landscapes like Savage Rapids Lake, some stakeholders, having formed their own sense of how the system worked, refused to believe in problems pointed out by scientists. Science was most useful to WaterWatch and its environmental and economic allies; they argued in terms of the fish and the river. The Rogue fishery had been devastated, and this dam was "the biggest fish-killer in the Rogue." This phrase quickly became a rallying cry, and environmental groups used it or some version of it consistently.[419] Dam defenders protested, but the frame stuck—even when people denied that the dam killed fish, listeners could not help but think of dead salmon.[420] As environmentalists saw it, the dam was built to provide irrigation water, which pumps could do with minimal disruption to fish.[421] It made little difference whether the fish were desired for recreation,[422] for business,[423] or for their environmental value. Removal advocates cast the dam in terms of its harms (great) and its production (marginal, and easily replaceable). The dam removal coalition wielded technical knowledge to make their case. Arguments were in quantities: 114,600 more salmon, $5 million per year to the regional economy.[424] Dam removal would lead to a 22 percent increase in fish, underlining the dam's label as a killer.[425] Throughout the issue, the fish and their well-being were politically unassailable, and no one spoke against them—note Dennis Becklin's concerted and partly successful effort to improve their passage over the dam.

At the same time, beneath environmentalists' arguments lay dams' long history as powerful political symbols of environmental degradation. As Bernie Moore of Rogue Flyfishers and the Governor's Task Force on Savage Rapids Dam said, "I have never been a fan of dams, period."[426] Dave Strahan, the area representative for the NSIA and a Grants Pass native, was motivated in part by his lifelong opposition to Savage Rapids and the changes it wrought on his home river.[427] These men were not members of environmental action groups as such—they represented industrial and fishing interests in the removal coalition—but their core values were the same as those of the environmentalists. WaterWatch's campaign slogan was

"Free the Rogue!"[428] Here was no reference to increased salmon returns or whitewater rafting dollars, but a plea for an imprisoned river that deserved freedom as if it were a person. This sort of construct, redefining liberty to fit a river, is present in many dam removals.[429]

Oregon law makes river water a publicly owned good, but to dam supporters, the water was their own, to use as they saw fit.[430] Dam supporters focused on the dam's status as private property and, somewhat incongruously, on its services to the public; at the same time, removal advocates focused on the dam's impacts on public resources like fish.[431] To Bob Hunter, the public was subsidizing GPID by granting it excess water for its inefficient system, and by putting some of the costs of GPID's operations onto the Rogue fishery instead of the district paying them itself.[432] Both sides believed that their rights were under attack by their opponents.

State and national environmental groups joined the Savage Rapids fight as part of a larger effort to remove dams and restore rivers nationwide.[433] Early in the process, Savage Rapids was one of fourteen "damnable dams" listed by the Oregon Natural Resources Council as candidates for removal.[434] In the 1990s, Interior Secretary Bruce Babbitt publicly expressed the desire to blow up a big dam and made something of a national dam removal tour, sledgehammer in hand.[435] He stopped in the Rogue Valley in 1998 to help take out a small dam in downtown Medford.[436] It was easy for these state and national environmentalists to target Savage Rapids as one more instance of a destructive dam, a victory for their movement and a stepping-stone to bigger things. At the same time, Bob Hunter's effective local leadership kept the Savage Rapids removal coalition from losing focus, allies, or direction despite the coalition's national-level expansion and its eventual embrace of its former opponents.[437] In the end, the removal coalition needed everyone. The animosity and ideological clashes among stakeholders overwhelmed one effort to create a venue for everyone when the task force failed, but in the end, Judge Hogan's order into mediation established a venue where they had to succeed, and where they had less distraction from the public. Wiser after years of policy conflict, gripped by the fear that GPID might collapse, and incentivized by the prospect of federal funding, the mega-coalition held together and worked out the consent decree and a unified path to dam removal.

The scale and impact of the New West phenomenon is ever shifting, but the fact that such changes occurred in Grants Pass and in GPID is indisputable. When GPID was founded during World War I, it is unlikely that its patrons anticipated a post-agricultural era for the district, or that they would have considered a free-flowing salmon stream superior to one that was dammed, despite protestations from anglers when the dam was built.[438] But sportfishing for salmon is the sort of amenity on which New West economies are built. Faced with an influx of people like Bob Hunter and Bernie Moore, dam savers appealed to local granges,[439] traditionally a potent source of political power in rural America.[440] Dam savers met in grange halls and connected with rotary clubs,[441] but these communal organizations did not possess the political clout they might once have wielded, and their role was very minor. Indeed, Patagonia, an extremely New West company[442] with headquarters in Santa Barbara, California, probably exerted as much influence as the granges.

Despite swimming against the sociohistorical tide, the dam savers managed to delay the dam removal for a decade, and then, in much the same way as their ideological mates in Port Angeles, got that removal on very advantageous terms for GPID. Although the political climate has changed since 2009, and funding has grown ever scarcer, it is likely that gathering a near-comprehensive array of stakeholders, and caring for their diverse needs and priorities, will remain a necessity for the removal of major dams anywhere. As Dan Shepard said in 2011, looking back on the whole issue of Savage Rapids Dam, politicians love to give out money when everyone is shaking hands.

5

The Friendly Battle of Bull Run

The Bull Run Hydroelectric Project was a Rube Goldberg machine on a landscape scale.[1] It sprawled for miles across the foothills of volcanic Mount Hood in a web of diversions, flumes, tunnels, and turbines. At its heart sat forty-seven-foot Marmot Dam, which caught the Sandy River and shot it across the mountains to be made into power. How to remove this?

Marmot Dam, and the rest of the Bull Run project, were proposed for removal more than a decade after the Elwha and Savage Rapids dams, but came out years earlier. How did it go so fast? This was not a matter of size—Marmot was taller than Savage Rapids. It was not physical simplicity—Marmot had a million cubic yards of silt plugged up behind it. It was not a matter of ecology—endangered fish management plagued the basin well after the dam removal. The same political issues and complexities of the Rogue and Elwha ran through the Sandy. And yet the process was far smoother and more amicable. The Marmot removal holds lessons for future river decisions as an efficient, effective negotiation wherein diverse stakeholders worked through serious political and technical challenges to achieve significant restoration for the watershed. Leadership from the dam owner, a focused and open approach to stakeholders' goals, and creative use of policy structures created the political conditions for success.

The Sandy River and the Bull Run Project

The Sandy River runs north and west from the slopes of 11,240-foot Mount Hood to the Columbia River. Its mouth is seventeen miles east of Portland, Oregon's largest city. A turbid stream, it was christened the Sandy by Lewis and Clark, in 1805.[2] The river is quite wild—there is very little development along its banks, and much of the river's watershed lies in Mount Hood National Forest. It is close enough to the city, though, that a Portlander can easily drive there after work, kayak or fish, and be home for dinner. It is one of the most popular fishing destinations in the state.[3] Not many big cities have such a river close at hand, and Oregonians cherish the

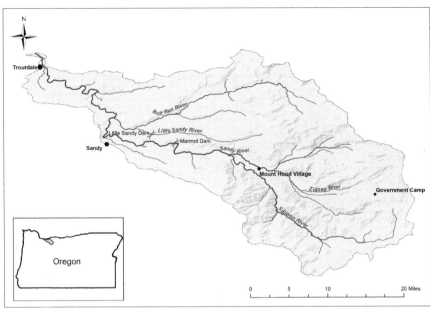

The Sandy River watershed. Map by Bradley Blackwell.

Sandy. The basin includes the Bull Run River, which provides Portland's municipal water.[4]

In 1906, the Mount Hood Company began work on a hydroelectric project in the Sandy Basin. In 1912, the project began to make power, as a sixteen-foot diversion dam on the Little Sandy River sent water through flumes to a forebay named Roslyn Lake. The next year, the thirty-foot Marmot Dam came online. The dam was a timber crib structure, made of logs with fill added. In 1924 the whole system—dams, powerhouse, lake, and flumes—was licensed as the Bull Run Hydroelectric Project.[5] Despite the convoluted layout, it worked, providing 22 megawatts of power. In the early twentieth century, this represented a significant electricity source.[6]

The Mount Hood Company merged with the Portland Railway, Light, and Power Company in 1912, and the new company eventually became Portland General Electric (PGE), which owned and operated the Bull Run project for the rest of its existence.[7] Bull Run provided power for the city's trolleys.[8] This was in the Progressive Era, when the political tide was turning away from private power providers like PGE; many of the Northwest's public utilities formed around the turn of the century.[9] This being the case, PGE knew that the city of Portland always had the option to form its own public utility, so it could not make its power too expensive.[10] Affordable power became even more important as the construction of the enormous Columbia River dams in the 1930s made northwestern electricity the cheapest in the United States.[11] So Bull Run was a small piece of the regional energy puzzle, just as the Sandy River forms a small part of the Columbia basin. By 2003, it produced 1 percent of PGE's generation.[12]

Fish, Dams, and the Sandy River

For most of history, the Columbia River Basin was the greatest salmon stream on earth, hosting somewhere between eleven and sixteen million returning adult salmon every year.[13] By the late 1800s, runs in the Lower Columbia basin, including the Sandy, began to decline under pressure from industrial development—timber, fishing, and urbanization.[14] People began to raise a question that has bedeviled northwestern rivers ever since: How to build up industry without losing fish? The balance tipped decidedly toward industry; by the twenty-first century, Columbia salmon populations were at roughly 12 percent of their historic levels.[15] Sandy River salmon and steelhead were no exception—the Sandy's runs dropped to 10 to 25 percent of historic levels.[16] The response, basin-wide and in the Sandy, was hatcheries. On the Sandy, people started collecting salmon eggs for artificial propagation as early as 1887.[17] The Oregon Fish Commission, as it was named then, built a permanent hatchery below the Marmot Dam in 1938.[18] The Sandy's fish have been a mixture of wild and hatchery stock ever since. Some 80 percent of Columbia salmon and steelhead are from hatchery stock.[19]

The Sandy's salmon runs declined, but salmon fishing continued. The town of Sandy sits along Oregon Highway 26, the main artery linking Portland to the skiing and hiking mecca of Mount Hood, and crowds of anglers dropped their lines in the river.[20] By the early 1980s, the Sandy was the second most productive fishing stream in Oregon.[21] Fly-fishing workshops were offered regularly in the area, and nearby Mt. Hood Community College offered fishing classes.[22] All this meant that the fish of the Sandy River enjoyed the support of two political constituencies—urban anglers who spent their leisure time on the Sandy, and fishing guides whose livelihoods depended on those anglers having fish to catch.

Over the decades, fishing on the Sandy evolved around the Marmot Dam and the hatchery. The hatchery program ensured the people an active year-round fishery by stocking winter and summer runs of steelhead, and spring Chinook and coho salmon. This was advantageous for anglers, shops, and guides, but the program drew criticism from wild fish advocates: there probably never was a significant native run of summer steelhead on the

Sandy, so ODFW used South Santiam River stock.[23] The wild fish lobby saw this run on the Sandy as artificial. The dam itself was used as a convenient collection point for hatchery brood stock.[24] It was also useful for separating hatchery and wild fish—you could gather all hatchery stock (which was marked at the hatchery) from ascending the dam's fish ladder, and keep the upper river wild.

The dam harmed Sandy River fish runs as well. Marmot's fish ladder allowed adult fish returning from the ocean to swim upstream, but originally, it did not have any system to guide juvenile fish downstream, or screens to keep fish from being diverted into canals and through the Roslyn Lake powerhouse.[25] Marmot Dam sent six hundred cubic feet per second[26] into the flume, leaving sharply reduced downstream flows in the Sandy—sometimes the Sandy ran at only 30 cfs below the dam.[27] This, along with the dam's retention of silt and organic material, degraded downstream fish habitat.[28] In 1948, the Oregon Fish and Game Commission[29] asked PGE to install screens to keep fish out of the Sandy diversion canal.[30] Combined with a juvenile bypass canal guiding them around the dam, these were effective for fish more than two inches long, but not smaller juveniles.[31] By 1976, PGE was required under the terms of its renewed FERC license to maintain minimum downstream flows of 520 cfs[32] from June 16 to October 16, 400 cfs from October 16 to 31, and 460 cfs from November 1 to June 15.[33] These sorts of ecologically driven shifts continued into the 1990s and reduced the dam's productivity.[34] PGE maintained their fish passage facilities regularly throughout this time.[35]

Such mitigation efforts were not enough to rescue northwestern salmon populations. In the early 1990s, Pacific salmon began to find their way onto the federal endangered species list (including, you'll remember, the Rogue's coho). In March 1998, NMFS listed Lower Columbia steelhead as threatened.[36] The next year, the Lower Columbia Chinook and chum followed,[37] as did bull trout.[38] The Lower Columbia/Southwest Washington Coast coho salmon (*O. kisutch*) was not listed, but was being considered as a candidate species; it would eventually be listed in 2005. Each of these fish ran up the Sandy River.

Relicensing and Surrender

Bull Run's FERC license, having been renewed in 1974, was scheduled to expire in 2004. But by 1988, Marmot Dam's original timber crib structure was in danger of collapse. Part of the dam's interior had fallen in, and water flowed through the structure.[39] PGE installed a new Marmot Dam of poured concrete.[40] At the ribbon-cutting ceremony, PGE CEO Peggy Fowler expressed the hope that "this dam could last for centuries."[41] She, like most people, was probably not anticipating the era of federally listed salmon that waited just around the corner.

In 1998, PGE began the process of renewing Bull Run's license. The utility assembled a broad stakeholder group with which to work on Bull Run, as well as its much larger Clackamas project, which was due for relicensing in 2006.[42] The assumption was that Marmot, like most dams, would be relicensed, presumably with some upgraded facilities, and would continue to operate for another thirty to fifty years.[43] However, after taking a close look at Bull Run's ecological issues in the newer, brighter light of the Endangered Species Act, and considering the projected value of its energy production, the company had second thoughts. Three other hydroelectric licenses were set to expire by 2006; these produced a combined 556 megawatts.[44] The company decided to focus its relicensing efforts on these more valuable projects and began to look at decommissioning Bull Run and its 22 megawatts.[45]

Making this move just nine years after rebuilding Marmot Dam was a major reversal. Looking back on the decision much later on, PGE hydroelectric project licensing manager John Esler laid out the situation in an informative article for the regional publication *Open Spaces*.[46] The most significant difference was the listing of the Lower Columbia salmon, which meant that PGE, if it kept the project, would need to replace its Sandy River fish ladder and install new fish screens for juveniles migrating downstream.[47] This would be expensive. Complicating the fish management problem, some Sandy River water was diverted into the Bull Run River, which, said ODFW, "confused migrating fish, who wrongly nosed up to the powerhouse outfall searching for their spawning grounds."[48] Another daunting expense, looking forward from the late 1990s, was future maintenance on the whole Rube Goldberg hydro project, with its flumes and tunnels flung across the forests and hills of northern Oregon.[49] The flume and the project's creosote lumber would have to be replaced by helicopter, there being no roads in much of that area.[50]

PGE would also have been required to release enough water below the Little Sandy Dam for fish to spawn there.[51] How much this would have required is unrecorded, but some indication can be found in PGE's later transfer of its water rights to in-stream flow, which sent 200 cfs to the Little Sandy;[52] 200 cfs represents a quarter of PGE's water right for the whole Bull Run project. PGE also expected to have to leave more water for fish in the Sandy River itself. The water downstream of Marmot Dam also exceeded 64° Fahrenheit, the Oregon Department of Environmental Quality's temperature standard for salmon rearing.[53] It would be difficult to re-operate the project in such a way as to reduce temperatures below Marmot Dam while producing enough electricity to make the investment worthwhile. All this would mean less water flowing through the power-house at Bull Run, less electricity from the project, less income for PGE— "cascading decisions," in the words of Julie Keil, PGE's widely respected director of hydro licensing and water rights.[54] Bull Run's production cost per megawatt-hour was already more than double PGE's hydro average.[55]

It is also notable that, in the 1990s, energy was cheap.[56] From 1990 to 2000, the price of electricity in Oregon was 4¢–5¢/kilowatt-hour—since then it has been between 6¢ and 8¢/kilowatt-hour.[57] Calculating the value of Bull Run's power over the decades of a renewed license, it was deter-mined the project was not worth keeping.[58] Had the license expired later, the math, and perhaps the decision, would have been different.[59] The total cost of a renewed license, including foregone power (but not including the landslides that crashed into the project flume once or twice a decade), was anticipated to be $30 million; early estimates indicated that the decommis-sioning cost would be $22 million. The company was also well aware of the public relations impact of performing such a dramatic and environmentally powerful action near the environmentally conscious city of Portland.[60]

Portland was (and is) a major presence in the Sandy Basin; the city gets its drinking water from the Bull Run River. Portland's massive (one-hundred- and two-hundred-foot-tall) dams on the Bull Run are impassable to fish, so under the Endangered Species Act, the city would have to mitigate their impact elsewhere. Further complicating matters, the Willamette River flows through the urban core of the five-hundred-thousand-person city, and is, of course, heavily affected. The late 1990s salmon listings meant that there were threatened fish in the Willamette, swimming through down-town Portland.[61] Mayor Vera Katz asked water commissioner Erik Sten to figure out how to respond.[62] The city already balanced some of its impact on salmon by helping fund ODFW hatchery production,[63] but the Endan-gered Species Act would demand more. Sten thought that the listings and PGE's FERC process might provide an opportunity to go beyond regulatory agencies' mandates and proactively benefit salmon.[64] Looking over at the larger Sandy watershed, the Bull Run hydro project seemed like one place where Portland could perhaps help restore salmon habitat without altering its own municipal water system.[65] The city and the utility began to discuss a collaborative decommissioning process. Early on, the focus was on the dewatered Little Sandy and its smaller dam,[66] but talks expanded to include the whole project. Oregon governor John Kitzhaber, heartily devoted to salmon conservation and feeling the same pressure from federal listings, also expressed his support, and promised $10 million in state money to make up for PGE's power loss.[67] This was a significant share of the $22 million decommissioning cost.[68] The stakeholders also harbored hopes of raising dam removal money from the federal government.[69]

In May 1999, the city of Portland, the governor's office, and PGE announced the Bull Run decommissioning in a joint press release.[70] Kitzhaber saw the decommissioning as a victory for nature, saying that, "for the first time in almost a century, Oregonians will see these two rivers flowing freely again," letting the salmon "return home." Fowler spoke of how the decommissioning would save money, restore the environment, and help the people of Portland. To Northwest Sportfishing Industry Association executive director Liz Hamilton, this was "a win-win for everyone."[71] The city would fulfill its ESA responsibilities (and burnish its reputation as a citadel of environmentalism), fish advocates would get more restored habitat and presumably more fish, and PGE would save on project renovations and possibly work out a long-term deal to buy power from Portland's dams.[72] The removals, only the second and third to take place in Oregon,[73] were full-"stream" ahead.

At a relicensing meeting the next month, Julie Keil addressed the Bull Run project stakeholders. She discussed the changes that had taken place for the project, explained that they would be planning a decommissioning, not a license renewal, and targeted 2000 as the year to remove the Little Sandy Dam; Marmot would come out in 2001.[74] On November 12, 1999, PGE filed a notice of intent not to renew the license.[75] Such a notice is irrevocable. At this point, other utilities could have competed for the license, but none did.[76] On March 9, 2000, FERC made public notice of PGE's decision. This established a hard deadline by which PGE had to file its application to surrender its license: November 21, 2002, two years before the license expired.[77] If there was no agreement on a course of action by then, the project would again be available to any other operator interested in applying to license it, and FERC might issue orders on what to do with the unused, unlicensed project.[78]

PGE's notice of intent essentially removed FERC from the decision process; going forward, its only roles would be to approve the surrender application and then, later, to decide whether or not to accept PGE's terms of surrender.[79] This was part of PGE's motivation to make a decommissioning deal; PGE wanted to control its project's future itself, as much as possible.[80] A FERC ruling might not have turned out as PGE hoped. The challenge became how to structure the conditions of surrender in such a way as to satisfy the necessary state and federal agencies, as well as the private stakeholders involved, and of course, PGE itself.

PGE knew that the path ahead would be complicated, given the physical and environmental scale of the project. Marmot's fish management role was in jeopardy, along with its power production. At a stakeholder meeting, the company asked representatives of the resource agencies if they would consider assuming liability for Marmot and its role in Sandy fish management. Kammy Kern-Korot of ODFW replied that the agencies, state and federal, had discussed this, and, while they were concerned about fish management, they supported dam removal and were not interested in operating Marmot Dam themselves.[81] Where this would leave the fish, post-dam, was not clear.

Eager to deal with the issue efficiently, PGE forged ahead toward decommissioning. The utility circulated a draft surrender application, preliminary draft environmental assessment, and draft decommissioning report in March 2000. Company representatives met with project stakeholders in Portland on April 17 and held a public meeting in the town of Sandy that same day. The intention was to seek input on the draft documents and incorporate the information into a final surrender application, which they planned to file on June 1. Said PGE consultant Tom Sullivan, "Today's meeting is really just a meeting to kind of see if folks have questions to clarify some of the things that were in the reports."[82]

They sure did have questions: the transcripts of the Portland and Sandy meetings are 66 and 109 pages long, respectively, and filled with concerns from alarmed stakeholders.[83] Additional written comments came in over the following weeks. PGE looked at the many complicated issues raised by commenters in these and other forums over the previous year, and realized that their timeline would not be feasible.[84] On May 17, 2000, the company called this phase of the stakeholder process to an end, pushed back their planned surrender filing date, and began to reassess the situation.[85] As PGE representative Mark Fryburg put it, "We found out breaching dams is very complicated and we were on a fast timeline. You could almost hear a collective sigh of relief when we decided to go slower."[86]

At the core of the issue was the simple novelty of the situation—PGE and the stakeholders were trying to do something that hadn't been done much before. Most of the stakeholders in the group were familiar with the

FERC relicensing process, but few of them had been through a license surrender and dam removal, certainly not one on this scale, and there was little sense of how to proceed—there was no template to follow.[87]

As everyone reconsidered, the idea arose of PGE simply surrendering the license and abandoning the project, leaving, as John Esler put it, "a cement waterfall in the river with a fish ladder."[88] But abandonment was distasteful all around.[89] As Julie Keil had already declared, "PGE's position on stewardship alone would dictate that they return to the stakeholders group to coordinate what would likely happen to the project in that event."[90] However, if concerns over fish and sediment management could not be resolved and nothing was done, orphaning the dam was the default option.

If this had happened, the Sandy would have flowed into a jurisdictional mess—it is uncertain just what authority regulatory or management agencies have once a license has been surrendered.[91] Surprisingly enough, this situation is not uncommon: nearly three thousand major dams in the United States have no recorded owner.[92] Undoubtedly many thousands, perhaps hundreds of thousands, of little dams have been built, operated, and abandoned without being recorded anywhere and now block up streams across America without anyone taking responsibility for them—"feral dams," in the words of some ODFW staff.[93]

Deliberations over removal of the Marmot Dam had raised three particularly important and difficult issues: fish management, silt management, and how to address the fate of Roslyn Lake. In the absence of concerted opposition to dam removal, these questions would shape the course of negotiations for the rest of the process.

The Silt

Behind Marmot Dam sat nearly a million tons of silt.[94] Fluvial geomorphologists in 2000 found it very difficult to say with confidence what would happen to that silt after dam removal.[95] If the dam was removed gradually, over the course of two working summers, they feared that, in the intervening winter, the loose slopes of Mount Hood would slough off and drop more silt behind the dam.[96] But if they opted to demolish the dam in a single season—"blow and go," as the technique is enjoyably known—the silt release might wreak severe ecological havoc as it burst downstream.[97]

Worse than either scenario was the possibility that the silt might fail to flush out at all. Stakeholders were haunted by visions of an unstable and uncontrollable silty mass plugging the river, leaking haphazardly

The Marmot Dam, pre-removal. PGE.

downstream, collecting upstream silt, raising turbidity, barring fish passage, and potentially collapsing catastrophically at some unknown future date.[98] With such high ecological stakes, PGE was leery about moving forward until they had a strong sense of what the river might look and act like afterward. Politically, the silt was pretty simple—everyone wanted it gone—but the hydrological models available in 2000 did not provide sufficient foundations for a solid decision.

In the winter of 2000–2001, as everyone wondered about the decommissioning, a lahar (a large flow of volcanic debris) from Mount Hood fortuitously dumped almost a million cubic yards of material into the Sandy.[99] Lahars are normal (but dramatic) events on geologically lively Mount Hood. There was a bit of damage to Bull Run's infrastructure,[100] but overall, the river consumed the lahar without making much trouble.[101] This was an encouraging indication that the silt release after dam removal might work—as some said, the river is called the Sandy for a reason[102]— but worries remained.[103] After all, no one can be held liable after a lahar.

Roslyn Lake

The fate of Roslyn Lake, the forebay for the Bull Run powerhouse, was more politically vexing. The lake was the main spot where the Sandy community interacted with PGE and its Bull Run project. The lake was in no way a natural feature—it had previously been a meadow, which PGE turned into a forebay by raising berms on all sides and diverting water into it.[104] Since 1957, PGE had maintained a park around Roslyn Lake, providing cheap ($3 on weekends, free on weekdays),[105] publicly accessible flat-water recreation and rainbow trout fishing.[106] There was an annual Polar Bear Swim.[107] The lake received up to sixty thousand visitors in the summertime,[108] and many in the community felt that Roslyn was a natural area—its connection to and dependence on hydropower infrastructure was not part of their perception.[109] Shortly after the decommissioning announcement, the Sandy City Council met to discuss their concern over the future of Roslyn Lake and decided to ramp up their involvement.[110] While the editors of the *Oregonian* and the local *Sandy Post* had both declared their support for dam removal, and the Sandy River Basin Watershed Council had as well, everyone wondered about the future of the lake.[111] Roslyn groundskeeper Caddy Grantz predicted that the community, faced with the loss of their lake, would "throw a big old fit."[112]

When PGE and the regulatory agencies held public meetings to share information and give local people a chance to express their views, they found that Caddy Grantz was right. The meetings quickly grew heated.[113] As the *Sandy Post* put it, "PGE [took] a punch from local residents."[114] The agencies, environmentalists, and anglers might be excited about dam removal, but in these meetings, "area residents' reactions . . . varied from poker-faced to enraged."[115] People decried the speed with which the decision was being made, expressing a sense of voicelessness, and asked whether there was any way to keep the lake without the dam.[116] People waxed nostalgic about the community's connection to the "pristine lake"[117] and worried about the wildlife that lived in and around it.[118] One Sandy citizen said, "This whole community seems to revolve around Roslyn Lake."[119] Rick Buhler, representing a group called the Bull Run Community Planning Association, worried about the loss of small streams and the decommissioning's effect on old-growth trees.[120] Overwrought letters to the *Sandy Post* editor flew in. People claimed that "it would be impossible to imagine life without Roslyn Lake," and warned that removal would leave a dust bowl spotted with tree stumps.[121] The hardest rhetorical blow was dealt by ten-year-old Molly Courtney: "If you want to hurt hundreds of little children's feelings, then go ahead and do it."[122]

While the people packing these meetings were concerned about Roslyn Lake, they were also skeptical about PGE's motives, and about the role of the city of Portland. One attendee asked whether there was some sort of cover-up, if it was about economics or fish runs, or something else entirely.[123] Those who spied the hand of Portland behind it all worried about a water rights grab by the growing city.[124] Alarmed, PGE scheduled more meetings for September 1999.

Lurking beneath Roslyn Lake was a related issue: groundwater. There were no homes on the lakeshore, which would have made a tricky political situation trickier for PGE, but there were up to fifty-eight wells around the Bull Run area that might be affected by shifting groundwater dynamics.[125] What might happen, and how could the community respond? It seemed unlikely that any wells would actually run dry (and in the end, none did), but in 2000 it was difficult to know.[126] PGE held a senior water right, and was not legally responsible for the water in private wells. To maintain public goodwill, it was prepared to provide bottled water, and perhaps even a "city" of Porta Potties, to be on the safe side,[127] but this was clearly not a long-term solution. A related concern was that Roslyn served as the primary water source for part of the Sandy Fire District, but this issue was easily addressed by connecting to Portland's water system.[128]

The alarmed defenders of Roslyn Lake began to make political moves: they constructed phone trees,[129] held forums,[130] and formed an advocacy group called the Keeping Water in the Lake Committee.[131] One committee member stated optimistically, "There will be a lake there. How that's going to finally work out, I don't know."[132] They hoped that the city of Portland, with its enormous water rights in the Bull Run basin, might be open to diverting enough of its water to keep the lake topped up even after the dams were gone. They also suggested digging a smaller, deeper, spring-fed lake.[133]

Somewhat alarmed by all this public anger, PGE began to explore ways that Roslyn might be saved. The utility was happy to have the lake continue as a park and wetland habitat, but there was no apparent economical way to keep water in the lake.[134] In April 2000, PGE held another meeting to take comments and further explain its position, saying that it was eager to preserve the lake if possible.[135] It began to look into the possibility of preserving a smaller lake, perhaps 50 acres instead of 160.[136] But the lake was a "leaky bathtub."[137] There had never been a natural lake at the site, and the earth was porous: five to seven cubic feet of water seeped out of the lake and into the soil every second.[138] Clackamas County Parks was proposed as a possible future park operator, but it lacked the revenue to take the site on.[139] PGE made the lake available to any other user willing to maintain it, but no one emerged who would keep it full of water.[140]

The *Sandy Post* editors, reflecting on the furor, astutely identified the crux of the problem: "The company owns Roslyn Lake, which has seemed like a public place, but, in reality, never was."[141] John Esler echoed this perspective, saying that he couldn't "see how our decision is at all going to be influenced. . . . We're not asking for input. We really don't have any choice."[142] Esler later noted that westerners love to have their say—look at all the region's ballot measures—but they couldn't do that here.[143] The historic and nostalgic role of the lake was not PGE's responsibility, and while the company was willing to listen to and work with lake proponents, those proponents did not, in the end, gain any power at the negotiating table.[144] Oregonians, the *Sandy Post* observed, were sometimes unwilling to pay the levies for public parks, but if they relied on private facilities like Roslyn Lake for their recreation, they were setting themselves up for disappointment.[145]

At the end of 1999, the dam removal was listed as one of the biggest stories of the year in the *Sandy Post*.[146] The community's anger had helped convince PGE to slow decommissioning down. In the summer of 2000, when PGE announced that it would step back and reconsider the situation, the *Post*'s headline was "Roslyn Lake Gets Reprieve from PGE."[147]

The Fish

The third and most difficult challenge for stakeholders was the management of fish runs. Marmot Dam separated the Sandy's hatchery fish, which anglers can harvest, from the genetically pure, federally listed, wild fish in the upper river. On May 30, 1999, Bill Monroe of the *Oregonian* laid out the decommissioning effort's fish issues in a perceptive passage worth quoting at length. He said,

> Depending on your politics, it's:
> a) An extraordinary opportunity to help restore threatened wild steelhead to one of Oregon's most pristine watersheds.
> b) A masterful public relations move that saves PGE a bundle.
> c) A diversion by Erik Sten and the city of Portland of public attention away from more gnarly urban threats to salmon and steelhead. This makes the city look good without risking a single hard feeling from constituents washing their cars with the river's water.
> d) A threat to Republicans in the Northwest congressional delegation who are fighting tooth and nail to keep all dams intact.

e) An enigma for the Oregon Department of Fish and Wildlife, which recently drafted a comprehensive plan for the Sandy's wild salmon and steelhead based on Marmot Dam's ability to intercept pesky hatchery fish and keep them out of the basin. All of the above? Or how about: f) A potential kick in the teeth to Portland steelhead anglers.[148]

The matter of hatchery versus wild fish afflicts, I would guess, most West Coast rivers of any significant size. It gets at the central issue in salmon management—that most people want there to be a lot of salmon in the river, in order that they might pull those salmon out of the river. Hatcheries allowed Sandy anglers to have their fish and eat them too. But it was controversial there, long before the Bull Run decision.[149] In 1997, hoping to exclude hatchery fish from the upper river, ODFW began to mark them by clipping their adipose fins.[150] The updated Sandy River Basin Fish Management Plan incorporated the Marmot Dam as the site at which to take out marked (harvestable) fish and allow unmarked (wild) ones. So when PGE announced its intention to remove Marmot, it jarred the fish stakeholders who had worked up the plan.[151] The question even affected the sedate hobby fishing on Roslyn Lake, as excess hatchery steelhead were sometimes put in the lake in an effort at "recycling fish."[152]

The local fishing industry, from guides to tackle shops, depended on a harvestable fishery. Anglers must release any wild fish they hook, but can take home hatchery-raised salmon, to mount above the mantelpiece or to eat for dinner.[153] As Jack Glass, a longtime guide and member of ODFW's Fisheries Restoration Enhancement Program board, pointed out, people see salmon as food, and when they catch one, they intend to eat it.[154] This shapes the economy of northwestern salmon fishing guides, and distinguishes salmon fishing from catching (and releasing) species like, for instance, brown trout in the Rocky Mountains. Hatchery-produced summer steelhead ensured a year-round harvestable Sandy River fishery.[155] The Association of Northwest Steelheaders and the Northwest Sportfishing Industry Association, not to mention local outfitters and guides, wanted to keep their year-round harvest, and would not support a dam removal plan unless it included some assurance that they and their clients would still be able to keep their catch; they lobbied hard for a gradual approach to restoration,[156] and to perhaps retain some sort of sorting mechanism in the Sandy.[157] In 1999 the Steelheaders, who had a long history of involvement with restoration efforts in the Sandy Basin, announced that they opposed removal because of the dam's important management role.[158] For the fishing community, the looming fear was a mixed-up fishery without hatchery stock, leading to a fishing ban on the entire river, leaving destitute fishing guides and furious anglers.[159] Without the dam, what kind of sorting would even be possible? How to keep hatchery fish out of the upper Sandy? On the opposing side, groups like Oregon Trout and the Native Fish Society aimed to promote and preserve wild, native fish runs. They argued that the endangered fish, and the river in general, would be better off in the long run with no hatchery fish at all.[160]

Caught in the middle were the agencies, NMFS and ODFW. ODFW, with its mission to support Oregon's fish and fishers alike, operates Oregon's hatcheries. NMFS was more enthusiastic about wild fish but was willing to accept hatchery stock.[161] Contradictory agency missions like ODFW's inevitably cause divisions in agencies. The case of Marmot Dam was no exception.[162] It is notable that ODFW is partly funded by fishing license sales, so effects on recreational fishing redound onto the agency. This opens ODFW to accusations of greed and mismanagement by wild fish activists.[163] Complicating the matter, PGE helped fund ODFW's Sandy hatchery as mitigation for the ecological impacts of its other operations, but if the Marmot Dam went away, so would those funds.[164] Early in the licensing process, PGE offered to give ODFW the dam, to be operated as a watershed management machine, but the state didn't want to take ownership.[165] NMFS suggested building a weir at the dam site to act as a sorting tool,[166] but PGE was loath to remove one dam and then, essentially, build another one.[167]

In 2001 ODFW released a plan, publicized in local newspapers, to eliminate stocking of summer steelhead and to dramatically reduce coho salmon and winter steelhead releases: smolt releases would drop from 1.465 million to between 310,000 and 660,000.[168] Local guides and tackle shop owners complained that this plan would hurt them badly:[169] the Sandy saw more than forty-two thousand fishing trips per year and contributed $4 million to the fishing economy.[170] ODFW, again, found itself in an awkward position: one state biologist who attended public meetings recalls law enforcement officers looking at the crowd and worrying aloud that they didn't have enough bullets to protect him.[171] Fish industry representatives Richard Allen and Debbi Schneider urged the restive crowd to show some respect, but they were angry too.[172] Allen said of the fishery, "It's ours and we'll fight to the death for it. I'll take it to Washington. I'll take it all the way." Letter-writing campaigns followed, and petitions circulated among those hoping to keep the fishery.[173] At the same time, the exchange of views that took place in these meetings did move the issue forward, and ODFW agreed to cut down on some of its hatchery programs without eliminating any of them, by way of encouraging compromise on the Sandy.[174]

But all of this was so much sound and fury without a decision on what would happen to the dam, the "linchpin" of Sandy River fish management.[175] As in the case of Roslyn Lake, PGE had no desire to hurt the Sandy River fishery, and the utility was amenable to working with ODFW, NMFS, and fish interests to find a broadly acceptable management plan. But how this would work without a sorting site was uncertain. Fishing guide Brian Silvey put it best: "On one hand, get rid of the hatchery fish, and the river's toast [as a fishing destination]. It's gone. On the other hand, I think you've got to protect the wild fish. It's a tough one."[176]

The heart of the issue was simply how to define salmon. Runs of the same species of salmon will vary from stream to stream—this is part of why NMFS lists them by evolutionarily significant unit rather than by river—and hatchery fish are different from wild ones. But at the same time, to a delighted weekend angler with a heavy rod, a hatchery-born coho looks, and tastes, just like one hatched in an upstream redd.

To Bill Bakke of the Native Fish Society, opening habitat and letting the wrong fish into it wastes that habitat and holds back the restoration of the wild run.[177] The crux, though, is that while people wait for wild populations to rise, what are fishing guides to do on a river containing only a few wild fish? The role of science is problematic as well—it is obviously crucial to ecological issues, but emotions and perceptions drive political decisions. Bakke recalls receiving a phone call asking him why he wasn't upset that Caspian terns were eating native salmon near the coast. He had to explain that Caspian terns are native to North America, despite the fact that they are named after a salt lake in Asia.[178]

Another issue, less politicized but crucial, arose during this time—the city of Sandy's municipal water right.[179] If PGE decommissioned the Bull Run project and converted its senior 800 cfs water right to in-stream flow, as environmental groups hoped it would,[180] the city's water, also drawn from the river, might be in jeopardy. In the summer months, the Sandy often flowed at less than 800 cfs, so all of it would have to stay in the river. Eventually, a wary city council negotiated a deal whereby they could keep their water, with an ironclad claim to 16.3 cfs, the amount they deemed necessary.[181]

Forming a Working Group

Between 2000 and 2002, the city of Portland drifted away from the dam removal process. The Clinton administration was making way for the Bush administration, and NMFS under President Bush was far less zealous in its enforcement of the Endangered Species Act. This released some of the pressure on the city to mitigate its impacts.[182] Governor Kitzhaber's $10 million in state money, never firmly promised, disappeared. PGE was left entirely responsible for funding the Bull Run decommissioning. However, the Sten-Kitzhaber combination created a climate in which the city and the governor had promoted dam removal and wanted to see PGE's decommissioning effort succeed—anyone who might have wanted to fight the dam removal could not expect to use Kitzhaber's office or Portland's clout.

For most of 2001, the issue quieted down—Marmot Dam does not appear in the Sandy City Council meeting minutes at all in that year—as PGE figured out its next move. Some stakeholders felt that PGE let things go during this time,[183] but PGE indicated that it was busy planning throughout.[184] By February 2001, the price of energy had risen well above its 1998 level,[185] but PGE's notice of surrender was irrevocable, no matter how valuable the Bull Run project's power looked now.[186]

In January 2002, with the deadline looming, PGE convened a diverse working group of twenty-three organizations and reopened deliberations over the Bull Run project. The group included every significant user or authority on the Sandy River, from the Oregon Governor's Office to American Rivers to Alder Creek Kayak Supply. The environmental organizations alone made a political mosaic. Bill Bakke notes that the Portland environmental community relies on one another for expertise in their various specialty issues and is well accustomed to working together.[187] Moreover, many of the groups and individuals involved had long collaborated to manage Oregon's watersheds and enjoyed a certain level of familiarity. Keith Jensen, to take one example, owned Alder Creek Kayak, was on the WaterWatch of Oregon Board, and had connections with American Rivers, American Whitewater, and Bill Bakke.[188] This created a thorough, knowledgeable, and diverse group with experience in all the Sandy River's issues.

Reflecting on the lessons of its abortive first attempt at decommissioning, PGE decided to take a different approach and hire a neutral mediator, Debra Nudelman of RESOLVE, to facilitate the negotiation. Nudelman's skillful approach probably made the difference between success and failure—perhaps between a thoroughly planned and managed removal and an orphaned dam.[189] She was goal-oriented, kept diverse stakeholders engaged and united, and, crucially, formed subgroups with the skills and regulatory responsibilities that would be needed to overcome the river's technical challenges.[190] These groups acted like "buckets"[191] into which stakeholders threw their needs, perspectives, and expertise on each particular issue. In this round of negotiations, it was decided to assemble a group of mid-level staff, who worked closer to the ground level but still had real decision-making power. Keith Kirkendall of NMFS[192] and Connie Athman of the US Forest Service identified the group's composition as a key to success.[193]

This working group opened a new political venue wherein all participants were more or less on equal footing. Nudelman's evenhanded oversight and stakeholders' uncertainty over what would occur in the case of an orphaned project leveled the playing field. The working-group venue was collaborative, not adversarial in the way that a lawsuit is or regulatory action can be. These stakeholders did not appeal to the public—no circulating petitions or furious op-eds—and there was very little coverage of negotiations during most of 2002 in the Post or the Oregonian. This likely served to hold down any politicization. While everyone stayed aware of the various agencies' mandatory authority and FERC's deadline, the working group afforded stakeholders political space that allowed them to solve problems in a collaborative manner. The group enjoyed a good deal of camaraderie; after the final agreement, participants gave one another whimsical awards honoring individuals' particular contribution to success.[194] The only oddity in the group was the dual role of John Esler—he served on Oregon's Fish and Wildlife Commission as well as working for PGE. This meant that he had to work differently with different stakeholders, depending on which hat he was wearing, but everyone was aware of this, and it did not derail the process.[195]

The experience of 1998–2000 had provided the stakeholders a good sense of the issues they were facing and what could be done to handle them. This meant that the subgroups were able to get to work efficiently. But Bull Run's expiring license meant that the group was working against the clock—a decision had to be made by November 21.

And it was. In ten months, the group hammered out an agreement to remove Marmot Dam, Little Sandy Dam, Roslyn Lake, and the other Bull Run infrastructure. As part of the agreement, PGE would run the project for an additional five years. This would allow stakeholders enough time to rework fish management, sort out an alternative future for Roslyn Lake, model the movement of silt after removal, and let PGE build up revenue to pay for the decommissioning. The funds for removal came from PGE's ratepayers.[196] With all stakeholders united in favor of dam removal, the process moved quickly.[197] On November 12, just before the deadline, PGE sent FERC its application to surrender the Bull Run license.

Moving the Silt

> Will it barge through the river like a pig in a python, or melt slowly like an ice cube?
> —Trevison, "Seeing Through the Silt," *Oregonian*, 2003.

The million-cubic-yard plug in the Sandy River frightened anglers and intrigued scientists. No one had intentionally released this much silt before.[198] There was the possibility of dredging the silt out before dam removal, but that would be expensive and laborious.[199] One cause for hope was that, as a diversion dam, Marmot had never collected fine sediment— the most problematic material for fish ecologists and engineers—making the plug a relatively sandy and unconsolidated load, and more likely to move easily.[200]

The situation was complicated somewhat by the Sandy's sensitive ecology and listed fishes—NMFS wouldn't allow engineers to keep a partial dam in the stream for two years, so removal would have to take place in one year.[201] PGE hired Stillwater Sciences to study the silt's composition and model its movement after Marmot was gone. The researchers built an operating physical model of the dam site, working in the widely respected St. Anthony Falls Laboratory in Minnesota. PGE made a conscious effort to support a strong team of scientists and ensure that the model of silt movement would be as accurate as possible.[202] The company receives credit for this commitment to good science from many stakeholders.[203] The scientists worked together smoothly during the process—hydrologist Gordon Grant describes the process as "collegial and congenial."[204] Julie Keil agreed: "I like making scientists happy."[205] The model also helped the rest of the coalition move forward. Deb Nudelman notes that physical visualization, especially of the sediment, was a powerful way to help nervous stakeholders feel comfortable about dam removal.[206]

Stillwater's hydrological models indicated that the silt would erode away relatively quickly and that the structure of the reach behind the dam would be in a comparable state to adjacent reaches within five to ten years.[207] This allowed the working group to proceed with confidence.[208] The geomorphological-aspect project also offered the opportunity to push riparian science into the future. According to Grant, "We joke[d] that the river science community would probably buy tickets just to get to watch it."[209]

Negotiating Away Roslyn Lake

Roslyn Lake was a paradox: an engineered component of a privately owned power-generation project and, at the same time, a widely beloved natural feature. During the decades of its existence, Roslyn had offered the same public uses—fire suppression, groundwater, swimming—as a natural lake. So in this sense it is only reasonable that the citizens of Sandy would have regarded it as natural and created emotional ties to it, as people do to any familiar recreational landscape. This sort of paradox is likely found in nearly any artificial water body near human population centers. Even years after Roslyn Lake went away, "most residents do not recognize PGE's right of ownership."[210]

Public support for Roslyn Lake faded after the initial burst of dismay in 1999–2000. This meant that in 2002, when the actual decision to remove was made, there was essentially no grassroots challenge to the removal. The Keeping Water in the Lake Committee does not appear in the *Sandy Post* or the *Oregonian* after 2000. Individual pleas to save the lake remained,[211] but they came to nothing. This successful diminution of the issue was likely due to PGE's straightforward approach and its good-faith efforts to keep the Roslyn area dedicated to community recreation.[212] While later scholars found some people who felt that they had not had a voice in the decision,[213] public meetings allowed enough Sandy-area citizens to express themselves and have their feelings taken into consideration that the issue did not reach critical mass.

Some of the community worried about not just the end of the lake, but also the possibility that the Roslyn Lake Park site would be logged and developed; PGE quelled these fears by refusing to sell the plot to logging interests.[214] After all the meetings and public attempts to find some way to retain the lake, no one who was involved in the issue could doubt that all options had been exhausted. PGE spokesman Mark Fryburg, reviewing PGE's efforts, noted empathetically that PGE employees enjoyed using Roslyn Lake, themselves, and would miss it along with the rest of the community.[215] At the end of the process, PGE held farewell events at Roslyn, offering free park access and hot dogs, and tours with a public historian.[216] As the lake shrunk down, people were encouraged to catch all the rainbows they could before the water disappeared.[217] When the final agreement was signed, Sandy city manager Scott Lazenby informed the city council that they could not keep the lake, but they could expect to keep recreation, of some sort.[218]

Partly to mitigate for the loss of wildlife habitat that accompanied the loss of Roslyn Lake, PGE donated 1,530 acres up and down the Sandy Basin to an organization called Western Rivers Conservancy. Western Rivers incorporated this land into a growing conservation area in the Sandy Basin, and eventually transferred most of it to be administered by the Bureau of Land Management (BLM) as public low-impact recreation land; the BLM owned the land under the actual dam.[219] This status forbids extractive uses, like logging, on protected land. Ultimately, these lands will be part of a large Area of Critical Environmental Concern in the Sandy Basin.[220] Some small parcels, near the mouths of the Bull Run and Little Sandy Rivers, were transferred to the Portland Water Bureau.[221]

The problem of groundwater, and surrounding properties' wells, which had kept PGE project manager Dave Heintzman awake at night,[222] evaporated as no such problems arose. This issue does provide an instructive illustration of the ancillary impacts of a dam, and the potential issues therewith. As Mark Fryburg put it, "We supplied a free benefit from the lake that was tied completely to us operating a power plant. They [the homeowners] will have to access the natural water table once the hydro project stops operating."[223] Homeowners complained that when they bought their homes they were not aware that their wells might rely on a privately operated forebay but this, of course, was not PGE's responsibility.[224] The company worked with Bull Run Community Planning to see if grants might be available for redrilling wells, but there was no intention of compensating anyone beyond offering stricken homeowners some bottled water and Porta Potties.[225]

The dams' physical location, far from the lake, altered the public perception and understanding of the Bull Run project.[226] Marmot Dam was remote in the consciousness of anyone who wasn't involved with Sandy River salmon—it did not form the lake directly, so it seemed feasible to keep Roslyn full without Marmot Dam. This disconnect probably worked in favor of dam removal. A dam that visibly serves as the guarantor of a community's weekend recreation—like Savage Rapids—might rally people to save it, but the removal of Marmot Dam would not drain Roslyn Lake right away. The lake's defenders looked to replace some of the dam's function, but not necessarily keep the dam. Had the people of Sandy gotten angrier about the demise of the lake, had some of them owned lakefront

Roslyn Lake, 2008. Photographer Sam Beebe. Wikimedia Commons.

property, had they formed a stronger advocacy organization with a creative, motivated leader, the course of the negotiations over the Bull Run project might have been quite different. But they didn't.

Managing the Fish

The hatchery/wild management situation was decided through creative scientific management, a shared desire to improve and restore Sandy River salmonids, and fear from both sides: environmentalists worried that they might lose a major dam removal, and sporting interests worried that they would lose a major fishing destination.[227] Thus motivated, they tackled the issues together, but their deliberations yielded a complex and unstable compromise.

Up until 2002, hatchery fish had been released at the Marmot Dam site, ensuring that they would return to that same site and be caught and separated before they managed to ascend the fish ladder. Without the dam, it was probable that these fish, especially Chinook, would swim beyond the former dam site and into the upper basin. The working group agreed that ODFW would attack this problem by replacing the out-of-basin Chinook, which the hatchery had previously supplied, with Sandy River fish.[228] The fish were also released lower in the basin, in a creek that allowed them to imprint with different water chemistry that would eventually draw them back to spawn.[229] The last cohort of fishes to be released at the dam would return in 2007, and after that the fish management slate would be clean—this was

The Roslyn Lake site, 2013. Jeff Felker, "Roslyn Lake, Bull Run, Marmot Dam History." Reprinted with permission.

one reason the dam removal would have to wait until then. Juvenile summer steelhead would also be released lower in the river, and at such times and in such conditions as to minimize interaction with wild fish.[230] The system the stakeholders agreed on was expected to result in 10 percent of hatchery fish straying into the upper basin.[231] This level of straying seemed as though it might be realistic without putting wild DNA in undue jeopardy.

PGE committed to monitoring river conditions as the silt moved and implementing contingency plans if anything went wrong—if the silt created a fish passage barrier, for instance.[232] In the end, all actors in the fishery issue hoped that the project would create better fish habitat and larger fish populations. As watershed council member George Hoyt said, "Who wouldn't want salmon swimming and spawning in the creek in their own back yard?"[233] This was a classic political compromise, an agreement that made no one entirely happy, but broadly seemed like the best way to reach their shared goal. Long afterward, some still harbor regrets about not holding out for a weir.[234]

Out of the fish debates arose some political structures that would facilitate ongoing collaborative management. In 2000, prompted by PGE's dam removal announcement and by the federal listing of Chinook and steelhead, some of the Sandy's stakeholders formed the Sandy River Basin Partners.[235] The partners included both anglers and wild fish advocates.

To this day, in 2017, the partners continue to engage in restoration and maintain a neutral forum for Sandy management issues.

Removal

The years between the final decision in 2002 and the actual removal in 2007 brought little political controversy, but there were some logistical challenges. PGE had to work quickly to obtain a Section 404 dredge and fill permit from the US Army Corps of Engineers and a fill and removal permit from Oregon's Division of State Lands, and to work with NOAA to handle the newly listed coho.[236] NMFS's Keith Kirkendall directed his staff to work hard to ensure that this wouldn't delay the process[237] and Esler[238] asked PGE's consultants to write the draft biological opinion quickly and completely. The Army Corps wanted a one-to-one mitigation ratio for the removal of the Roslyn Lake wetland,[239] but John Esler noted that PGE had not removed a natural wetland, only drained an artificial lake: wet land, not a wetland. They did wait until the former lakebed dried up on its own before regrading the area.[240]

All permits secured, removal work began in 2007. Some of the silt load was used to build a cofferdam, which allowed for dry working conditions at the dam site, and the actual Marmot removal started in July. To prepare for the immediate impact of the silt release, ODFW held a "salmon rodeo" in which agency personnel gathered all the fish from the dam site and sent them to the hatchery, safely away from the silt blast.[241]

Portland General Electric corporate culture was a key component: PGE strives to be a friendly environmental steward, a "green company."[242] It sees itself as a "cute old" Portland, Oregon-based company[243] that lives in a world where it needs to be "good corporate citizens."[244] The utility's sustainable energy projects are featured in local newspapers, and its employees are lauded for volunteering in the community.[245] While local citizens sometimes did cast PGE as a corporate villain, as in the Roslyn Lake issue,[246] the local nature of the company made it a neighbor as well. It handled the Roslyn issue adroitly and openly, and any potential Marv Chastains or Dennis Becklins living in Sandy did not rise to power.

So it was not surprising that the cute old company, with the other Sandy River stakeholders, built the Marmot removal into a media event.[247] As the cameras rolled, CEO Peggy Fowler pushed a plunger and the top of the dam exploded in a cloud of smoke. This was slightly dramatized—the explosion was actually triggered by a demolition professional standing behind Fowler, and the smoke blast, which would not have looked impressive on its own, was embellished with some sort of powder—perhaps kitty litter—scattered on top of the dam.[248] But PGE had worked hard to make the removal happen, nearly everyone felt that it was a triumph, and there were no objections to a larger and more dramatic blast. Time-lapse cameras immortalized the explosion on YouTube. The concrete dam was gone by the end of the summer.

The crux of the removal came three months later, with the disposal of the silt plug and cofferdam. The hydrological models were promising, but no one really knew what would actually happen to the million tons of silt. The plan was to cut a notch in the cofferdam, release the river, and blast the silt away—but this required big, fast water. The planners decided to wait for a large storm up on Mount Hood, which would fill the river and, they hoped, do the job. On October 19, after a very tense wait, such a storm gathered on the mountain, and the notch was cut.[249] The river thundered through, and the next morning, when Gordon Grant came to inspect the dam site, he was exuberant to find that the cofferdam had vanished and the river had flushed out an enormous amount of silt—far more, far faster, than anyone expected.[250] Some two hundred thousand tons of material, one-fifth of the total load, was excavated in the first forty-eight hours.[251] Two days later, when John Esler made a discreet visit to some downstream fishing holes, the anglers there told him that fishing was just fine.[252] By 2012, 50 to 60 percent of the silt had eroded downstream, with much of the rest of it sitting on the terraces above the river, out of circulation.[253] The real-life result was better than the model.[254]

Afterward

The concrete that had once been Marmot Dam was mostly rendered into rubble for a new road to the former dam site.[255] This area is popular with mountain bikers and, in the view of Scott Lazenby, has become a real public resource.[256] A little of the dam became "souvenir bits" for onlookers.[257] Some of them are displayed in stakeholders' offices to this day. PGE also worked with filmmaker Jeff Gersh and National Geographic to create a movie about the dam removal and restoration on the Sandy River.[258] All of this served to further cement PGE as the "good guy" utility.[259]

The next summer, with minimal hullabaloo, fifteen-foot Little Sandy Dam came out, and Roslyn Lake was drained. The Sandy and Portland newspapers ran wistful articles about the last days of the lake.[260] Sandy mayor Linda Malone requested aerial photos of the lake site before and after draining for the historical record.[261]

Marmot Dam removal, 2007. PGE. Reprinted with permission.

The old Bull Run Powerhouse and part of the Roslyn Lake site were bought by a private consortium, which has moved to develop it as a historic museum.[262] In 2009, the facility was featured in a project called Art Contemplates Industry, a creative reexamination of the Northwest's recent past.[263] This land is deed-restricted to keep it from being used for timber harvest or development.[264] It has also been used for environmental education programs.[265] The other half of the former Roslyn Lake land is still owned by PGE, which is seeking to sell it on.[266] It was seriously considered as a rest and recreation spot for the elephants of the Portland zoo.[267] Sadly, this did not work out.[268] An old tunnel that had guided the flume through the hillside is envisioned as bat habitat.[269] The exposed silt from behind the dam, which now makes up the Sandy's riverbanks, turned out to be full of alder and willow seeds—native vegetation, just waiting to reemerge. This saved anyone from having to go to the effort of replanting the site.[270]

Coho salmon swam above the dam site the day after the barrier fell.[271] In the Sandy, returning fish are brooding longer over their redds than they had in the past, while the Little Sandy, empty for decades, saw immediate returns of Chinook, coho, and steelhead.[272] In 2017, ten years after Marmot Dam blew up, ODFW biologists announced, in a celebratory press release, that Sandy salmon and steelhead were thriving, with many more fish than before removal, even as runs in other rivers struggled.[273] While they were

The Marmot Dam site, October 2007. PGE. Reprinted with permission.

careful to note the complexity of salmon populations, the success of the Sandy's fish speaks to conditions in the stream itself, as opposed to in the ocean, making the difference. There is hope that the wild fish population in the upper Sandy might eventually triple or quadruple in size.[274]

As part of the surrender agreement, PGE monitored revegetation and noxious weed control, turbidity and sediment movement (with regard to fish passage and habitat), and the transformation of the Roslyn Lake wetlands, submitting annual monitoring reports to FERC for five years.[275] Habitat requirements were overseen by the monitoring implementation team of NMFS, ODFW, the US Fish and Wildlife Service, and PGE biologists.[276] In 2014, all monitoring requirements were fulfilled, and FERC signed off on the end of the project, the license surrender process, and PGE's responsibilities in the Sandy.[277] The contingency plans that would have been triggered if anything had gone awry post-removal (such as emergency fish rescue) never occurred, and everyone, PGE most of all, breathed a sigh of relief.[278] Resource and land agencies continue to monitor salmonids and other ecological changes as part of their overall responsibilities in the basin.

The hatchery issue lingers. Despite the carefully calculated post-removal management plan, hatchery-bred spring Chinook strayed above the former dam site in greater numbers than projected.[279] The Native Fish

The Little Sandy Dam, 2007. PGE. Reprinted with permission.

Society dropped out of the decommissioning agreement, presumably to maintain its ability to sue[280]—and, indeed, in 2014 the society, along with a fly-fishing group, filed an injunction against NMFS and ODFW. It argued that Sandy River Hatchery operations violated the Endangered Species Act.[281] A federal judge agreed but did allow a reduced number of hatchery fish to be released.[282] The adjustment may have worked; as of 2016, the stray rate for Chinook has come down from 75 percent to 10 percent.[283] With the removal of Marmot Dam, the fish can indeed now "migrate from the Pacific all the way up the slopes of Mount Hood,"[284] but what kind of fish swim to the mountain, and how they'll be managed, remains a political and ideological question.

Conclusions

The Marmot Dam removal, despite divisions among its stakeholders, did not turn into an antagonistic competition between coalitions, and the removal occurred less than ten years after the idea was first raised. This is because no stakeholders' values or core beliefs were contrary enough to overturn the idea of dam removal. The overall question for much of the time was not so much *whether* to remove the dam, but rather *how* to go about it. The issues of Roslyn Lake and fish management created tension but did not create long-term concerted opposition to the dam removal.

The Little Sandy River, 2012. Photographer Steve Terrill. Western Rivers Conservancy. Reprinted with permission.

Stakeholders attacked problems, rather than each other, and facilitated a relatively efficient process. To understand it, then, I focus on what didn't happen as much as on what did.

Other major dam removal negotiations quickly become adversarial because stakeholders differed over core or ideological values, which cannot be easily negotiated, and because they failed to account for one another's perspectives. In these cases, issues only resolved when pro-dam advocates exhausted their tactical options and, where possible, received some substitution for their accustomed river uses (sometimes referred to as being "made whole"). This allowed for the creation of mega-coalitions sufficiently broad and deep to secure political support and funding. But that became possible only after many years of expensive conflict drove the sides together and the most ideological removal opponents were politically exhausted and then marginalized.

The primary reason that this did not happen on the Sandy was PGE's leadership.[285] The dam owner provides a natural base on which an anti-removal coalition might build, so the fact that PGE suggested and then vigorously pursued decommissioning and dam removal meant that any political challengers to the removal plan would lack a crucial ally.

To John Esler, the decommissioning was "a moment of history for the company. . . . Nobody's looking back at the decision—it was the right

decision to make—but at the same time, there's the loss of a neat old powerhouse, a neat lake and one of the area's oldest parks."[286] There were some
internal regrets over the end of this "legacy project."[287] Julie Keil noted that
while you might expect utility people to be cold and rational about such
decisions, they were emotional; engineers are not robots.[288] At a ceremony
two days after the breach, a photo of Marmot was re-created in such a way
as to make the dam appear to fade into the river. Some spectators cheered
and clapped, but not PGE people.[289] John Esler notes that PGE's fish biologists felt that they had spent their careers making dams work with the
Sandy River's fish, and that overall, they had done a pretty good job.[290] The
company had taken pride in its management of the Bull Run project.

At the same time, though, PGE had built itself into the sort of corporate citizen that would be likely, even expected, to restore a river. Many
of the Sandy River stakeholders, veterans of northwestern river politics,
note that different utilities have different "personalities," and that PGE's
is among the best.[291] The utility framed itself as both a virtuous citizen of
the environment and community and a business that was responsible to
its ratepayers. This made it easy for PGE to connect effectively with many
other stakeholder groups. Its rhetoric was borne out by its actions, before
and during negotiations, and this added to its credibility for most users.
Kirkendall employed the metaphor of sitting on the same side of the table,
not different sides.[292] Users as contrary to one another as NFS's Bill Bakke
and Steelheader Norm Ritchie praised PGE's work with the stakeholder
group.[293]

The political approach and eventual agreement made room for every
interest. The removal plan included enough possibilities on fish management and recreational use of Roslyn Lake to let everyone reasonably hope
that their goals could be met. Even outside groups like the Keeping Water
in the Lake Committee, which was not politically substantial enough to
get a seat in Deb Nudelman's working group, had many opportunities to
engage publicly with PGE, express itself, have PGE's position as the property owner explained, and see that all options for keeping water in the
lake had been exhausted without the park site turning into condominiums
or clear-cuts. The leadership of Julie Keil was essential. Though there was
some blowback from other utilities for not fighting to keep the project,[294]
Keil's role won her widespread respect. In 2003, the year after the decommissioning agreement, she received the Dr. Kenneth Henwood Award from
the National Hydropower Association.[295] Among other qualities, nominees
display "persistence in the face of institutional obstacles, appreciation and

understanding of the relationships among project engineering, environment, and economics, and a strong commitment for fair dealing and plain speaking."[296]

Once PGE decided to go forward with removal, the only interest groups that might feasibly have stopped the removal process were the supporters of Roslyn Lake (who had very little actionable claim to the lake but whose cultural brethren enjoyed great success on the Elwha and Rogue) and fish advocates. But the issue for these groups was more a matter of economic advantage or recreational preferences, not core values. PGE and the relevant agencies were very open to maintaining these stakeholders' uses throughout, and explored a variety of creative avenues to do so. At the same time, PGE also made it clear that their options were limited by economics. This prompted some grumbling but no real opposition—the Bull Run project was PGE's private property, and there was no very concrete argument for giving priority to ancillary uses in the decision over how to dispose of the project. The fact that the wild fish advocates and angling advocates opposed one another after the agreement was signed is a testimony to PGE and Deb Nudelman's ability to work effectively with all stakeholders, even ones with important disagreements, to achieve decommissioning and dam removal.

Unsatisfied stakeholders often respond to political reverses by expanding the conflict into new venues and incorporating new allies and resources. The most likely group to do this would have been the Roslyn defenders. But they would have found only a dead end. State-level political venues were close at hand in the cities of Portland and Salem. In neither of these venues, though, were removal opponents likely to find support—Governor Kitzhaber and Commissioner Sten had heartily endorsed dam removal, and while they withdrew from the decommissioning process by 2002, they could not be expected to oppose it. Local state senator Rick Metsger (D-Welches) was present at some of the Roslyn Lake meetings,[297] but again, these did not take on an adversarial tone, and Metsger did not push the issue in the state legislature. Moreover, PGE's working group was broad enough to already occupy most of the other political venues that stakeholders might reasonably have sought—no one from outside the group would have had strong grounds on which to successfully sue or lobby legislators. With NMFS, the US Fish and Wildlife Service, and the US Forest Service working on decommissioning, there was also no realistic path by which removal opponents might have called on the federal government to save the dam.

PGE's identity as John Esler's "cute old" company seems to have played well in Portland and in Sandy. People in urban and suburban Portland skew toward "cute," in the sense of being socially conscious and environmentally caring—and supportive of ecological restoration. The city of Sandy identifies strongly with its river. Although some anti-environmental sentiment was expressed during the process,[298] by and large people in the area appear to have been environmentally engaged, with river clean-ups and nature festivals forming regular parts of Sandy's public life.[299] Salmon statues are prominently displayed in the town's main plaza.

For many advocates, the Sandy River, like the Rogue and Elwha, took on human qualities. To Amy Kober of American Rivers, the issue was about balance and fairness in assessing a river: "I think we're learning how to strike a better balance. There are dams that don't make sense any more, and by removing them, we can have healthy, free-flowing rivers."[300] She said, "We see the Sandy as symbol of our country's changing relationship with rivers. We settled on the banks of rivers so that we could harness their power with dams, but rivers have other powers as well. A free-flowing river has the power to renew our souls."[301] To Keith Jensen, "there is nothing more special than a free-flowing river."[302] The theme of freedom and release was a constant theme. The *Oregonian*'s editorial after the dam breaching was headlined "A River Released to the Wild,"[303] and the *Sandy Post* editorial after the cofferdam notching proclaimed, "Sandy River Runs Free."[304] The historic return of the river's living identity resonates even with scientists. Gordon Grant said, "We borrowed the river's energy for a hundred years. We used it to light our houses, to run our computers. Yesterday, the river took it back."[305]

How should we see the Marmot Dam in reflections of other removals? People on both sides of the debate over dam removal draw connections, hopeful or foreboding, between the Bull Run decommissioning and ongoing high-profile disputes on rivers like the Klamath and Snake.[306] If this one goes down, people thought, maybe these others will as well. PGE disagrees, saying that this situation was unique, that its good faith effort on the Sandy has helped its credibility and streamlined the process of renewing its other licenses on other hydroelectric projects, and noting that many old hydroelectric projects are productive enough to earn their keep, their upgrades and renewed licenses, and not be considered for removal.[307]

Of course, both sides are correct. Removals like Marmot Dam have made and are making dam removal into something approaching a routine option for the end of infrastructural life, through both political learning on the part of the stakeholders and scholarly learning on the part of the scientists. The next time some dam with a big slug of silt behind it is considered for removal, the planners will surely read Gordon Grant's work on flushing out the Sandy. But at the same time, each dam has its own idiosyncrasies. Many older hydro dams are indeed productive and worth relicensing—managers are learning how to mitigate fish passage impacts and how to operate dams in closer tune with the river, as well as how to take them down. The one major lesson of the Sandy, though, is that dam removal doesn't need to be a long and expensive fight. The Bull Run decommissioning, with its amicability and openness, may be a landmark in the move toward a more textured, less politicized, more united politics of dam removal.

Dam removals 2009–2017. Rivers, American (2017): American Rivers Dam Removal Database. figshare. https://doi.org/10.6084/m9.figshare.5234068.v2. Retrieved: 12:37pm, 12/2/2018.

6
What Lies Downstream

Times were changing. Business-as-usual ran headlong into powerful new environmental laws and the ghosts of millions of vanished salmon.
—Burke, "River of Dreams," *High Country News*, 2001

Salmon weren't the only ghosts hanging watchfully over the negotiating tables and press conferences of dam removal. The minds and the hearts of political stakeholders were haunted by the shades of wild rivers and ancient tribal fishers, and of booming industry towns and lakeside summer days.

It's in the nature of restoration to confront ghosts. The pre-Columbian or preindustrial river (or forest, or grassland, or whatever) is gone, and will not reappear any more than a wooly mammoth or a *Tyrannosaurus rex*. But this, to greater or lesser degrees, is just what restorationists are setting out to accomplish. When Elwha activists spoke of pink salmon filling the river from bank to bank, or environmentalists condemned Savage Rapids as the biggest fish killer on the Rogue, the message, sometimes quite explicitly, was that the dam stood in the way of a future that enjoyed the abundance of the past.

But the most powerful ghosts are the ones who built the dams. The communities that had been served by dams and lakes for decades were just as gone, in their ways, as the wild rivers. GPID doesn't really serve farmers anymore. Port Angeles doesn't need hydropower to keep its forest economy afloat. Portland doesn't even have the rail line whose cars were once charged up via Roslyn Lake and Marmot Dam. But as people fought for their dams they saw, in their minds, their towns as they used to be, where rivers ran through turbines and canals without bothering anyone and where a young person might go swimming in the lake on a hot afternoon.

So, to take out dams, we must learn to contend with ghosts, and to somehow put them to rest. But ghosts, by definition, do not die easily. And a ghost that haunts one person may be invisible to another.

In the Meantime

The old saying that you can't step in the same river twice, attributed to the ancient Greek philosopher Heraclitus, is more completely cited as follows: "No man ever steps in the same river twice, for it is not the same river, and he is not the same man." Just as the Rogue, Sandy, and Elwha will never be quite the same as they were before the dams, people who care about them, and people who care about rivers in general, will never be the same as they were before dam removal.

Out on the rivers of America, dams keep falling. In 2016 and 2017, a total of 158 dams were removed—more than in the entire decade of the 1990s.[1] More than a thousand dams have been removed since 1999.[2] The trend will only roll on in the future, as dam removal becomes a more and more normal decision for resource managers and river stakeholders. The dams keep getting older—an estimated 2.1 million dams will be more than fifty years old by 2020.[3] An ODFW biologist on the Rogue once told me that the basin, with its many small dams on tributaries, was a "target-rich environment."[4] For dam removal advocates, nearly any watershed in the country presents a target-rich environment.

Everyone thinks that their situation is special—the people I interviewed insisted that the situation on the Elwha or Sandy or Rogue was a one-off, unrelated and inapplicable to the Klamath or the Snake or to anyplace else. Technically, they were right—not many dams have the Elwha's giant salmon or the Rogue's hobby irrigators. But they were also wrong. Six weeks after the Elwha removal, contractors blew a hole in the foot of 125-foot Condit Dam, and the White Salmon River thundered through. On the White Salmon, just like the Rogue, Sandy, and Elwha, local people wanted to keep their lake, and the owners had to move carefully.[5] But in the end it, too, yielded to the ghosts of tribal fishers and salmon, and the result, enshrined on YouTube by National Geographic, was a river exploding through its concrete wall and draining a ninety-eight-year-old reservoir in about six hours.[6] Steelhead swam above the dam site and spawned the next year. Condit certainly had its own special details, but it shared a lot of political features with Elwha, Savage Rapids, and Marmot Dams. And so do thousands of other dams all across the country.

The experience, technical knowledge, and political comfort created by one dam removal inevitably facilitate others. Many of the stakeholders who took part in these northwestern removals were members of national or regional organizations. Sometimes the effect is direct; soon after the Savage

Rapids removal decision, three other major dams came down on the Rogue. Some attributed this to the Savage Rapids experience.[7] According to Bob Hunter, "thinking on the Rogue [had] changed."[8] But more broadly, the experience of dam removals in the interconnected, globalized twenty-first century will shape the future on rivers across the country and world. Just as scientists and managers use hydrological and ecological data to improve future dam removals, political activists apply political knowledge.[9] No matter the protestations of local stakeholders, one thing does lead to another.

The most basic political lesson has been learned. Although dam removal was seen as exceptional and extreme as recently as 2003, even by salmon advocates,[10] those days are past. Dam removal, as a concept, will never shock people again. It will continue to anger them, though. Out of that anger is born controversy, delay, expense, and personal animus. But no one wants this. Just as Bill Lowry saw in 2003, success depends on fostering receptivity.[11] The fate of rivers, dams, fisheries, and the people who care about them will depend on how skillfully activists approach the situation. But first they need to understand each other, and the ungainly policy subsystem they've begun to build. Here, I offer hypotheses about dam removal politics. It would be great if they were tested by future scholars, and even better if they were applied by future restorationists.

Framing

Hypothesis: The most important frames in dam removal politics are cultural and emotional.

For an introduction to the complexities of dam removal framing, all you have to do is turn on the radio. Song after song, you'll hear about rivers—rivers as fishing holes, rivers as love spots, rivers as youth, rivers as old age, rivers as eternity, rivers as monstrous, rivers as sublime. You'll hear about river infrastructure, too—Chevys at levees, teenage boys taking girls down to the reservoir, dams rising in Colorado, dams falling in Pennsylvania. Rivers make people feel everything there is to feel. Those feelings, expressed through political frames, make politics and policy.

Feelings collided on the Rogue, the Sandy, and the Elwha, as stakeholders looked at the dam, the reservoir, the river, the fish, and felt different things. Of course, this is true of nearly any land issue: forests can be valuable habitat or valuable timber. If everyone felt the same way about their landscapes and resources . . . well, environmental policy scholars wouldn't have much to talk about. But dam removal goes beyond other such issues in two ways.

The first is simply the public nature of rivers. You can buy and possess a forest or a grassland or a farm,[12] but your purchase ends on the riverbank, and the water flowing past it belongs to everyone. The public nature of rivers allows all parties—upstream, downstream, and even beyond the watershed—to see the river as their business. And there is room, in America's political and legal system, for each of them to pursue and promote their vision of the river.

The other frame that distinguishes dam removal was that the environmentalists, fishers, and tribes did not see a threatened landscape in need of protection; rather, they saw a degraded watershed or fishery in need of restoration. As recently as 1990, Friends of the Earth's Jim Baker said, "For all our hard work just to keep the status quo, we have never successfully struck a blow for nature, and forced the removal of a dam that developers never should have built in the first place."[13] Now, during the last three decades, dam removal advocates have been on a rescue mission.

The frame through which the dam removers portrayed their mission was simple and durable—a wild river full of fish. Many people who were still alive in the 1980s and 1990s remembered the enormous surges of fish that had once been the pride of the Pacific Northwest. These fish were culturally charismatic, economically valuable, ecologically powerful, and strongly representative of the region and its rivers. It's hard to imagine a more effective policy image than a returning salmon leaping—crash!—into a dam as it strives to reach its ancient spawning grounds. Dam removal alliances had a variety of reasons for supporting removal efforts—restoring wilderness, improving fishing, carrying out their regulatory and management responsibilities—but no matter their motivation, the frame of the dams as harmful, and of the river as a natural system that should be allowed to return to its natural state, worked. The environmentalists' rhetoric about freeing the river, and the tribe's efforts to return the salmon-based prosperity that had been stolen from them, were different from the agencies' or the fishing groups' less emotional frames, but at bottom they demanded the same thing: a free-flowing river and a restored ecosystem.

Opponents were always slower to establish themselves and publicize their own frames. In each case, dam removal was decided on early—1992 for the Elwha dams, 1994 for Savage Rapids, 1999 for Marmot. Conflict ramped up afterward, as a reaction. This meant that the most important frames in the dam removal debate became those through which anti-removal stakeholders viewed and portrayed the situation. These advocates saw dams' functions and dam removal through two frames—economics and culture. Woven into these was science—how the geology, hydrology, and ecology of the river worked, and what they meant for people.

Economics

For some people, the dams were moneymakers. For others, they provided employment. For still others, they secured a water supply, or real estate values, or recreation. Each of these was at least partly a matter of economics.

Naturally, the central figures in this wing of the issue were the dam owners. You might expect, as I did, that the companies that owned the dams would take a hardheaded look at the costs and benefits of the structure and go forward in a businesslike way, taking leadership of the process by which they would dispose of their property. But in fact GPID, Crown Zellerbach and its successors, and (to a lesser extent) PGE were all torn, not confident of how to proceed. This opened up political space for other players to jump into the fray and lead the way. It would be wise for future dam owners to take a firm stand on the issue, and to do it quickly.

At the start, as it began to dawn on the owners that their dam situation would need some sorting out, all of them planned to keep the dams and the power or irrigation water they provided. But none of these dams provided much economic value. If they had, then the Elwha/Glines Canyon and Bull Run projects would probably have survived the FERC licensing process, and Savage Rapids Dam, filling GPID's full water right, would have nullified environmentalists' initial attacks. But they did not do these things, and did not make enough money to pay for the upgrades and mitigation FERC or OWRD demanded.

Poor economic production is a necessary condition for dam removal.[14] Productive dams, like the Columbia River's Bonneville or The Dalles, make enough money to pay for required maintenance and mitigation.[15] Should a big dam become controversial, political decision-makers will be less likely to support removal—like Slade Gorton on the Snake. The dams on the Elwha, Rogue, and Sandy weren't valuable enough to keep, so after various efforts to find an affordable way out, each dam owner joined (or, in PGE's case, formed) the removal coalition.

Really, this should have been no surprise. Century-old dams become pretty decrepit, and the owners were well aware of Burke's powerful new environmental laws. America takes much better care of our waters now than we did when Thomas Aldwell was throwing together the Elwha Dam. So why, when they looked at their low-production dams and the daunting demands of ecological mitigation, did owners drag their feet? Because it was hard for them to look beyond the status quo, that's why. Economically, the dams had always been productive parts of their operations, and the owners would have preferred for them to remain so. Crown Zellerbach spun out the situation for decades, keeping its dams running on temporary licenses, rather than face up to the demands of licensing. In Savage Rapids, allegiance to the dam—even as a community service and cultural symbol—overcame economic analyses in the eyes of the GPID Board. The board members, too, had enjoyed summer afternoons at Savage Rapids Lake.

But sentimentality could go only so far. The owners were, after all, businesses, and once they took a colder look at their dams, market value makes a pretty simple frame: if the dam becomes expensive and removal is cheaper (or free), then the business's core value—service provision and profit—will compel it to support dam removal. In this sense, dam removal advocates were able, indeed eager, to work within the dam owners' frame and co-opt their opposition. Economic value is inherently negotiable, and it was successfully negotiated to removal in all three cases. Post-removal, the dams' functions were replaced through other means, and PGE, Daishowa,[16] and GPID continued to operate much as they had before.

In the Savage Rapids and Elwha cases, the carrot of public money to replace the dams' function joined the stick of legal action and ended the companies' resistance. The process of gathering federal money exposed an important contrast between frames: who should be responsible for the end of a dam's life. Again, this broke down into those who saw the matter as one of private property (who should tell a dam owner what to do with their own dam?) versus those who saw it as a matter of public property (who were dam owners to degrade the public's rivers?).

To dam defenders, if the government (and the environmentalists) wanted to remove the dam, they should have to pay for it.[17] Even cute old PGE openly considered abandoning Marmot Dam—partly in order to preserve its role in fish management, but the utility was naturally aware of the money that it could save by doing this. On the other hand, some environmentalists felt that dam owners should take care of their dams just as car owners are not allowed to leave their clapped-out sedans on the highway. They were happy to have the federal government pay for removal, but the government cannot be relied upon to pay for big dam removals whenever they occur. Federal appropriations will remain a possibility for big removal projects, but will not be easy to acquire, and there will probably be no reprise of the federal stimulus that helped put Elwha and Savage Rapids over the top. A federal law demanding that old dams be refurbished or removed by their owners is not going to happen in the foreseeable future, so the undefined status quo is likely to endure. Financial responsibility for dam removal will remain a source of difficulty, as it is for a lot of ecological restoration projects.[18]

Future funding will probably have to rely on state-level action, public and private grants, and the willingness of dam owners to take out their own older dams, perhaps as mitigation for other actions or as a dramatic public relations move. Nothing establishes a company's environmental values like exploding concrete. One potentially attractive option for funding future removals, demonstrated on the Sandy River, is to let the dam operate a few more years after the removal agreement and fund its own removal. This would have the advantage of giving local people a few more years on the lake, as well.

The economic issue that created the most fear was the potential destruction of business. Some dam removal opponents framed the Savage Rapids and Elwha removals as threatening the existence of the paper mill or of the irrigation district, and the people who depended on them for their livelihoods.[19] An alarming prospect, but the worst was never likely to happen. Politically, a dam removal that threw a lot of people out of work would be an absolute nonstarter, unlikely to find support from lawmakers at any level. Removal advocates knew this, and they framed dam removal as a "win-win" scenario that would boost the local economy as well as restore the environment. They argued that dam removal would help local employment in both the short term, through (de)construction jobs, and the long term, as larger runs of fish would be pursued by larger runs of fly-fishing tourists, though these benefits were somewhat diffuse and uncertain. The phrase "win-win" was used in each case, disrupting the traditional anti-environmentalist formulation of fish versus jobs or rivers versus jobs.

The gnarlier economic problem was the dams' ancillary impacts. As the dams became part of their landscapes, other people and businesses relied on them as if they were permanent features. Marmot Dam was not built to keep hatchery fish downstream and support the local angling economy, but this was what happened, and it became one of the toughest issues stakeholders faced. The removal's repercussions, especially on fly-fishing, are still playing out. The Elwha dams' role as settling basins that provided water for Port Angeles, and the silt that would mess this up during removal, became a huge problem; the most expensive part of the Elwha restoration project, $79 million, was building Port Angeles's new water treatment facilities.[20] Without guaranteed clean water, the town of Port Angeles would not have accepted any dam removal plan, and the Elwha Act would never have passed into law. On Savage Rapids, some of the early resistance to dam removal came from small-business people who benefited from recreation at Savage Rapids Lake. These interests had very little formal standing—inn owners could not reasonably have expected a privately owned dam to guarantee stable conditions forever—but their grievances attracted sympathy, and they extended, expanded, and inflamed the debate. They could, perhaps, have made some political progress over a potential decline in the value of their real estate—this has been a concern elsewhere.[21] It's not clear why they didn't.

Science

Everyone knew that it was necessary to understand the dam, the river, and the fish through the technical fields of ecology, hydrology, and engineering. To echo Vogel's insightful point, the public cannot effectively add much to technical decisions. However, rather than bowing to science and meekly accepting the word of experts, the stakeholders seized it as one more political stick with which to beat their political opponents.[22] We all take biology classes in high school, but most of us don't cover "combat biology" on the way to the AP test. But in the calculus of dam removal science, ecology plus politics equals fury.

Removal advocates saw science as a powerful weapon. Their goals were supported by and founded on the findings of agency, tribal, and academic researchers. This was countered by consultants hired by GPID and, on the Elwha, by consultants for the various dam owners and for REAL. Some pro-removal advocates were skeptical of these consultants,[23] and suspected that their science was not a disinterested search for truth but a conscious effort to get results that supported their clients' goal of keeping the dam.

To be fair, rivers are complex systems, so it was easy for people to focus on one aspect of the river and craft believable explanations for why their perspective was correct and opposing science was insufficient. The public doesn't have much technical training, so ideas like REAL's scheme for fish passage over the Elwha dams could feel quite reasonable, especially to a person with a preexisting preference for keeping the dam. On the Rogue, there was even a high school student who pieced together his own plan for how passage might work at Savage Rapids Dam and had his ideas seriously considered by some adult stakeholders.[24] In the Marmot removal, PGE invested in science and gained respect from other stakeholders for it; as a result, this sort of technical confusion was mostly avoided on the Sandy.

In each of these removals, and probably in every major dam removal that will ever be, the silt behind the dams presented a massive problem. On the Sandy, PGE's emphasis on good science made this into a stressful hydrological issue but not a political problem. Not so on the Elwha and Rogue. REAL looked at the gigantic loads of silt behind the Elwha dams and confidently predicted that there would be flooding and failure.[25] On the Rogue, Dennis Becklin was so worried about contaminants in the silt that he personally paid for a study on it. Even after the Savage Rapids removal, a local conspiracy theorist stoked public fear by claiming that there were dangerous metals in the silt.[26] All professional studies indicated that the Savage Rapids silt was pretty clean, and subsequent research has confirmed that it hasn't contaminated the ecosystem—the river's invertebrates, for example, bounced back swiftly.[27] But the idea of poison lurking under the water scared people, and it was easy for fear to outweigh scientific studies.

A nastier problem, on the Sandy and the Elwha, was how to deal with hatcheries.[28] Hatcheries have long played a central part in managing Pacific salmon. Hatchery fish, at least in some places, can be managed to serve various goals—fishing in the short term, wild native runs in the long term. But how these goals should be balanced, and what this balance should mean for decisions like the use of stocks originating in other rivers, the fishes' management regime in the hatchery, the timing and location of their release into the river, and the numbers in which they are released are all live issues. For some people, no hatchery would be acceptable—rivers should be managed only with wild fish, which would presumably thrive in their ancestral stream and perhaps lead to better restoration outcomes, but over a longer time period. Groups on both sides will pull out of deals and go to court over these questions.

The hatchery question came down to how people saw restoration. How wild did the fish need to be? A hatchery fish is kind of feral, not quite wild, but not quite tame—they're not farmed fish, after all. So are they acceptable for restoration purposes? Would it be enough to simply restore the size of the fish population, or would it be necessary for the restored fishery to be evolutionarily consistent and genetically pure? Anglers and, on the Elwha, the tribe, wanted a fishable stream, in the short term. Some of the environmentalists, whose core value was their own vision of environmental quality, disagreed. Both sides, of course, were sure that their science was best. But although this question complicated the removal, it didn't stop it—all fishing interests wanted the dam out and were willing to wait on the hatchery issue. Restoration is often beset by such controversies, as definitions and goals can be similar enough for people to agree on the overall project, but not on the definition of ultimate success.[29] Hatcheries' role in western rivers will undoubtedly remain a thorny problem for many years.

Fishing transcends all sorts of sociopolitical boundaries, and rural conservatives who might not otherwise have much in common with urban environmentalists often like to fish. Pretty much everyone framed fish restoration as positive and important—whatever happened with the dam, they all said, we ought to help the fish. The terms of the debate were such that a stakeholder would have lost some face by admitting that they didn't care if the fish lived or died. For the dam removal advocates, of course, salmon restoration was a core value, their reason for being involved in the issue at all. On the Sandy, the universal desire for a stronger fishery was a given, and the prospect of healthier salmon populations compelled skeptical anglers to agree to removal despite the management problems they knew would come later. On the Rogue and Elwha, removal opponents asserted that they, not the environmental groups, were the ones who wanted the best for the fish—they just felt that it was best to achieve this goal with the dams in place. GPID's Dennis Becklin board, the Elwha paper companies, and REAL all created and promoted their own plans for getting salmon past the dam—a win-win, to them.

But while everyone agreed that lower fish populations were a problem, no one agreed about who was to blame for it. It was common for dam defenders to point at foreign fishing fleets, marine mammals, and, in some cases, gillnets. These claims were reasonable enough—there is no doubt that fishing, on the open sea or in the river, impacts salmon populations, or that sea lions eat fish—but these factors were not well documented and therefore made a difficult frame for advocates to promote. To dam removers, the dams were "fish killers" and stood as the most specific and controllable factors harming the fish. But in the end, the clash over responsibility didn't much matter; having publicly committed themselves to restoring the salmon, pro-dam advocates were forced to argue against the many scientists who had concluded that removal was necessary for restoration. In the case of agency scientists, these conclusions directly affected the legal status of the dam, the river, and the fish. This was a battle that dam defenders could not win.

The science of deciding for dam removal is different from the science of understanding its effects.[30] Those effects remain largely uncertain even after years of study and millions of research dollars. The big question, of course, is whether dam removal helped restore the ecosystem. On well-monitored Elwha Dam (and also on the small and simple Little Sandy), dam removal seems to be living up to expectations, and salmon and steelhead have returned to their ancestral spawning grounds. On Savage Rapids and Marmot, though indications are good, the quality of the fish ladders was never measured, so there is no baseline from which to measure those removals' effects. This is a common problem for northwestern dam removals.[31] Do more fish swim upstream now than before the dam came down? Probably. It is likely that most removals have benefited fish by easing access to upstream habitat and restoring natural material flows and temperatures, but it would be better to have a firmer basis for evaluation. Future projects should build in funds for long-term monitoring. This would not only help evaluate the removal, it would also inform future restoration decisions elsewhere. As James Lichatowich points out, this would demand a cultural shift, in management agencies and in society as a whole,[32] but the growth of dam removal is one example of how such cultural shifts are possible, and happening.

Culture

Everyone loves their local lake, whether it was formed naturally, by geology, or technologically, by engineers. For local communities, the dams were central to the social and recreational landscape. This frame grew from their cultural preferences. When people who lived near Roslyn or Aldwell or Savage Rapids Lakes looked at the reservoir, they saw a natural feature around which they had spent joyous summer afternoons with their parents and with their children. The names of anti-removal pressure groups demonstrate this: the Keeping Water in the Lake Committee, Rescue Elwha Area Lakes, the Association to Save Savage Rapids Dams and Lake. This became the most difficult political problem in dam removal.

It's important to remember that the lake-using public had no legal standing—people are not entitled to views of an impoundment any more than they are to views of grain silos or train stations. But the impoundments felt like natural lakes, and many people felt the same way about the lakes that Sierra Club members feel about wild forests and mountains. This meant that thousands of local people wanted to keep the lake, massively broadening and strengthening the anti-removal coalition. This recreational relationship, which didn't weigh how much water the dams diverted or how much power they made, separated the public from the question of the dam's operations and its environmental or economic impacts. As Bob Hunter pointed out, a dam's operational and structural lives are not the same thing.[33] A dam can stand and seem the same as ever while no longer functioning effectively. So when people fought to keep the dam, they weren't fighting to keep the same dam as the owners were.

Another fear was over what the lake site would look like without the lake. If a beloved swimming hole turns into a scar on the landscape, a community may be skeptical the next time someone suggests a restoration project.[34] People feared that their beloved blue lake would become an ugly mud flat.[35] This fear was somewhat irrational—landscapes are dynamic, and mud flats eventually sprout into forests—but the image of a mucky wasteland intensified locals' defense of their old lake. This has been true in a variety of places, from Wisconsin to Catalonia.[36] It would be wise for future restorationists to show skeptics photographs of reblooming riverbanks from other dam removals when considering a new one. And it would be wise for anyone involved in restoration to use good science to give themselves a better chance of political success, to satisfy people who will judge the project with their eyes and their hearts, as well as ecological success.

For environmentalists, the emotionally resonant frame of the impoundment as a beautiful lake with happy families swimming and fishing was very difficult to combat. Dam removal advocates found themselves opposing "little children" and "the images that tug at our hearts." Similar situations are to be found across the country; there are over a million artificial lakes and ponds in the American West alone.[37] In the absence of a dam, flat water can be very difficult to access. If people in Grants Pass wish to water-ski now, they must drive an hour to Lost Creek Lake.[38] Many states have few natural lakes, or none.

On a subtler note—lake scenery (and in Grants Pass, the verdant irrigated landscape reaching out along the canals) matched community members' sense of what their environment should look like. This clashed directly with removal advocates' belief in restoration. To dam defenders, removal would blight the landscape and return it to the bad old days when Grants Pass was "the brown desert."[39] Just as removal advocates felt that they were rescuing the river from the dam, dam advocates believed that the dam had redeemed the wild river. As Doremus and Tarlock found in similar rural communities in the nearby Klamath basin, people "can be just as emotionally attached to the water filling an arrow-straight irrigation ditch as to water swiftly flowing from mountains to sea."[40] For people who had prospered through Marc Reisner's go-go years, the Savage Rapids, Elwha, and Marmot dams were guarantors of progress and prosperity. This was a core value, central to people's worldviews. Beauty is classically in the eye of the beholder, and as such is not subject to negotiation. Natural resource lawyer James Buchal, who represented GPID in the 1990s, had a photograph of Savage Rapids Dam up on his office wall as late as 2011.[41] A local historian documenting the Savage Rapids removal wrote two books entitled *The Death of Savage Rapids Dam*.[42] On each river, the dams and their infrastructure were lauded as historic monuments, testimony to the labor and ingenuity of the people who built them in an earlier America.[43] It was hard for local people to imagine that others didn't see the dams that way.

In the wake of disbelief came conspiracy theories. On the Rogue, some could not believe that the dam removal issue was really about the river and the fish. It seemed more plausible that the United Nations was engineering the dam removal—or maybe it was the British royal family.[44] Fear of the UN flared on the Olympic Peninsula as well.[45] Dam removals were seen as part of a campaign to return the landscape to wilderness by a pagan earth religion.[46] Even on the more politically amicable Sandy, people suspected the shadowy hand of the city of Portland, reaching greedily up Route 26.[47] Dam removal's conspiracy theories, wherein ordinary small-town dam advocates pitted themselves against wicked, immensely powerful opponents, created something of a hero complex: Dennis Becklin compared himself to the famous college student who stood in the way of tanks in Tiananmen Square,[48] and so did some dam defenders on the Elwha.[49] Dam savers cast themselves in the traditional political role of environmentalists—scrappy underdogs struggling to save beloved landscapes from destruction.

All this fit into a larger antienvironmentalist narrative that has been strong in the rural West for many decades—that environmental activists really care about controlling regular people, that there is more to it than a simple desire to preserve nature. This sort of conspiracist mind-set has grown increasingly strong in the American right-wing in recent decades.[50] These conspiracy theories have little factual basis, but they were, and are, earnestly held and passionately expressed. Conspiracy theories were a thorny challenge for removal advocates, one that by its nature could not be overcome through rational arguments. Even offers of financial compensation would probably have riled conspiracists that much more—their narrative includes deep-pocketed environmental backers and reckless government spending. The phenomenon of a "devil shift," where opponents are harshly vilified and their power inflated, is common in coalition politics.[51] In the Northwest, this had already happened with the spotted owl wars.

The spotted owl reshaped environmental politics in the Northwest, and perhaps in the United States, for the foreseeable future.[52] It hovers over landscape and species questions as the symbol of environmental conflict. The owl had two primary effects on these dam removals. The first was to embitter the conflict. Communities in rural Washington and Oregon had seen the suffering of the owl wars, which made some people hate and fear environmentalists and federal agencies no matter what. The owl experience boosted conspiracy theories and fueled popular uprisings that halted the progress of dam removal. At the same time, though, the fearsome memory of the owl wars probably pushed some stakeholders toward a negotiated solution. They did not want their rivers to be shaped by a sweeping decision from the Ninth Circuit. As many people noted, a court case is a blunt instrument, one that creates defeat and resentment. Politicians were eager to offer their help in order to avoid this sort of conflict. Al Swift, John Kitzhaber, and Slade Gorton all strove to ensure a negotiated solution rather than risk a devastating legal ruling. A federal judge ordered the Savage Rapids stakeholders into mediation rather than allow litigation to create winners and losers. No one wanted to be responsible for creating the next spotted owl.

Coalition Dynamics

Hypothesis: Stakeholders must form mega-coalitions in order to win political backing, raise money, and stave off opposition.

Dam removals are like the battlefield of Thermopylae,[53] where a small but vigorous force can fight off an army. Without the political platoons of ASS and the Three Rivers Watershed Council to rally the community, the Savage Rapids Dam Act might have passed through Congress in 1994, been funded through Senator Hatfield, and enabled dam removal by, say, 1998. REAL, a small group that raised only a few thousand dollars,[54] added years to the life of the Elwha dams—without REAL, Slade Gorton wouldn't have had much political justification for opposing dam removal. In 2002, it would have been easy for some stakeholders to withdraw from the Bull Run working group and for negotiations to collapse, as they had two years before. Someone can always say no. This sort of resistance can make it politically impossible to gain political approval, and funding. It became necessary for every powerful stakeholder to join in support of dam removal and to approach decision-makers as a comprehensive mega-coalition, in which it was imperative to understand not only the law but also one another.

Despite the stark, intense pressures that form mega-coalitions, they are combustible and difficult to hold together. In each case, the presence of steady and dedicated players who commanded the respect of other stakeholders was crucial: Julie Keil, Bob Hunter, and Orville Campbell, among others, are widely credited for their demeanors and interpersonal skills in working with diverse interests. These personalities likely made the difference between a successful mega-coalition and a failed negotiation. Mega-coalitions are liable to rupture post-removal, as they did over hatchery fish on the Elwha and Sandy, but while they hold together—and in each case they did hold, through the years between the decision and the actual removal—they are politically unbeatable for the simple reason that no one is left to beat them.

At the coalitions' core sat the stakeholders that began the fight to remove the dam. Salmon anglers and environmentalists and, on the Elwha, native tribes, had always been against the dams and deplored their effects on rivers. As American society moved toward environmentalism and a more receptive attitude toward dam removal, and as native tribes gained a stronger political voice, these stakeholders gathered strength and created a critical community[55] in the Northwest. This societal transition was eventually reflected in resource and land agencies, as their understanding of their missions, the values of the personnel who carried out those missions, and sometimes the laws that defined agency missions evolved in the direction of ecological restoration. Even the Bureau of Reclamation, the environmental villain in more than one popular book,[56] worked to facilitate dam removal on both the Rogue and the Elwha.

The common direction of agencies, environmental and fishing groups, and (on the Elwha) the tribe made for advocacy coalitions that worked effectively despite—indeed, because of—their diverse perspectives and functions. Environmental advocates, of course, have no power to order a dam removal, but they were able to stimulate action from the agencies, not least by making it clear that they would sue to enforce laws like the Endangered Species Act. They were also able to be proactive in the face of challenges—the formation of the CAG, which marked the beginning of the end for the Elwha dams, was the sort of creative innovation that is not as likely to be suggested by a resource agency. Problems came when the coalitions had to combine with local stakeholders whose values clashed with their own. But local people were what made the difference between forming a successful mega-coalition or not.

Every landscape issue begins locally, with the problem rooted in some specific place, and ends locally, with the problem being addressed (or not) in that same place. This means that local people are likely to play an important role—they're the ones who live with the river and the lake, and they have an obvious claim and connection to it that is quite different from that of the park or river's nationwide or statewide constituency. But aside from a certain moral authority, local people and their city- or county-level representatives may not have much actual power over these resources. As Brian Winter observed, a national park belongs to all Americans, and is not managed by or for the people who happen to live nearby.[57] The same is true of rivers, which are owned by the state. Their waters are used, but not fully possessed, by the interests along their banks. The poorly defined role of local communities is a major problem in American ecological politics.

Despite their political disadvantages, local people did have the power to raise a ruckus, to attract political allies who believe in small government and, through these things, to delay and perhaps veto dam removal. This meant that it behooved the dam removal coalition to establish its local credibility. On the Elwha, the creation of Friends of the Elwha and the activism of Dick Goin, and on the Rogue, the formation of Citizens for Responsible Irrigation and the voice of fishing professional Dave Strahan, born and bred in Grants Pass, showed that the removal was not simply foisted on the community from the outside.[58] Sandy's close proximity to Portland meant that PGE was something of a local community member itself, and the gap between the town and the company was easier to bridge.

The most difficult interest group to wrangle was the conspiracy theorists. Conspiracists were present in all three removals.[59] Dam removers could help replace the dams' production, and express sympathy about lake recreation, but they could not reasonably agree that yes, the UN was using dam removal to subjugate the American West. Conspiracy theories like this reflect core values, essential expressions of how their believers understand the world and its workings. The mega-coalition had no room for these people—they had to be, and were, politically neutralized and excluded.

In the Advocacy Coalition Framework sense, policies indicate belief—people make the policy because they believe in its goals—but the policies governing dams and rivers are layered in such a way as to reflect many beliefs. Agency missions, the FERC relicensing process, and even the Endangered Species Act serve many constituencies. Environmental policies tend to be relatively new and are challenging to interpret in the context of dam removal. While the most powerful and absolute policies—FERC relicensing and the Endangered Species Act—played important roles in guiding dam removal advocates, even they did not specifically force removal.

Until the creation of some defining federal law, dam removal will continue to be everybody's business.

The clearest-cut policy for dam removal is FERC relicensing, especially after the 1986 Electric Consumers Protection Act, which enshrined dam removers' beliefs in the licensing process. FERC licensing presents a clear opportunity for removal proponents to inject themselves into the future of a dam. It's no surprise that the new era of dam removal began with the FERC-driven removal of Maine's Edwards Dam. But the way it actually works is unpredictable—each dam is different, and a lot can happen across the fifty years of a hydropower license. Consider the idiosyncrasies of the FERC process as it played on the Elwha and the Sandy. On the Elwha, it tied itself into a snarled jurisdictional knot, and the lower dam never was licensed. The question is still unresolved, having been truncated by the Elwha Act. The Bull Run removal was a voluntary license surrender by PGE, not an environmentalist mission. The role of the FERC licensing process in dam removal is what the stakeholders, and the dams, make of it.

The Endangered Species Act drives a lot of environmental politics, but was only a contributor in these cases. All three removals involved runs of endangered salmonids, but only on the Sandy was the listing necessary to trigger removal (though PGE's proprietary calculations, the actual basis for the decision, make it hard to say this with total certainty). The ESA was a strong motivating factor for the Savage Rapids removal, but given the presence of the unresolved water right issue, it may not have been necessary. The removal effort was well under way, with good chances of success, before any fish in the Rogue or the Elwha was federally listed.

The fluid nature of dam removal politics and policy means that in these cases we can see Sabatier and Jenkins-Smith's policy subsystem under construction.[60] The years between the beginning of the Savage Rapids issue in the early 1980s and the end of the Elwha removal in 2014—well over the ACF's suggestion of a decade—saw a massive shift in the way dam removal was perceived and who would be willing to support it. As Margaret Bowman said, removals "started as a super wacky weird idea that everyone laughed at,"[61] but they ended as the subject of broad if begrudging consensus. However, these decades have not nearly been sufficient to form a stable, predictable policy subsystem, at least in the case of large dams. Advocacy coalitions are unstable; fishers, environmentalists, and tribes coalesce to push for dam removal, then cleave asunder over hatcheries. In the anti-removal coalition, dam owners were quite easily split off from their culturally motivated allies. The role of science is crucial, as the ACF suggests, but it is continuously developing. The endangered salmonids that drive much of northwestern river management have for the most part been listed only since the 1990s, and as noted above, most of the dam removals that have occurred have not been monitored well enough to define their effects or effectiveness. Nonetheless, we can assemble a cast of characters that will take part in nearly all dam removal negotiations: dam owners, environmental groups, fishing groups, state water agencies, federal wildlife and water agencies, and (unless the dam is very small or remote) local lake users. If they are proactive and fortunate, they may coalesce into a permanent mega-coalition that could take out (or re-operate, or mitigate for) future dams before things get out of hand. But they need to find a venue in which to do it.

Venues

Hypothesis: Dam removal conflicts end when they reach a venue that can accommodate everyone.

Dam removals are guided by the policies and actors governing water, energy, and species—three complex and heavily layered political arenas. Moreover, dams' public cultural roles inspire citizens to protest against removal and to bring their grievances to sympathetic politicians like Brady Adams or Slade Gorton. In the case of Savage Rapids, political venues included the GPID Board, the Oregon water right adjudication process, the governor's task force, federal court (in the SONCC takings case), the Oregon legislature, and the federal legislature, with its subsequent appropriations process, as well as some smaller and more personal legal suits. The removal was also, of course, hotly debated in the court of public opinion, through petitions, public meetings, op-eds, and letters to the editor. The Elwha case also moved through a broad and diverse array of venues, including tribal treaties and their associated politics, though with less litigation and a much smaller role for the State of Washington than Oregon had in Savage Rapids. So there are a multiplicity of political venues available,[62] and dam removal activists use them all.

For the dam removal coalition, the biggest venue-shopping challenges come at the beginning and the end—finding a place to begin the dam removal process, and then one to end it (i.e., pay for it). For aspiring dam removers, there are not many reliable spots to set their political lever, and their options change depending on the specifics of their targeted dam. The FERC process is the clearest option, but there aren't that many hydroelectric dams. On Savage Rapids, the Oregon water right system created the necessary opening but this, again, doesn't apply to many dams. Future advocates might push for dam removal as mitigation, or using the Endangered Species Act, or perhaps, in some places, under the terms of tribal treaties, but there is no reliable venue to which they can go. Each of these cases demanded creative thinking to get off the ground at all. This instability will continue to challenge dam removal advocates for the foreseeable future.

Advocates hoping to save their dams tended to focus on state-level venues. This was productive in the case of Savage Rapids, where Brady Adams and Bob Repine wielded some power over the Oregon Water Resources Department, but futile in the case of the Elwha. There was very little role for Olympia in the Elwha, particularly as no state water right was being adjudicated, but REAL hoped to gain resources and legitimacy there anyway. As noted by the *Peninsula Daily News,* REAL's appeal to the Washington legislature was something of a puzzling political decision, as any state effort to manage the river the way REAL wanted would have to operate through the same federal agencies that had already rejected its ideas.[63] State legislatures don't have the power to waive federal laws. REAL presumably understood this, but a state law, even one as unworkable as theirs would have been, would have had some symbolic weight and expanded the anti-removal coalition. As partisans of local resource control, REAL members probably saw state action as more legitimate than federal action. They also had better access to power through local representatives like Jim Buck than they did through Senator Gorton or Representative Dicks. It was a bit like the man who drops his keys in the park but looks for them under the street lamp because that's where the light is. On the Sandy, although some local representatives did attend meetings and keep abreast of the issue, any effort by them to stop dam removal would have run into pro-removal Governor Kitzhaber.[64] By the time Kitzhaber left office in 2001, PGE was clearly open to preserving the lake if possible, and there was no need for lake defenders to seek help in Salem.

The dam defenders who looked for salvation in Olympia or Salem didn't seriously consider the costs of victory. Would state governments have chosen to take on the costs of operating and upgrading the dams? Most state legislators don't readily throw around this kind of money. A state might contribute to dam removal, or fund small ones, but would probably not spend the tens of millions of dollars it took to remove these dams, let alone to keep them and pay for expensive upgrades. It might conceivably waive some regulations to make dam retention cheaper, but this would have to be very artfully done to avoid a bad precedent, or an environmental lawsuit. Moving the issue to higher-level venues, be they state or federal, unleashed forces beyond locals' control. The closest the Savage Rapids defenders came to success was Senator Brady Adams' bills, but not only did Adams run into Governor Kitzhaber, he also ran into state-wide irrigation interests that wouldn't approve of such sweeping precedent being set on behalf of a little nonagricultural district.

This loss of power was that much greater when the issue went to Washington, DC—now the dams' fates were tied up with such national and even global issues as the Gingrich revolution and the war on terror. Moving the conflict to Congress meant that decision-makers were account-able to all stakeholders and therefore driven to achieve a balanced solu-tion—Oregon's delegation represents all Oregonians, irrigators, anglers, and environmentalists alike. For the Elwha and Rogue, DC was the only place to gather enough money to remove the dams and make everyone else more or less whole. It was worth sacrificing control for that.

The pro-removal coalitions on the Rogue or the Elwha could have taken a simpler, less tortuous path to defeating their opponents: litigation. Had they pushed their issue in the courts, using the Endangered Species Act or the FERC jurisdiction process, they probably would have won. This has been the model for success in other times and places; witness the Boldt Decision, or the spotted owl wars. But while removal advocates did file suits in both cases, in both cases they abandoned them. The most important reason was that, had they won in this sort of adversarial venue, their opponents—GPID, the paper companies, dam savers from the local communities—would have had no interest in helping lobby for federal dam removal money. Prying money out of Washington, DC, would not be pos-sible without a mega-coalition. They might, just possibly, have been able to sue and get a ruling that forced the dam owner to pay for removal—but probably not. Regardless, lawsuits would surely have had a chilling effect on inter-stakeholder relations in the Rogue or Elwha regions for the fore-seeable future. If WaterWatch wanted a sustainable working relationship with the people of Grants Pass, it would be necessary to conclude the issue in a collaborative setting and satisfy everyone as much as possible.

In each case, stakeholders eventually created original, inclusive venues in which to work out their issues. The Bull Run working group facilitated by Deb Nudelman was one such, and so was the mediated ne-gotiation that resulted in the Savage Rapids consent decree. It is difficult to form these venues—the Savage Rapids Task Force, RVCOG facilitation, and PGE's first working group all failed—but eventually, each dam removal reached a successful point, entering a new venue where a mega-coalition could take shape. A certain amount of pressure—the threat of a lawsuit or an abandoned dam—was necessary to coax everyone to work together, but in the end, it did prove effective. These groups were somewhat corporatist, creating conditions where the various interests could resolve the situation together, relatively insulated from public scrutiny and politicking. The creation of the CAG in Port Angeles was a key step toward forging a mega-coalition as well, but it produced only information and recommendations. The CAG's main contribution was to create a political space in which something credibly resembling the local community's opinion could form, be embraced by the pro-removal coalition, and be presented to Slade Gorton, Norm Dicks, and their fellow appropriators.

The creation of a permanent venue in which the mega-coalition could work—a watershed council, or something like it—is perhaps the most promising development in the modern-day River Republic. The power and potential embodied in watershed councils vary a lot from situation to situation, of course, but they can, at least, be a forum for sharing information, fostering discussion, and building relationships and trust—things that were lacking on the Rogue and Elwha. Ideally, a watershed council would incorporate the local community, which would likely have little formal claim to a dam or reservoir (aside from connections to municipal water supply) but, as we have seen, a great deal of sociocultural connection to and political energy for it. Such a body would not just help incorporate local views and allow the community to learn from other stakeholders, it could also facilitate citizen-scientists' monitoring and other ground-level engagement with the watershed. As many others have found, community engagement and monitoring are important components in a successful restoration project.[65] And indeed, a main purpose of the venues created in these dam removals was to incorporate local communities.

To do this, though, dam removers had to face hostile opponents and marginalize some anti-removal zealots. These advocates' claim to represent their communities was the source of their political power. While the environmental impact statement process offers the public a chance to comment, some local people felt that they had been ignored and silenced. As Brady Adams said, for many people "it's not that they necessarily have to express themselves, but people have to be able to feel that they have the ability to express themselves."[66] The likes of REAL and the Three Rivers Watershed Council were able to wave this flag for some years, and there is no doubt that they did express the feelings of many local people. But when it came down to it, these groups were only selected by, and beholden to, their members; they did not have the credibility to gain a seat at the final table. But their ability to exercise, to inspire, and to enrage enough people from the community, and to gain public attention, permanently altered the terms of their dam removal debates. One reason that the Marmot removal process was so much smoother than others was PGE's strenuous efforts to work with the Sandy-area community. The final Savage Rapids and Elwha settlements might not have included their generous terms for Port Angeles and Grants Pass if not for the work of the dam savers.

Each case left major policy questions unanswered. Would the State of Oregon or the federal government have forced the removal of Savage Rapids Dam because of the water right, or the coho? If the state had not ordered the removal, and GPID had collapsed under the weight of federal fines or a reduced water right, whose responsibility would the dam have been, and would it have been removed at all? After the Elwha Act, it is still uncertain whether FERC may license a preexisting dam in a national park.[67] It was pretty clear that Marmot Dam could have been abandoned by PGE, but would John Esler's "cement waterfall"[68] have been maintained or operated by anyone? Who would have been liable in the event of a future dam failure? In each case, stakeholders avoided these questions through negotiated resolutions. In the Kingdon sense,[69] dam removal's problem and politics streams flow ahead of a meandering and inconsistent policy stream. The policy subsystem that governs dam removal will not be fully formed until such questions are resolved.

The River Flows On

This book has focused on Pacific salmon in the Northwest, and of course, those fish and that region are remarkable in many ways. But this book could just as easily have been about Atlantic salmon in Maine, or bass in Wisconsin. The history, politics, and ecology of many places are as unique and meaningful as those in Washington and Oregon. The degradation of American rivers by dams, and the restoration of those rivers by dam removal, is a national story. Indeed, it is an international one, as the politics of dam removal have reared up in France,[70] in Spain,[71] in Sweden,[72] in Tasmania,[73] and will surely continue throughout and beyond the industrialized (which is to say, dammed-up) world. And as the developing world looks to dam up its rivers, stakeholders from the Mekong to the Amazon may look at the failures, successes, and lessons learned in the United States and perhaps shape their own rivers, and their own politics, a little differently.

For river stakeholders are stuck with each other. As long as water flows into irrigation ditches and salmon return from the sea, competing stakeholders will have to deal with each other to manage their shared resource. The age when dams were built with minimal consideration for ecology has passed, the environmental explosion of the 1960s and 1970s has passed as well, and in the River Republic[74] stakeholders are adjusting to a more complicated political era. In twenty-first-century America, it is very difficult for one political antagonist to conclusively defeat another, and if they do, they'll find it hard to work with an enemy when the next river issue arises.

The most important difference between the efficient, relatively amicable Marmot removal and the tortuous battles of Savage Rapids and Elwha was that the Sandy community didn't rally around Marmot Dam with the fury that characterized the other removals. The difference may have been PGE's proactive, conciliatory approach,[75] or it may have been the regional culture, or it may have been a matter of there being no Dennis Becklins or Marv Chastains in Sandy—it is difficult to prove the negative. But in each case, the dams' actual functions were not as politically difficult as the public's relationship to the landscape the dams created. Researchers have been finding these sorts of frames and conflicts across the nation and world—people love and identify with their dammed landscapes.[76] It would be interesting to see studies that looked specifically at dams' unintended functions—flat-water recreation, fish management, lake-like scenery—and see the history of how local communities' relationship to the watershed has grown around its dam.

Dam removal advocates eventually learned that when other interest groups were powerful enough to stop removal, they needed to incorporate former opponents in their coalitions. This did not require friendship, but it was an early move toward an ongoing working relationship. Mega-coalitions may break apart upon the completion of the dam removal project, but at the same time, the connections and relationships formed in the course of the removal negotiation can have lasting effects on the watershed. Trust, a quality that is rare and crucial in land politics, may be built in these ways.[77] All dam removal stakeholders are likely to have continuing interests in the health and management of the watershed. On each river, many of the same organizations and individuals continue to work together on fish and water questions. On August 1, 2012, three years after the removal of Savage Rapids Dam, I was surprised to see Bob Hunter, the face of dam removal, stride into the GPID office for a friendly discussion of some ongoing issues in the Middle Rogue Valley.

In each case, stakeholders sought and eventually found a "win-win" solution. To do this, given the expense of dam removal and the importance of maintaining services for demanding stakeholders post-removal, it was necessary for everyone to work in unison and craft a plan that they all could support. This demanded the creation of new venues, such as the CAG and the Bull Run working group. On the Rogue and Elwha, this eventually forced moves to the federal level, which was the only venue able to accommodate all stakeholders and fund massive restoration projects that included water treatment facilities, pumping plants, and hatcheries, as well as dam removal. PGE was able to contain the issue by funding the project itself, partly by running the dam for an additional five years. For large dams with complex uses, it is likely that such an inclusive, resource-rich venue will be necessary in order for restoration to proceed.

A major concern is that, after dam removal, people will figure that the job is done now—the dam is gone, the fish will come back, hurrah. If this becomes the case, then just as hatcheries were a techno-utopian solution a century ago,[78] so dam removal will be in the present. The ecological and social complexity of salmon and rivers demands ongoing monitoring and adaptive management.

Fortunately, this sort of broad engagement is growing. It is becoming increasingly apparent that rivers are social and ecological systems at the same time.[79] Multi-stakeholder basin-scale management is the future, and the present, for many American rivers. Watershed groups are no guarantor of success—often they're poor, sometimes they fail—but it is hard to successfully handle complex river problems without one. A well-run watershed council, like the one that has emerged on the Sandy, in a strong political framework essentially maintains and solidifies the mega-coalition, and its successful operation may prevent future controversies from becoming controversies at all.

In the decades since the Savage Rapids, Marmot, and Elwha Dams were built, land and water use were rethought by every industry and in every landscape. The environmental movement successfully redefined the value of wilderness, nature, and wildlife across the United States.[80] Nature has gained legal and political power, and there are legions of advocates dedicated to representing it. Nationwide, policies regulating fisheries and water allocation have trended toward the environmental perspective.[81] These societal changes created the conditions and the demand for dam removal. Now dam removal and ecological restoration overall are becoming normal.

As a sector of the economy, ecological restoration is estimated to be worth $9.5 billion and directly employ 126,000 people. More people are presently employed in restoration than in logging or coal mining.[82] As Bendor and colleagues point out, the restoration economy, while rooted in the local areas being restored, spreads itself across society, employing people with a wide range of educational backgrounds, skills, and training. In the case of dam removal, we can expect economic knock-on benefits if fish populations rise as hoped. Perhaps a new generation of Clark Gables will fly up from Los Angeles to fish the Rogue, and Seattle restaurants will serve Elwha Chinook instead of Alaskan sockeye.

But the value of restoration goes beyond contractors' paychecks and fishing guides' tips and into the emotional buoyancy of knowing that the nation's natural heritage has been restored. Loomis found that the aggregate benefit of the Elwha dam removal to households across the United States, most of which will never use the river in any tangible way, was between $3 billion and $6 billion.[83] Ecological restoration stands as the furthest evolution of the relationship between nature and American society.[84] As more restoration projects occur, and as ongoing projects produce data to guide future practice, it seems likely that ecological restoration will only grow, as a business, as a science, and as a part of American environmental culture.

In a closely related transition, Americans have increasingly understood their landscapes to be culturally and economically valuable for beauty and ecological function, not just resource extraction. Natural amenities are a source of increasing interest[85] and increasing political and economic dynamism. Whitewater organizations mattered in western rivers by the 1990s, and Patagonia, an apparel company founded by a famous rock climber, was (and still is) active in funding and publicizing dam removal efforts, including on the Elwha and Rogue. At the same time, traditional economies, Wilkinson's "lords of yesterday,"[86] were crumbling along with the concrete in the dams: by 1990, agriculture in Grants Pass was almost gone, and timber in the Olympic Peninsula was challenged by new laws and new values.[87] While this transition was not clear-cut or immediate—there have always been lovers of scenery, and resource extraction remains a crucial activity in many places—it is unquestionably happening, and continues to happen, in each of these cases. In some analyses, natural amenities are the American West's greatest economic assets.[88] The rise of the "New West" has altered politics, culture, and economics in many communities, including in each watershed I discuss here, but it's important to keep in mind that the kinds of processes—and tensions—that make the New West are playing out nationwide, from the Hill Country of Texas to northern Vermont to western North Carolina. The presence of Olympic National Park, Wild and Scenic designation for the Rogue, streams of amenity-driven retirees to Southern Oregon and the Olympic Peninsula,[89] and Sandy's importance as a fishing destination for Portlanders all altered the political calculus on these rivers—but every river has its own special situations. As society and culture change, it will become increasingly politically necessary for all the people in a watershed, old and new, to work with one another.

In the fall of 2015, Hetch Hetchy restoration was on the ballot in San Francisco.[90] In 2017, the Nevada legislature discussed the removal of 710-foot Glen Canyon Dam—the one whose demolition was previously considered mostly through Edward Abbey novels. Neither of these things is likely to happen in the near or medium future, but it wasn't long ago that such suggestions would have been laughable. Dam removal is buoyant. People all across the country are beginning to think that we can regain what was lost—that we can boat and fish in something like the rivers our great-grandparents did. They will not be the same rivers, but they will have some of the same qualities.

If you're like most Americans, every landscape you've ever seen has been transformed and managed by humans, and its natural features and functions degraded. Whatever watershed you live in, there are almost certainly dams, upstream and downstream from you, defining your home waterways. I type these words from a cabin in a remote village in Vermont. The brook fifty yards below me has been dug out, straightened, and deepened—it no longer floods its meadow. Half a mile up the road, a little dam holds in the pond where people canoe and catch bass. There is restoration potential everywhere. The politics of dam removal will only grow and spread, and it's not likely that they'll be easy—my neighbors would surely mourn the demolition of our pond's dam. But as national values and regional economies shift and scientific knowledge develops, ecological restoration is becoming a nationwide political priority. The question that faces us is, how to do it?

Notes

Substantive notes and note numbers are italicized.

CHAPTER 1

1 Major 2007.
2 Pohl 2002.
3 American Rivers 2017.
4 Eliot 1944.
5 Gupta 2013.
6 Helmholz 1999.
7 US Census Bureau 2016.
8 Babbitt was referring to dams on the National Inventory of Dams, which are, as a rule, at least six feet tall.
9 Babbitt 1998.
10 Graf 2003.
11 Thoreau 2004.
12 Anon. 2018b.
13 Gomez and Sullivan 2016.
14 Barlow Knives 2018.
15 National Museum of American History 2018.
16 Anon. 2018a.
17 Cronon 1992.
18 Andrews 1999.
19 Of course, they had long relied on the government for security through the extension of American military control across the West, and the destruction of the tribal societies that were already there.
20 Reisner 1993.
21 Reisner 1993; Andrews 1999.
22 McKinley and Frank 1996.
23 Andrews 1999.
24 Nash 2001.
25 Originally a state park, ceded to California by the federal government.
26 National Park Service 2018.
27 Worster 2008.
28 Worster 2008.
29 Muir 1912.
30 Worster 2008.
31 Sierra Club n.d.
32 This is extremely unlikely to happen in the lifetime of anyone reading this. All other considerations aside, the project would be tremendously expensive.
33 US Bureau of Reclamation 2017.
34 US Bureau of Reclamation 2015.
35 Reisner 1993.
36 As opposed to the native tribes, who had of course lived there for thousands of years.
37 Reisner 1993; Babbitt 2002; Grossman 2002.
38 US Census Bureau 2012.
39 Alt 2005.
40 Dietrich 1995.
41 Dietrich 1995.
42 Dietrich 1995.
43 Dietrich 1995.
44 Dietrich 1995.
45 US Army Corps of Engineers 2018.
46 Reisner 1993.
47 McPhee 1971.
48 National monuments are run by the Park Service; they are essentially national parks, but are created by the president rather than by Congress.
49 DeVoto 1950; Stegner 1955.
50 McPhee 1971.
51 Brower 1997.
52 Porter 1963.
53 BOR 1965.
54 McPhee 1971.
55 But Abbey wrote on a typewriter and drove a truck.

56 *The exclamation point is a component of the group's name.*

57 Bowden 1990.

58 *Though it came frighteningly close to failing in the big melt year of 1983.*

59 Babbitt 1982.

60 McCarthy 2002.

61 McCarthy 2002.

62 Lichatowich 1999, 2013.

63 *Egan 1991. This definition would embrace much of California into the PNW, something that many northwesterners would rather not do in any setting. But Northern California, especially the Klamath basin and the many coastal streams in the northern reaches of the state, has as much in common with Oregon as it does with Hollywood.*

64 *This anadromous lifestyle, spawning in the river but living in the ocean, probably evolved because the ocean is a far richer source of food than the river: 90 percent of a salmon's body mass is added in the ocean.*

65 Moulton n.d.; Montgomery 2003.

66 Yoshiyama et al. 1998; Augerot and Foley 2005; Lackey et al. 2006.

67 Ward et al. 2008.

68 Norgaard and Reed 2017, for example.

69 Taylor 1999.

70 Blumm and Swift 1998.

71 Dietrich 1995.

72 Dietrich 1995; Yoshiyama et al. 1998.

73 Dietrich 1995.

74 Montgomery 2003.

75 Dietrich 1995; Lichatowich 1999; Northwest Power and Conservation Council 2018.

76 Montgomery 2003.

77 Lichatowich 1999, 2013.

78 Dietrich 1995; Nicole 2012.

79 Montgomery 2003.

80 Montgomery 2003.

81 Freyhof 2014.

82 Montgomery 2003.

83 Montgomery 2003.

84 Montgomery 2003.

85 NOAA Fisheries 2016.

86 NOAA Fisheries 2016.

87 Montgomery 2003.

88 Thoreau 2004.

89 Miller et al. 2014.

90 Gende et al. 2002; Naiman et al. 2002; Helfield and Naiman 2001.

91 Halverson 2011.

92 Boughton et al. 2006; Pearse et al. 2009.

93 *In this book, it would often be more correct for me to refer to "salmonids" rather than to "salmon," because steelhead and cutthroat are not salmon. But because these fish play a similar ecological, political, and cultural role, I use "salmon," simply because "salmonids" is an unwieldy term.*

94 Lichatowich 1999; Taylor 1999; Montgomery 2003.

95 Lichatowich 1999; Taylor 1999.

96 Taylor 1999.

97 Zeug et al. 2010; McClure et al. 2008; Lichatowich 1999.

98 Nehlsen et al. 1991.

99 Sherwood, personal communication.

100 *Twenty-eight ESUs were listed as of 2017; two ESUs have been de- and relisted.*

101 NOAA 2015.

102 Lichatowich 1999; Taylor 1999.

103 Taylor 1999.

104 Taylor 1999.

105 Lichatowich 1999, 2013; Taylor 1999.

106 Lichatowich 2013.

107 Trushenski et al. 2018.

108 Lichatowich 1999, 2013; Taylor 1999.

109 Lichatowich 1999, 2013.

110 Lichatowich 2013.

111 Stickney 1994.

112 National Research Council 1992.

113 Chasan 2015.

114 National Research Council 1996; Lichatowich 2013; Trushenski et al. 2018.

115 White 1995.

116 Montgomery 2003.

117 US Army Corps of Engineers 2018.
118 National Research Council 1992.
119 Doyle et al. 2003.
120 US Army Corps of Engineers 2018.
121 Lanz Oca 2011.
122 US Army Corps of Engineers 2018.
123 *This is a human-rights issue, not just an ecological one, as people who live in the future reservoirs behind big dam projects have often been forced to leave their homes.*
124 Bushaw-Newton et al. 2002; Bednarek 2001.
125 Gregory et al. 2002; Bednarek 2001; Collier et al. 2000.
126 Bednarek 2001; Collier et al. 2000.
127 Ligon et al. 1995; Stevens et al. 2001; Shafroth et al. 2002.
128 Song et al. 2018.
129 *For example, Stoecker, personal communication; Goin, personal communication.*
130 Noonan et al. 2012.
131 Sheer and Steel 2006.
132 Gende et al. 2002.
133 Gresh et al. 2000.
134 Turner et al. 1983.
135 Arman and Woolridge 1982.
136 *Some turbines are safer for fish, and better maintained, than others.*
137 *Backman and Evans 2002. This is much like the bends, which sometimes kills human SCUBA divers.*
138 Schmidt et al. 1998; Bartholow et al. 2004.
139 Myrick and Cech 2005; Ray et al. 2012.
140 Lowry 2003; American Rivers 2009; Crane 2009.
141 American Rivers 2017.
142 Heinz Center 2003.
143 *Fox et al. (2016) and Magilligan et al. (2017) have shown some interesting political angles to New England and, to some extent, Upper Midwest dam removal. Some scholar should look into what's going on in Pennsylvania, which has removed many more dams than any other state (Bellmore et al. 2016; Duda et al. 2016; American Rivers 2017).*
144 *Californian dam removals are concentrated in the northern half of that state and share similar eco-cultural settings and restoration goals with those in Oregon and Washington.*
145 American Rivers 2017; US Army Corps of Engineers 2018.
146 USEIA 2014.
147 Brewitt 2016.
148 Van Dyke, personal communication.
149 Press 1994.
150 Shields 1925; Cole 1986; Vencill 1987.
151 *Scalia (2017) suggests that FERC could make a rule that would force the dam owner to pay for removal. It would be surprising to see FERC take this sort of contentious step in the foreseeable future.*
152 US Army Corps of Engineers 2018.
153 Hardin 1968; Ostrom 1990.
154 *There are a few states that use a mixed approach, or other regimes entirely—remnants of Spanish and Mexican law in California, for instance—but riparian rights and prior appropriation dominate American water law.*
155 Hundley 2001.
156 Pittock and Hartmann 2011.
157 US Army Corps of Engineers 2018.
158 Light and Higgs 1996; Gross 2006.
159 *As opposed to indigenous history, which is, of course, much deeper than American history.*
160 Gross 2008.
161 Nash 2001; Gross 2008.
162 Light and Higgs 1996; Crutzen 2002.
163 Layzer 2012; Klyza and Sousa 2013.
164 Van Wieren 2008.
165 *The productive life of a concrete dam is reckoned to be roughly fifty to one hundred years, after which the concrete begins to break down (National Research Council 1992). The overwhelming majority of dams (~86 percent) are earthen dams, and more susceptible to erosion than concrete (US Army Corps of Engineers 2018).*

166 *Momsen 2010. This is one way to make a dam removal happen, but it is not exactly political.*

167 Mahoney 2000.

CHAPTER 2

1 Rutz, personal communication.

2 Curtis, personal communication.

3 Keil 2009.

4 Palmer et al. 2005; Palmer and Ruhl 2015, for example.

5 Society for Ecological Restoration 2004; Hilderbrand et al. 2005; Palmer et al. 2005; Hobbs et al. 2011; Palmer and Ruhl 2015.

6 Cronon 1983; Pyne 1990; Dietrich 1995; Lichatowich 1999; Mann 2005.

7 Cronon 1995.

8 As opposed to Native Americans.

9 *Other than flooding, which has always been an obvious concern. Reisner 1993; McCool 2012.*

10 Cronon 1983.

11 Wiley 2008.

12 McCool 2012.

13 Klyza and Sousa 2013.

14 Clarke and McCool 1996; Center of the American West 1997; Lowry 2003; Clark 2009; McCool 2012.

15 Clark 2009.

16 American Rivers 2017.

17 Duda et al. 2016.

18 This is why I first began to research it.

19 Symmes 2003.

20 Sabatier and Jenkins-Smith 1993.

21 Weible et al. 2011.

22 Sabatier and Jenkins-Smith 1993.

23 Weible et al. 2009.

24 Baumgartner and Jones 1993; Kingdon 1995.

25 Schon and Rein 1994.

26 Klyza and Sousa 2013.

27 *BLM National Science and Technology Center 2011. In 1992, they were required to pay the government $100 a year for each mining claim.*

28 Earthworks 2016.

29 Stone 2002.

30 Worster 1992; Reisner 1993; Hundley 2001; Pincetl 2003.

31 Nash 2001; Lowry 2003.

32 Schon and Rein 1994.

33 Hirschman 1970.

34 Stone 2002.

35 Rochon 1998.

36 Baumgartner and Jones 1993; Birkland 2006.

37 *The term is taken from an evolutionary theory promoted by the famous paleontologist Stephen Jay Gould.*

38 Baumgartner and Jones 1993; Pralle 2006.

39 Baumgartner and Jones 1993; Stone 2002.

40 Lejano 2006; Rochon 1998; Pralle 2006.

41 Repetto 2006.

42 Allen 2010.

43 Doremus and Tarlock 2008.

44 In Jasanoff and Wynne 1998.

45 Vogel 1986.

46 *There are, of course, many arguments to be had about whether this openness is better or worse for American politics; that is a question for other people to answer.*

47 Merrill 2005.

48 Schattschneider 1960; Baumgartner and Jones 1993; Pralle 2006.

49 Pralle 2006.

50 Hobbs et al. 2011.

51 *Condit Dam, on the White Salmon River, was larger than Savage Rapids or Marmot Dams. It came out in the fall of 2011. However, at the time I selected my cases, there was some lingering uncertainty about its removal. As I learned at the earliest stage of my work, dam removal politics is fraught with delays.*

52 Pralle 2006.

53 Pralle 2006.

54 Coleman 1958.

55 Mahoney 2000; Goertz and Mahoney 2012.

CHAPTER 3

1 Dicks, personal communication.
2 Aldwell 1950.
3 *At present, three Klallam bands live on the Olympic Peninsula—the Port Gamble S'Klallam Tribe, the Jamestown S'Klallam Tribe, and the Lower Elwha Klallam Tribe. The anglicization of the tribal name; its being used, in a different form, for Clallam County; and the atomized nature of the various Klallam bands have created a slightly confused naming situation. They are commonly known as the Elwhas. I call them that here.*
4 Blumm and Swift 1998.
5 Gresh et al. 2000.
6 USDOI et al. 1994.
7 Goin, personal communication; Dickerson 2010c.
8 Ging, personal communication; Hawkins-Hoffman, personal communication; Gende et al. 2002; Naiman et al. 2002; Helfield and Naiman 2001.
9 USDOI et al. 1994.
10 USDOI NPS 2011.
11 Gottlieb 2010c.
12 Ward et al. 2008.
13 Brown 1982.
14 *Elwha tribal member Bea Charles, in Lundahl 2002.*
15 Stevens and Native Signatories 1855.
16 Egan 2007; Crane 2011.
17 Aldwell 1950; Crane 2011.
18 Aldwell 1950.
19 Aldwell 1950; Sadin and Vogel 2011.
20 Yes, Halloween.
21 Egan 2007.
22 Aldwell 1950.
23 Crane 2011.
24 Crane 2011.
25 Crane 2011.
26 Crane 2011.
27 USDOI et al. 1994.
28 USDOI NPS 1995; Citizen's Advisory Committee 1996.

29 *The North Olympic Peninsula, which includes Washington's Clallam and Jefferson Counties, is the commonly used term for the region in which Port Angeles and the Elwha River lie.*
30 Goin, personal communication; Jackson 2011.
31 Goin, personal communication.
32 Fausch and Northcote 1992; Quinn 2005.
33 McHenry and Pess 2008.
34 USDOI NPS 1995.
35 *USDOI NPS 1996. This was important partly because the US Coast Guard has a base at the end of the Hook.*
36 Erb 1988; Crane 2011.
37 Crane 2011.
38 Rachel Kowalski, Lower Elwha Klallam Tribe, in Joint Fish and Wildlife Agencies 1989.
39 Sampson-Sherbeck 1985.
40 Aldwell 1950.
41 *Goin would emerge as a passionate local voice for river restoration, speaking with a deep personal knowledge of the Olympic Peninsula's human and natural communities (Goin, personal communication; Hawkins-Hoffman, personal communication).*
42 Goin, personal communication.
43 Crane 2011.
44 Goin, personal communication.
45 Hard et al. 1996.
46 USDOI NPS 1995.
47 *The government had rejected earlier requests for a reservation at the river mouth partly because some local people worried that this would hurt the fishing in the Elwha (Sadin and Vogel 2011).*
48 FERC 1991; Busch 2007.
49 Brown 1982.
50 US Army Corps of Engineers 1986.
51 Elofson, personal communication.
52 Busch 1990, 2007; Elofson, personal communication.
53 Burke 2001b; Lundahl 2002.

54 Busch 1990; Norgaard and Reed 2017.

55 Guarino 2013.

56 Crown Zellerbach 1986.

57 FERC 1991.

58 USDOI et al. 1994.

59 The wheels of bureaucracy turn slowly.

60 Crown Zellerbach and Washington Department of Fisheries 1975.

61 Crown Zellerbach 1986.

62 *This language is from the 1855 Treaty of Point Elliot, a treaty with tribes from the eastern shores of Puget Sound. Other treaties, including the Treaty of Point No Point, include very similar language.*

63 Belsky 1996.

64 Taylor 1999.

65 Jensen, personal communication; Bogaard, personal communication; Broman, personal communication; Hughes 2011.

66 Sampson-Sherbeck 1985; Tizon 1999.

67 Busch and Ralph 1986.

68 Tom Jensen, in Egan 2007.

69 Meyer Resources 1991.

70 Sadin and Vogel 2011.

71 Lower Elwha Klallam Tribe 2014.

72 *Egan 2007. At that time, the Elwhas lacked the resources to intervene in the Glines Canyon licensing process (Plumb 1986).*

73 FERC 1991.

74 Crown Zellerbach 1986.

75 Meierotto 1980.

76 Rutz, personal communication; Ortman, personal communication.

77 Rutz, personal communication.

78 Ortman, personal communication; Dyer, personal communication.

79 *Jensen, personal communication; Broman, personal communication; McNulty, personal communication; Rossotto, personal communication; Cantrell, personal communication. Brown himself did not take much political action during the Elwha debate, though he did speak at some*

environmental meetings *(Nafziger 1988; Friends of the Elwha 1991).*

80 Ortman, personal communication; Cantrell, personal communication; O'Keefe, personal communication; Camara 1994c.

81 Rutz, personal communication.

82 Rutz, personal communication.

83 Rutz, personal communication; Cantrell, personal communication; O'Keefe, personal communication.

84 Rutz, personal communication.

85 Cantrell, personal communication; Ortman, personal communication.

86 Rutz, personal communication; Ortman, personal communication.

87 Barson, personal communication.

88 Rutz, personal communication.

89 Barson, personal communication.

90 Campbell, personal communication.

91 McNulty, personal communication; Ralph, personal communication.

92 *The Elwhas left the PNPTC later, and for most of the debate the tribe was the primary Native actor.*

93 Rutz, personal communication; McNulty, personal communication.

94 Derick 1986.

95 Rutz, personal communication.

96 Sadin and Vogel 2011.

97 Cantrell, personal communication.

98 Clarke and McCool 1996; Gross 2008.

99 Cantrell, personal communication; Ging, personal communication; Hawkins-Hoffman, personal communication.

100 Ging, personal communication.

101 Joint Fisheries Agencies 1985; Egan 2007.

102 Bodi, personal communication; Ralph, personal communication; Winter, personal communication.

103 Winter, personal communication.

104 Winter, personal communication.

105 Baker, personal communication; Barson, personal communication; Hawkins-Hoffman, personal communication.

106 Hawkins-Hoffman, personal communication.
107 Crown Zellerbach 1986; Adamire 1990a; Deacon 1991; American Public Power Institute et al. 1992; Derick 1992.
108 *16 U.S.C. 1920; Anon. 1986. If this suggestion had been taken up in the 1980s, it would have saved a lot of trouble, and made this book considerably shorter.*
109 Mentor, personal communication.
110 Adamire 1986; Holden 1986.
111 Socolar 1990.
112 Socolar 1990.
113 Friends of the Earth-Northwest 1990.
114 Derick 1990c.
115 Anon. 1987a.
116 Anon. 1988.
117 *The mill is, as of 2018, owned and operated by Nippon Paper Industries, which bought DA in 2003. Bracy, personal communication.*
118 Weland, personal communication; Bracy, personal communication; Finnerty, personal communication.
119 Rutz, personal communication.
120 Anon. 1986.
121 Derick 1990a; Hosey and Associates 1990.
122 Ralph, personal communication; Elwha Conservation Interveners 1989a.
123 Harris 1990a.
124 Bodi et al. 1989.
125 Busch 1990.
126 Joint Fish and Wildlife Agencies 1989.
127 Riski 1990.
128 Hard et al. 1996.
129 Baker 1990a; Bodi et al. 1990.
130 Michaels 1988.
131 Harris 1991a; Moeller et al. 1991.
132 Elwha Conservation Interveners 1991.
133 Moeller et al. 1992.
134 Shelton 1990.
135 Dawson 1997.
136 Bodi et al. 1987.
137 For example, Anon. 2001 and 1987b.
138 Ross 1987.
139 USDOI NPS 2005.
140 Wunderlich, personal communication.
141 Wunderlich, personal communication; Anon. 2001.
142 Joint Fisheries Agencies 1988.
143 For example, Henry 2011; Tuttle 2000.
144 Ross 1989b.
145 Chastain, personal communication; Holman 1994; Parsons 1998; Spees 2006; Stoddard 2010.
146 Ross 1989a; Harris 1990b; Chastain 1995a; Lauderback 1996.
147 Garrity, personal communication; Mossman 1991; Seideman 1993.
148 *Forks would later become known for other sorts of wildlife, as the vampires and werewolves of the popular Twilight series attended high school there. This boosted the region's economy, as vampire kitsch was sold around the North Olympic Peninsula.*
149 Dietrich 1992.
150 Dietrich 1992.
151 Baker, personal communication; Cantrell, personal communication; Garrity, personal communication; McNulty, personal communication; Mentor, personal communication; Swift, personal communication.
152 Derick 1990b.
153 Derick 1987.
154 Harris 1991d; Busch 2007.
155 Busch 2007.
156 Busch 2007.
157 Robinson, personal communication; Rutz, personal communication; Cantrell, personal communication.
158 Erb 1991b.
159 Associated Press 1999.
160 Swift, personal communication.
161 Derick 1990b.
162 Elwha Conservation Interveners 1989a; Derick 1990a.
163 USDOI NPS 1995.
164 Harza Engineering 1991.

165 Elwha Conservation Interveners 1989a.
166 Dolan 1987a, b; Patterson 1988; Anon. 1990b; Baker 1990a.
167 Dolan 1987b; Curnew 1990c.
168 Sierra Club 1989.
169 Olympic Park Associates 1989.
170 Baker, personal communication.
171 Wiggins, personal communication; Curnew 1990b; Harris 1990b; Wright 1990.
172 Broman, personal communication; Rossotto, personal communication.
173 Jensen, personal communication; Baker, in *Friends of the Earth Magazine*, 1991; Johnson 1990; Perkins 1993.
174 Finnerty, personal communication; Rutz, personal communication; Curnew 1990a; Harris 1991b.
175 Finnerty, personal communication.
176 Charles n.d.
177 Kowalski 1989; Busch 2007.
178 Curnew 1990c; Lundahl 2002.
179 Ralph 1988.
180 Busch 1990.
181 Meyer Resources 1991.
182 Christman 1989b.
183 Campbell, personal communication; Cantrell, personal communication; Chastain, personal communication; Swift, personal communication.
184 *Peninsula Daily News* Staff 1988.
185 Anon. 1990a.
186 Nafziger 1988.
187 Derick 1989.
188 Riski 1990.
189 Amundson 1988.
190 Bodi 1989.
191 Cantrell, personal communication; Wold 1989.
192 Patterson 1987.
193 Dolan 1987a; Patterson 1987.
194 Dolan 1987b.
195 United Press International 1987; Barlow 2011.
196 Keim 1987.
197 Lebo 1990.
198 Griffing 1990.
199 Griffing 1990; Machenheimer 1991; Rains 1994.
200 Buxton 1990.
201 Smith 1990.
202 Bergman 1990; USDOI NPS 1996.
203 USDOI NPS 1996; Citizens' Advisory Committee 1996.
204 Campbell, personal communication; Riski 1989b.
205 Riski 1989b.
206 Riski 1989a.
207 Erb 1989.
208 Camara 1994a.
209 Baker, personal communication; McNulty, personal communication.
210 Unsigned n.d.
211 Erb 1990b.
212 Anon. 1989; Patterson 1989.
213 Swift, personal communication; Amundson 1989.
214 Christman 1989a; Erb 1990b.
215 Baker, personal communication.
216 Baker, personal communication.
217 Rutz, personal communication; Baker, personal communication.
218 BPA was involved because it had been mandated to seek efficiency in the region's power under the 1980 Northwest Power Planning Act. Reviews like this were one of their options for doing so.
219 Rossotto, personal communication; Baker 1990b.
220 Rutz, personal communication; Baker 1990b. The company later had Port Angeles City Light audit the mill. This audit showed 1.1 MW in conservation. The CIs thought that a better audit would have shown more savings (Erb 1991a).
221 The phrase "win-win" would be constantly repeated by dam removal advocates in the years to come. Baker, personal communication; Adams 1991; Christman 1989b.
222 Hawkins-Hoffman, personal communication; Erb 1990a; Patterson 1987.
223 Baker, personal communication; Finnerty, personal communication; Hawkins-Hoffman, personal communication; Elofson, personal communication; Thaler 1985.

224 USDOI NPS 1990.
225 Erb 1990a.
226 Hawkins-Hoffman 1990.
227 Dawson 1990.
228 Winter, personal communication.
229 Ging, personal communication.
230 Erb 1990b.
231 Swift, personal communication.
232 Deacon 1991.
233 Egan 1990.
234 Cantrell, personal communication.
235 Bradley, personal communication.
236 Bradley, personal communication.
237 Bradley 2011.
238 Jensen, personal communication;
    Finnerty, personal communication.
239 Jensen, personal communication;
    Bradley, personal communication.
240 Anonymous 1990.
241 LaChasse 1988b.
242 LaChasse 1988a.
243 Hollis and Knutson 1992.
244 *These are wells that draw on water
    from the ground below active water
    bodies, like rivers. This meant that
    they draw on surface water, not on
    aquifers.*
245 Harris 1990d.
246 Hollis and Knutson 1992.
247 Modaff, personal communication;
    Harris 1991a.
248 Egan 2007.
249 Baker 1991b.
250 USDOI NPS 2014c.
251 Harris 1991b.
252 Harris 1992a.
253 Campbell, personal communication.
254 Busch 2007.
255 Swift, personal communication;
    Anon. 1991b.
256 *Though few sex scandals could be
    called "savory."*
257 Cantrell, personal communication;
    Egan 2007; Schaefer 1992.
258 Friends of the Earth-Northwest et
    al. 1992.
259 Cantrell 1992b.
260 Bea Charles, in Sadin and Vogel
    2011.
261 Editor 1992.

262 Evans 1991; Cantrell 1992a.
263 Harris 1992e.
264 Harris 1992c.
265 Anon. 1992b; Morgan and
    Teniguchi 1992.
266 Adamire 1992.
267 Nowak 1992.
268 Terry Bracy, in Egan 2007.
269 Weland, personal communication;
    Jensen, personal communication;
    Egan 2007; Sonner 1992.
270 102nd Congress 1992.
271 Swift, personal communication;
    Cantrell, personal communication.
272 Fultz 1992; US General Accounting
    Office 1992a, b.
273 Dingell 1992.
274 Cantrell, personal communication.
275 Egan 2007.
276 Swift, personal communication;
    Cantrell, personal communication.
277 Olympic Park Associates 1992.
278 Cantrell and Elofson 1992.
279 Anon. 1992c.
280 Elwha Conservation Interveners
    1992b.
281 Elwha Conservation Interveners
    1992a.
282 Ortman 1992.
283 Catterson 1994.
284 Finnerty, personal communication.
285 Cantrell 1994b.
286 Cantrell, personal communication.
287 Cantrell 1994b.
288 Cantrell 1993b; Finnerty 1993.
289 Cantrell 1993c.
290 Cantrell 1993a.
291 USDOI et al. 1994.
292 Wunderlich et al. 1994; USDOI
    NPS 1995; Wunderlich, personal
    communication; Baker, personal
    communication.
293 Murray 1994.
294 Camara 1994d.
295 Chastain, personal communication;
    Camara 1994b.
296 Chastain, personal communication;
    Sisson 1993.

297 *Jordan 1990. The Trumpeter Society later distanced itself from REAL (Gillete and Jordan 1994).*

298 Chastain 2014b.

299 Brannin 1990.

300 Anon. 1995b, "Endangered Rivers List Names Elwha;" McNeece and McNeece 1995; Mosiman 1996b.

301 Chastain, personal communication.

302 REAL n.d. Dam Removal = Environmental Destruction; Towslee 1994.

303 Adamire 1990b.

304 Chastain, personal communication; Chastain 1995b.

305 Camara 1996.

306 Hewett, personal communication; Lundsford 1990; Short 1999; Smith 1990.

307 *These are islands of private property that, through the vagaries of history, sit within the borders of Olympic National Park.*

308 Associated Press 1997; Robinson 1999.

309 Hewett, personal communication.

310 Lundsford 1990.

311 Chastain, personal communication.

312 Mentor, personal communication; Robinson, personal communication; McNulty, personal communication.

313 Chastain 1994; Pryne 1994.

314 Chastain 1994.

315 Chastain 1995b.

316 *Chastain 2014a. The Wildlands Project, now called the Wildlands Network, is an initiative attempting to increase habitat connectivity for wildlife (Wildlands Network 2014). Any more nefarious motivations are difficult to establish.*

317 USDOI NPS 1995.

318 Noonan 1994.

319 Editor 1994.

320 Winter, personal communication.

321 Gorton 1992.

322 Anon. 1994b.

323 Mentor, personal communication.

324 Camara 1995a.

325 Anon. 1996b.

326 Mosiman 1996a.

327 Cantrell 1997a, b.

328 Gorton 1995.

329 Jensen, personal communication.

330 McNulty, personal communication; Gorton, personal communication.

331 REAL n.d. Letter to Friends of REAL.

332 Robinson, personal communication.

333 Eberhard, personal communication; Bohman 1995; Cantrell 1996b.

334 Robinson, personal communication.

335 Robinson, personal communication; Bohman 1994.

336 Broman, personal communication; Cantrell 1994a.

337 Anon. 1992a; Harris 1992d.

338 Short 1996.

339 Anon. 1994a.

340 Anon. 1995a.

341 Mosiman 1994; Northwest Conservation Act Coalition 1994; Trout Unlimited-Northwest Steelhead and Salmon Council 1994.

342 Campbell, personal communication.

343 Phillips, personal communication; Robinson, personal communication; Campbell, personal communication.

344 Mentor, personal communication; Phillips, personal communication; Robinson, personal communication.

345 Anon. 1996a; Citizen's Advisory Committee 1996.

346 Robinson, personal communication.

347 Winter, personal communication; Mosiman 1996f.

348 Robinson, personal communication.

349 *It did not wish to be called a "committee" to emphasize the ad hoc nature of the organization (Egan 2007).*

350 Phillips, personal communication.

351 Winter, personal communication.

352 Citizens' Advisory Committee 1996.

353 Mentor, personal communication.

354 CAG 1996.

355 Egan 2007; Hughes 2011.

356 Cantrell 1996a.

357 Pearl 1996.

358 Cantrell, personal communication.

359 Mosiman 1996f.

360 Kelly 1996.
361 Winter, personal communication.
362 Campbell, personal communication.
363 Gussman, personal communication; Winter, personal communication.
364 Mosiman 1996f.
365 Chastain 1996; Mosiman 1996d; Rudolph 1996.
366 Mosiman 1996d.
367 USDOI NPS 2005.
368 Mosiman 1996c.
369 USDOI NPS 1996; Mosiman 1996c.
370 USDOI NPS 1995.
371 Mosiman 1996e.
372 Mosiman 1996c.
373 USDOI NPS 1996.
374 Govtrack 2014.
375 Associated Press 1996.
376 Mosiman 1997c.
377 Editor 1997.
378 Mosiman 1997b.
379 Mosiman 1997a.
380 Mosiman 1996f.
381 USDOI NPS 1996.
382 Cantrell 1996b.
383 Mosiman 1996g; Murray 1996.
384 Hughes 2011.
385 Associated Press 1998b.
386 Lincoln 1998a.
387 Associated Press 1998a.
388 Anon. 1998b.
389 Associated Press 1998d; Lincoln 1998b.
390 Dicks, in Associated Press 1998c.
391 Associated Press 1998e.
392 Associated Press 1998c.
393 *It's worth noting that President Clinton was far more popular in 1999 than he'd been in 1995 (Gallup 2017).*
394 Morey 1999.
395 Anon. 1999.
396 Bogaard, personal communication.
397 Gottlieb 1999.
398 Bill Robinson, in Dawson 1998.
399 Ramzy 2000a.
400 Ramzy 2000b.
401 *He still expects the lake sites to be "eyesore(s)" for the many years to come (Gorton, personal communication).*

402 *Babbitt had a green sledgehammer that he liked to carry to dam removal events around the country.*
403 Ramzy 2000b.
404 Johnson 1999.
405 Hamilton, personal communication
406 *Ramzy 2000a. Though it would later be beaten to this mark by the Sandy River dam removals, in 2007–2008; see chapter 5.*
407 Weland, personal communication; Robinson, personal communication; Finnerty, personal communication.
408 Ramzy 2000d.
409 Ramzy 2000d.
410 Ollikainen 2010a.
411 Editor 2000; Kitz 2000.
412 Editor 2000.
413 Editor 2000.
414 Rudolph 2000.
415 Ramzy 2000c.
416 Beaumariage 2001.
417 McConnell 1969.
418 Penn 2000; McNulty 2007.
419 Short 2000.
420 Anon. 2000a.
421 Editor 2000; McKeown 2000.
422 Gottlieb 2000.
423 Gottlieb 2011a.
424 Harris 2006.
425 Ollikainen 2010a.
426 Dicks, personal communication; Anon. 2002d.
427 Dicks, personal communication.
428 Jensen, personal communication; McNulty, personal communication; Morris, personal communication; Bracy, personal communication; Bradley, personal communication; Rutz, personal communication; Cantrell, personal communication.
429 USDOI NPS 2014b.
430 Cantrell, personal communication; Broman, personal communication.
431 USDOI NPS 2014a.
432 USDOI NPS 2014b.
433 Shared Strategy Development Committee 2007.
434 Peters, personal communication; Pess, personal communication;

Hawkins-Hoffman, personal
communication.

435 Anon. 2005; de la Paz 2008.

436 Anon. 2002b.

437 Silliman 2001.

438 For example, Callis 2011; Anon.
2002c.

439 Hanson, personal communication;
Cokelet 2004.

440 Bogaard, personal communication.

441 Bogaard, personal communication;
Garrity, personal communication;
Masonis, personal communication;
Anon. 2006b.

442 Chew 2007.

443 Gorton, personal communication;
Rudolph 1995.

444 Green 2010; Lamoureux 2010.

445 USDOI NPS 2014d.

446 Gawley 2007b.

447 Elofson personal communication;
Gawley 2007b.

448 Gottlieb 2006.

449 Gawley 2007a.

450 Anon. 2007a.

451 Baker, personal communication;
Dicks, personal communication;
Finnerty, personal communication.

452 Anon. 2006c.

453 For example, Gawley 2007b.

454 Hanson, personal communication.

455 Anon. 2007b.

456 Gawley 2007c.

457 Dickerson 2010a.

458 Dickerson 2010b.

459 Gottlieb 2010d.

460 Callis 2010.

461 Gottlieb 2010a.

462 Gottlieb 2010b.

463 Ollikainen 2010b.

464 Gottlieb 2011b.

465 Brewitt, personal observation.

466 Hamilton, personal communication.

467 Gottlieb 2011c.

468 Mentor, personal communication;
Bogaard, personal communication;
Elofson, personal communication;
Hawkins-Hoffman, personal
communication; Winter, personal
communication.

469 de la Paz 2011.

470 Bradley 2011.

471 Ward et al. 2008.

472 Erdman Video Systems and USDOI
NPS 2014; Rubin et al. 2017.

473 Mapes 2017.

474 Mapes 2016; Major 2018; Ollikainen
2018.

475 Anderson and Hoffmann 2017.

476 National Marine Fisheries Service et
al. 2012.

477 Gottlieb 2017.

478 Anderson and Hoffmann 2017;
Mapes 2017.

479 Brian Winter, in Kelly 1997.

480 Crain, personal communication.

481 Lichatowich 1999, 2013;
Montgomery 2003.

482 Egan 2007.

483 American Rivers 2017.

484 Harris 1992b; USDOI NPS 1996.

485 O'Keefe, personal communication.

486 Casey 2007.

487 American Public Power Institute et
al. 1992; Camara 1995b; Rudolph
1996.

488 Baker, personal communication.

489 Cantrell 1993b.

490 Bodi, personal communication.

491 Baker, personal communication;
Bodi, personal communication;
Crain, personal communication;
Rossotto, personal communication.

492 Baker, personal communication.

493 Ralph, personal communication.

494 Lowry 2003.

495 Finnerty, personal communication.

496 Lowry 2003.

497 Hawkins-Hoffman, personal
communication.

498 Wilson and Magraw 1987.

499 Hawkins-Hoffman, personal
communication; Rutz, personal
communication; Elofson, personal
communication.

500 Modaff, personal communication.

501 Bracy, personal communication;
Mentor, personal communication;
Ralph, personal communication.

502 Masonis, personal communication.

503 Baker, personal communication;
    Bogaard, personal communication;
    Rutz, personal communication;
    Mentor, personal communication.
504 Dicks 2011.
505 Mapes 2016.
506 Mosiman 1996b; Chastain 2010.
507 *At least, it is in the I-5 corridor
    where most Washingtonians live and
    vote.*
508 Gardner 1992.
509 Chastain 1995b.
510 Editor 1998.
511 Egan 2007.
512 *In 1994, the wise use movement
    released an announcement urging
    dam removal as the wisest use of the
    resource, and saying that any other
    course of action would be illegal
    and a waste. This was not due to a
    change of heart on the part of perhaps
    the foremost antienvironmentalist
    movement in America, but rather
    was because the wise use movement
    had never claimed the name legally.
    David Ortman of Friends of the
    Earth realized this, incorporated
    under the name, and sometimes
    used it to release pro-environmental
    statements (Ortman, personal
    communication).*
513 Chastain, personal communication.
514 Lowry 2003.
515 Elofson, personal communication.
516 Eberhard, personal communication;
    Charles 1994.
517 Busch 2007.
518 Fox et al. 2017.
519 Busch 2007.
520 Cantrell, personal communication;
    Eberhard, personal communication;
    Jensen, personal communication;
    Weland, personal communication;
    Guarino 2013.

CHAPTER 4

 1 USDOI BOR 1995.
 2 Editor 1920b.
 3 *In the 1930s, GPID's service
   area was cut to 12,600 acres in*

   *acknowledgement that roughly 6,000
   of its high-elevation acres were not
   feasible to irrigate (USDOI BOR
   1995).*
 4 Editor 1920a; Anon. 1921a, b.
 5 Momsen 2010.
 6 Momsen 2009.
 7 Strahan, personal communication;
   Arman and Woolridge 1982;
   Barnard 1998.
 8 Gove 1998.
 9 USDOI BOR 1995.
10 Martin, personal communication.
11 USDOI BOR 1995.
12 USDOI BOR 1995; Benik et al. 2010.
13 *There was some hope at the time that
   potential hydropower development at
   the site, and the associated demands
   of upgrading the dam to receive a federal energy license, would force GPID
   to take care of fish passage without
   costing the government anything (B.
   Hamilton, personal communication).
   This never happened.*
14 Henderson 1982.
15 Fattig 1980; USDOI BOR 1995.
16 Strahan 2001; Waterwatch of
   Oregon 2009; Learn 2010; Hunter,
   personal communication; Kerr,
   personal communication; Phippen,
   personal communication; Strahan,
   personal communication; Tehan,
   personal communication.
17 L. Hamilton, personal
   communication.
18 Dodds 2011.
19 Rogue Web 2014.
20 Dodds 2011.
21 Hunter, personal communication;
   Momsen 2009.
22 Dodds 2011.
23 Norcross 2013.
24 Araki et al. 2008.
25 Duewel 1986.
26 David J. Newton Associates 1994.
27 *The slogan is still proudly displayed
   on a large arch over a busy downtown
   street. It feels like mockery on a
   hundred-degree July day.*

28 Shepard, personal communication; McMurray, personal communication; USDOI BOR 1995.
29 Shepard, personal communication.
30 Nelson 2005.
31 Shepard, personal communication.
32 Smith, personal communication.
33 GPID 1999c; Duewel 2000f.
34 Brandon 1980.
35 Raush 1975.
36 Huntington 1986.
37 Stone 2002.
38 David J. Newton Associates 1994.
39 GPID 1978, 1979b, 1981a.
40 GPID 1978, 1979a.
41 GPID 1980.
42 GPID 1981b.
43 Hanh 1986.
44 USDOI BOR 1995; Ledbetter 1997; Koch 2005.
45 LaBounty 1994a; Long 1998w; Duewel 2000h.
46 McMurray, personal communication.
47 *The tribes that had previously inhabited the region were devastated in the Rogue River Wars of the 1850s, and they have essentially no organized presence in or around Grants Pass. Although native tribes are very important in many dam questions in the Northwest, they were not part of the Savage Rapids issue in any active way.*
48 GPID 1997g.
49 GPID 1985.
50 GPID 1987a.
51 GPID 1987b.
52 USDOI BOR 1995.
53 *The project eventually came to focus primarily on GPID, as Josephine County lost the funding that had allowed it to take part in the study (USDOI BOR 1995; GPID 1988).*
54 GPID 1997f.
55 Cauble, personal communication.
56 GPID 1990, 1991c.
57 GPID 1990.
58 GPID 1989a.
59 Hunter, personal communication.

60 GPID 1989b.
61 Whitworth 2001.
62 Sherwood, personal communication; Adams, personal communication; Hunter, personal communication; Pagel, personal communication.
63 Reeves, personal communication.
64 Tom McMurray, in GPID 1997g; Cauble, personal communcation; Shepard, personal communication.
65 Associated Press and the *Daily Courier* 1991.
66 Associated Press and the *Daily Courier* 1991; USDOI BOR 1995.
67 Anon. 1991a.
68 Martin, personal communication.
69 Tienson, personal communication. The mouth of the Rogue is in Curry County.
70 Gregory 1993c.
71 Kirtley, personal communication; GPID 1993b; Lucas 1993b.
72 Beyerlin, personal communication; Hunter, personal communication.
73 Beyerlin, personal communication; Curtis, personal communication; Raabe, personal communication; Strahan, personal communication.
74 Shepard, personal communication.
75 Anon. 1991a.
76 Gregory 1994c.
77 Lucas 1993.
78 Anon. 1993a; GPID 1993f; Lucas 1993; Gregory 1994a.
79 Kirtley, personal communication.
80 GPID 1992b, 1993a.
81 Bender 1997.
82 In Bender 1997.
83 Staff 1994.
84 Bender 1997.
85 Canan 1989.
86 Staff 1994.
87 Lucas 1993.
88 Adams, personal communication; Greenwood, personal communication; Kirtley, personal communication; McMurray, personal communication; Spickler, personal communication.
89 Gregory 1994c; GPID 1999b.

90 Anon. 1993a; USDOI BOR 1995
91 USDOI BOR 1995.
92 GPID 1993d.
93 GPID 1993d, 1994c; Gregory 1994d.
94 Cauble, personal communication; Moore, personal communication; Shepard, personal communication.
95 Gregory 1994d.
96 Cauble, personal communication.
97 *The presence of ownerless dams, sitting unused in America's waterways, remains a tricky restoration challenge.*
98 GPID 1993f; USDOI BOR 1995.
99 GPID 1993d.
100 Anon. 1993a; Gregory 1994a; USDOI BOR 1995.
101 Gregory 1994c.
102 GPID 1994c.
103 GPID 1994d.
104 USDOI BOR 1995.
105 Beyerlin, personal communication; Hunter, personal communication; Pagel, personal communication; GPID 1993b.
106 USDOI BOR 1995.
107 Kerr, personal communication; Adams, personal communication; Cauble, personal communication; B. Hamilton, personal communication; Moore, personal communication; Polsky, personal communication.
108 Roberts 1991.
109 Hunter, personal communication; Lavigne 2005; Reisner 1993.
110 Kagan 2009.
111 Hunter, personal communication; Anon. 1993b and 1991a; Gregory 1994a.
112 GPID 1994c.
113 GPID 1993f; Gregory 1994c.
114 Huntington 1997.
115 Hayden 2014; Hayden, personal communication.
116 Hayden 1994, 1997.
117 GPID 1995a.
118 Gregory 1994f.
119 Gregory 1994a.
120 GPID 1994d.
121 Hiljus 1994a.
122 USDOI BOR 1995.
123 GPID 1995e.
124 *Savage Rapids Lake was indeed sometimes used as a water source by firefighters.*
125 Huntington 1994.
126 Lavigne 2005.
127 Shepard, personal communication.
128 Kirtley, personal communication.
129 GPID 1999b.
130 GPID 1994a; Gregory 1994b.
131 Hunter, personal communication; GPID 1995b.
132 Hiljus 1994b.
133 Greenwood 1994.
134 O'Loughlin 1995a.
135 Adams, personal communication.
136 Adams, personal communication.
137 Tappan, personal communication.
138 Repine, personal communication.
139 Buck 1995.
140 O'Loughlin 1995b.
141 GPID 1995d.
142 GPID 1995c.
143 GPID 1995d.
144 Associated Press 1995.
145 *This was asserted more than once but has not been confirmed by John Kitzhaber. Curtis, personal communication; Buchal, personal communication.*
146 O'Loughlin 1995c.
147 O'Loughlin 1995e.
148 O'Loughlin 1995e; Bender 1997.
149 Thomas 2003; Pralle 2006; Walker 2006.
150 *In the case of the Library Group, the selection of a library as an actual physical venue in which to gather disparate stakeholders was important because in libraries, you are not allowed to shout (Moore 1997).*
151 Pralle 2006.
152 State of Oregon 2014.
153 Solliday, personal communication; O'Loughlin 1996b.
154 O'Loughlin 1995d.
155 Adams, personal communication.
156 O'Loughlin 1996a.
157 Long 1996b.

158 *There have been issues with contaminated sediment in other dam removals, most notably Fort Edwards, in New York's Hudson River.*
159 Long 1996c, 1997o; Peattie 2011.
160 Long 1996a; Savage Rapids Dam Task Force 1996.
161 Savage Rapids Dam Task Force 1996.
162 Savage Rapids Dam Task Force 1996.
163 Savage Rapids Dam Task Force 1996.
164 Hunter, personal communication; Moore, personal communication.
165 Kitzhaber 1997.
166 Shepard, personal communication; GPID 1996a, b; Hayden 1997.
167 Webster, personal communication.
168 Adams 1999.
169 Long 1997b.
170 Long 1996b.
171 GPID 1991a; Gregory 1993a.
172 *GPID 1995g. Nearby Gold Ray Dam, since removed, included a fish counter that tracked the salmon populations of the Rogue every year. This is how people knew about the large coho run.*
173 GPID 1997f; Pickett 1997.
174 Deland 1997; GPID 1997f.
175 USDOC NMFS 1991.
176 McMurray, personal communication.
177 Long 1997h.
178 GPID 1997f; Long 1997h.
179 GPID 1997g.
180 Long 1997p.
181 GPID 1997d.
182 Long 1997g.
183 GPID 1997g, f; Long 1997a.
184 GPID 1997i.
185 Long 1997p.
186 Long 1997p.
187 Lundgren 1997.
188 Anon. 1997b.
189 GPID 1997i.
190 GPID 1997h.
191 *The statement was transcribed at the time by GPID's assistant manager from a tape of the district board meeting, hence the inconsistencies.*
192 GPID 1997h.
193 McMurray, personal communication; GPID 1997c.
194 GPID 1997b.
195 Long 1997c, e.
196 Long 1997e.
197 Long 1997m.
198 Long 1997m.
199 McMurray 1997.
200 Long 1997L.
201 GPID 1997e; Long 1997f.
202 Anon. 1997c; Huntington 1997; Long 1997i.
203 Hofstadter 1964.
204 Gregory 1993b.
205 Kaeser 1997.
206 Sloan 1997.
207 Sloan 1997.
208 GPID 1997a.
209 Gregory 1993b.
210 GPID 1997f.
211 Snyder 1998.
212 USDOI BOR 1995; Woodcock 1997.
213 Woodcock 1997.
214 Tappan, personal communication.
215 Brewitt, personal observation.
216 Davis 1952.
217 Davis 1952; Laufer 2014.
218 Laufer 2014; Wiles 2018.
219 Anon. 2018c; Branson-Potts 2018; Wiles 2018.
220 Laufer 2014.
221 GPID 1994c.
222 Thomas 2003.
223 *Grants Pass is near the well-known Oregon Caves, and its high school teams are called the Cavemen, offering antagonists a tailor-made epithet. Barr, personal communication; Hayden, personal communication.*
224 GPID 1994c.
225 Long 1997h; GPID 1999b.
226 Clarke and McCool 1996.
227 Smith 1994.
228 GPID 1993e.
229 Associated Press and the *Daily Courier* 1991; Martin, personal communication.
230 Martin, personal communication.
231 Adams, personal communication.

232 B. Hamilton, personal communication; GPID 1998i.
233 Duewel 1999c.
234 Clarke and McCool 1996.
235 Long 1997j.
236 Long 1997n.
237 GPID 1997c.
238 Long 1997k.
239 GPID 1995f, 1998f, 2001b.
240 Long 1997d.
241 Long 1997d.
242 Buck 1998.
243 Buck 1998.
244 Buck 1998.
245 Buck 1998.
246 GPID 1998b.
247 GPID 1998b.
248 Harper, personal communication; GPID 1998a.
249 GPID 1998j, 1999c.
250 Hunter, personal communication; Long 1998a.
251 Long 1998g.
252 Long 1998w.
253 GPID 1998b.
254 Pellissier 2001.
255 Hunter, personal communication; Long 1998d.
256 Spickler 1998.
257 GPID 1998d, g; Long 1998g.
258 Gaar 1997; Morris 1997, 1998; Stelle 1998.
259 Long 1998b.
260 Becklin 1998b; Long 1998b.
261 Long 1998o, x.
262 Becklin 1998a; Long 1998a.
263 Becklin 1998a.
264 Long 1998n.
265 *Becklin later admitted that they did not meet the agency's criteria (Long 1998t, v).*
266 Duewel 1999e.
267 Long 1998g.
268 Long 1998p.
269 Polsky, personal communication.
270 Long 1998h.
271 Long 1998q.
272 Long 1998r, s.
273 Long 1998m.
274 Anon. 1998a; GPID 1998m.
275 Tienson, personal communication.
276 Gove 1998; GPID 1998L; Long 1998c, L.
277 Long 1998k.
278 Becklin 1999.
279 GPID 1998L.
280 GPID 1998e.
281 Gove 1998; Vejtasa 1998.
282 Gove 1998.
283 GPID 1998n.
284 GPID 1998c, h, k.
285 GPID 1998L; Long 1998e, f.
286 *Becklin refused repeated interview requests. As of 2011, he was writing his own account of the Savage Rapids controversy. Guillotte, personal communication; Strahan, personal communication; Adams, personal communication; Hunter, personal communication; Greenwood, personal communication; Kirtley, personal communication.*
287 Evans 2005.
288 Roler 1998.
289 Hunter, personal communication; Strahan, personal communication; Long 1997e.
290 Guillotte, personal communication; Hunter, personal communication; Moore, personal communication.
291 Long 1998f.
292 Tappan, personal communication.
293 Robbins et al. 2009.
294 USDOI BOR 1995.
295 GPID 1995e.
296 Geiske 1979; GPID 1994b.
297 GPID 2002c.
298 Hunter, personal communication; Shepard, personal communication.
299 Hunter, personal communication; Shepard, personal communication; Duewel 2000a.
300 Long 1997d.
301 Martin, personal communication.
302 Shepard, personal communication.
303 GPID 1998L, 2001b.
304 GPID 1998L, 2001b, 2003.
305 Sheehan and Strahan 1999; Strahan 1999.

306 Kirtley, personal communication; Gregory 1994a; LaBounty 1994b; USDOI BOR 1995.
307 Gregory 1994g; GPID 1998L; Duewel 2001b.
308 Ingram 1994.
309 Gregory 1994a.
310 Guston 2001; Doremus and Tarlock 2008.
311 McMurray, personal communication.
312 Duewel 1985; GPID 1991b; Woodcock 1997.
313 Duewel 1985.
314 Duewel 1986; Gregory 1994g.
315 Duewel 1999e.
316 USDOI BOR 1995.
317 Hunter 1999.
318 Long 1998u.
319 Roler 1999.
320 Associated Press and the *Daily Courier* 1999; Hunter 1999; Roler 1999.
321 Associated Press and the *Daily Courier* 1999.
322 Shepard, personal communication.
323 Duewel 2000j.
324 Funk, personal communication.
325 Duewel 1999L.
326 Duewel 1999j.
327 Duewel 1999g; Gove 1999.
328 Duewel 1999g.
329 Duewel 1999i, k.
330 Guillotte, personal communication; Duewel 1999e.
331 Duewel 1999h; GPID 1999c.
332 GPID 1999a.
333 Duewel 1999b.
334 Duewel 1999d.
335 Duewel 1999a.
336 Duewel 1999c.
337 Duewel 1999c.
338 GPID 2000b.
339 Shepard, personal communication.
340 Greenwood, personal communication.
341 Hunter, personal communication.
342 Duewel 2000c.
343 Hunter 2000.
344 Duewel 2000g; Roler and Snyder 2000; Whitworth 2001.
345 Duewel 2000g.
346 Duewel 2000d.
347 Duewel 2000i.
348 Duewel 2000e.
349 Duewel 2000e.
350 Duewel 2000a.
351 Duewel 2000b, 2001d; Widdison 2001.
352 Smith and Wyden 2000.
353 GPID et al. 2000.
354 GPID 2000a.
355 Duewel 2001c.
356 GPID 2001a.
357 Duewel 2001b.
358 Duewel 2001b.
359 Duewel 2001b.
360 GPID 2001b.
361 Duewel 2001a.
362 Associated Press 2001.
363 Strahan, personal communication.
364 Giguere and James, personal communication.
365 Bowman, personal communication; Raabe, personal communication.
366 Curtis, personal communication.
367 Bowman, personal communication; Curtis, personal communication; Hunter, personal communication.
368 Beyerlin, personal communication; L. Hamilton, personal communication; Strahan, personal communication.
369 Polsky, personal communication.
370 GPID 2002a.
371 Giguere and James, personal communication.
372 GPID 2002b.
373 Howard 2005; Skevington 2005.
374 Beyerlin, personal communication.
375 Giguere and James, personal communication; Repine, personal communication.
376 Giguere and James, personal communication.
377 Strahan, personal communication.
378 Giguere and James, personal communication.

379 Giguere and James, personal communication.
380 Giguere and James, personal communication.
381 Duewel 2002b.
382 Smith et al. 2005.
383 Duewel 2005b, 2006c.
384 Giguere and James, personal communication; Bierly, personal communication; Shepard, personal communication.
385 Bierly, personal communication.
386 Giguere and James, personal communication; Duewel 2002b.
387 Duewel 2004, 2005b.
388 Duewel 2005a, 2006b.
389 Duewel 2006a.
390 GPID 2014.
391 Raabe, personal communication.
392 *Becklin 2005. As of 2018, the editorial was still available on a property rights advocacy website.*
393 Becklin 2005.
394 Duewel 2008.
395 *Shepard, personal communication; GPID 1998k. The pumps inside the dam had been powered by the river.*
396 Duewel 2009b.
397 Momsen 2009.
398 Duewel 2002b.
399 Duewel 2009a; Hunter, personal communication; Moore, personal communication; Polsky, personal communication; Tienson, personal communication.
400 Polsky, personal communication.
401 Freeman 2013; Van Dyke, personal communication.
402 Van Dyke, in Grable 2014.
403 Strahan, personal communication.
404 Grable 2014.
405 Adams, personal communication.
406 Shepard, personal communication.
407 McMurray, personal communication.
408 Shepard, personal communication.
409 Curtis, personal communication; Martin, personal communication; Tehan, personal communication;

Moore, personal communication; Shepard, personal communication.
410 Martin, personal communication.
411 Frego 2011.
412 Brewitt, personal observation.
413 Stone 2002.
414 WaterWatch of Oregon 2014.
415 GPID 1997b.
416 For example, Woodcock 1997.
417 Long 1997n.
418 Guston 2001; Doremus and Tarlock 2008.
419 Hunter, personal communication; USDOI BOR 1995.
420 In the sense of Lakoff 2008.
421 Hunter, personal communication.
422 Moore, personal communication.
423 Beyerlin, personal communication; Strahan, personal communication.
424 Hunter 1999.
425 USDOI BOR 1995.
426 Moore, personal communication.
427 Strahan, personal communication.
428 WaterWatch of Oregon 2011.
429 American Whitewater 2014; White Salmon River 2014.
430 Long 1998w.
431 Spickler 1998; GPID 1999a.
432 GPID 1992a.
433 Bowman, personal communication.
434 Koberstein 1994.
435 Bender 1997; Babbitt 1998.
436 Barnard 1998.
437 Giguere and James, personal communication; Raabe, personal communication; Shepard, personal communication.
438 Momsen 2010.
439 Anon. 1993b; GPID 1993e; Duewel 2001e.
440 McConnell 1969.
441 GPID 1993c.
442 Chouinard 2012.

CHAPTER 5

1 Esteve 1999c.
2 American Whitewater et al. 2007.
3 Alsbury, personal communication.

4 *It is important to distinguish between PGE's Bull Run Project and the city of Portland's dams on the Bull Run River, which also produce electricity. They are different dams on different rivers.*

5 *It is also important to be clear about the distinction between Marmot Dam itself and the rest of the Bull Run Hydroelectric Project. The dam was the main issue in decommissioning, but it existed as part and parcel of the larger project, which stakeholders considered and dealt with as a whole. The Little Sandy Dam was also removed as part of the process, but its removal was essentially an appendage to the Marmot removal.*

6 Keil, personal communication.

7 Taylor 1998.

8 Wollner 1990.

9 Wollner 1990; Kirkendall, personal communication.

10 Kirkendall, personal communication; Jensen, personal communication.

11 Wollner 1990.

12 FERC 2003.

13 Bottom et al. 2005.

14 Dietrich 1995; White 1995; Taylor 1998.

15 Bottom et al. 2005.

16 Taylor 1998.

17 Taylor 1998.

18 The Oregon Department of Fish and Wildlife operates it now.

19 Bonneville Power Administration 2010.

20 For example, Cade 2007; Keller 1997.

21 Goranson 1989c.

22 For example, Anon. 2006a and 1997a.

23 ODFW 2013.

24 Taylor 1998.

25 Taylor 1998.

26 *The typical flow level at Marmot Dam is between about 1,030 cfs (in the early spring) and 266 cfs (in the late summer) (FERC 2003).*

27 Taylor 1998.

28 *The entire Little Sandy was diverted to the powerhouse, totally dewatering that stream except during very high flows—above 800 cfs (FERC 2003). This, of course, eliminated its salmon runs.*

29 *Broadly, the commission makes management programs and policies, which ODFW carries out.*

30 Taylor 1998.

31 FERC 2003.

32 *FERC's draft Environmental Impact Statement (2003) says 5,200, but this is likely a typo, given the river's typical flow levels.*

33 FERC 2003.

34 Kirkendall, personal communication.

35 Taylor 1998.

36 NMFS 2011.

37 *Chum salmon occasionally run in the Sandy, but the population is not there consistently enough to warrant evaluation in the Bull Run EIS (Taylor 1998; FERC 2003). The other three species are well established in the river.*

38 USFWS 2002; NMFS 2011.

39 Goranson 1988.

40 *This was partly to meet seismic criteria (Heintzman, personal communication; Goranson 1988).*

41 Goranson 1989b.

42 Portland General Electric 1999.

43 Esler 2009; Esler, personal communication; Heintzman, personal communication.

44 Keil 2009.

45 Keil 2009.

46 Esler 2009.

47 Young, personal communication; Burchfield, personal communication.

48 *Jensen 2003. Fish imprint on the chemistry of their natal stream— hence (in part) their famous ability to return there to spawn.*

49 Keil 2009.

50 Prather, personal communication.

51 Athman, personal communication.

52 FERC 2003.

53 FERC 2003.

54 Kirkendall, personal communication; Nudelman, personal communication; Heintzman, personal communication; Esler, personal communication; Grant, personal communication.

55 Keil 2009.

56 Esler, personal communication.

57 US Energy Information Administration 2014.

58 *Heintzman, personal communication. PGE's specific calculations are proprietary.*

59 Esler, personal communication.

60 City of Portland Oregon and Portland General Electric 1999b; Esler, personal communication; Heintzman, personal communication.

61 Sten, personal communication.

62 Sten, personal communication.

63 Taylor 1998.

64 Jones 1998a; Sten, personal communication.

65 Sten, personal communication.

66 Jones 1998a.

67 City of Portland Oregon and Portland General Electric 1999a.

68 City of Portland Oregon and Portland General Electric 1999b.

69 Menard, personal communication.

70 City of Portland Oregon and Portland General Electric 1999a.

71 Brinckman 1999.

72 Brinckman 1999.

73 Brinckman 1999.

74 Portland General Electric 1999.

75 FERC 2003.

76 Keil 2009; Mitchnick, personal communication.

77 Mitchnick, personal communication.

78 Keil 2009; Heintzman, personal communication.

79 Mitchnick, personal communication.

80 Esler, personal communication.

81 Portland General Electric 1999.

82 Nageli Reporting Corporation 2000b.

83 Nageli Reporting Corporation 2000a, b.

84 Heintzman, personal communication.

85 Portland General Electric 2000; Keil, personal communication; Esler, personal communication.

86 McMullen 2000b.

87 Esler, personal communication; Keil, personal communication; Keil 2009.

88 Irving 2000a.

89 Keil 2009; Nageli Reporting Corporation 2000b; Kirkendall, personal communication; Esler, personal communication; Kucas, personal communication.

90 Portland General Electric 1999.

91 Keil 2009.

92 US Army Corps of Engineers 2018.

93 Van Dyke, personal communication.

94 Stillwater Sciences 2000.

95 Grant, personal communication.

96 Esler, personal communication; Plaeger, personal communication.

97 Keil, personal communication.

98 Esler 2009; Trevison 2003; Heintzman, personal communication.

99 Braudrick and Vick 2001.

100 Kirkendall, personal communication.

101 Athman, personal communication.

102 Prather, personal communication; Burchfield, personal communication.

103 Braudrick and Vick 2001.

104 Portland General Electric 1999.

105 Esteve 1999c.

106 Jones 1998b; FERC 2003; Anon. 2008.

107 Eno 2007.

108 Trevison 2005.

109 Heintzman, personal communication; Esler, personal communication; Reese 1999.

110 City of Sandy 1999.

111 Editor 1999a, b; McMullen 1999c.

112 Esteve 1999c.

113 Reese 1999; Rowley 1999.
114 Lewis 1999b.
115 McMullen 1999a.
116 Austin et al. in prep.; Editor 1999b.
117 Rowley 1999.
118 Lewis 1999b.
119 Lewis 1999b.
120 City of Sandy 1999.
121 Reese 1999.
122 Lewis 1999b.
123 McMullen 1999d.
124 Esteve 1999b; Lewis 1999b; Merlich 1999.
125 Cox 2000.
126 Heintzman, personal communication.
127 Heintzman, personal communication.
128 FERC 2003.
129 Esteve 1999c.
130 McMullen 1999d.
131 Irving 2000b.
132 Irving 2000b.
133 Esteve 1999d.
134 McMullen 1999d.
135 Irving 2000b; McMullen 2000a.
136 Anon. 2000b.
137 Plaeger, personal communication.
138 FERC 2003.
139 McMullen 2000b.
140 Esler, personal communication.
141 Lewis 1999a.
142 Esteve 1999c.
143 Esler, personal communication.
144 Keil, personal communication; Esler, personal communication.
145 Lewis 1999a.
146 McMullen 1999b.
147 McMullen 2000b.
148 Monroe 1999.
149 Monroe 1997.
150 *ODFW 2011a, 2012, 2013; Alsbury, personal communication. This is the fin low on a fish's back. Its removal is a standard salmonid marking technique. The fin is not thought to be important for swimming (Vander Haegen et al. 2005).*
151 Glass, personal communication; Ritchie, personal communication.
152 Ewing 2002.
153 Jensen, personal communication; Glass, personal communication.
154 Glass, personal communication.
155 Glass, personal communication; Ritchie, personal communication.
156 L. Hamilton, personal communication.
157 Glass, personal communication; Ritchie, personal communication.
158 Monroe 1999.
159 Brinckman and Irving 2000.
160 Esteve 1999c.
161 Monroe 2000; Prather, personal communication.
162 Kern-Korot, personal communication.
163 Bakke 2001; Bakke, personal communication.
164 Esler, personal communication; Esler, in City of Sandy 1999.
165 Keil, personal communication.
166 Tehan, personal communication.
167 Esler, personal communication; Keil, personal communication.
168 O'Dell 2001a.
169 Irving 2001c.
170 Irving 2001c.
171 Muck, personal communication.
172 O'Dell 2001b.
173 Cox 2001.
174 Muck, personal communication.
175 Editor 2001.
176 Irving 2001a.
177 Bakke, personal communication.
178 Bakke, personal communication.
179 Lazenby, personal communication.
180 City of Sandy 2002.
181 Lazenby 2002.
182 Sten, personal communication.
183 Young, personal communication; Gray, personal communication.
184 Heintzman, personal communication.
185 Irving 2001b.
186 Keil, personal communication.
187 Bakke, personal communication.
188 Jensen, personal communication.
189 Keil 2009; Young, personal communication; Heintzman, personal

communication; Jensen, personal communication; Muck, personal communication; Lazenby, personal communication.

190 Kucas, personal communication; Lazenby, personal communication; Plaeger, personal communication.

191 Nudelman, personal communication.

192 Kirkendall, personal communication.

193 Athman, personal communication.

194 *Muck, personal communication; Plaeger, personal communication. As a political scientist, I would suggest that awarding one another silly prizes is a telling indicator of an effective multi-stakeholder collaboration.*

195 Burchfield, personal communication; Kern-Korot, personal communication.

196 Heintzman, personal communication.

197 Mitchnick, personal communication.

198 Major et al. 2012.

199 Trevison 2003; Kern-Korot, personal communication.

200 Esler, personal communication; Grant, personal communication.

201 Grant, personal communication.

202 Major et al. 2012.

203 Pagel, personal communication; Swift, personal communication; Athman, personal communication; Grant, personal communication; Kern-Korot, personal communication.

204 Grant, personal communication.

205 Keil, personal communication.

206 Nudelman, personal communication.

207 Major et al. 2012.

208 Grant, personal communication.

209 Trevison 2003.

210 Austin et al. in prep.

211 Janssens 2007b; Roper 2008.

212 Esteve 1999c.

213 Austin et al. in prep.

214 Rowley 1999; Janssens 2007a.

215 Trevison 2007e.

216 Trevison 2007d.

217 Anon. 2008.

218 Woods 2002.

219 *FERC 2003; Kling, personal communication. It is common to include a third party when transferring land to the federal government (Prather, personal communication).*

220 Kling, personal communication.

221 Kling, personal communication.

222 Heintzman, personal communication.

223 Trevison 2007a.

224 Trevison 2007a.

225 Trevison 2008.

226 Young, personal communication; Austin et al. in prep.

227 Muck, personal communication.

228 Esler, personal communication.

229 Alsbury, personal communication; Trevison 2007a.

230 ODFW 2013.

231 ODFW 2011a.

232 Heintzman, personal communication; FERC 2003; Esler 2009.

233 Anon. 2002a.

234 Glass, personal communication.

235 Anon. 2014.

236 Keil 2009.

237 Monroe 2007.

238 Esler, personal communication.

239 Keil, personal communication.

240 Esler, personal communication.

241 Trevison 2007c.

242 Athman, personal communication; Lazenby, personal communication; Kirkendall, personal communication; Muck, personal communication; Nudelman, personal communication.

243 Esler, personal communication.

244 Jensen, personal communication.

245 For example, Anon. 2003 and 2006d; Van Fleet 2008; Curtis, personal communication.

246 Trevison 2007b.

247 Kirkendall, personal communication.

248 Kober, personal communication;
    O'Keefe, personal communication.
249 Gersh 2011.
250 Gersh 2011; Alsbury, personal
    communication.
251 Parks 2009.
252 Esler, personal communication.
253 Grant, personal communication.
254 Newell, personal communication.
255 Kling, personal communication.
256 Lazenby, personal communication.
257 Trevison 2007d; Kober 2009.
258 Gersh 2011.
259 Nudelman, personal
    communication.
260 Trevison 2007a, 2008; Hatchcock
    2008.
261 City of Sandy 2007.
262 Smith 2012.
263 Goetze 2009.
264 Kling, personal communication.
265 Trackers Earth 2018.
266 Esler, personal communication.
267 Sandy Area Chamber of Commerce
    2013; Esler, personal com-
    munication; Lazenby, personal
    communication.
268 Garber-Simon 2015.
269 Lazenby personal communication;
    Cornforth Consultants and Crockett
    Environmental 2005.
270 Esler, personal communication.
271 Zauner, personal communication.
272 Arendt, personal communication.
273 Oregon Department of Fish and
    Wildlife 2017.
274 Alsbury, in Trevison 2007a.
275 Heintzman, personal
    communication.
276 FERC 2003.
277 Heintzman, personal
    communication.
278 Heintzman, personal
    communication.
279 Alsbury, personal communication.
280 Ritchie, personal communication.
281 Native Fish Society 2014.
282 Davis 2014a, b.
283 Sandy River Basin Watershed
    Council 2017.

284 Fryburg, in Trevison 2005.
285 Tehan, personal communication;
    Grant, personal communication;
    O'Keefe, personal communica-
    tion; Kirkendall, personal
    communication; Swift, personal
    communication.
286 Hatchcock 2008.
287 Heintzman, personal
    communication.
288 Keil, personal communication.
289 Heintzman, personal
    communication.
290 Esler, personal communication.
291 Gray, personal communication;
    Bakke, personal communication;
    Burchfield, personal commu-
    nication; Kern-Korot, personal
    communication.
292 Kirkendall, personal
    communication.
293 Bakke, personal communication;
    Ritchie, personal communication.
294 Esler, personal communication.
295 National Hydropower Association
    2014; Nudelman, personal
    communication.
296 National Hydropower Association
    2014.
297 McMullen 1999d.
298 Rowell 2001a.
299 For example, Anon. 2002e; Woods
    2003.
300 Trevison 2007f.
301 Sherman and Guibord 2007.
302 McMullen 1999a.
303 Editor 2007.
304 Guibord 2007.
305 Gersh 2011.
306 Rowell 2001b; Sherman 2007; Kober
    2009.
307 Esler 2009; Keil 2009; Trevison
    2003.

CHAPTER 6

1 Pohl 2002; American Rivers 2017;
  Thomas-Blate 2018.
2 American Rivers 2017.
3 National Research Council 1992;
  Doyle et al. 2003.

4 Van Dyke, personal communication.
5 Blumm and Erickson 2012; Hamilton, personal communication; O'Keefe, personal communication.
6 National Geographic 2011.
7 *Hunter, personal communication; Phippen, personal communication; Tehan, personal communication. But at the same time, the forces opposing dam removal on rivers like the Klamath have surely learned from the experience of the nearby Rogue as well (Strahan, personal communication).*
8 Hunter, personal communication.
9 *Of course, technical challenges will always be important in the removals of major dams. But these challenges are not political (though they are sometimes politicized), and in this sense they are no different than technical challenges of any large engineering project.*
10 Montgomery 2003.
11 Lowry 2003.
12 *Or even an endangered animal, unfortunately.*
13 Baker 1990a.
14 *The only exception would be a productive dam that posed some sort of imminent safety risk, but a lot of the time, even that doesn't seem to matter.*
15 Barr, personal communication.
16 And its successor, Nippon Paper Industries.
17 Office of Rep. Carl Wilson 1999; Office of Senator Brady Adams 1999.
18 Holl and Howarth 2000.
19 *It is notable that actually operating each dam only demanded a handful of employees, and their jobs were not much of an issue.*
20 USDOI NPS 2014e.
21 Provencher et al. 2008.
22 Vogel 1986.
23 Hunter, personal communication.
24 Duewel 1999c. His ideas wouldn't actually have worked.
25 Chastain, personal communication.
26 Peattie 2011; Cope, personal communication.
27 Tullos et al. 2014.
28 *There are hatchery fish in the Rogue as well—you'll recall that they caused dam defenders to question the coho listing—but hatchery operations were not important in the Savage Rapids settlement.*
29 Hilderbrand et al. 2005.
30 Winter and Crain 2008.
31 Brewitt 2016.
32 Lichatowich 2013.
33 Hunter, personal communication.
34 Reid et al. 2017.
35 Bowman, personal communication.
36 Sarakinos and Johnson 2003; Lejon and Nilsson 2009; Fox et al. 2016; Brummer et al. 2017.
37 Whitworth 2001.
38 Duewel 2008.
39 Greenwood 1994.
40 Doremus and Tarlock 2008.
41 Brewitt, personal observation.
42 Momsen 2013.
43 USDOI NPS 1996; Long 1997e; Smith 2012.
44 Spickler, personal communication.
45 Hewett, personal communication.
46 Chastain 1995b.
47 McMullen 1999e; Lewis 1999b.
48 Barnard 1998.
49 Editor 2000.
50 Layzer 2012. Indeed, it presently occupies the White House.
51 Sabatier et al. 1987.
52 *Even in 2013, the spotted owl was prominently mentioned in the Oscar-nominated movie* The Wolf of Wall Street, *a film mostly devoted to the hedonistic excesses of white-collar criminals.*
53 *The memory of which was recently defiled by the cartoon 300.*
54 Chastain, personal communication.
55 In the sense of Rochon 1998.
56 McPhee 1971; Reisner 1993.
57 Winter, personal communication.
58 Strahan, personal communication.

59 Chastain, personal communication; Spickler, personal communication; McMullen 1999e.

60 Sabatier and Jenkins-Smith 1993.

61 Bowman, personal communication.

62 Klyza and Sousa 2013.

63 Editor 1997.

64 McMullen 1999d.

65 Mansourian and Vallauri 2014; Reid et al. 2017.

66 Adams, personal communication.

67 *It would be extremely interesting to see what would happen if another old dam in a national park came up for relicensing—but it's not likely that there are many such dams.*

68 Irving 2000a.

69 Kingdon 1995.

70 Le Lay 2017.

71 Brummer et al. 2017.

72 Lejon and Nilsson 2009.

73 Crowley 1999.

74 McCool 2012.

75 Pagel, personal communication.

76 Lejon and Nilsson 2009; Fox et al. 2016.

77 Leach et al. 2002; Thomas 2003; Thomas and Koontz 2008.

78 Lichatowich 2013.

79 Lichatowich 2013; Grabowski et al. 2017.

80 Reisner 1993; Nash 2001.

81 Hundley 2001; Whitworth 2001.

82 Bendor et al. 2015.

83 Loomis 1996.

84 Gross 2008.

85 Schaeffer and Dissart 2018.

86 Wilkinson 1992.

87 *Sandy, too, had been a timber town, but by the late 1990s that history was remote enough that it was not a significant factor in the Bull Run debate.*

88 Hansen et al. 2002.

89 Peninsula Daily News Staff 1987.

90 It was soundly defeated.

Interviews

Many interviewees changed organizations or played several roles in dam removal. The affiliation identified here is their most prominent as it related to the issue.

CHAPTER 1

Dick Goin	Olympic Peninsula subsistence fisher	12/18/12
Matt Stoecker	Stoecker Ecological	4/7/12
Daniel Van Dyke	Oregon Department of Fish and Wildlife	3/29/12

CHAPTER 2

Jeff Curtis	WaterWatch of Oregon	11/26/12
Rick Rutz	Conservation Interveners	11/8/11

CHAPTER 3

Jim Baker	Friends of the Earth	3/4/12
Len Barson	Conservation Interveners	3/27/12
Lori Bodi	National Marine Fisheries Service	2/15/12
Joseph Bogaard	Save Our Wild Salmon	2/2/12
Terry Bracy	Daishowa America	4/1/13
Eric Broman	Sierra Club	3/1/12
Orville Campbell	Crown Zellerbach/James River	11/9/11
Shawn Cantrell	Friends of the Earth	9/14/11
Marv Chastain	Rescue Elwha Area Lakes	9/9/11
Pat Crain	Lower Elwha Klallam Tribe	3/5/12
Norm Dicks	US House of Representatives	10/7/13
Polly Dyer	Olympic Park Associates	3/27/12
Eric Eberhard	Senate Indian Affairs Committee	4/30/13
Robert Elofson	Lower Elwha Klallam Tribe	11/9/11
Maureen Finnerty	National Park Service	6/21/12
Michael Garrity	American Rivers	9/8/11
Gwill Ging	US Fish and Wildlife Service	12/6/12
Dick Goin	Olympic Peninsula subsistence fisher	12/18/12
Slade Gorton	US Senate	2/28/12
John Gussman	Double Click Productions	3/3/12
Bob Hamilton	US Bureau of Reclamation	2/21/12
Kim Hanson	Naturebridge	5/7/14
Cat Hawkins-Hoffman	National Park Service	12/18/12
Pearl Hewett	Olympic National Park inholder	11/10/11
Tom Jensen	Senate Energy and Natural Resources Committee	4/25/13
Robert Masonis	American Rivers	2/29/12

Tim McNulty	Olympic Park Associates	11/29/12
Joe Mentor	CAG Organizer	1/24/13
Pete Modaff	Staff of Norm Dicks	6/22/12
Judith Morris	Staff of Norm Dicks	3/2/12
Tom O'Keefe	American Whitewater	9/13/11
David Ortman	Friends of the Earth	12/7/12
George Pess	National Marine Fisheries Service	3/1/12
Roger Peters	US Fish and Wildlife Service	2/13/13
Bart Phillips	Clallam County Economic Development Council	3/15/12
Steve Ralph	Point No Point Treaty Council	12/13/12
Bill Robinson	Trout Unlimited	2/6/12
Michael Rossotto	Friends of the Earth	11/8/12
Rick Rutz	Conservation Interveners	11/8/11
Al Swift	US House of Representatives	6/20/12
Mike Weland	Staff of Brock Adams	5/6/13
Glenn Wiggins	CAG Member	3/3/12
Brian Winter	National Park Service	11/10/11
Bob Wunderlich	US Fish and Wildlife Service	4/3/12

CHAPTER 4

Brady Adams	Oregon Senate	8/31/11
Bill Bakke	Native Fish Society	2/20/12
Brian Barr	World Wildlife Fund	8/3/11
Steve Beyerlin	Oregon Guides and Packers	7/23/12
Ken Bierly	Oregon Watershed Enhancement Board	8/12/11
Margaret Bowman	American Rivers	8/16/12
James Buchal	Murphy and Buchal LLP	8/11/11
Chris Cauble	Grants Pass Irrigation District Counsel	8/29/11
Jeff Curtis	WaterWatch of Oregon	11/26/12
Laird Funk	Grants Pass Irrigation District	7/20/12
Michelle Giguere*	Ball Janik	8/20/12
Don Greenwood	Grants Pass Irrigation District Board	9/12/11
Leon Guillotte	Grants Pass Irrigation District Board	7/23/12
Bob Hamilton	US Bureau of Reclamation	7/25/11
Liz Hamilton	Northwest Sportfishing Industry Association	12/15/12
Craig Harper	Rogue Valley Council of Governments	7/19/11
Curtis Hayden	*Sneak Peak* Newspaper	7/18/12
Bob Hunter	WaterWatch of Oregon	4/19/11, 6/16/11, 7/19/12, 5/5/14
Dan James*	Ball Janik	8/20/12
Andy Kerr	Oregon Natural Resources Council	8/24/12
L. H. Kirtley	Grants Pass Irrigation District Board	8/19/11, 8/24/11
Jim Martin	Oregon Department of Fish and Wildlife	8/7/12
Tom McMurray	Grants Pass Irrigation District Board	8/5/11
Bernie Moore	Rogue Flyfishers	8/24/11
Martha Pagel	Oregon Water Resources Department	9/6/11
Ken Phippen	National Marine Fisheries Service	8/2/11
Claudia Polsky	Earthjustice	9/17/12
Peter Raabe	American Rivers	7/31/12
Meg Reeves	Oregon Water Resources Department	11/5/12

Bob Repine	Oregon House of Representatives	8/8/12
Dan Shepard	Grants Pass Irrigation District	7/13/11, 7/3/12, 7/23/12, 7/30/12
Mike Sherwood	Earthjustice	10/17/12
Kathy Smith	Oregon Water Resources Department	8/26/11
Louise Solliday	Governor Kitzhaber's Office	9/1/11
Marjorie Spickler	Grants Pass Irrigation District Board	8/21/11
Dave Strahan	Northwestern Sportfishing Industry Association	7/16/12
Nancy Tappan	Grants Pass Irrigation District Board	8/30/11
Michael Tehan	National Marine Fisheries Service	5/8/13
Thane Tienson	Copeland, Landye, Bennett, and Wolf, LLP	11/5/12
Daniel Van Dyke	Oregon Department of Fish and Wildlife	7/30/12
Julie Webster	Grants Pass Irrigation District	7/5/2012

* Giguere and James were interviewed together. Their answers were often mutual, and I cite them as a unit.

CHAPTER 5

Todd Alsbury	Oregon Department of Fish and Wildlife	3/12/12, 12/4/12
Kathryn Arendt	US Forest Service	3/16/12
Connie Athman	US Forest Service	1/26/12
Bill Bakke	Native Fish Society	2/20/12
Stephanie Burchfield	National Marine Fisheries Service	3/9/12
Jeff Curtis	WaterWatch of Oregon	11/26/12
John Esler	Portland General Electric	1/30/12, 7/19/13, 4/5/13, 5/18/18
Jack Glass	Hook-Up Guide Service	12/3/12
Gordon Grant	US Forest Service	3/7/12
Ann Gray	US Fish and Wildlife Service	2/10/12
Liz Hamilton	Northwest Sportfishing Industry Association	12/15/12
David Heintzman	Portland General Electric	3/19/12, 8/8/12, 2/25/13, 4/14/14, 4/15/14, 5/6/14
Keith Jensen	Alder Creek Kayak Supply	1/25/12
Julie Keil	Portland General Electric	9/6/11
Kammy Kern-Korot	Oregon Department of Fish and Wildlife	8/9/12
Keith Kirkendall	National Marine Fisheries Service	9/2/11
Josh Kling	Western Rivers Conservancy	8/6/12, 5/17/18
Amy Kober	American Rivers	11/6/12
Steve Kucas	Portland Water Bureau	11/6/12
Scott Lazenby	City of Sandy	2/8/12
Rosemary Menard	Portland Water Bureau	4/4/13
Alan Mitchnick	Federal Energy Regulatory Commission	2/7/12
Jim Muck	Oregon Department of Fish and Wildlife	9/7/12
Avis Newell	Oregon Department of Environmental Quality	8/13/12
Debra Nudelman	RESOLVE	11/7/12
Tom O'Keefe	American Whitewater	9/13/11
Martha Pagel	Oregon Water Resources Department	9/6/11
Ken Phippen	National Marine Fisheries Service	8/2/11
Russell Plaeger	Sandy River Basin Watershed Council	8/20/12
Dick Prather	US Bureau of Land Management	2/17/12
Norm Ritchie	Association of Northwest Steelheaders	1/25/12

Mike Sherwood	Earthjustice	10/17/12
Erik Sten	City of Portland	4/3/13
Brett Swift	American Rivers	8/12/11
Michael Tehan	National Marine Fisheries Service	5/18/13
Dan Van Dyke	Oregon Department of Fish and Wildlife	7/30/12
Doug Young	US Fish and Wildlife Service	11/18/11
John Zauner	Oregon Department of Fish and Wildlife	3/29/12

CHAPTER 6

Brady Adams	Oregon Senate	8/31/11
Brian Barr	World Wildlife Fund	8/3/11
Margaret Bowman	American Rivers	8/16/12
Marv Chastain	Rescue Elwha Area Lakes	9/9/11
Michael Cope*	Informal Geologist	7/?/11
Bob Hamilton	US Bureau of Reclamation	2/21/12
Pearl Hewett	Olympic National Park Inholder	11/10/11
Bob Hunter	WaterWatch of Oregon	6/16/11
Tom O'Keefe	American Whitewater	9/13/11
Martha Pagel	Oregon Water Resources Department	9/6/11
Ken Phippen	National Marine Fisheries Service	8/2/11
Marjorie Spickler	Grants Pass Irrigation District	8/21/11
Dave Strahan	Northwestern Sportfishing Industry Association	7/16/12
Michael Tehan	National Marine Fisheries Service	5/8/13
Daniel Van Dyke	Oregon Department of Fish and Wildlife	7/30/12
Brian Winter	National Park Service	11/10/11

* Cope happened in to the Josephine County Historical Society building on one of the many occasions when I was doing research there. Unprompted, he shared his theory about contaminants in the silt with me. I did not record the date, as I did not expect that his ideas had any political importance. Later, I read articles about his ideas and heard other people mention them, and I concluded that Mr. Cope had had more influence that I'd thought.

Works Cited

While researching this book, I was fortunate to work in several valuable archives. To source my citations, and to acknowledge their help, I list them here.

ELWHA

The University of Washington's Allen Library (hereafter UW) has a wonderful archive on the Elwha, and while it was hard to spend my days underground there and barely see Mount Rainier at all, I learned an enormous amount about the dam removal.

The Port Angeles branch of the North Olympic Library System (hereafter NOLS) contains the archives of the *Peninsula Daily News* and assorted other documents on the Elwha.

ROGUE

In Grants Pass, Oregon, the Josephine County Historical Society (hereafter JCHS) is a wonderful resource for anyone interested in the history of that interesting region. Joan Momsen was a great help to me there, but really, everyone there was terrific.

The Grants Pass Irrigation District (hereafter GPID) keeps thorough records of its past, and I spent many, many hours in the GPID offices, going through old binders. Dan Shepard's thoughtful and entertaining perspective added a lot to my time there, as did Julie Webster's recollections.

Jeff Duewel of the *Grants Pass Daily Courier* shared with me a collection of newspaper articles on Savage Rapids Dam. They and other *Daily Courier* articles are found at the offices of that newspaper, in Grants Pass.

Bob Hunter, of WaterWatch, shared some of the documents (hereafter BH) he'd amassed through his decades of involvement with Rogue politics.

SANDY

Portland General Electric personnel John Esler, Dave Heintzman, and the late Julie Keil were extremely helpful in every way, providing me with a variety of documents (hereafter PGE) about the Bull Run decommissioning.

I was able to study the *Sandy Post* archives with the help of reporter Lisa Anderson. These were housed in the *Post* offices. I also found them in the Gresham, Oregon, branch of the Multnomah County Public Library.

102nd Congress. 1992. H.R. 4844—Elwha River Ecosystem and Fisheries Restoration Act.

16 U.S.C. 1920. Federal Water Power Act. American Electric Power, United States of America. https://www.aep.com/about/IssuesAndPositions/governmentaffairs/docs/fpa.pdf.

Adamire, B. 1986. "Park Expansionists Selfish." *Peninsula Daily News*, September 26, A7.

Adamire, B. 1990a. "Elwha Dam Decision Absurd." *Peninsula Daily News*, April 11.

Adamire, B. 1990b. "What's Behind Dam Decisions?" *Peninsula Daily News*, July 11, A9.

Adamire, B. 1992. "Give Elwha Dam Land Back to Public." *Peninsula Daily News*, April 19, A9.

Adams, B. 1991. Statement at FERC Hearing, Port Angeles, WA, 4/3/91. UW.

Adams, B. 1999. HB3065. 70th Oregon Legislative Assembly—1999 Regular Session, Salem, OR. State Library of Oregon, 1999 Summary of Major Legislation. http://library.state.or.us/repository/2010/201010061538333/1999.pdf.

Aldwell, T. 1950. *Conquering the Last Frontier*. Seattle: Mountaineer Books.

Allen, N. 2010. "Texas Governor Calls Louisiana Oil Spill 'Act of God.'" *Telegraph*, May 5. http://www.telegraph.co.uk/news/worldnews/northamerica/usa/7679189/Texas-Governor-calls-Louisiana-oil-spill-act-of-God.html.

Alt, D. 2005. "Inside Glacial Lake Missoula." *NOVA*. http://www.pbs.org/wgbh/nova/earth/inside-glacial-lake-missoula.html.

American Public Power Institute, Edison Electric Institute, and National Rural Electric Cooperative Association. 1992. Amicus Briefs in Olympic Park Associates et al. vs. FERC/James River 2, April 22. UW.

American Rivers. 2009. "The 10th Anniversary of the Removal of Maine's Edwards Dam." July 1. http://www.americanrivers.org/initiative/dams/projects/the-10th-anniversary-of-the-removal-of-mainea%25C2%2589uas-edwards-dam/.

American Rivers. 2017. Map of U.S. Dams Removed since 1916. Accessed November 7, 2017. https://www.americanrivers.org/threats-solutions/restoring-damaged-rivers/dam-removal-map/.

American Whitewater. 2014. "Project-Elwha Restoration (WA)." Accessed February 6, 2014. http://www.americanwhitewater.org/content/Project/view/id/elwha/.

American Whitewater, American Rivers, and Trout Unlimited. 2007. "Restoring the Sandy River: Dam Removal and River Restoration in Portland's Backyard." https://www.tu.org/sites/default/files/sandy_river_AW_AR_TU.pdf.

Amundson, M. 1988. "License Battle Heats Up." *Peninsula Daily News*, December 4, A1/A2.

Amundson, M. 1989. "Swift Proposes Study of Elwha Fish Runs, Dams." *Peninsula Daily News*, January 22, A1/A2.

Anderson, J., and A. Hoffmann. 2017. "Elwha River Dam Removal, Fish Status Update, and Fishing Moratorium." Washington Fish and Wildlife Commission, Port Angeles, WA. https://wdfw.wa.gov/commission/meetings/2017/09/sep0817_14_presentation.pdf.

Andrews, R. 1999. *Managing the Environment, Managing Ourselves: A History of American Environmental Policy*. New Haven, CT: Yale University Press.

Anon. 1921a. "Arranging for Celebration." *Grants Pass Courier*. November 1. JCHS.

Anon. 1921b. "Complete Power House Walls." *Grants Pass Courier*. September 27. JCHS.

Anon. 1986. "City Council Surprised by Plan for Elwha River Dam Takeover." *Peninsula Daily News*, September 17.

Anon. 1987a. "James River Keeps Ownership of Dams." *Peninsula Daily News*, November 27, A1/A2.

Anon. 1987b. "Parasite Causing Large Salmon Kill." *Peninsula Daily News*, September 3, A1/A2.

Anon. 1988. "Daishowa Gives $36,000 to Build PA Play Fields." *Peninsula Daily News*, February 3.

Anon. 1989. "Adams Gets a Look." *Peninsula Daily News*, March 24, A9.

Anon. 1990a. "PA Council OKs Taking Out Log Dam." *Peninsula Daily News*, April 4, A3.

Anon. 1990b. "Sierra Club to Hear of Elwha Dams." *Peninsula Daily News*, April 10, A3.

Anon. 1991a. "Supporters of Dams Hold Vigil Saturday." *Grants Pass Daily Courier*, February 8.

Anon. 1991b. "Swift Sees Little Hope for Dams." *Peninsula Daily News*, June 20, A1/A2.

Anon. 1992a. "City Mixed on Stance." *Peninsula Daily News*, July 10, A1/A2.

Anon. 1992b. "Daishowa Likes Bill to Oust Dams." *Peninsula Daily News*, April 5, A5.

Anon. 1992c. "Swift Bids Farewell to Peninsula Constituents." *Peninsula Daily News*, December 18, A4.

Anon. 1993a. "Dam Backers Will Meet Wednesday." *Grants Pass Daily Courier*, October 12.

Anon. 1993b. "Granges Gear for Dam Fight." *Grants Pass Daily Courier*, November 24.

Anon. 1994a. "Dams Draw Both Sides." *Peninsula Daily News*, December 18, A1.

Anon. 1994b. "GOP Likely to Ax Dams' Destruction; Elwha Fish-Run Plan Would Be Expensive." *Tacoma News-Tribune*, November 18, B7.

Anon. 1995a. "Dams Plan Hits Snag." *Peninsula Daily News*, July 27, A1.

Anon. 1995b. "Endangered Rivers List Names Elwha." *Peninsula Daily News*, April 18, A2.

Anon. 1996a. "Committee to Study Elwha Dam Removal." *Peninsula Daily News*, February 26, A3.

Anon. 1996b. "Dam Money in Budget." *Peninsula Daily News*, A1.

Anon. 1997a. "Fly-Fishing Workshop Presented by Lauzon." *Sandy Post*, February 19, 5A.

Anon. 1997b. "GPID: Tear Out the Dam." *Grants Pass Daily Courier*, August 5.

Anon. 1997c. "Rogue River City Council to Debate Dam Support Issue." *Grants Pass Daily Courier*, September 16.

Anon. 1998a. "Environmental Group Says It Will Sue GPID If Dam Isn't Removed." *Grants Pass Daily Courier*, October 10.

Anon. 1998b. "Gorton Has Hopes for Elwha Deal." *Peninsula Daily News*, October 11, A3.

Anon. 1999. "This Might Be Year for Action on the Elwha Dam." *Peninsula Daily News*, July 7, A7.

Anon. 2000a. "Dam Removal Position Letter Tabled for Now." *Peninsula Daily News*, August 15, A3.

Anon. 2000b. "PGE Puts Together Site Assessment of Lake." *Sandy Post*, June 14, 3A.

Anon. 2001. "Officials Seek Cause of Fish Kill on Elwha." *Peninsula Daily News*, October 12, A9.

Anon. 2002a. "$45,000 Grant Will Help Council Improve Salmon Habitat in Creek." *Sandy Post*, June 26, 3A.

Anon. 2002b. "Historic Salmon Count Under Way on Elwha River." *Peninsula Daily News*, August 18, A1.

Anon. 2002c. "Looking Up Close at Young Elwha Salmon." *Peninsula Daily News*, May 27, A3.

Anon. 2002d. "Panel Clears Funds for Elwha Project." *Peninsula Daily News*, June 26, A1.

Anon. 2002e. "Winter Steelhead Course at College." *Sandy Post*, December 24, 3A.

Anon. 2003. "PGE Employees Earn Grants for Groups." *Sandy Post*, April 30, 1A.

Anon. 2005. "Post-Dam Plantings Envisioned." *Peninsula Daily News*, April 7, A1.

Anon. 2006a. "Blue Lake Hosts Fly Fishing Seminar." *Sandy Post*, March 8.

Anon. 2006b. "How Will It Look When the Dams Are Gone?" *Peninsula Daily News*, September 3, C1.

Anon. 2006c. "Middle Schoolers Share Findings." *Peninsula Daily News*, November 20, A5.

Anon. 2006d. "Portland General Electric Becomes an Independently Owned Company." *Sandy Post*, April 5, 3A.

Anon. 2007a. "Delay Disappoints Many Connected with Dams Project." *Peninsula Daily News*, March 5, A6.

Anon. 2007b. "Elwha Volunteers Rid Valley of Weeds." *Peninsula Daily News*, June 17, A6.

Anon. 2008. "Catch All You Want at Roslyn Lake." *Sandy Post*, January 30, 1A.

Anon. 2014. Sandy River Basin Partners. http://www.sandyriverpartners.org/partners.html/.

Anon. 2018a. "Colt Collection." Museum of Connecticut History. http://museumofcthistory.org/colt-collection/.

Anon. 2018b. Millpond Dam, Concord River. Waymarkingcom. http://www.waymarking.com/waymarks/WMD589_Millpond_Dam_Concord_River_Billerica_MA.

Anon. 2018c. Official State of Jefferson Movement. Accessed May 5, 2018. http://soj51.org/.

Anonymous. 1990. Olympic Peninsula Families Solidarity Rally. UW.

Araki, H., B. A. Berejikian, M. J. Ford, et al. 2008. "Fitness of Hatchery-Reared Salmonids in the Wild." *Evolutionary Applications* 1:342–355. http://doi.wiley.com/10.1111/j.1752-4571.2008.00026.x.

Arman, F., and G. Woolridge. 1982. *The Rogue: A River to Run*. Grants Pass, OR: Wildwood Press.

Associated Press. 1995. "GPID Chief Asks Lawmakers to Back Dam." *Grants Pass Daily Courier*, April 6.

Associated Press. 1996. "Official Pushes for Dam Removal." *Peninsula Daily News*, May 6, A1.

Associated Press. 1997. "Wolves Out, Dam In." *Peninsula Daily News*, June 28, A1.

Associated Press. 1998a. "Elwha Dam Removal Funded." *Peninsula Daily News*, February 3, A1.

Associated Press. 1998b. "Elwha Removal Depends on Gorton." *Peninsula Daily News*, October 26, A2.

Associated Press. 1998c. "Gorton Denies Elwha Funding." *Peninsula Daily News*, October 16, A1.

Associated Press. 1998d. "Gorton to Foes: Fish or Cut Bait." *Peninsula Daily News*, A1.

Associated Press. 1998e. "Salmon Swim with Politics." *Peninsula Daily News*, April 12, A6.

Associated Press. 1999. "Different Doomed Dams Show Uneven Financing." *Peninsula Daily News*, September 27, A1.

Associated Press. 2001. "Governor Signs Death Warrant for Dam." *Grants Pass Daily Courier*, October 13.

Associated Press and the *Daily Courier*. 1991. "Savage Rapids Dam on State Official's Hit List." *Grants Pass Daily Courier*, February 7.

Associated Press and the *Daily Courier*. 1999. "It's Official: Governor Sinks GPID Water Permit." *Grants Pass Daily Courier*, June 30.

Augerot, X., and D. Foley. 2005. *Atlas of Pacific Salmon: The First Map-Based Status Assessment of Salmon in the North Pacific*. Berkeley: University of California Press.

Austin, T., L. House-Peters, and D. Skees-Gregory. In Preparation. "Valuing Cultural Ecosystem Services in the Planning Process: A Case Study on the Decommissioning of Oregon's Bull Run Hydroelectric Project and the Draining of Roslyn Lake."

Babbitt, B. 1982. "Federalism and the Environment: An Intergovernmental Perspective of the Sagebrush Rebellion." *Environmental Law* 12:847–861.

Babbitt, B. 1998. "Dams Are Not Forever." In *Ecological Society of America Annual Meeting*. Baltimore, MD: Ecological Society of America.

Babbitt, B. 2002. "What Goes Up, May Come Down." *BioScience* 52:656–658.

Backman, T. W. H., and A. F. Evans. 2002. "Gas Bubble Trauma Incidence in Adult Salmonids in the Columbia River Basin." *North American Journal of Fisheries Management* 22:579–584.

Baker, J. 1990a. Letter to Friends of the Earth, October 22. UW.

Baker, J. 1990b. Letter to the Hon. Al Swift and Midori Okazaki, September 11. UW.

Baker, J. 1991. Letter to Elwha Conservation Interveners, June 28. UW.

Bakke, B. 2001. "Story Fails To Put Sandy Fish Situation In Proper Context." *Oregonian*, February 22, 02.

Barlow, Z. 2011. "A Graffiti Taunt to Tear Down Matilija Dam." *Ventura County Star*, September 13.

Barlow Knives. 2018. "History of Barlow Knives." http://barlow-knives.com/history. htm.

Barnard, J. 1998. "Reversing the Course of History." *Grants Pass Daily Courier*, August 22.

Barson, L. 1990. Letter to Priscilla Derick, Perkins Coie, introducing Jim Baker, April 19. UW.

Bartholow, J. M., S. G. Campbell, and M. Flug. 2004. "Predicting the Thermal Effects of Dam Removal on the Klamath River." *Environmental Management* 34:856–874. http://www.ncbi.nlm.nih.gov/pubmed/15726283.

Baumgartner, F., and B. Jones. 1993. *Agendas and Instability in American Politics*. Chicago: University of Chicago Press.

Beaumariage, R. 2001. "Dam Removal." *Peninsula Daily News*, August 13, A5.

Becklin, D. 1998a. "GPID Board Has Fought Courageous Battle." *Grants Pass Daily Courier*, October 28.

Becklin, D. 1998b. Letter to Steven Morris, NMFS, October 16. GPID.

Becklin, D. 1999. "Remove the Dam on GPID's Terms." *Grants Pass Daily Courier*, December 1.

Becklin, D. 2005. "$30-Million and Counting the Stupidity—Removing Oregon's Savage Rapids Dam—An Enviro's Wet Dream." Our Klamath Basin Water Crisis, May 25. http://www.klamathbasincrisis.org/Poweranddamstoc/savagerapids-dam052505.htm.

Bednarek, A. T. 2001. "Undamming Rivers: A Review of the Ecological Impacts of Dam Removal." *Environmental Management* 27:803–814. http://www.springer-link.com/Index/10.1007/s002670010189.

Bellmore, J. R., J. J. Duda, L. S. Craig, et al. 2016. "Status and Trends of Dam Removal Research in the United States." *WIREs Water* 4:e1164.

Belsky, M. 1996. "Indian Fishing Rights: A Lost Opportunity for Ecosystem Management." *Journal of Land Use and Environmental Law* 12:45–65.

Bender, P. 1997. "Restoring the Elwha, White Salmon, and Rogue Rivers: A Comparison of Dam Removal Proposals in the Pacific Northwest." *Journal of Land, Resources and Environmental Law* 189:1–48.

Bendor, T., T. W. Lester, A. Livengood, et al. 2015. "Estimating the Size and Impact of the Ecological Restoration Economy." *PLoS ONE* 10:1–15. http://dx.doi.org/10.1371/journal.pone.0128339.

Benik, R. D., R. Hamilton, and J. Redding. 2010. "Removing Savage Rapids Dam." *International Water Power and Dam Construction*. February 8. http://www.waterpowermagazine.com/features/featureremoving-savage-rapids-dam.

Bergman, B. 1990. "Elwha River Dams Important to Area." *Peninsula Daily News*, July 16, A7.

Birkland, T. 2006. *Lessons of Disaster: Policy Change after Catastrophic Events*. Washington, DC: Georgetown University Press.

BLM National Science and Technology Center. 2011. Mining Claims and Sites on Federal Lands. https://www.blm.gov/download/file/fid/7476.

Blumm, M., and A. Erickson. 2012. "Dam Removal in the Pacific Northwest: Lessons for the Nation." *Environmental Law* 4:1043.

Blumm, M., and B. Swift. 1998. "Indian Treaty Piscary Profit and Habitat Protection in the Pacific Northwest: A Property Rights Approach." *University of Colorado Law Review* 69:407.

Bodi, L., R. Busch, W. Frymire, et al. 1987. Letter to Kenneth Plumb, FERC, June 17. UW.

Bodi, L. 1989. Letter to Lois Cashell, FERC. Scope of Work for Evaluation of Fish Restoration Alternatives for the Elwha River, Including Dam Removal, March 20. UW.

Bodi, L., S. Driver, R. Busch, et al. 1990. Letter to Richard Fleming, Hosey and Associates, representing James River 2. June 12. UW.

Bodi, L., S. Driver, R. Busch, et al. 1989. Joint Fish and Wildlife Agencies' Supplemental Petition Regarding Application and Information Deficiencies. June 27. UW.

Bohman, J. 1994. Letter to Elwha Stakeholders re: REAL Newsletters, April 21. UW.

Bohman, J. 1995. Letter to Joe Mentor, May 3. UW.

Bonneville Power Administration. 2010. "Columbia River Hatcheries: An Evolving Role." http://www.salmonrecovery.gov/Hatchery/HatcheryReform.aspx.

BOR. 1965. *Lake Powell, Jewel of the Colorado*. Washington, DC: US Government Printing Office.

Bottom, D. L., C. A. Simenstad, J. Burke, et al. 2005. Salmon at River's End: The Role of the Estuary in the Decline and Recovery of Columbia River Salmon. NOAA Technical Memorandum, National Marine Fisheries Service-NWFSC 68. https://repository.library.noaa.gov/view/noaa/3432.

Boughton, D. A., C. Adams, Peter B. Anderson, Eric Fusaro, Craig Keller, Edward Kelley, Elise Lentsch, et al. 2006. Steelhead of the South-Central/Southern California Coast: Population Characterization for Recovery Planning. NOAA Technical Memorandum 394. https://pubs.er.usgs.gov/publication/70175741.

Bowden, C. 1990. "Last Will and Monkeywrench: Hayduke Lives! by Edward Abbey." *Los Angeles Times*, January 7. http://articles.latimes.com/1990-01-07/books/bk-259_1_edward-abbey.

Bradley, B. 2011. Keynote Address at Lower Elwha Klallam Tribe dam removal dinner, Port Angeles, WA, September 16, 1–6. http://www.billbradley.com/assets/PDF/Elwha-River-Celebration-Speech_9-16-2011.pdf.

Brandon, P. 1980. Letter to Larry Jebousek, OWRD, December 10. GPID.

Branin, A. 1990. Letter to Orville Campbell, James River, February 5. UW.

Branson-Potts, H. 2018. "In California's Rural, Conservative North, There Are Big Dreams for Cleaving the State." *Los Angeles Times*, March 17. http://www.latimes.com/local/lanow/la-me-ln-state-of-jefferson-activists-20180317-htmlstory.html.

Braudrick, C., and J. Vick. 2001. Observed Geomorphic and Ecological Impacts of October 2000 Lahars on the Sandy River, OR. Memorandum from Stillwater Sciences to John Esler, PGE. http://www.sandyriverpartners.org/reports/StillwaterSandyLahar01.pdf.

Brewitt, P. 2016. "Do the Fish Return? A Qualitative Assessment of Anadromous Pacific Salmonids' Upstream Movement after Dam Removal." *Northwest Science* 90:433–449.

Brinckman, J. 1999. "PGE Agrees to Remove 2 Dams." *Oregonian*, May 26, A01.

Brinckman, J., and D. Irving. 2000. "Oregon Considers Closing Fishery." *Oregonian*, October 3, A01.

Brower, D. 1997. "Let the River Run Through It." *Sierra Magazine*. https://vault.sierraclub.org/sierra/199703/brower.asp.

Brown, B. 1982. *Mountain in the Clouds*. New York: Simon and Schuster.

Brummer, M., B. Rodríguez-Labajos, T. T. Nguyen, et al. 2017. "'They Have Kidnapped Our River': Dam Removal Conflicts in Catalonia and Their Relation to Ecosystem Services Perceptions." *Water Alternatives* 10:744–768.

Buck, H. 1995. "Savage Rapids Will Be Around a While Longer." *Grants Pass Daily Courier*, April 1.

Buck, H. 1998. "GPID On New Course to Save Dam." *Grants Pass Daily Courier*, January 7, 1A/2A.

Burke, A. 2001a. "Hydro(power) Had No Friends." *High Country News*, September. http://www.hcn.org/issues/211/10751/print_view.

Burke, A. 2001b. "River of Dreams: The 30-Year Struggle to Resurrect Washington's Elwha River and One of Its Spectacular Salmon Runs." *High Country News*, September 24.

Busch, R. 1990. Comments of the Elwha Klallam Tribe on Scoping Document 1, February 28. UW.

Busch, R. W. 2007. "Justice Delayed: A Tribal Attorney's Perspective on Elwha River Dam Removal and Ecosystem Restoration." In *Natural Resources Law Center 25th Anniversary Conference*. Boulder: University of Colorado Law School.

Busch, R., and S. Ralph. 1986. Lower Elwha Indian Tribe's Motion for Intervention, Consolidation, A Conference, and Other Relief. January 24. UW.

Bushaw-Newton, K. L., D. D. Hart, J. E. Pizzuto, et al. 2002. "An Integrative Approach towards Understanding Ecological Responses to Dam Removal: The Manatawny Creek Study." *Journal of the American Water Resources Association* 38:1581–1599.

Buxton, S. 1990. "Fish Ladders Just Might Work." *Peninsula Daily News*, July 26, A9.

Cade, M. 2007. "The Sandy River's Guide and Guardian." *Sandy Post*, June 20, 10A.

Callis, T. 2010. "National Parks Chief Lauds Tribe." *Peninsula Daily News*, July 4, A1/A8.

Callis, T. 2011. "Elwha Dam Removals: Researchers Use Giant Fish Weir to Study Salmon." *Peninsula Daily News*, September 4.

Camara, C. 1994a. "Many Favor Dam Removal." *Peninsula Daily News*, November 15, A1.

Camara, C. 1994b. "REAL Fights to Keep Elwha Dams, Lakes in Place." *Peninsula Daily News*, April 9, A5.

Camara, C. 1994c. "Removal Gets Strong Support." *Peninsula Daily News*, November 16, A1.

Camara, C. 1994d. "Support at Meeting Runs Deep to Keep 2 Elwha River Dams." *Peninsula Daily News*, November 16, A3.

Camara, C. 1995a. "Dams' Removal Not Likely, Dicks Says." *Peninsula Daily News*, August 27, A1.

Camara, C. 1995b. "Realtor Group Supports Dams." *Peninsula Daily News*, February 5, A1.

Camara, C. 1996. "Group Offers Plan to Preserve Dams." *Peninsula Daily News*, January 21, A1.

Canan, P. 1989. "The SLAPP from a Sociological Perspective." *Pace Environmental Law Review* 7:23–32.

Cantrell, S. 1992a. Letter to Elwha Conservation Interveners, May 19. UW.

Cantrell, S. 1992b. Letter to Environmental Interveners, March 27. UW.

Cantrell, S. 1993a. Letter to Brian Winter, August 5. UW.

Cantrell, S. 1993b. Letter to Brian Winter and Jeff Bohman, NMFS and LEKT, December 23. UW.

Cantrell, S. 1993c. Letter to Elwha Stakeholders, April 13. UW.

Cantrell, S. 1994a. Elwha Litigation Theories, Letter to Brooke Drury, The Mountaineers, December 21. UW.

Cantrell, S. 1994b. Letter to Environmental Group Interveners, January 25. UW.

Cantrell, S. 1996a. Comments on Elwha Citizen's Advisory Committee Report, June 5. UW.

Cantrell, S. 1996b. Letter to Elwha Conservation Interveners, October 3. UW.

Cantrell, S. 1996c. Letter to Elwha Conservation Interveners re: Elwha Letter and Meeting with White House, February 16. UW.

Cantrell, S. 1997a. Letter to Elwha Environmental Group Contacts, August 7. UW.

Cantrell, S. 1997b. Letter to Katie McGinty, August 3. UW.

Cantrell, S., and C. Elofson. 1992. "Elwha River Restoration Bill Signed into Law." Press Release, Conservation Interveners and Lower Elwha Klallam Tribe. UW.

Casey, J. 2007. "Permits Granted for Dam Removal." *Peninsula Daily News*, February 15, A1.

Catterson, C. 1994. OPA et al. vs. FERC/James River, US DOC et al. vs. FERC/James River, September 14. UW.

Center of the American West. 1997. *Atlas of the New West*. Edited by W. Riebsame. New York: W.W. Norton.

Charles, D. 1994. "Indians Not to Blame for Salmon Shortage." *Peninsula Daily News*, A10.

Charles, G. n.d. Testimony to Be Presented before Appropriations Committee, US House of Representatives. UW.

Chasan, D. J. 2015. "Hatcheries Flow on Despite the Evidence They Harm Salmon Recovery." *Crosscut*, March 30. https://crosscut.com/2015/03/hatcheries-part-2.

Chastain, M. 1994. Letter to Friends of REAL, February 9. UW.

Chastain, M. 1995a. "Alternatives Exist to Elwha Dam Removal." *Peninsula Daily News*, September 29, A10.

Chastain, M. 1995b. Letter to Friends of REAL, September 7. UW.

Chastain, M. 1996. "Elwha Politics Get Weird." *Peninsula Daily News*, May 9, A10.

Chastain, M. 2010. "R.E.A.L. and History of Planned Removal of Elwha Dams." *Citizens Review Online*. http://www.citizenreviewonline.org/2010/Jun/elwha_dams_history.html.

Chastain, M. 2014a. "Back to 1492." *North Olympic Bulletin Board.* http://www.marvchastain.com/BackTo1492.htm.

Chastain, M. 2014b. "Elwha Synopsis." *North Olympic Bulletin Board.* http://www.marvchastain.com/ElwhaSynop.html.

Chastain, M. 2014c. "Index2." *North Olympic Bulletin Board.* http://www.marvchastain.com/.

Chew, J. 2007. "Noted Artist Envisions Future of Elwha River." *Peninsula Daily News,* February 26, A1.

Chouinard, Y. 2012. "Dammed If We Don't." *Patagonia.* Mountain 2012 Catalog. Accessed February 6, 2014. http://www.patagonia.com/us/patagonia.go?assetid=67738.

Christman, T. 1989a. "Elwha Dams Catch On as Major Political Issue." *Peninsula Daily News,* May 22, A1/A2.

Christman, T. 1989b. "Elwha Plan: Save Power, Oust Dams." *Peninsula Daily News,* July 7, A1/A2.

Citizens' Advisory Committee. 1996. "The Elwha River and Our Community's Future: Recommendations of the Elwha Citizens' Advisory Committee." Port Angeles, WA. NOLS.

City of Portland Oregon, and Portland General Electric. 1999a. Governor Announces Plan to Remove Dams, Restore Habitat to Sandy River Basin. Press Release. PGE.

City of Portland Oregon, and Portland General Electric. 1999b. "Sandy River Basin Habitat Restoration Plan Fact Sheet." PGE.

City of Sandy. 1999. 7 June 1999 City Council Minutes Regular Meeting Approved Minutes. http://archive.cityofsandy.com/WebLink/DocView.aspx?id=2714&searchid=d72c29f3-854f-4ef5-942b-f2f4172389c6&dbid=1.

City of Sandy. 2002. November 2001 to December 2002 Approved Minutes. http://archive.cityofsandy.com/WebLink/DocView.aspx?id=8408&searchid=82a5a34c-9a82-49fb-9620-447bfbcdc312&dbid=1.

City of Sandy. 2007. 21 May 2007 City Council Minutes Regular Meeting Approved Minutes. http://archive.cityofsandy.com/WebLink/DocView.aspx?id=15839&searchid=2b6c3813-0a04-4988-96c1-f4c15ee7ba49&dbid=1.

Clark, B. 2009. "River Restoration in the American West: Assessing Variation in the Outcomes of Policy Change." *Society and Natural Resources* 22:401–416. http://www.informaworld.com/openurl?genre=article&doi=10.1080/08941920801914528&magic=crossref%7C%7CD404A21C5BB053405B1A640AFFD44AE3.

Clarke, J., and D. McCool. 1996. *Staking Out the Terrain: Power and Performance among Natural Resource Agencies.* Albany: State University of New York Press.

Cokelet, E. 2004. "Students Aid Watershed Study." *Peninsula Daily News,* October 14, A4.

Cole, D. H. 1986. "Reviving the Federal Power Act's Comprehensive Plan Requirement: A History of Neglect and Prospects for the Future." Indiana University Maurer School of Law. https://www.repository.law.indiana.edu/facpub/927/.

Coleman, J. S. 1958. "Relational Analysis: The Study of Social Organizations with Survey Methods." *Human Organization* 17:28–36.

Collier, M., R. Webb, and J. Schmidt. 2000. *Dams and Rivers: A Primer on the Downstream Effects of Dams.* Darby, PA: Diane Publishing Company.

Cornforth Consultants and Crockett Environmental. 2005. "Turbidity Managment Plan, Bull Run Hydropower Project Decommissioning." Portland, OR. http://www.deq.state.or.us/wq/sec401cert/docs/hydropower.

Cox, J. 2000. "Future of Roslyn Lake Dubious as Power Plant Is Taken Off-Line." *Sandy Post*, September 20, 1A/2A.

Cox, J. 2001. "Fish Plan Modified." *Sandy Post*, February 21, 1A/2A.

Crane, J. 2009. "'Setting the River Free': The Removal of the Edwards Dam and the Restoration of the Kennebec River." *Water History* 1:131–148. http://link. springer.com/10.1007/s12685-009-0007-2.

Crane, J. 2011. *Finding the River: An Environmental History of the Elwha*. Corvallis: Oregon State University Press.

Cronon, W. 1983. *Changes in the Land: Indians, Colonists and the Ecology of New England*. New York: Hill and Wang.

Cronon, W. 1992. *Nature's Metropolis: Chicago and the Great West*. New York: W.W. Norton.

Cronon, W. 1995. "The Trouble with Wilderness, or, Getting Back to the Wrong Nature." In *Uncommon Ground: Rethinking the Human Place in Nature*, edited by W. Cronon, 69–90. New York: W.W. Norton.

Crowley, K. 1999. "Lake Pedder's Loss and Failed Restoration: Ecological Politics Meets Liberal Democracy in Tasmania." *Australian Journal of Political Science* 34:409–424.

Crown Zellerbach. 1986. Response to Comments from DOI and FERC Intervenors, June 27. UW.

Crown Zellerbach and Washington Department of Fisheries. 1975. Agreement Covering Contribution Toward Cost of Construction and Operation of Salmon Rearing Pond and Appurtenant Facilities on Elwha River.

Crutzen, P. J. 2002. "Geology of Mankind." *Nature* 415:23. http://www.ncbi.nlm.nih. gov/pubmed/11780095.

Curnew, J. 1990a. All About Fish in the Elwha River. UW.

Curnew, J. 1990b. "Elwha Dam Problems Not That Complex." *Peninsula Daily News*, November 12, A7.

Curnew, J. 1990c. "Group Urges That Dams on Elwha Come Down." *Peninsula Daily News*, July 24, A7.

Curnew, J. 1991. Letter to Friends of the Elwha, September 9. UW.

David J. Newton Associates. 1994. *Grants Pass Irrigation District Water Management Study*. Salem, OR. Southern Oregon University Library, Ashland, OR.

Davis, R. 2014a. "Federal Judge Allows Sandy Hatchery Fish to Be Released This Spring." *Oregonian*. http://www.oregonlive.com/environment/index.ssf/2014/03/ federal_judge_allows_sandy_hat.html.

Davis, R. 2014b. "Releasing Sandy River Hatchery Steelhead, Salmon Thrown into Flux by Federal Judge." *Oregonian*. http://www.oregonlive.com/environment/ index.ssf/2014/01/releasing_sandy_river_hatchery.html.

Davis, W. N. 1952. "State of Jefferson." *California Historical Society Quarterly* 31:125–138.

Dawson, M. 1990. "New Agency Urges Removal of Elwha Dams." *Peninsula Daily News*, July 4, A1.

Dawson, M. 1997. "Senator Snags Elwha Funding." *Peninsula Daily News*, July 4, A1.

Dawson, M. 1998. "Dam Removal Close to Reality." *Peninsula Daily News*, February 4, A1.

Deacon, J. 1991. Letter to Lois Cashell, FERC, June 12. UW.

Deland, R. 1997. "Coho in Danger Only of Becoming Cat Food." *Grants Pass Daily Courier*, November 6.

de la Paz, D. 2008. "Botanist Turns to Native Species." *Peninsula Daily News*, February 20, C1.

de la Paz, D.U. 2011. "'Prayers Answered': National Figures Join Peninsula Leaders at Dam Ceremony." *Peninsula Daily News*, September 18.

Derick, P. 1986. Crown Zellerbach Corporation's Answer in Opposition to Motion for Late Intervention by Seattle Audubon Society, Friends of the Earth, Olympic Park Associates, and the Sierra Club, June 2. UW.

Derick, P. 1987. James River II Response to Request for Information Pursuant to Amended Section 15 of Federal Power Act, May 29. UW.

Derick, P. 1989. James River II Comments on NEPA Alternatives and Additional Information, July 14. UW.

Derick, P. 1990a. James River II Comments Regarding Scoping of Environmental Impact Statement, February 28. UW.

Derick, P. 1990b. James River II Response to FERC's Request for Additional Information Item 3, and Information Regarding Regional Need for Power, March 29. UW.

Derick, P. 1990c. James River II Response to Request for Ruling on Petition for Declaratory Order in Connection with Expiration of Annual License, June 5. UW.

Derick, P. 1992. Letter to Lois Cashell, FERC, April 13. UW.

DeVoto, B. 1950. *Shall We Let Them Ruin Our National Parks?* Philadelphia, PA: Curtis Publishing.

Dickerson, P. 2010a. "Be Among the First with a Dam Button." *Peninsula Daily News*, April 6, A1/A4.

Dickerson, P. 2010b. "Interactive Model of Dam Removal Coming to Feiro." *Peninsula Daily News*, March 16, A9.

Dickerson, P. 2010c. "Removal of Dams Hurt Trout?" *Peninsula Daily News*, March 11, A1/A6.

Dicks, N. 2011. "Remarks." In *2011 Elwha River Science Symposium*, September 14–16, Peninsula College, Port Angeles, WA.

Dietrich, W. 1992. *The Final Forest: The Battle for the Last Great Trees of the Pacific Northwest*. New York: Simon and Schuster.

Dietrich, W. 1995 [2016]. *Northwest Passage: The Great Columbia River*. Seattle: University of Washington Press.

Dingell, J. 1992. Letter to Martin Allday, FERC, July 2. UW.

Dodds, G. B. 2011. "The Fight to Close the Rogue." *Oregon Historical Quarterly* 60:461–474.

Dolan, K. 1987a. "Elwha Dams Not Needed, Earth First! Group Says." *Peninsula Daily News*, June 29, A3.

Dolan, K. 1987b. "Unknown Earth First! Artist Paints 'Crack' on Elwha Dam." *Peninsula Daily News*, September 3, A1.

Doremus, H., and A. Tarlock. 2008. *Water War in the Klamath Basin: Macho Law, Combat Biology, and Dirty Politics*. Washington, DC: Island Press.

Doyle, M. W., J. M. Harbor, and E. H. Stanley. 2003. "Toward Policies and Decision-Making for Dam Removal." *Environmental Management* 31:453–465. http://www.ncbi.nlm.nih.gov/pubmed/12677292.

Duda, J. J., D. J. Wieferich, R. S. Bristol, et al. 2016. Dam Removal Information Portal (DRIP)—A Map-Based Resource Linking Scientific Studies and Associated Geospatial Information about Dam Removals. United States Geological Survey. Open File Report 2016-1132.

Duewel, J. 1985. "Dam Concerns Prompt Study." *Grants Pass Daily Courier*, January 18.

Duewel, J. 1986. "Volunteers Will Try Rebuilding Savage Rapids Dams Fish Ladder." *Grants Pass Daily Courier*, February 5.

Duewel, J. 1999a. "Becklin Lining Up Marquee Supporters for Dam Plan." *Grants Pass Daily Courier*, November 18.

Duewel, J. 1999b. "Dam Foe Elected to GPID Board." *Grants Pass Daily Courier*, November 10.

Duewel, J. 1999c. "Dam Supporters Come Out in Force." *Grants Pass Daily Courier*, December 7.

Duewel, J. 1999d. "Details of Dam Removal Plan Aired." *Grants Pass Daily Courier*, November 10.

Duewel, J. 1999e. "GPID: We Want to Save Fish." *Grants Pass Daily Courier*, May 20, 1A/2A.

Duewel, J. 1999f. "GPID's Supplemental Water Right Is On the Line." *Grants Pass Daily Courier*, August 26.

Duewel, J. 1999g. "GPID Patrons Split on Becklin Deal." *Grants Pass Daily Courier*, July 9.

Duewel, J. 1999h. "GPID Sues Patrons Who Jump Ship." *Grants Pass Daily Courier*, October 1, 1A.

Duewel, J. 1999i. "Irrigators' Profits Drying Up." *Grants Pass Daily Courier*, July 15, 1A/3A.

Duewel, J. 1999j. "Plan to Scrap Dam Unveiled." *Grants Pass Daily Courier*, July 7.

Duewel, J. 1999k. "South Highline Canal Running but 'Chaotic.'" *Grants Pass Daily Courier*, July 27.

Duewel, J. 1999L. "State Fines GPID Boss $2,000." *Grants Pass Daily Courier*, October 8, 1A/3A.

Duewel, J. 2000a. "Canal Should Be OK Tonight." *Grants Pass Daily Courier*, June 14.

Duewel, J. 2000b. "Congress Begins Push to Remove Dam." *Grants Pass Daily Courier*, October 24, 1A/2A.

Duewel, J. 2000c. "Dam Removal Plan Passes." *Grants Pass Daily Courier*, January 19, 1A/2A.

Duewel, J. 2000d. "GPID Faces Expensive Repair Cost for Turbine." *Grants Pass Daily Courier*, May 30.

Duewel, J. 2000e. "GPID Patrons Combust Over Dry Ditches." *Grants Pass Daily Courier*, June 14.

Duewel, J. 2000f. "GPID Repairs Hold Up; D.C. Mum on Dam Plan." *Grants Pass Daily Courier*, July 12.

Duewel, J. 2000g. "GPID Water Is Running, and So Is Courtroom Battle." *Grants Pass Daily Courier*, June 26.

Duewel, J. 2000h. "New GPID's Chief's a 13-Year Vet of Dam War." *Grants Pass Daily Courier*, January 11.

Duewel, J. 2000i. "Savage Rapids Dam Repair Bill: $225,000." *Grants Pass Daily Courier*, June 7, 1A/2A.

Duewel, J. 2000j. "Study Shows Little Sediment Behind Dam." *Grants Pass Daily Courier*, August 7.

Duewel, J. 2001a. "Days of Annual Ritual Numbered." *Grants Pass Daily Courier*, October 11.

Duewel, J. 2001b. "GPID Approves Dam Settlement." *Grants Pass Daily Courier*, July 25, 1A/2A.

Duewel, J. 2001c. "Removal of Savage Rapids Dam an Uphill Battle." *Grants Pass Daily Courier*, June 13.

Duewel, J. 2001d. "State Chips In to Help Prepare for Dam Removal." *Grants Pass Daily Courier*, May 7.

Duewel, J. 2001e. "Supporters of the Savage Dams Unite." *Grants Pass Daily Courier*, February 22, 1A/2A.

Duewel, J. 2002a. "Congress Unlikely To Re-introduce Dam Removal Bill." *Grants Pass Daily Courier*, October 9, 6A/8A.

Duewel, J. 2002b. "Savage Rapids Dam Removal Bill Gets New Name." *Grants Pass Daily Courier*, April 27.

Duewel, J. 2004. "GPID Gets $2.2 Million for Dam's Demise." *Grants Pass Daily Courier*, November 22, 1A/2A.

Duewel, J. 2005a. "2008 Projected as Date for Dam Removal." *Grants Pass Daily Courier*, September 17.

Duewel, J. 2005b. "Congress Appropriates $1.5 Million for Removal of Savage Rapids Dam." *Grants Pass Daily Courier*, November 12.

Duewel, J. 2006a. "$28 Million Savage Rapids Dam Pump Station Contract Awarded." *Grants Pass Daily Courier*, August 9, 1A/3A.

Duewel, J. 2006b. "Broken Fish Screens Cause Problems For GPID." *Grants Pass Daily Courier*.

Duewel, J. 2006c. "GPID, Enviros Pleased with Dam Removal Funding." *Grants Pass Daily Courier*, February 16.

Duewel, J. 2008. "Local Lake Will Soon Be Gone." *Grants Pass Daily Courier*, September 4.

Duewel, J. 2009a. "Many Celebrate River's Release." *Grants Pass Daily Courier*, October 12.

Duewel, J. 2009b. "Problems Surface with Pumps at Savage Rapids Dam." *Grants Pass Daily Courier*, July 9.

Earthworks. 2016. "Tell Your Senator to Support 1872 Mining Law Reform." Accessed January 1, 2016. http://org.salsalabs.com/o/676/p/dia/action3/common/public/?action_KEY=18701&tag=action.

Editor. 1920a. "No State Guarantee." *Rogue River Courier*, September 28, weekly edition. JCHS.

Editor. 1920b. "Water Everywhere." *Rogue River Courier*, June 1, weekly edition. JCHS.

Editor. 1992. "A Step Closer—Congress Should Agree to Remove Elwha Dams." *Seattle Times*, May 11. http://community.seattletimes.nwsource.com/archive/?date=199 20511&slug=1491187.

Editor. 1994. "Elwha Dam Removal." *Peninsula Daily News*, September 6, A8.

Editor. 1997. "Elwha Issues Not Simple: New Fish Ladder Legislation Really Is Too Good to Be True." *Peninsula Daily News*, February 2, A8.

Editor. 1998. "Gorton's Elwha Dance Steps on Many Toes." *Peninsula Daily News*, October 21, A6.

Editor. 1999a. "Giving Salmon a Route to the Sea." *Oregonian*, May 27, D14.

Editor. 1999b. "Removal of Dams Appears to Be OK." *Sandy Post*, June 2, 4A.

Editor. 2000. "Collected Letters to the Editor." *Peninsula Daily News*, February 20, A8–9.

Editor. 2001. "Commission Should Delay Fish Decision." *Sandy Post*, February 14, 4A.

Editor. 2007. "A River Released to the Wild." *Oregonian*, July 29, E04.

Egan, T. 1990. "Dams May Be Razed So the Salmon Can Pass." *New York Times*, January 7.http://www.nytimes.com/1990/07/15/us/dams-may-be-razed-so-the-salmon-can-pass.html.

Egan, T. 1991. *The Good Rain: Across Time and Terrain in the Pacific Northwest*. New York: Knopf Doubleday.

Egan, V. G. 2007. Restoring the Elwha: Salmon, Dams and People on the Olympic Peninsula, a Case Study of Environmental Decision-Making. PhD Thesis. Antioch University New England, Keene, NH.

Eliot, T. S. 1944. *The Dry Salvages.* London: Faber and Faber.

Elwha Conservation Interveners. 1989a. Comments on Response to Request for Additional Information of May 28, 1987, and Supplemental Response to May 28, 1987 Request For Additional Information, October. UW.

Elwha Conservation Interveners. 1989b. Letter to the Hon. Al Swift, April 18. UW.

Elwha Conservation Interveners. 1991. Letter to Gov. Booth Gardner, Sen. Brock Adams, Sen. Slade Gorton, and the Hon. Al Swift, March 15. UW.

Elwha Conservation Interveners. 1992a. Certificate of Appreciation Presented by Olympic Park Associates, Friends of the Earth, The Mountaineers, Seattle Audubon Society, Sierra Club and the Entire Northwest Conservation Community to Richard Rutz. UW.

Elwha Conservation Interveners. 1992b. "It's Time to Celebrate Our Victory." UW.

Eno, M. 2007. "One Last Plunge into Roslyn Lake: Final Polar Bear Dip on Jan. 1." *Sandy Post*, December 31, 2A.

Erb, G. 1988. "Mill's Water Use Explored." *Peninsula Daily News*, June 21, A1/A2.

Erb, G. 1989. "Rough Water." *Peninsula Daily News*, December 22, A1/A2.

Erb, G. 1990a. "Park Takes Stand against Dams." *Peninsula Daily News*, June 18, A1/A2.

Erb, G. 1990b. "Swift Warns Agency on Dam Stance." *Peninsula Daily News*, June 19, A1/A2.

Erb, G. 1991a. "City Light Ends Daishowa Study." *Peninsula Daily News*, October 13, A1.

Erb, G. 1991b. "Peninsula Leaders Cautious about Elwha Dam Proposal." *Peninsula Daily News*, August 17, A1/A2.

Erdman Video Systems and USDOI NPS. 2014. "Elwha River Restoration Project." http://video-monitoring.com/construction/olympic/js.htm.

Esler, J. 2009. "Going, Going, Gone: Reflections on the Retirement of the Bull Run Hydroelectric Project." *Open Spaces* 9:21–25.

Esteve, H. 1999a. "Fish Debate on Sandy." *Oregonian*, August 19, 01.

Esteve, H. 1999b. "PGE Takes Heat from Audience about Roslyn Lake." *Oregonian*, June 15, C02.

Esteve, H. 1999c. "Residents Rally to Fight Roslyn Lake Closure; A Project Manager for PGE Says the Company Will Not Halt Demolition of the Dams Feeding the Popular Recreation Spot." *Oregonian*, June 14, E01.

Esteve, H. 1999d. "Supporters Rally to Preserve Lake." *Oregonian*, August 2, E01.

Evans, B. 2005. "We're Supposed to Feel Sorry for Becklin?" *Grants Pass Daily Courier*, March 1.

Evans, D. 1991. KIRO (Seattle, WA). Weekly Radio Broadcast, April 5.

Ewing, G. 2002. "Hatchery Moves Steelhead into Roslyn." *Oregonian*, February 28, B02.

Fattig, P. 1980. "What Do You Want to Do with Savage Rapids Dam?" *Grants Pass Daily Courier*, June 20, 1A/2A.

Fausch, K., and T. Northcote. 1992. "Large Woody Debris and Salmonid Habitat in a Small Coastal British Columbia Stream." *Canadian Journal of Fisheries and Aquatic Sciences* 49:682–693.

FERC. 1991. "Draft Environmental Impact Statement: Glines Canyon (FERC No. 588) and Elwha (FERC No. 2683)." Washington, DC: Hydroelectric Projects, Washington.

FERC. 2003. "Final Environmental Impact Statement: Bull Run Project, Oregon, FERC No. 477-024." Washington, DC. https://searchworks.stanford.edu/view/5568575.

Finnerty, M. 1993. Draft Elwha Report for Rick Rutz, July 2. UW.

Fox, C. A., N. James, R. Dale, et al. 2017. "'The River Is Us; The River Is in Our Veins': Re-defining River Restoration in Three Indigenous Communities." *Sustainability Science* 12 (4): 521–533.

Fox, C. A., F. J. Magilligan, and C. S. Sneddon. 2016. "'You Kill the Dam, You Are Killing a Part of Me': Dam Removal and the Environmental Politics of River Restoration." *Geoforum* 70:93–104.

Freeman, M. 2013. "There's a Redd Revival on the Rogue." *Medford Mail-Tribune*, November 19. http://www.mailtribune.com/apps/pbcs.dll/article?AID=%252F2 0131119%252FNEWS%252F311190306.

Frego, J. 2011. "Savage Rapids Dam Fiasco." *Oregonian*, May 19. http://blog.oregon-live.com/myoregon/2011/05/savage_rapids_dam_fiasco.html.

Freyhof, J. 2014. "*Salmo salar* (Atlantic Salmon)." *The IUCN Red List of Threatened Species.* http://www.iucnredlist.org/details/19855/1.

Friends of the Earth Magazine. 1991. "An Upstream Battle," 21(4).

Friends of the Earth-Northwest. 1990. "GAO Finds for Removal of Elwha River Dams." Press Release. UW.

Friends of the Earth-Northwest, Sierra Club, Seattle Audubon Society, et al. 1992. Mailing, May. UW.

Friends of the Elwha. 1991. Public flyer announcing public meeting with Bruce Brown.

Fultz, K. 1992. "Hydroelectric Dams: Proposed Legislation to Restore Elwha River Ecosystem and Fisheries." Washington, DC: US General Accounting Office.

Gaar, E. 1997. Letter to Dennis Becklin, GPID, June 6. GPID.

Gallup. 2017. Presidential Approval Ratings—Bill Clinton. Accessed September 4, 2017. http://www.gallup.com/poll/116584/presidential-approval-ratings-bill-clinton.aspx.

Garber-Simon, J. 2015. "Roslyn Lake Off the Table but Remote Elephant Center for Oregon Zoo Still Under Consideration." *Oregon Metro*, August 18. https://www.oregonmetro.gov/news/roslyn-lake-table-remote-elephant-center-oregon-zoo-still-under-consideration.

Gardner, B. 1992. Letter to Shawn Cantrell, Friends of the Earth, November 3. UW.

Gawley, B. 2007a. "Elwha Dams Removal Date Clouded." *Peninsula Daily News*, April 26, A1.

Gawley, B. 2007b. "First Step in Elwha Dam Removal Starts." *Peninsula Daily News*, September 16, A4.

Gawley, B. 2007c. "How Elwha Will Change after Dams." *Peninsula Daily News*, August 19, C1.

Gawley, B. 2007d. "Peninsula in Spending Bill." *Peninsula Daily News*, December 20, A1.

Gawley, B. 2007e. "Water Plant Set for Construction." *Peninsula Daily News*, May 17, A7.

Geiske, H. 1979. Letter to James Sexson, Oregon Water Resources Department, April 12. GPID.

Gende, S. M., R. T. Edwards, M. F. Willson, et al. 2002. "Pacific Salmon in Aquatic and Terrestrial Ecosystems." *BioScience* 52:917–928.

Gersh, J. 2011. MegaStructures: Dam Busters. Video. National Geographic. https://www.youtube.com/watch?v=7RtjISTizx4.

Gillete, L., and M. Jordan. 1994. Letter to the Hon. Al Swift, May 14. UW.

Goertz, G., and J. Mahoney. 2012. *A Tale of Two Cultures: Qualitative and Quantitative Research in the Social Sciences*. Princeton, NJ: Princeton University Press.

Goetze, J. 2009. "Bull Run River: A Tour for Creatives Leads to a New Exhibit." *Oregonian*, October 7. http://www.oregonlive.com/clackamascounty/index. ssf/2009/10/bull_run_river_a_tour_for_crea.html.

Gomez and Sullivan Engineers. 2016. "Concord River Diadromous Fish Restoration: Feasibility Study." Final report prepared for Commonwealth of Massachusetts Division of Marine Fisheries. http://archives.lib.state.ma.us/handle/2452/626310.

Goranson, E. 1988. "PGE Crews Keep Wary Eye on Marmot Dam." *Oregonian*, December 14, E01.

Goranson, E. 1989a. "New Concrete Structure to Replace Marmot Dam." *Oregonian*, January 18, B02.

Goranson, E. 1989b. "New Stronger Dam on Sandy River to Be Dedicated by PGE on Saturday." *Oregonian*, October 27, E13.

Goranson, E. 1989c. "PGE Officials Dedicate New Dam on Sandy." *Oregonian*, October 29, E01.

Gorton, S. 1992. Testimony before Congress, June 4.

Gorton, S. 1995. Senate Acts on Elwha and Glines Dams, July 26. Press Release. UW.

Gottlieb, P. 1999. "Dam Pact Includes Water System Funds." *Peninsula Daily News*, October 21, A5.

Gottlieb, P. 2000. "Gorton: Glines Dam Decision Should Wait." *Peninsula Daily News*, June 4, A1.

Gottlieb, P. 2006. "Why the Elwha Dams Are Still There." *Peninsula Daily News*, January 27, A10.

Gottlieb, P. 2010a. "Breaking News: Montana Company Wins Contract to Remove Elwha River Dams." *Peninsula Daily News*, August 26.

Gottlieb, P. 2010b. "Dam Removal Contract Comes in $13 Million under Estimate." *Peninsula Daily News*, August 27.

Gottlieb, P. 2010c. "Elwha River's 100-Pound Salmon: Did They Exist? Will They Return?" *Peninsula Daily News*, May 22. http://archive.peninsuladailynews.com/ article/20100523/news/305239991/elwha-rivers-100-pound-salmon-did-they-exist-will-they-return.

Gottlieb, P. 2010d. "GOP Candidates Criticize Removal of Elwha Dams." *Peninsula Daily News*, May 26, A4.

Gottlieb, P. 2011a. "Boulders Shore Up Elwha Levee to Prepare for Dams' Demolition." *Peninsula Daily News*, January 12.

Gottlieb, P. 2011b. "Elwha Dams Electrical Turbines Turned Off for Good." *Peninsula Daily News*, May 31.

Gottlieb, P. 2011c. "Obama? Bon Jovi? Redford? Olympic National Park Seeks Big Names to Celebrate Start of Dam Removals." *Peninsula Daily News*, January 30.

Gottlieb, P. 2017. "Court of Appeals Supports Hatchery Fish in Elwha River in Decision." *Peninsula Daily News*, August 27. http://www.peninsuladailynews. com/news/court-of-appeals-supports-hatchery-fish-in-elwha-river-in-decision/.

Govc, B. 1998. "GPID Board Endangering the District." *Grants Pass Daily Courier*, May 5.

Gove, B. 1999. "GPID Proposal Intentionally Ludicrous." *Grants Pass Daily Courier*, December 30.

Govtrack. 2014. Richard "Rick" White. Civic Impulse, LLC. https://www.govtrack. us/congress/members/richard_white/411550.

GPID. 1978. December 12 Meeting. Board Meeting Minutes. GPID.

GPID. 1979a. January 24 Meeting. Board Meeting Minutes. GPID.

GPID. 1979b. January 31 Meeting. Board Meeting Minutes. GPID.

GPID. 1980. April 9 Meeting. Board Meeting Minutes. GPID.

GPID. 1981a. February 10 Meeting. Board Meeting Minutes. GPID.

GPID. 1981b. May 12 Meeting. Board Meeting Minutes. GPID.

GPID. 1985. December 10 Meeting. Board Meeting Minutes. GPID.

GPID. 1987a. November 18 Meeting. Board Meeting Minutes. GPID.

GPID. 1987b. August 11 Meeting. Board Meeting Minutes. GPID.

GPID. 1988. March 8 Meeting. Board Meeting Minutes. GPID.

GPID. 1989a. January 13 Meeting. Board Meeting Minutes. GPID.

GPID. 1989b. February 14 Meeting. Board Meeting Minutes. GPID.

GPID. 1990. December 28 Meeting. Board Meeting Minutes. GPID.

GPID. 1991a. December 20 Meeting. Board Meeting Minutes. GPID.

GPID. 1991b. February 12 Meeting. Board Meeting Minutes. GPID.

GPID. 1991c. February 28 Meeting. Board Meeting Minutes. GPID.

GPID. 1992a. December 3 Meeting. Board Meeting Minutes. GPID.

GPID. 1992b. February 9 Meeting. Board Meeting Minutes. GPID.

GPID. 1993a. January 5 Meeting. Board Meeting Minutes. GPID.

GPID. 1993b. October 12 Meeting. Board Meeting Minutes. GPID.

GPID. 1993c. November 9 Meeting. Board Meeting Minutes. GPID.

GPID. 1993d. December 14 Meeting. Board Meeting Notes. GPID.

GPID. 1993e. March 9 Meeting. Board Meeting Minutes. GPID.

GPID. 1993f. September 14 Meeting. Board Meeting Minutes. GPID.

GPID. 1994a. January 11 Meeting. Board Meeting Minutes. GPID.

GPID. 1994b. January 26 Meeting. Board Meeting Notes. GPID.

GPID. 1994c. January 5 Meeting. Board Meeting Minutes. GPID.

GPID. 1994d. "Here Are the Facts about the Savage Rapids Dam." *Grants Pass Daily Courier*, February 4, 1994.

GPID. 1995a. January 13 Meeting. Board Meeting Minutes. GPID.

GPID. 1995b. February 14 Meeting. Board Meeting Minutes. GPID.

GPID. 1995c. February 16 Meeting. Board Meeting Minutes. GPID.

GPID. 1995d. February 21 Meeting. Board Meeting Minutes. GPID.

GPID. 1995e. March 28 Meeting. Board Meeting Minutes. GPID.

GPID. 1995f. April 25 Meeting. Board Meeting Minutes. GPID.

GPID. 1995g. April 5 Meeting. Board Meeting Minutes. GPID.

GPID. 1996a. April 9 Meeting. Board Meeting Minutes. GPID.

GPID. 1996b. September 10 Meeting. Board Meeting Minutes. GPID.

GPID. 1997a. October 14 Meeting. Board Meeting Minutes. GPID.

GPID. 1997b. October 16 Meeting. Board Meeting Minutes. GPID.

GPID. 1997c. November 17 Meeting. Board Meeting Minutes. GPID.

GPID. 1997d. May 13 Meeting. Board Meeting Minutes. GPID.

GPID. 1997e. June 6 Meeting. Board Meeting Minutes. GPID.

GPID. 1997f. July 22 Meeting. Board Meeting Minutes. GPID.

GPID. 1997g. July 29 Meeting. Board Meeting Minutes. GPID.

GPID. 1997h. August 12 Meeting. Board Meeting Minutes. GPID.

GPID. 1997i. August 5 Meeting. Board Meeting Minutes. GPID.

GPID. 1998a. January 20 Meeting. Board Meeting Minutes. GPID.

GPID. 1998b. January 6 Meeting. Board Meeting Minutes. GPID.

GPID. 1998c. October 31 Meeting. Board Meeting Minutes. GPID.

GPID. 1998d. February 18 Meeting. Board Meeting Minutes. GPID.

GPID. 1998e. February 24 Meeting. Board Meeting Minutes. GPID.

GPID. 1998f. February 6 Meeting. Board Meeting Minutes. GPID.

GPID. 1998g. March 17 Meeting. Board Meeting Minutes. GPID.

GPID. 1998h. March 3 Meeting. Board Meeting Minutes. GPID.

GPID. 1998i. May 28 Meeting. Board Meeting Minutes. GPID.

GPID. 1998j. June 9 Meeting. Board Meeting Minutes. GPID.

GPID. 1998k. July 14 Meeting. Board Meeting Minutes. GPID.

GPID. 1998L. August 11 Meeting. Board Meeting Minutes. GPID.

GPID. 1998m. September 25 Meeting. Board Meeting Minutes. GPID.

GPID. 1998n. September 8 Meeting. Board Meeting Minutes. GPID.

GPID. 1999a. November 15 Meeting. Board Meeting Minutes. GPID.

GPID. 1999b. December 6 Meeting. Board Meeting Minutes. GPID.

GPID. 1999c. September 2 Meeting. Board Meeting Minutes. GPID.

GPID. 2000a. November 30 Meeting. Board Meeting Minutes. GPID.

GPID. 2000b. Press Release, January 18. GPID.

GPID. 2001a. June 12 Meeting. Board Meeting Minutes. GPID.

GPID. 2001b. August 14 Meeting. Board Meeting Minutes. GPID.

GPID. 2002a. January 8 Meeting. Board Meeting Minutes. GPID.

GPID. 2002b. December 10 Meeting. Board Meeting Minutes. GPID.

GPID. 2002c. December 17 Meeting. Board Meeting Minutes. GPID.

GPID. 2003. June 10 Meeting. Board Meeting Minutes. GPID.

GPID. 2014. History. Accessed February 6. http://gpid.com/history/.

GPID, Waterwatch of Oregon, and Trout Unlimited. 2000. Press Release, October 23.

Grable, J. 2014. "After the Flood." *Earth Island Journal*. http://www.earthisland.org/journal/index.php/eij/article/after_the_flood/.

Grabowski, Z. J., A. Denton, M. A. Rozance, et al. 2017. "Removing Dams, Constructing Science: Coproduction of Undammed Riverscapes by Politics, Finance, Environment, Society, and Technology." *Water Alternatives* 10:769–795. www.water-alternatives.org.

Graf, W. L. 2003. "The Changing Role of Dams in Water Resources Management." *Water Resources Update* 126:54–59.

Green, M. 2010. "Elwha Dams." *Peninsula Daily News*, April 8, A7.

Greenwood, D. 1994. "Grants Pass Will Suffer If Irrigation District's Dam Removed." *Grants Pass Daily Courier*, November 8.

Gregory, G. 1993a. "Bad News Given on Savage Rapids." *Grants Pass Daily Courier*, October 30, 6A/7A.

Gregory, G. 1993b. "GPID Hears Tough Talk on Savage Rapids." *Grants Pass Daily Courier*, December 15.

Gregory, G. 1993c. "GPID Invites Dam Foes to Come Visit." *Grants Pass Daily Courier*, October 14.

Gregory, G. 1994a. "Backers Plot Strategies to Save Dam." *Grants Pass Daily Courier*, January 26.

Gregory, G. 1994b. "Bid to Recall GPID Board Flowing Along, Backers Say." *Grants Pass Daily Courier*, March 21.

Gregory, G. 1994c. "Dam Fans Scratch Heads, Raise Fists." *Grants Pass Daily Courier*, January 15.

Gregory, G. 1994d. "Official Calls GPID Decision Good One." *Grants Pass Daily Courier*, January 29.

Gregory, G. 1994e. "Packwood Hears Dam Concerns." *Grants Pass Daily Courier*, February 15, 1A/2A.

Gregory, G. 1994f. "Some See Dam as the First Domino." *Grants Pass Daily Courier*, January 29.

Gregory, G. 1994g. "SR's Fish-Killing Rap Is Ancient." *Grants Pass Daily Courier*.

Gregory, S., H. Li, and J. Li. 2002. "The Conceptual Basis for Ecological Responses to Dam Removal." *BioScience* 52:713–723.

Gresh, T., J. Lichatowich, and P. Schoonmaker. 2000. "An Estimation of Historic and Current Levels of Salmon Production in the Northeast Pacific Ecosystem: Evidence of a Nutrient Deficit in the Freshwater Systems of the Pacific Northwest." *Fisheries* 25:15–21.

Griffing, M. 1990. "Don't Forget Dam-Property Rights." *Peninsula Daily News*, January 15, A7.

Gross, M. 2006. "Beyond Expertise: Ecological Science and the Making of Socially Robust Restoration Strategies." *Journal for Nature Conservation* 14:172–179. http://linkinghub.elsevier.com/retrieve/pii/S1617138106000239.

Gross, M. 2008. "Return of the Wolf: Ecological Restoration and the Deliberate Inclusion of the Unexpected." *Environmental Politics* 17:115–120. http://www.tandfonline.com/doi/abs/10.1080/09644010701643159.

Grossman, E. 2002. *Watershed: The Undamming of America*. New York: Counterpoint.

Guarino, J. 2013. "Tribal Advocacy and the Art of Dam Removal: The Lower Elwha Klallam and the Elwha Dams." *American Indian Law Journal* 2:114–145.

Guibord, G. 2007. "Sandy River Runs Free." *Sandy Post*, October 24, 1A/14A.

Gupta, A. 2013. "The World's Oldest Dams Still in Use." Water Technology. https://www.water-technology.net/features/feature-the-worlds-oldest-dams-still-in-use/.

Guston, D. H. 2001. "Boundary Organizations in Environmental Policy and Science: An Introduction." *Science, Technology, and Human Values* 26:399–408.

Halverson, A. 2011. *An Entirely Synthetic Fish*. New Haven, CT: Yale University Press.

Hanh, B. 1986. "Agencies to Explore Savage Rapids Dam Options." *Grants Pass Daily Courier*, January 8.

Hansen, A. J., R. Rasker, B. Maxwell, et al. 2002. "Ecological Causes and Consequences of Demographic Change in the New West." *BioScience* 52:151–162.

Hard, J., R. Kope, W. Grant, et al. 1996. Status Review of Pink Salmon from Washington, Oregon, and California. NOAA Technical Memorandum NMFS-NWFSC-25.

Hardin, G. 1968. "The Tragedy of the Commons." *Science* 162:1243–1248.

Harris, E. 2006. "Dam Removal Images." *Peninsula Daily News*, September 4, A7.

Harris, L. 1990a. "Anti-Dam Forces Dig In." *Peninsula Daily News*, July 13, A1/A2.

Harris, L. 1990b. "Elwha Dams Likely to Be Big Turf War." *Peninsula Daily News*, November 8, A3.

Harris, L. 1990c. "Elwha Proposal Brings Mixed Views." *Peninsula Daily News*, August 15, A1/A2.

Harris, L. 1990d. "Little Dam-Water Data in Pipeline." *Peninsula Daily News*, September 14, A1/A2.

Harris, L. 1991a. "Dam Study Brings Optimism, Caution." *Peninsula Daily News*, March 1, A1/A2.

Harris, L. 1991b. "Groups Want Dam Removal." *Peninsula Daily News*, June 2, A1/A2.

Harris, L. 1991c. "Lawmaker Tries to Ease Dam Concerns." *Peninsula Daily News*, January 19, A3.

Harris, L. 1991d. "U.S. Looks at Buying Elwha Dams." *Peninsula Daily News*, August 16, A1/A2.

Harris, L. 1992a. "Adams Has Bill to Remove Dams." *Peninsula Daily News*, January 9, A1.

Harris, L. 1992b. "Dicks Is Wary of Dam Cost." *Peninsula Daily News*, April 17, A1.

Harris, L. 1992c. "Elwha Dam Bill Protects PA Water, Hook." *Peninsula Daily News*, October 7, A1/A2.

Harris, L. 1992d. "PA Council Pans Bill to Buy, Remove Dams." *Peninsula Daily News*, January 29, A3.

Harris, L. 1992e. "PA Mayor Says Elwha Bill Addresses City Water Costs." *Peninsula Daily News*, March 19, A3.

Harza Engineering. 1991. Comments on FERC's DEIS of February, June 28. UW.

Hatchcock, M. 2008. "PGE Sets Drain Date for Roslyn Lake." *Sandy Post*, March 26, 1A/4A.

Hawkins-Hoffman, C. 1990. Letter to Polly Dyer, OPA, October 22. UW.

Hayden, C. 1994. "Battle for the Dam Heats Up." *Sneak Preview*, August.

Hayden, C. 1997. "The Saving of Savage Rapids Dam: A Band of Local Activists Fight a Heroic Battle to Keep the Dam." *Sneak Preview*. January.

Hayden, C. 2014. "A Brief History of the Sneak Preview." *Sneak Preview*. Accessed January 6, 2014. http://www.sneakpre.com/about.

Heinz Center. 2003. *Dam Removal Research: Status and Prospects*. (W. Graf, Ed.) Washington, DC: The H. John Heinz III Center for Science, Economics and the Environment.

Helfield, J. M., and R. J. Naiman. 2001. "Effects of Salmon-Derived Nitrogen on Riparian Forest Growth and Implications for Stream Productivity." *Ecology* 82:2403–2409.

Helmholz, R. H. 1999. "Magna Carta and the IUS Commune." *University of Chicago Law Review* 66:297–371.

Henderson, B. 1982. "Steelhead Saved; Casualties Eaten." *Grants Pass Daily Courier*, March 10.

Henry, B. 2011. "Boldt's Impact." *Peninsula Daily News*, February 25, A10.

Hilderbrand, R. H., A. C. Watts, and A. M. Randle. 2005. "The Myths of Restoration Ecology." *Ecology and Society* 10:19.

Hiljus, B. 1994a. "Savage Rapids Dam Defies Fixing." *Grants Pass Daily Courier*, February 4.

Hiljus, B. 1994b. "Saving the Dam Could Doom the District." *Grants Pass Daily Courier*, November 5.

Hirschman, A. O. 1970. *Exit, Voice and Loyalty: Responses to Decline in Firms, Organizations and States*. Cambridge, MA: Harvard University Press.

Hobbs, R. J., L. M. Hallett, P. R. Ehrlich, et al. 2011. "Intervention Ecology: Applying Ecological Science in the Twenty-First Century." *BioScience* 61:442–450. https://academic.oup.com/bioscience/article-lookup/doi/10.1525/bio.2011.61.6.6.

Hofstadter, R. 1964. "The Paranoid Style in American Politics." *Harper's Magazine*, November, 77–86.

Holden, P. 1986. "Finding an Effective Balance." *Peninsula Daily News*, October 3, A7.

Holl, K. D., and R. B. Howarth. 2000. "Paying for Restoration." *Restoration Ecology* 8:260–267.

Hollis, S., and C. Knutson. 1992. "City of Port Angeles' Motion to Intervene Out of Time in Elwha Relicensing." March 5. UW.

Holman, G. 1994. "Protect Elwha Dams, Lakes." *Peninsula Daily News*, October 28, A10.

Hosey and Associates. 1990. "Agency Review Draft Response to February 1, 1990 Request for Additional Information Item 1. Fish Passage and Restoration Plan." UW.

Howard, D. 2005. Letter to Rogue River City Council, February 23. GPID.

Hughes, J. 2011. *Slade Gorton: A Half Century in Politics*. Olympia: Washington State Heritage Center.

Hundley, N. 2001. *The Great Thirst: Californians and Water—A History*. Berkeley: University of California Press.

Hunter, B. 1999. "Savage Rapids Dam a Big Harm to Fish." *Grants Pass Daily Courier*, June 22.

Hunter, R. 2000. GPID vs. WRD et al., June 30. BH.

Huntington, H. 1986. "Steelheaders Rise Up against Planned Hydroplant." *Grants Pass Daily Courier*, April 30.

Huntington, H. 1994. "Save Dam, Says County." *Grants Pass Daily Courier*, September 14.

Huntington, H. 1997. "County Commissioners Support Keeping Dam." *Grants Pass Daily Courier*, September 24.

Ingram, R. 1994. Letter to Don Greenwood, GPID, August 19. BH.

Irving, D. 2000a. "PGE Stalls Scuttling of Bull Run Plant Because of Dam: Concerns Have Arisen about How Fish Spawning Will Be Affected by Bringing Down the Marmot Structure." *Oregonian*, May 22.

Irving, D. 2000b. "Roslyn Lake Backers Want To Tap Portland Supply." *Oregonian*, April 11, B02.

Irving, D. 2001a. "Anglers Attack Cuts in Sandy's Hatchery Runs." *Oregonian*, February 6, B02.

Irving, D. 2001b. "Officials Rethink Hatchery Fish Plan." *Oregonian*, February 17, C01.

Irving, D. 2001c. "Sandy Hatchery Fish Threatened." *Oregonian*, January 17.

Jackson, J. 2011. "Jennifer Jackson's Port Townsend Neighbor Column: Capturing the Legacy of the Elwha King." *Peninsula Daily News*, September 21.

Janssens, E. 2007a. "Roslyn: It's Not Over 'Til It's Over." *Sandy Post*, 12A, September 12.

Janssens, E. 2007b. "Save Roslyn Park for the Future." *Sandy Post*, 12A, October 3.

Jasanoff, S., and B. Wynne. 1998. "Science and Decisionmaking." In *Human Choice and Climate Change: The Societal Framework*, edited by S. Rayner and E. Malone, 1–87. Columbus, OH: Batelle Press.

Jensen, R. 2003. "The Sandy River Basin." *Oregonian*, June 11, E12.

Johnson, E. 1990. "Elwha River Dams Should Come Down." *Peninsula Daily News*, January 4, A7.

Johnson, E. 1999. "Gorton and Salmon." *Peninsula Daily News*, April 12, A4.

Joint Fish and Wildlife Agencies. 1989. Supplemental Petition for Interim Relief for Fish and Wildlife. October 12. UW.

Joint Fisheries Agencies. 1985. Elwha Dams Relicensing Steering Committee Meeting. November 13. UW.

Joint Fisheries Agencies. 1988. Joint Fishery Agencies' Comments to Response to FERC Request for Additional Information of May 28, 1987, August 16. UW.

Jones, J. 1998a. "PGE, Public Officials Work on Little Sandy Preservation." *Sandy Post*, November 18, 2A.

Jones, J. 1998b. "Roslyn Lake Hosts Diverse Group." *Sandy Post*, August 5, 2A.

Jordan, M. 1990. Letter to Curt Smitch, Washington Department of Wildlife, May 17. UW.

Kaeser, C. 1997. "GPID Need Injunction." *Grants Pass Daily Courier*, November 29.

Kagan, N. 2009. "The Elk Creek Dam Story." *Pace Environmental Law Review* 26:9–11.

Keil, J. 2009. "Bull Run Decommissioning: Paving the Way for Hydro's Future." *Hydroworld* 28.

Keim, C. 1987. "Mime, the Dam Issue and Earth Firsters." *Peninsula Daily News*, July 3, A11.

Keller, J. 1997. "Recreation on the River." *Sandy Post*, November 5, 1A.

Kelly, C. 1996. "Tribe Likes Dam Proposal." *Peninsula Daily News*, May 17, A3.

Kelly, C. 1997. "Babbitt Seeks Dam Consensus." *Peninsula Daily News*, August 8, A1.

Kingdon, J. 1995. *Agendas, Alternatives, and Public Policies*. New York: Addison-Wesley Educational.

Kitz, W. 2000. "Water Questions." *Peninsula Daily News*, February 10, A4.

Kitzhaber, J. 1997. Press Release, August 15. GPID.

Klyza, C., and D. Sousa. 2013. *American Environmental Policy: Beyond Gridlock*. 2nd ed. Cambridge, MA: MIT Press.

Kober, A. 2009. "Ringing in New Life for Rivers." *Open Spaces* 9.

Koberstein, P. 1994. "Damnable Dams." *High Country News*, February 7, 11–12.

Koch, M. 2005. Letter to Senator Gordon Smith. GPID.

Kowalski, R. 1989. Review of the December 2, 1988 (JR2) supplemental Response to May 28, 1987 Request for Additional Information, January 20. UW.

LaBounty, M. 1994a. "Fate of Savage Rapids Rides on GPID Race." *Grants Pass Daily Courier*, November 4.

LaBounty, M. 1994b. "Fish-Kill Figures: Fact or Fancy?" *Grants Pass Daily Courier*, September 21.

LaChasse, C. 1988a. "Elwha Dams Senate Bill Dies." *Peninsula Daily News*, February 23, A3.

LaChasse, C. 1988b. "Hargrove, Jones Not Ready to Ask Support for Fish Bills." *Peninsula Daily News*, January 21, A3.

Lackey, R. T., D. H. Lach, and S. L. Duncan. 2006. "Wild Salmon in Western North America: The Historical and Policy Context." In *Salmon 2100: The Future of Wild Pacific Salmon*, edited by R. T. Lackey, D. H. Lach, and S. L. Duncan, 13–55. Bethesda, MD: American Fisheries Society.

Lakoff, G. 2008. *Don't Think of an Elephant: Know Your Values and Frame the Debate*. White River Junction, VT: Chelsea Green.

Lamoureux, P. 2010. "Ever-Brown Lawns." *Peninsula Daily News*, August 26, A9.

Lanz Oca, E. 2011. "Manufacturing a New Hydroscape Era: Semantics of Restoration in the Elwha Waters." In *Proceedings of the 2011 Elwha River Science Symposium*, edited by K. Barbero, T. Morrow, A. Shaffer, et al. Port Angeles, WA: USGS.

Lauderback, B. 1996. "Leave the Dams." *Peninsula Daily News*, August 26, A6.

Laufer, P. 2014. "All We Ask Is to Be Left Alone." *Humboldt Journal of Social Relations* 36:17–33.

Lavigne, P. M. 2005. "Dam(n) How Times Have Changed..." *William and Mary Environmental Law and Policy Review* 29:451–480.

Layzer, J. 2012. *Open For Business: Conservatives' Opposition to Environmental Regulation*. Cambridge, MA: MIT Press.

Lazenby, S. 2002. Marmot Dam Removal and Water Rights Transfer, Memorandum to City Council. http://archive.cityofsandy.com/weblink/1/doc/5194/Page1.aspx.

Leach, W. D., N. W. Pelkey, and P. A. Sabatier. 2002. "Stakeholder Partnerships as Collaborative Policymaking: Evaluation Criteria Applied to Watershed Management in California and Washington." *Journal of Policy Analysis and Management* 127:378–385.

Learn, S. 2010. "After Dam Removals, Oregon's Rogue River Shows Promising Signs for Salmon." *Oregonian*, October 28. http://www.oregonlive.com/environment/index.ssf/2010/10/early_signs_good_for_dam_remov.html.

Lebo, F. 1990. "Elwha Dams Deserve Tablets." *Peninsula Daily News*, August 2, A9.

Ledbetter, L. 1997. "Wake Up before the Dam Is Gone at Our Expense." *Grants Pass Daily Courier*, November 26.

Lejano, R. 2006. *Frameworks for Policy Analysis: Merging Text and Context*. New York: Routledge.

Lejon, A. G. C., and C. Nilsson. 2009. "Conflicts Associated with Dam Removal in Sweden." *Ecology And Society* 14.

Le Lay, Y.-F. 2017. "Remove Energy Infrastructure Installations? The Case of Dams on the River Sélune (Manche, France)." *Annales de geographie* 715:259–286.

Lewis, S. 1999a. "PGE Fumbles PR Ball at Roslyn Lake." *Sandy Post*, June 16, 1A/3A.

Lewis, S. 1999b. "PGE Takes a Punch from Local Residents over Dam Breachings." *Sandy Post*, June 16, 1A/3A.

Lichatowich, J. 1999. *Salmon without Rivers: A History of the Pacific Salmon Crisis*. Washington, DC: Island Press.

Lichatowich, J. 2013. *Salmon, People, and Place: A Biologist's Search for Salmon Recovery*. Corvallis: Oregon State University Press.

Light, A., and E. S. Higgs. 1996. "The Politics of Ecological Restoration." *Environmental Ethics* 18:227–247.

Ligon, F. K., W. E. Dietrich, and W. J. Trush. 1995. "Downstream Ecological Effects of Dams: A Geomorphic Perspective." *BioScience* 45:183–192.

Lincoln, B. 1998a. "Gorton Bill Seeks Elwha Dam Removal." *Peninsula Daily News*, February 8, A1.

Lincoln, B. 1998b. "Reaction Varies." *Peninsula Daily News*, April 3, A1.

Long, C. 1996a. "Dam Decision: Let's Keep It." *Grants Pass Daily Courier*, October 10.

Long, C. 1996b. "Dam Group Gets the Scoop on Endangered Fish." *Grants Pass Daily Courier*, June 4.

Long, C. 1996c. "Retain, Don't Remove, Savage Rapids Dam." *Grants Pass Daily Courier*, August 30.

Long, C. 1997a. "Adams Tells Board: State Funding's Slim." *Grants Pass Daily Courier*, July 30.

Long, C. 1997b. "Coho Could Doom Savage Rapids." *Grants Pass Daily Courier*, June 11.

Long, C. 1997c. "Dam Flip-Flop Makes Waves." *Grants Pass Daily Courier*, August 6, 1A/2A.

Long, C. 1997d. "Dam Supporters Earn District Board Slots." *Grants Pass Daily Courier*, November 13.

Long, C. 1997e. "Dam Vote Sets Off Flood of Activity." *Grants Pass Daily Courier*, August 9.

Long, C. 1997f. "Feds Want Dam Removal Plan." *Grants Pass Daily Courier*, September 8.

Long, C. 1997g. "Funding Savage Rapids." *Grants Pass Daily Courier*, August 13.

Long, C. 1997h. "GPID Backs Savage Rapids." *Grants Pass Daily Courier*, July 22, 1A/2A.

Long, C. 1997i. "GPID Board Adds Staunch Foe of Saving Dam." *Grants Pass Daily Courier*, September 17, 1A/2A.

Long, C. 1997j. "GPID Called before Water Commission." *Grants Pass Daily Courier*, October 1.

Long, C. 1997k. "GPID Election Offers Clear Choice: Keep Dam or Tear It Out." *Grants Pass Daily Courier*, November 7.

Long, C. 1997L. "GPID Faces Lawsuit over Dam Decision." *Grants Pass Daily Courier*, September 8.

Long, C. 1997m. "GPID Flooded with Cost Estimates for Dam Plans." *Grants Pass Daily Courier*, September 30.

Long, C. 1997n. "GPID Patrons Vote to Oust Board Chairman." *Grants Pass Daily Courier*, November 4.

Long, C. 1997o. "GPID System Still Goes with the Flow." *Grants Pass Daily Courier*, August 22.

Long, C. 1997p. "New GPID Rates Scary." *Grants Pass Daily Courier*, July 30, 1A/2A.

Long, C. 1998a. "Adams Asks E-Board to Help Fund Fish Screens." *Grants Pass Daily Courier*, September 16, 1A/2A.

Long, C. 1998b. "Agency Orders GPID to Get Rid of the Dam." *Grants Pass Daily Courier*, February 13, 1A/2A.

Long, C. 1998c. "Can the Dam Battle Be Won?" *Grants Pass Daily Courier*, May 2, 1A–3A.

Long, C. 1998d. "Few Coho Showing Up in Savage Rapids Traps." *Grants Pass Daily Courier*, July 2.

Long, C. 1998e. "GPID Bills about to Go Up." *Grants Pass Daily Courier*, August 12, 1A/2A.

Long, C. 1998f. "GPID Board Recall Under Way." *Grants Pass Daily Courier*, August 14.

Long, C. 1998g. "GPID Bracing for Dam Fight." *Grants Pass Daily Courier*, April 23, 1A/2A.

Long, C. 1998h. "GPID Brief Calls NMFS 'Dambuster.'" *Grants Pass Daily Courier*, May 14.

Long, C. 1998i. "GPID Case to Drag On." *Grants Pass Daily Courier*, April 2.

Long, C. 1998j. "GPID Closer to Installing New Fish Screens at Dam." *Grants Pass Daily Courier*, October 22.

Long, C. 1998k. "GPID Gets a Week to OK Removal Plan." *Grants Pass Daily Courier*, April 17, 1A/2A.

Long, C. 1998L. "GPID Patrons Quiz Board on Water Battles." *Grants Pass Daily Courier*, April 3.

Long, C. 1998m. "GPID Water Will Flow—For Now." *Grants Pass Daily Courier*, May 29.

Long, C. 1998n. "GPID Will Get Money for Fish Screens." *Grants Pass Daily Courier*, September 18, 1A/2A.

Long, C. 1998o. "GPID Yet to Address Order to Yank Dam." *Grants Pass Daily Courier*, March 4.

Long, C. 1998p. "Injunction Seeks to Pull Plug on GPID." *Grants Pass Daily Courier*, April 22, 1A/2A.

Long, C. 1998q. "Irrigation District Readies for '98 Season." *Grants Pass Daily Courier*, May 4.

Long, C. 1998r. "Judge Halts GPID Irrigation for at Least 10 Days." *Grants Pass Daily Courier*, May 21.

Long, C. 1998s. "Judge Tells GPID, NMFS: Stop Bickering." *Grants Pass Daily Courier*, May 22, 6A/7A.

Long, C. 1998t. "NMFS: Building GPID Fish Screens a Waste of Money." *Grants Pass Daily Courier*, September 25.

Long, C. 1998u. "Patrons with More Acres Get GPID Break." *Grants Pass Daily Courier*, August 22, 1A/2A.

Long, C. 1998v. "Rain Ends Irrigation Season." *Grants Pass Daily Courier*, October 14.

Long, C. 1998w. "Ruling Takes Away One-Third of Supply; District Can Still File an Appeal." *Grants Pass Daily Courier*, November 6.

Long, C. 1998x. "Silt Study Turns Up No Toxic Problems." *Grants Pass Daily Courier*, July 1, 1A/2A.

Loomis, J. 1996. "Measuring the Economic Benefits of Removing Dams and Restoring the Elwha River: Results of a Contingent Valuation Survey." *Water Resources Research* 32:441–447.

Lower Elwha Klallam Tribe. 2014. "Timeline of the Elwha River Dams and Removal Efforts." *Elwha River Restoration*. http://www.elwha.org/riverrestorationtimelin. html.

Lowry, W. 2003. *Dam Politics: Restoring America's Rivers*. Washington, DC: Georgetown University Press.

Lucas, K. 1993. "Savage Rapids Saviors Meet." *Grants Pass Daily Courier*, October 14.

Lundahl, R. 2002. *Unconquering the Last Frontier*. Bullfrog Films. http://www. bullfrogfilms.com/catalog/ulf.html.

Lundgren, L. 1997. "Mayor Rude about Dam." *Grants Pass Daily Courier*, August 1.

Lundsford, C. 1990. "Let's Keep Dams and the Goats." *Peninsula Daily News*, July 3, A7.

Machenheimer, F. 1991. "Don't Take Out the Elwha Dams." *Peninsula Daily News*, June 23, A11.

Magilligan, F., C. Sneddon, and C. Fox. 2017. "The Social, Historical, and Institutional Contingencies of Dam Removal." *Environmental Management* 6:982–994. http:// dx.doi.org/10.1007/s00267-017-0835-2.

Mahoney, J. 2000. "Strategies of Causal Inference in Small-N Analysis." *Sociological Methods and Research* 28:387–424. http://smr.sagepub.com/cgi/doi/10.1177/0049 124100028004001.

Major, J. J. 2007. "Marmot Dam Removal, Sandy River." United States Geological Survey. Accessed July 17, 2017. https://www.youtube.com/ watch?v=CaNb2wouYUk.

Major, J. 2018. "Meeting with Federal Officials Focuses on Elwha Water Facility Impasse." *Peninsula Daily News*, April 20. http://www.peninsuladailynews.com/ news/meeting-with-federal-officials-focuses-on-elwha-water-facility-impasse/.

Major, J. J., J. E. O'Connor, C.J. Podolak, et al. 2012. Geomorphic Response of the Sandy River, Oregon, to Removal of Marmot Dam. United States Geological Survey Professional Paper 1792, i–64. https://pubs.usgs.gov/pp/1792/.

Mann, C. 2005. *1491: New Revelations of the Americas before Columbus*. New York: Alfred A. Knopf.

Mansourian, S., and D. Vallauri. 2014. "Restoring Forest Landscapes: Important Lessons Learnt." *Environmental Management* 53:241–251.

Mapes, L. V. 2016. "Port Angeles, Tribe Say Elwha Water Plant Never Worked, Still Doesn't." *Seattle Times*, July 16. https://www.seattletimes.com/seattle-news/ port-angeles-tribe-say-elwha-water-plant-never-worked-still-doesnt/.

Mapes, L. 2017. "At Elwha River, Forests, Fish and Flowers Where There Were Dams and Lakes." *Seattle Times*, July 3.

McCarthy, J. 2002. "First World Political Ecology: Lessons from the Wise Use Movement." *Environment and Planning* A 34:1281–1302.

McClure, M. M., S. M. Carlson, T. J. Beechie, et al. 2008. "Evolutionary Consequences of Habitat Loss for Pacific Anadromous Salmonids." *Evolutionary Applications* 1:300–318. http://doi.wiley.com/10.1111/j.1752-4571.2008.00030.x.

McConnell, G. 1969. *The Decline of Agrarian Democracy*. New York: Atheneum.

McCool, D. 2012. *River Republic: The Fall and Rise of America's Rivers*. New York: Columbia University Press.

McHenry, M. L., and G. Pess. 2008. "An Overview of Monitoring Options for Assessing the Response of Salmonids and Their Aquatic Ecosystems in the Elwha River Following Dam Removal." *Northwest Science* 82:29–47.

McKeown, T. J. 2000. "Elwha River, Hospital." *Peninsula Daily News*, April 4, A4.

McKinley, G., and D. Frank. 1996. "Stories on the Land: An Environmental History of the Applegate and Upper Illinois Valleys." Medford, OR. https://archive.org/details/storiesonlandenv00mcki.

McMullen, D. 1999a. "Dam Breachings Not Bad News for Everyone." *Sandy Post*, July 7, 1A/3A.

McMullen, D. 1999b. "District Budget Cuts Is the Top Story of the Year." *Sandy Post*, December 29, 1A.

McMullen, D. 1999c. "Little Sandy, Marmot Dams to Be Breached." *Sandy Post*, June 2, 1A.

McMullen, D. 1999d. "Roslyn Lake Forum Attracts 40 Citizens." *Sandy Post*, September 15, 1A–2A.

McMullen, D. 1999e. "Residents discuss proposed dam breachings." *Sandy Post*, June 9.

McMullen, D. 2000a. "PGE Says Roslyn Lake Is a Priority." *Sandy Post*, April 19, 2A.

McMullen, D. 2000b. "Roslyn Lake Gets Reprieve from PGE." *Sandy Post*, June 14, 1A/3A.

McMurray, T. 1997. "Let's Face the Facts on Doomed Dam." *Grants Pass Daily Courier*, September 19.

McNeece, B., and S. McNeece. 1995. "Won't Silt Kill All Fish?" *Peninsula Daily News*, October 4, A10.

McNulty, T. 2007. "Thank You, Norm." *Peninsula Daily News*, July 1, A10.

McPhee, J. 1971. *Encounters with the Archdruid*. New York: Farrar, Straus, and Giroux.

Meierotto, L. 1980. Letter to William Lindsay, Director, Office of Electric Power Regulation, FERC, discussing Elwha relicensing, September 19. UW.

Merlich, M. 1999. "PGE Dam Decision Ups Disillusion." *Sandy Post*, June 30, 4A.

Merrill, T. W. 2005. "The Story of SWANCC: Federalism and the Politics of Locally Unwanted Land Uses." In *Environmental Law Stories*, edited by Richard Lazarus and O. Houck, 283–319. New York: Foundation Press.

Meyer Resources. 1991. Review of Socio-Economic Aspects of the Draft Environmental Impact Statement FERC/EIS-0059D. Report developed for the Lower Elwha Tribal Council. UW.

Michaels, J. L. 1988. Letter to Richard Fleming, Hosey and Associates, April 12. UW.

Miller, D., J. Van Zyle, and J. Eiler. 2014. *A King Salmon Journey*. Fairbanks: University of Alaska Press.

Moeller, N., S. Driver, R. Busch, et al. 1991. Joint Fish and Wildlife Agencies' response to JR2's comments on Draft Environmental Impact Statement, March 27. UW.

Moeller, N., S. Driver, R. Busch, et al. 1992. Joint Fish and Wildlife Agencies' comments on FERC's draft environmental impact statement, March 27. UW.

Momsen, J. 2009. *The Dam Picture Book*. Grants Pass, OR: Josephine County Historical Society.

Momsen, J. 2010. *Another Dam Picture Book*. Grants Pass, OR: Josephine County Historical Society.

Momsen, J. 2013. *The Death of Savage Rapids Dam 1*. Grants Pass, OR: Josephine County Historical Society.

Monroe, B. 1997. "State Plan to Manage Sandy Fish Gets OK." *Oregonian*, September 27, C05.

Monroe, B. 1999. "Fishermen Cast Out Some Alternatives to Proposal to Remove Marmot Dam." *Oregonian*, May 30, E11.

Monroe, B. 2000. "The Words Must Flow Freely, Too." *Oregonian*, January 23, C02.

Monroe, B. 2007. "Dam's Removal Still Faces Hurdle." *Oregonian*, April 2, D09.

Montgomery, D. R. 2003. *King of Fish: The Thousand-Year Run of Salmon*. Boulder, CO: Westview Press.

Moore, D. 1997. "Who Is the Quincy Library Group?" Feather Publishing. Accessed August 4, 2018. http://www.qlg.org/pub/miscdoc/whoistheqlg.htm.

Morey, M. 1999. "Gorton Changes Course." *Peninsula Daily News*, June 21, A1.

Morgan, R., and S. Teniguchi. 1992. Testimony before Congress, June 4. UW.

Morris, S. 1997. Letter to Dennis Becklin, GPID, April 8. GPID.

Morris, S. 1998. Letter to Dennis Becklin, GPID, October 15. GPID.

Mosiman, D. 1994. "Senator to Break Impasse?" *Peninsula Daily News*, July 20, A1.

Mosiman, D. 1996a. "Dam Report Predicts Huge Money Injection." *Peninsula Daily News*, November 17, A1.

Mosiman, D. 1996b. "Delay Dam Decision, Sequim Group Urges." *Peninsula Daily News*, April 19, A1.

Mosiman, D. 1996c. "Draft Plan Looks at Elwha without Dams." *Peninsula Daily News*, April 25, A1.

Mosiman, D. 1996d. "Elwha Plan Irks Group." *Peninsula Daily News*, May 17, A3.

Mosiman, D. 1996e. "Park Responds to Questions about Dams." *Peninsula Daily News*, November 14, A2.

Mosiman, D. 1996f. "Peninsula Panel Backs Dam Removal." *Peninsula Daily News*, July 5, A1.

Mosiman, D. 1996g. "Senator Touts Dam Funds." *Peninsula Daily News*, July 12, A1.

Mosiman, D. 1997a. "Clallam Clear: No Nod to One Elwha Plan." *Peninsula Daily News*, February 5, A4.

Mosiman, D. 1997b. "Clallam Leaders Deny Stand on Dam Removal." *Peninsula Daily News*, February 4, A1.

Mosiman, D. 1997c. "Lawmakers Want Elwha Fish Ladder." *Peninsula Daily News*, January 22, A1.

Mossman, B. 1991. "Finnerty Fails in Understanding." *Peninsula Daily News*, July 25, A4.

Moulton, G. E., ed. *The Journals of the Lewis and Clark Expedition*. Lincoln: University of Nebraska Press.

Muir, J. 1912. *The Yosemite*. New York: Century Company.

Murray, P. 1994. Letter to Craig Rowley, The Mountaineers, September 6. UW.

Murray, P. 1996. "Legislative Update: Senator Patty Murray Works to Restore Salmon Runs on the Elwha River." Mailing from Senator Patty Murray. Washington, DC. UW.

Myrick, C., and J. Cech. 2005. "Effects of Temperature on the Growth, Food Consumption, and Thermal Tolerance of Age-0 Nimbus-Strain Steelhead." *American Journal of Aquaculture* 67:324–330.

Nafziger, C. 1988. "Author Says Salmon Need Help." *Peninsula Daily News*, November 11, A1/A2.

Nageli Reporting Corporation. 2000a. Bull Run Public Meeting, April 17, 1–109. PGE.

Nageli Reporting Corporation. 2000b. Bull Run Stakeholder Meeting. April 17, 1–66. PGE.

Naiman, R. J., R. E. Bilby, D. E. Schindler, et al. 2002. "Pacific Salmon, Nutrients, and the Dynamics of Freshwater and Riparian Ecosystems." *Ecosystems* 5:399–417. http://link.springer.com/10.1007/s10021-001-0083-3.

Nash, R. 2001. *Wilderness and the American Mind*. New Haven, CT: Yale University Press.

National Geographic. 2011. "Spectacular Time Lapse Dam 'Removal' Video." YouTube. November 2. https://www.youtube.com/watch?v=4LxMHmw3Z-U.

National Hydropower Association. 2014. "Dr. Kenneth Henwood Award 2014." http://www.hydro.org/wp-content/uploads/2014/03/Henwood-Award-2014-Call-for-Nominations-FINAL.pdf.

National Marine Fisheries Service, National Park Service, and Bureau of Indian Affairs. 2012. "Environmental Assessment to Analyze Impacts of NOAA's National Marine Fisheries Service Determination that Five Hatchery Programs for Elwha River Salmon and Steelhead as Described in Joint State-Tribal Hatchery and Genetic Management Plans and One Tribal Harvest Plan Satisfy the Endangered Species Act Section 4(d) Rule." http://www.westcoast.fisheries.noaa.gov/publications/nepa/hatchery/elwha-hatchery-ea.pdf.

National Museum of American History. 2018. "Conestoga Wagon." *Smithsonian*. http://americanhistory.si.edu/collections/search/object/nmah_842999.

National Park Service. 2018. "Yosemite National Park." NPS Stats. https://irma.nps.gov/Stats/SSRSReports/Park Specific Reports/Park YTD Version 1?Park=YOSE.

National Research Council. 1992. *Restoration of Aquatic Ecosystems: Science, Technology, and Public Policy*. Washington, DC: National Academies Press.

National Research Council. 1996. *Upstream: Salmon and Society in the Pacific Northwest*. Washington, DC: National Academies Press. http://www.nap.edu/catalog/4976.

Native Fish Society. 2014. Victory for Wild Fish on the Sandy River. Press Release. https://s3-us-west-2.amazonaws.com/nativefishsocietyauction/Save+Sandy+Salmon+Documents/SANDY-PRESSRLS.pdf.

Nehlsen, W., J. E. Williams, and J. A. Lichatowich. 1991. "Pacific Salmon at the Crossroads." *Fisheries* 16:4–21.

Nelson, P. B. 2005. "Migration and the Regional Redistribution of Nonearnings Income in the United States: Metropolitan and Nonmetropolitan Perspectives from 1975 to 2000." *Environment and Planning* A 37:1613–1636. http://www.envplan.com/abstract.cgi?id=a37170.

Nicole, W. 2012. "Lessons of the Elwha River: Managing Health Hazards during Dam Removal." *Environmental Health Perspectives* 120:430–435.

NMFS. 2011. "5-Year Review: Summary and Evaluation of Lower Columbia River Chinook, Columbia River Chum, Lower Columbia River Coho, Lower Columbia River Steelhead." Portland, OR: NMFS. http://www.westcoast.fisheries.noaa.gov/publications/status_reviews/salmon_steelhead/multiple_species/5-yr-lcr.pdf.

NOAA. 2015. "West Coast Salmon and Steelhead Listings." Accessed January 1, 2015. http://www.westcoast.fisheries.noaa.gov/protected_species/salmon_steelhead/salmon_and_steelhead_listings/salmon_and_steelhead_listings.html.

NOAA Fisheries. 2016. "Atlantic Salmon." Protected Resources: Species. http://www.nmfs.noaa.gov/pr/species/fish/atlantic-salmon.html.

Noonan, D. 1994. "Mill Wants Dams Out." *Peninsula Daily News*, October 25, A1.

Noonan, M. J., J. W. Grant, and C. D. Jackson. 2012. "A Quantitative Assessment of Fish Passage Efficiency." *Fish and Fisheries* 13:450–464.

Norcross, G. 2013. "How Zane Grey Put the Rogue River on the Map." Oregon Public Broadcasting. http://www.opb.org/news/article/how-zane-grey-put-the-rogue-river-on-the-map/.

Norgaard, K. M., and R. Reed. 2017. "Emotional Impacts of Environmental Decline: What Can Native Cosmologies Teach Sociology about Emotions and Environmental Justice?" *Theory and Society* 46:463–495.

Northwest Conservation Act Coalition. 1994. "Still Hope for Elwha If Costs Can Be Cut." *Northwest Conservation Act Report*, December 23, 5–6. UW.

Northwest Power and Conservation Council. 2018. "First-Salmon Ceremony." https://www.nwcouncil.org/reports/columbia-river-history/firstsalmonceremony.

Nowak, G. P. 1992. "Motion of ITT Rayonier Inc. to file comments on the Draft Environmental Impact Statement and to intervene out of time." UW.

O'Dell, T. 2001a. "Hatchery Fish Program Faces Drastic Cut." *Sandy Post*, January 17, 3A.

O'Dell, T. 2001b. "Sandy Crowd Grills State Officials in Meeting." *Sandy Post*, February 7, 1A/2A.

ODFW. 2011a. "Final Hatchery and Genetic Management Plan, Sandy River Spring Chinook. Sandy River, Lower Columbia River Basin." ODFW. https://digital.osl.state.or.us/islandora/object/osl%3A18730/datastream/OBJ/view.

ODFW. 2011b. "Final Hatchery and Genetic Management Plan, Sandy River Winter Steelhead Program. Sandy River Basin." ODFW. https://digital.osl.state.or.us/islandora/object/osl%3A85176/datastream/OBJ/view.

ODFW. 2012. "Final Hatchery and Genetic Management Plan, Sandy River Coho Salmon Program. North Willamette Watershed, NW Region." ODFW. https://digital.osl.state.or.us/islandora/object/osl%3A18731/datastream/OBJ/view.

ODFW. 2013. "Final Hatchery and Genetic Management Plan, Sandy River Summer Steelhead Program. North Willamette Watershed, NW Region." ODFW. https://www.dfw.state.or.us/fish/HGMP/docs/2013/Sandy_STS_HGMP_10-28-13_FinalUpdate.pdf.

Office of Rep. Carl Wilson. 1999. Press Release, November 16. GPID.

Office of Senator Brady Adams. 1999. Letter, November 15. GPID.

Ollikainen, R. 2010a. "200 Gather for Hatchery Groundbreaking." *Peninsula Daily News*, February 7, A4.

Ollikainen, R. 2010b. "Olympic National Park Unveils Its Elwha River Project Logo, Slogan." *Peninsula Daily News*, November 17.

Ollikainen, R. 2018. "Port Angeles City Council Prepares to Fight Park Service over Water Treatment." *Auburn Reporter*, May 10. https://www.auburn-reporter.com/northwest/port-angeles-city-council-prepares-to-fight-park-service-over-water-treatment/.

O'Loughlin, D. 1995a. "Fate of Dam All But Sealed." *Grants Pass Daily Courier*, February 14.

O'Loughlin, D. 1995b. "GPID Board Won't Study Dam-Saving Possibilities." *Grants Pass Daily Courier*, March 2.

O'Loughlin, D. 1995c. "GPID Chair Fighting Lonely Battle." *Grants Pass Daily Courier*, April 7.

O'Loughlin, D. 1995d. "Savage Rapids Problem Still Not Addressed." *Grants Pass Daily Courier*, October 28.

O'Loughlin, D. 1995e. "State Assembling Savage Rapids Task Force." *Grants Pass Daily Courier*, August 8.

O'Loughlin, D. 1996a. "Dam Panel Selects Becklin as Chairman." *Grants Pass Daily Courier*, February 19.

O'Loughlin, D. 1996b. "Kitzhaber Pledges More Watershed Money." *Grants Pass Daily Courier*, February 21.

Olympic Park Associates. 1989. "Free the Elwha/Elwha River Project." Mailing. UW.

Olympic Park Associates. 1992. "Congress Passes Elwha Legislation." *Voice of the Wild Olympics*. October. UW.

Oregon Department of Fish and Wildlife. 2017. "Ten Years after Oregon's Largest Dam Removal, Salmon and Steelhead Rebounding on the Sandy." News Release, October 19. https://www.dfw.state.or.us/news/2017/10_Oct/101917b.asp.

Ortman, D. 1992. Tribute to the Elwha. Celebratory recitation. November 14. UW.

Ostrom, E. 1990. *Governing the Commons*. New York: Cambridge University Press.

Palmer, M. A., E. S. Bernhardt, J. D. Allan, et al. 2005. "Standards for Ecologically Successful River Restoration." *Journal of Applied Ecology* 42:208–217. http://doi.wiley.com/10.1111/j.1365-2664.2005.01004.x.

Palmer, M. A., and J. B. Ruhl. 2015. "Aligning Restoration Science and the Law to Sustain Ecological Infrastructure for the Future." *Frontiers in Ecology and the Environment* 13.

Parks, N. 2009. "A Ravenous River Reclaims Its True Course: The Tale of Marmot Dam's Demise." *PNW Science* Findings 111.

Parsons, J. S. 1998. "Keep the Dams." *Peninsula Daily News*, October 23, A6.

Patterson, K. 1987. "Protest of Elwha Dams Planned Sunday." *Peninsula Daily News*, June 26, A3.

Patterson, K. 1988. "Lowry Flies through PA." *Peninsula Daily News*, November 4, A1/A2.

Patterson, K. 1989. "Adams Tours Elwha Dams." *Peninsula Daily News*, March 23, A1/A2.

Pearl, P. 1996. Letter to Joe Mentor and Shawn Cantrell, Elwha Conservation Interveners, June 3. UW.

Pearse, D. E., S. A. Hayes, M. H. Bond, et al. 2009. "Over the Falls? Rapid Evolution of Ecotypic Differentiation in Steelhead/Rainbow Trout (*Oncorhynchus mykiss*)." *Journal of Heredity* 100:515–525.

Peattie, C. 2011. "Rogue River-Heavy Metals Are Being Churned Up from Dam Removals." Examiner.com/Klamath Basin Crisis, July 17. http://www.klamath-basincrisis.org/dams/rogueriverheavymetals101411.htm.

Pellissier, R., and S. Cramer. 2001. "Monitoring of Juvenile Fish Passage at Savage Rapids Dam, 2000." S.P. Cramer and Associates. https://www.researchgate.net/profile/Steven_Cramer2/publication/242171065_MONITORING_OF_JUVENILE_FISH_PASSAGE_AT_SAVAGE_RAPIDS_DAM_2000/links/54414f8a0cf2e6f0c0f60ee9/MONITORING-OF-JUVENILE-FISH-PASSAGE-AT-SAVAGE-RAPIDS-DAM-2000.pdf?origin=publication_detail.

Peninsula Daily News Staff. 1987. "Forget Miami: Peninsula Rates as Retirement Hotspot." *Peninsula Daily News*, September 8, A1.

Peninsula Daily News Staff. 1988. "Lawmaker Pursues Fisheries Department." *Peninsula Daily News*, January 15, A1/A2.

Penn, C. 2000. "Seals, Sea Lions, Salmon." *Peninsula Daily News*, March 5, A8.

Perkins, J. 1993. Letter to Friends of the Earth, June 27. UW.

Pickett, J. 1997. "Dam's Good Points Outweigh Fish Deaths." *Grants Pass Daily Courier*, August 14.

Pincetl, S. 2003. *Transforming California: A Political History of Land Use and Development*. Baltimore, MD: Johns Hopkins University Press.

Pittock, J., and J. Hartmann. 2011. "Taking a Second Look: Climate Change, Periodic Relicensing and Improved Management of Dams." *Marine and Freshwater Research* 62:312–320.

Plumb, K. 1986. Notice Granting Late Interventions, November 20. UW.

Pohl, M. M. 2002. "Bringing Down Our Dams: Trends in American Dam Removal Rationales." *Journal of the American Water Resources Association* 38:1511–1519.

Porter, E. 1963. *The Place No One Knew: Glen Canyon on the Colorado.* Edited by D. Brower. San Francisco: Sierra Club.

Portland General Electric. 1999. Bull Run and Oak Grove/North Fork Projects FINAL Relicensing Meeting Summary, June 22, 1–11. PGE.

Portland General Electric. 2000. Bull Run Hydroelectric Project Stakeholder Group Meeting May 17, 1–2. PGE.

Pralle, S. 2006. *Branching Out, Digging In: Environmental Advocacy and Agenda Setting.* Washington, DC: Georgetown University Press.

Press, D. 1994. *Democratic Dilemmas in the Age of Ecology: Trees and Toxics in the American West.* Raleigh-Durham, NC: Duke University Press.

Provencher, B., W. Sarakinos, and T. Meyer. 2008. "Does Small Dam Removal Affect Local Property Values? An Empirical Analysis." *Contemporary Economic Policy* 26:187–197.

Pryne, E. 1994. "Elwha Dams Won't Be Coming Down Anytime Soon." *Seattle Times.* http://community.seattletimes.nwsource.com/archive/?date=19940519&slug=1911315.

Pyne, S. J. 1990. "Firestick History." *Journal of American History* 76:1132–1141.

Quinn, T. 2005. *The Behavior and Ecology of Pacific Salmon and Trout.* Bethesda, MD: American Fisheries Society.

Rains, G. C. Sr. 1994. "To the People of Clallam County and Elsewhere." *Peninsula Daily News,* November 6, C3.

Ralph, S. 1988. Comments on the Draft Response by James River to the FERC Request for Additional Information on the Hydropower License Applications for the Elwha Project (No. 2638) and the Glines Project (No. 588), April 14. UW.

Ramzy, A. 2000a. "Countdown on the Elwha." *Peninsula Daily News,* April 2, A1.

Ramzy, A. 2000b. "Interior Chief Touts Razing Elwha Dams." *Peninsula Daily News,* February 13, A1.

Ramzy, A. 2000c. "Opposition Still Flowing Freely." *Peninsula Daily News,* April 2, A6.

Ramzy, A. 2000d. "Tribe Eagerly Awaits Restored River Flow." *Peninsula Daily News,* April 2, A1.

Raush, R. 1975. "Fishway Plan Gets Support." *Grants Pass Daily Courier,* June 4.

Ray, R. A., R. A. Holt, and J. L. Bartholomew. 2012. "Relationship between Temperature and *Ceratomyxa shasta*–Induced Mortality in Klamath River Salmonids." *Journal of Parasitology* 98:520–526.

REAL. n.d. Dam Removal = Environmental Destruction. Mailing. UW.

REAL. n.d. Letter to Friends of REAL. UW.

Reese, P. 1999. "Removing Dams Is Irresponsible." *Sandy Post,* June 23, 4A.

Reid, J. L., S. J. Wilson, G. S. Bloomfield, et al. 2017. "How Long Do Restored Ecosystems Persist?" *Annals of the Missouri Botanical Garden* 102:258–265. http://www.bioone.org/doi/10.3417/2017002.

Reisner, M. 1993. *Cadillac Desert.* New York: Penguin.

Repetto, R. 2006. *Punctuated Equilibrium and the Dynamics of U.S. Environmental Policy.* New Haven, CT: Yale University Press.

Riski, R. 1989a. "Critics Blast Elwha Dams." *Peninsula Daily News,* December 21, A1/A2.

Riski, R. 1989b. "Crowd: Help Fish in Elwha." *Peninsula Daily News,* June 28, A1/A2.

Riski, R. 1990. "Debate on Dams Goes On." *Peninsula Daily News,* January 2, A1/A2.

Robbins, P., K. Meehan, H. Gosnell, et al. 2009. "Writing the New West: A Critical Review." *Rural Sociology* 74:356–382. http://openurl.ingenta.com/content/xref?genre=article&issn=0036-0112&volume=74&issue=3&spage=356.

Roberts, B. 1991. Letter to Bob Buckmaster, GPID, December 20. GPID.

Robinson, R. 1999. "Suggested Solution." *Peninsula Daily News*, April 13, A4.

Rochon, T. 1998. "Culture Moves: Ideas, Activism, and Changing Values." Princeton, NJ: Princeton University Press.

Rogue Web. 2014. "The Rogue River in Southern Oregon—Profile." http://www.rogueweb.com/river/.

Roler, D. 1998. "GPID Finances Could Be in the Red for Awhile." *Grants Pass Daily Courier*, August 22.

Roler, D. 1999. "Dam-Razing Fans Avoid Question: Who Foots Bill?" *Grants Pass Daily Courier*, May 19.

Roler, D., and P. Snyder. 2000. "Ruling Endangers One-Third of GPID Water." *Grants Pass Daily Courier*, June 24.

Roper, J. 2008. "Inevitable?" *Sandy Post*, March 26, 16A.

Ross, R. 1987. "Elwha Dams Help Boost Salmon Run." *Peninsula Daily News*, October 14, A3.

Ross, R. 1989a. "Goin Fishin'." *Peninsula Daily News*, August 15, B1.

Ross, R. 1989b. "Tribal Waters." *Peninsula Daily News*, August 16, B1.

Rowell, M. 2001a. "Enough Is Enough in Regulating Land Use." *Sandy Post*, September 9, 4A.

Rowell, M. 2001b. "Land Use Laws Have Created a Mess." *Sandy Post*, September 5, 4A.

Rowley, D. 1999. "Draining Roslyn Will Ruin Memories." *Sandy Post*, August 4, 4A.

Rubin, S. P., I. M. Miller, M. M. Foley, et al. 2017. "Increased Sediment Load during a Large-Scale Dam Removal Changes Nearshore Subtidal Communities." *PLoS ONE* 12 (12): e0187742

Rudolph, D. 1995. "Dam Foes Feel the Pinch." *Peninsula Daily News*, September 26, A8.

Rudolph, D. 1996. "Elwha Panel Off Track." *Peninsula Daily News*, May 10, A10.

Rudolph, D. 2000. "Don't Destroy Dams." *Peninsula Daily News*, February 15, A4.

Sabatier, P., S. Hunter, and S. McLaughlin. 1987. "The Devil Shift: Perceptions and Misperceptions of Opponents." *Western Political Quarterly* 40:449–476.

Sabatier, P., and H. Jenkins-Smith, eds. 1993. *Policy Change and Learning: An Advocacy Coalition Approach*. San Francisco: Westview Press.

Sadin, P., and D. Vogel. 2011. "An Interpretive History of the Elwha River Valley and the Legacy of Hydropower on Washington's Olympic Peninsula." Historical Research Associates. Port Angeles, WA: US National Park Service. https://www.nps.gov/olym/learn/nature/elwha-river-restoration-research-publications.htm.

Sampson-Sherbeck, V. 1985. "Dirty White Boys." *Peninsula Daily News*, November 4.

Sandy Area Chamber of Commerce. 2013. "The Elephants Are Coming! The Elephants Are Coming!" http://www.sandyoregonchamber.org/news/the-elephants-are-coming-the-elephants-are-coming/.

Sandy River Basin Watershed Council. 2017. "State of the Sandy." http://sandyriver.org/wp-content/uploads/2017/12/State-of-Sandy-Report-Dec2017.pdf.

Sarakinos, H., and S. Johnson. 2003. "Social Perspectives on Dam Removal." In *Dam Removal Research: Status and Prospects*, edited by W. Graf, 40–55. Washington, DC: H. John Heinz III Center for Science, Economics and the Environment.

Savage Rapids Dam Task Force. 1996. "Final Report and Recommendations." Grants Pass, OR.

Scalia, D. R. 2017. "I'll Take the Benefits If You Pay the Costs: Weighing the Equities of Public and Private Funding Sources for Hydroelectric Dam Decommissioning." *American Indian Law Journal* 2:354–372.

Schaefer, D. 1992. "Adams' Legacy: He Kept On Working—Senator's Effectiveness Was Limited by Charges of Sexual Misconduct." *Seattle Times*, December 20. http://community.seattletimes.nwsource.com/archive/?date=19921220&slug=1530996.

Schaeffer, Y., and J. C. Dissart. 2018. "Natural and Environmental Amenities: A Review of Definitions, Measures and Issues." *Ecological Economics* 146:475–496.

Schattschneider, E. E. 1960. *The Semi-Sovereign People*. New York: Holt, Rinehart, and Winston.

Schmidt, J. C., R. H. Webb, R. A. Valdez, et al. 1998. "Science and Values in River Restoration in the Grand Canyon." *BioScience* 48:735–747.

Schon, D., and M. Rein. 1994. *Frame Reflection*. New York: BasicBooks.

Seideman, D. 1993. *Showdown at Opal Creek: The Battle for America's Last Wilderness*. New York: Carrol and Graf.

Shafroth, P. B., J. M. Friedman, G. T. Auble, et al. 2002. "Potential Responses of Riparian Vegetation to Dam Removal." *BioScience* 52:703–712.

Shared Strategy Development Committee. 2007. *Puget Sound Salmon Recovery Plan*. Vol. 1. Seattle: NMFS. http://www.westcoast.fisheries.noaa.gov/publications/recovery_planning/salmon_steelhead/domains/puget_sound/chinook/puget-soundchinookrecoveryplan.pdf.

Sheehan, M., and D. Strahan. 1999. "Sportsfishing Interests Decry Dam Plan." *Grants Pass Daily Courier*, November 29.

Sheer, M. B., and E.A. Steel. 2006. "Lost Watersheds: Barriers, Aquatic Habitat Connectivity, and Salmon Persistence in the Willamette and Lower Columbia River Basins." *Transactions of the American Fisheries Society* 135:1654–1669.

Shelton, S. 1990. Reply of Environmental Intervenors to Response to 2/1/90 FERC request for Additional Information. May 7. UW.

Sherman, P., and G. Guibord. 2007. "Power Outage: End of an Era for the Bull Run Hydroelectric Project." *Sandy Post*, May 30, 1A/4A.

Sherman, R. 2007. "In My Opinion: The Lower Klamath Dams—An Economic Case for Dam Removal." *Oregonian*, August 6, C07.

Shields, J. F. 1925. "The Federal Power Act." *University of Pennsylvania Law Review and American Law Register* 73:142–157.

Short, K. 1996. "PA Chamber Makes Own Pitch for Elwha Dams." *Peninsula Daily News*, June 20, A4.

Short, K. 1999. "Water Talks on Tap." *Peninsula Daily News*, May 23, A1.

Short, K. 2000. "Panel Endorses Dam Removal." *Peninsula Daily News*, September 6, A4.

Sierra Club. 1989. "Rivers Be Dammed?" *Cascade Crest* 8 (November 8). UW.

Sierra Club. n.d. "The Hetch Hetchy Restoration Task Force." Restore Hetch Hetchy. http://vault.sierraclub.org/ca/hetchhetchy/hetch_hetchy_task_force.html.

Silliman, D. 2001. "Elwha Hatchery Back to Nature." *Peninsula Daily News*, August 9, A1.

Sisson, J. 1993. "Save Aldwell, Mills Lakes." *Peninsula Daily News*, August 1, A10.

Skevington, D. 2005. Letter to GPID Board, February 28. GPID.

Sloan, W. 1997. "Dam a Monument to All the Propaganda." *Grants Pass Daily Courier*, November 12.

Smith, B. 1994. Letter to Elizabeth Gaar, NMFS, March 2. GPID.

Smith, D. 1990. "Writer Knows Little about Dams." *Peninsula Daily News*, August 9, A9.

Smith, G., and R. Wyden. 2000. S. 3227—106th Congress: Savage Rapids Dam Act of 2000. Govtrack.us. Accessed February 6, 2014. https://www.govtrack.us/congress/bills/106/s3227.

Smith, G., R. Wyden, G. Walden, et al. 2005. Letter to John Ashcroft, Gale Norton, and Joshua Bolten, Bush Administration, January 21. GPID.

Smith, Q. 2012. "The Century-Old Bull Run Powerhouse Finds New Life, Thanks to 3 Portland Preservationists." *Oregonian*, December 6. http://www.oregonlive.com/gresham/index.ssf/2012/12/the_century-old_bull_run_power.html.

Snyder, P. 1998. "Overflow Crowd Debates GPID Issues." *Grants Pass Daily Courier*, May 9.

Society for Ecological Restoration International Science and Policy Working Group. 2004. "The SER International Primer on Ecological Restoration." Society for Ecological Restoration International, Tucson, AZ. www.ser.org.

Socolar, M. 1990. General Accounting Office Report to the Hon. John Dingell, February 16. Washington, DC: Comptroller General of the United States. https://www.gao.gov/assets/170/168417.pdf.

Song, C., K. H. Gardner, S. J. W. Klein, et al. 2018. "Cradle-to-Grave Greenhouse Gas Emissions from Dams in the United States of America." *Renewable and Sustainable Energy Reviews* 90:945–956. https://doi.org/10.1016/j.rser.2018.04.014.

Sonner, S. 1992. "Bush Balks at High Cost to Save Fish." *Peninsula Daily News*, July 10, A1/A2.

Spees, K. 2006. "Salmon Issues." *Peninsula Daily News*, October 1, A10.

Spickler, M. 1998. "Dam Supporters Fight for Our Rights, Too." *Grants Pass Daily Courier*, May 7.

Staff. 1994. "A Savage SLAPP Suit." *High Country News*. May 30.

State of Oregon. 2014. "Oregon Plan for Salmon and Watersheds." Oregon.gov. Accessed January 6, 2014. http://www.oregon.gov/OPSW/Pages/about_us.aspx.

Stegner, W., ed. 1955. *This Is Dinosaur: Echo Park Country and Its Magic Rivers*. New York: Knopf.

Stelle, W. 1998. Letter to Dennis Becklin, GPID, December 22. GPID.

Stevens, I., and Native Signatories. 1855. Point No Point Treaty of 1855. Point No Point Treaty Council. https://goia.wa.gov/tribal-government/treaty-point-no-point-1855.

Stevens, L. E., T. J. Ayers, J. B. Bennett, et al. 2001. "Planned Flooding and Colorado River Riparian Trade-Offs Downstream from Glen Canyon Dam, Arizona." *Ecological Applications* 11:701–710.

Stickney, R. 1994. "Use of Hatchery Fish in Enhancement Programs." *Fisheries* 19:6–13.

Stillwater Sciences. 2000. "Numerical Modeling of Sediment Transport in the Sandy River, OR Following Removal of Marmot Dam." Berkeley, CA. https://www.google.com/search?q=b4668a5d-2d42-4876-8001-e16fac396b5f&ie=utf-8&oe=utf-8&client=firefox-b-1-ab.

Stoddard, C. 2010. "Nippon Project." *Peninsula Daily News*, October 19, A7.

Stone, D. 2002. *Policy Paradox: The Art of Political Decision Making*. New York: W.W. Norton and Company.

Strahan, D. 1999. "Dam Puts Plug in Economic Benefits." *Grants Pass Daily Courier*, July 31.

Strahan, D. 2001. "Special Addition Savage Rapids Dam." *Fin Clips*, November. NSIA newsletter. GPID.

Symmes, P. 2003. "River Impossible." *Outside Magazine* 28 (8): 64–68, 108–111. http://www.outsideonline.com/1821746/river-impossible.

Taylor, B. 1998. Salmon and Steelhead Runs and Related Events of the Sandy River Basin—A Historical Perspective. Portland, OR. Report prepared for Portland General Electric.

Taylor, J. 1999. *Making Salmon: An Environmental History of the Northwest Fisheries Crisis*. Seattle: University of Washington Press.

Thaler, T. 1985. Memo to Olympic Park Associates Board, March 25. UW.

Thomas, C. 2003. *Bureaucratic Landscapes: Interagency Cooperation and the Preservation of Biodiversity*. Cambridge, MA: MIT Press.

Thomas, C. W., and T. M. Koontz. 2008. Does Collaborative Governance Improve Environmental Performance? Presentation at the Annual Research Conference of the Association for Public Policy Analysis and Management. Los Angeles, CA, November 6–8.

Thomas-Blate, J. 2018. "Dam Good Year for Dam Removal in 2017." American Rivers. https://www.americanrivers.org/2018/02/dam-removal-in-2017/.

Thoreau, H. D. 2004. *A Week on the Concord and Merrimack Rivers*. Princeton, NJ: Princeton University Press.

Tizon, A. 1999. "The Boldt Decision / 25 Years—The Fish Tale That Changed History." *Seattle Times*, February 7.

Towslee, C. 1994. "Why Drain Lake Aldwell?" *Peninsula Daily News*, September 16, A10.

Trackers Earth. 2018. Bull Run Education Center. Facebook. https://www.facebook.com/BullRunCenter/.

Trevison, C. 2003. "Seeing Through the Silt." *Oregonian*, June 11, E12.

Trevison, C. 2005. "Plan to Remove Marmot Dam and Roslyn Lake Flows Forward." *Oregonian*, November 15, B04.

Trevison, C. 2007a. "As Lake Drains, Wells May, Too." *Oregonian*, October 4, 01.

Trevison, C. 2007b. "Dams' Demolition Will Give NW's Wild Salmon a Break." *Oregonian*, May 23, D01.

Trevison, C. 2007c. "Marmot Dam Explodes into Souvenir Bits." *Oregonian*, July 25, C01.

Trevison, C. 2007d. "PGE Offers Farewell Events for Dams, Lake." *Oregonian*, May 28, B02.

Trevison, C. 2007e. "Roslyn Lake—One Last Time." *Oregonian*, September 6, 01.

Trevison, C. 2007f. "This Is the Way the Dam Crumbles." *Oregonian*, July 23, A01.

Trevison, C. 2008. "As Roslyn Lake Drains, Fond Times Ebb and a River Renews." *Oregonian*, May 9, C01.

Trout Unlimited-Northwest Steelhead and Salmon Council. 1994. "Gorton Now Wants Deadline on Elwha Dam Removal." *Trout and Salmon Leader*, September/October, 1–2. UW.

Trushenski, J. T., G. E. Whelan, and J. D. Bowker. 2018. "Why Keep Hatcheries? Weighing the Economic Cost and Value of Fish Production for Public Use and Public Trust Purposes." *Fisheries*. https://onlinelibrary.wiley.com/doi/abs/10.1002/fsh.10084.

Tullos, D. D., D. S. Finn, and C. Walter. 2014. "Geomorphic and Ecological Disturbance and Recovery from Two Small Dams and Their Removal." *PLoS ONE* 9.

Turner, A., J. Kuskie, and K. Kostow. 1983. "Evaluation of Adult Fish Passage at Little Goose and Lower Granite Dams, 1981." Portland, OR. https://scholarworks. umass.edu/fishpassage_unpublished_works/202/.

Tuttle, E. 2000. "Sea Lions and Salmon." *Peninsula Daily News*, January 30, A8.

United Press International. 1987. "'Really a Work of Art': Vandal Paints Crack on Park Dam." *Los Angeles Times*. http://articles.latimes.com/1987-07-21/news/ mn-5359_1_o-shaughnessy-dam.

Unsigned. n.d. Letters to the Editor of the *Peninsula Daily News*. Friends of the Elwha.

US Army Corps of Engineers. 1986. Elwha River, Washington Flood Damage Reduction Draft Study. UW.

US Army Corps of Engineers. 2018. "National Inventory of Dams." CorpsMap National Inventory of Dams. http://nid.usace.army.mil/cm_apex/f?p=838:12.

US Bureau of Reclamation. 2015. "The Story of Hoover Dam—Essays." https://www. usbr.gov/lc/hooverdam/history/essays/artwork.html.

US Bureau of Reclamation. 2017. Frequently Asked Questions. Hoover Dam. https:// www.usbr.gov/lc/hooverdam/faqs/powerfaq.html.

US Census Bureau. 2012. Table 361: Flows of Largest U.S. Rivers-Length, Discharge, and Drainage Area. Washington, DC. https://www2.census.gov/library/publica- tions/2011/compendia/statab/131ed/tables/12s0365.xls.

US Census Bureau. 2016. "Frequently Occurring Surnames from the 2010 Census." https://www.census.gov/topics/population/genealogy/data/2010_surnames.html.

USDOC NMFS. 1991. "Policy on Applying the Definition of Species Under the Endangered Species Act to Pacific Salmon." *Federal Register* 56, 58612–58618.

USDOI BOR. 1995. "Fish Passage Improvements, Savage Rapids Dam. Planning Report and Final Environmental Impact Statement: Josephine County Water Management Improvement Study, Oregon." Rogue River Basin, Oregon. Southern Oregon University Library, Ashland, OR.

USDOI NPS. 1990. "National Park Service Calls for Restoration of All Native Fish Species to the Elwha River." Press Release, June 15. UW.

USDOI NPS. 1995. "Final Environmental Impact Statement: Elwha River Ecosystem Restoration." Denver. https://www.nps.gov/olym/learn/nature/upload/ ElwhaFinalEIS1.pdf.

USDOI NPS. 1996. "Final Environmental Impact Statement: Elwha River Ecosystem Restoration Implementation." Denver. https://www.nps.gov/olym/learn/nature/ upload/ElwhaFinalEIS2.pdf.

USDOI NPS. 2005. "Elwha River Ecosystem Restoration Implementation: Final Supplement to the Final Environmental Impact Statement." Denver. https://www.nps.gov/olym/learn/nature/loader.cfm?csModule=security/ getfile&PageID=136240.

USDOI NPS. 2011. Elwha River Restoration Webisode 1. Olympic National Park. http://www.nps.gov/media/video/view.htm?id=FD6764AB-FB65-DB8A- 5777A01401066473.

USDOI NPS. 2014a. Dam Removal Blog. Olympic National Park. http://www.nps.gov/ olym/naturescience/damremovalblog.htm.

USDOI NPS. 2014b. Frequently Asked Questions. Olympic National Park. http:// www.nps.gov/olym/naturescience/elwha-faq.htm.

USDOI NPS. 2014c. "Timeline of the Elwha 1940 to 1992." Olympic National Park. http://www.nps.gov/olym/historyculture/timeline-of-the-elwha-1940-to-1992. htm.

USDOI NPS. 2014d. "Timeline of the Elwha 1992 to Present." Olympic National Park. http://www.nps.gov/olym/historyculture/timeline-of-the-elwha-1992-to-present. htm.

USDOI NPS. 2014e. "Water Treatment-Overview." Olympic National Park. http:// www.nps.gov/olym/naturescience/water-treatment-overview.htm.

USDOI, USDOC, and LEKT. 1994. "The Elwha Report: Restoration of the Elwha River Ecosystem and Native Anadromous Fisheries." https://archive.org/details/ elwhareportresto94nati.

USEIA. 2014. "State Profile and Energy Estimates." Accessed April 3, 2014. http:// www.eia.gov/state/.

US Energy Information Administration. 2014. Sales (Consumption), Revenue, Prices, and Customers. Electricity-Data. http://www.eia.gov/electricity/data.cfm#sales.

USFWS. 2002. "Lower Columbia Recovery Unit, Washington." In *US Fish and Wildlife Service. Bull Trout (*Salvelinus confluentus*) Draft Recovery Plan*, i-89. Portland, OR: USFWS.

US General Accounting Office. 1992a. "Electric Consumers Protection Act's Effects on Licensing Hydroelectric Dams." September 18. Washington, DC. https://www. gao.gov/products/RCED-92-246.

US General Accounting Office. 1992b. "Interior Favors Removing Elwha River Dams, but Who Should Pay Is Undecided." June 5. Washington, DC. https://www.gao. gov/products/147071.

Vander Haegen, G., H. Blankenship, A. Hoffmann, et al. 2005. "The Effects of Adipose Fin Clipping and Coded Wire Tagging on the Survival and Growth of Spring Chinook Salmon." *North American Journal of Fisheries Management* 5:1161–1170.

Van Fleet, T. 2008. "PGE Buys More Turbines to Complete Biglow." *Sandy Post*, C15.

Van Wieren, G. 2008. "Ecological Restoration as Public Spiritual Practice." *Worldviews* 12:237–254. https://www.jstor.org/stable/43809391.

Vasquez, R. 2005. "Elwha River Group Receives $1 Million for Dams Study." *Peninsula Daily News*, April 27, A1.

Vejtasa, S. 1998. "Dam Supporters Ignore a Slew of Facts." *Grants Pass Daily Courier*, June 30.

Vencill, B. 1987. "The Federal Power Act and Western Water Law-Can States Maintain Their Own Water Use Priorities." *Natural Resources Journal* 27:213–234.

Vogel, D. 1986. *National Styles of Regulation: Environmental Policy in Great Britain and the United States*. Ithaca, NY: Cornell University Press.

Walker, P.A. 2006. "How the West Was One: American Environmentalists, Farmers and Ranchers Learn to Say 'Howdy, Partner.'" *Outlook on Agriculture* 35:129–135.

Ward, L., P. Crain, B. Freymond, et al. 2008. Elwha River Fish Restoration Plan, Developed Pursuant to the Elwha River Ecosystem and Fisheries Restoration Act, Public Law 102-495. NOAA Technical Memorandum. National Marine Fisheries Service-NWSC-90.

WaterWatch of Oregon. 2009. Press Release. "Rogue River Runs Free at Savage Rapids." Ashland, Oregon. http://waterwatch.org/pressroom/press-releases/ rogue-river-runs-free-at-savage-rapids.

WaterWatch of Oregon. 2011. The Campaign to Free the Rogue River. Powerpoint Presentation. BH.

WaterWatch of Oregon. 2014. Waterwatch of Oregon. Accessed February 6, 2014. Waterwatch.org.

Weible, C., P. Sabatier, H. Jenkins-Smith, et al. 2011. "A Quarter Century of the Advocacy Coalition Framework: An Introduction to the

Special Issue." *Policy Studies Journal* 39:349–360. http://doi.wiley.
com/10.1111/j.1541-0072.2011.00412.x.

Weible, C., P. Sabatier, and K. McQueen. 2009. "Themes and Variations: Taking Stock of the Advocacy Coalition Framework." *Policy Studies Journal* 37:121–140.

White, R. 1995. *The Organic Machine: The Remaking of the Columbia River.* New York: Hill and Wang.

White Salmon River. 2014. "Restoring the White Salmon River by Removing Condit Dam." Free the White Salmon River. Accessed February 6, 2014. http://www.whitesalmonriver.org/index.php.

Whitworth, J. 2001. "A Relic Dam Dislodged by a Dormant Doctrine: The Story of Beneficial Use and Savage Rapids Dam." *University of Denver Water Law Review* 183:1–29.

Widdison, K. 2001. "'Very Substantial Step' Taken Toward Dam Solution." *Grants Pass Daily Courier*, July 20.

Wildlands Network. 2014. FAQ—Wildlands Network. About Us. http://www.twp.org/about-us/faq.

Wiles, T. 2018. "A Separatist State of Mind." *High Country News*, January 22. https://www.hcn.org/issues/50.1/communities-rural-discontent-finds-a-home-in-the-state-of-jefferson.

Wiley, R. W. 2008. "The 1962 Rotenone Treatment of the Green River, Wyoming and Utah, Revisited: Lessons Learned." *Fisheries* 33:611–617.

Wilkinson, C. 1992. *Crossing the Next Meridian: Land, Water, and the Future of the West.* Washington, DC: Island Press.

Wilson, R., and C. Magraw. 1987. Memorandum to Sierra Club Cascade Chapter, December 2. UW.

Winter, B., and P. Crain. 2008. "Making the Case for Ecosystem Restoration by Dam Removal in the Elwha River, Washington." *Northwest Science* 82:13–28.

Wold, E. 1989. Letter to Ronald McKittrick, FERC. Re: Elwha/Glines Canyon Projects, Washington, FERC Nos. 2683 and 588, July 31. UW.

Wollner, C. 1990. *Electrifying Eden: Portland General Electric 1889–1965.* Portland: Oregon Historical Society Press.

Woodcock, L. 1997. "Extortion at Center of Dam Removal Issue." *Grants Pass Daily Courier*, September 18.

Woods, L. 2002. "Officials Sign Pact to Remove Dams." *Sandy Post*, October 30, 1A.

Woods, L. 2003. "Festival to Highlight Mushrooms, Salmon, and Music." *Sandy Post*, October 1, 1A/2A.

Worster, D. 1992. *Rivers of Empire: Water, Aridity, and the Growth of the American West.* New York: Pantheon Books.

Worster, D. 2008. *A Passion for Nature: The Life of John Muir.* Oxford, UK: Oxford University Press.

Wright, R. 1990. Trout Unlimited's Motion for Late Intervention, April 2. UW.

Wunderlich, B. R. C., B. D. Winter, and J. H. Meyer. 1994. "Restoration of the Elwha River Ecosystem." *Fisheries* 19:11–19.

Yoshiyama, R., F. Fisher, and P. Moyle. 1998. "Historical Abundance and Decline of Chinook Salmon in the Central Valley Region of California." *North American Journal of Fisheries Management* 18:487–521.

Zeug, S. C., L. K. Albertson, H. Lenihan, et al. 2010. "Predictors of Chinook Salmon Extirpation in California's Central Valley." *Fisheries Management and Ecology* 18 (1): 61–71.

Index